THE POLITICS OF BELONGING IN CONTEMPORARY INDIA

This volume looks at the emerging forms of intimacies in contemporary India. Drawing on rigorous academic research and pop culture phenomena, the volume:

- Brings together themes of nationhood, motherhood, disability, masculinity, ethnicity, kinship, and sexuality, and attempts to understand them within a more complex web of issues related to space, social justice, marginality, and communication;
- Focuses on the struggles for intimacy by the disabled, queer, Dalit, and other subalterns, as well as people with non-human intimacies, to propose an alternative theory of the politics of belonging;
- Explores the role of social and new media in understanding and negotiating intimacies and anxieties.

Comprehensive and thought-provoking, this book will be useful to scholars and researchers of political studies, sociology, sexuality and gender studies, women's studies, cultural studies, and minority studies.

Kaustav Chakraborty is Assistant Professor at the Department of English, Southfield (formerly Loreto) College, Darjeeling. He was formerly a fellow at the Indian Institute of Advanced Study. Dr Chakraborty has edited *Indian Drama in English*, *Tagore and Nationalism* (co-edited with K.L. Tuteja), and is the author of *Indigeneity, Tales and Alternatives: Revisiting Select Tribal Folktales*. In addition, he has published articles in journals such as *Feminist Theology*, *Studies in Humanities and Social Sciences*, and many other reputed journals. His research interests include indigenous literature and culture, queer theory, and cultural studies.

THE POLITICS OF BELONGING IN CONTEMPORARY INDIA

Anxiety and Intimacy

Edited by Kaustav Chakraborty

Routledge
Taylor & Francis Group
LONDON AND NEW YORK

First published 2020
by Routledge
2 Park Square, Milton Park, Abingdon, Oxon OX14 4RN

and by Routledge
52 Vanderbilt Avenue, New York, NY 10017

Routledge is an imprint of the Taylor & Francis Group, an informa business

British Library Cataloguing-in-Publication Data
A catalogue record for this book is available from the British Library

Library of Congress Cataloging-in-Publication Data
A catalog record for this book has been requested

ISBN: 978-1-138-56294-3 (hbk)
ISBN: 978-0-367-27307-1 (pbk)
ISBN: 978-0-429-29598-0 (ebk)

Typeset in Bembo
by Apex CoVantage, LLC

MIX
Paper from responsible sources
FSC™ C013985
FSC
www.fsc.org

Printed in the United Kingdom
by Henry Ling Limited

To My Students of Southfield, Darjeeling

CONTENTS

CONTRIBUTORS

Shilpaa Anand is Assistant Professor, Department of English, Maulana Azad National Urdu University (MANUU), Hyderabad, India. She completed her PhD in the Interdisciplinary Program in Disability Studies at the University of Illinois at Chicago, U.S.A.

Sayan Bhattacharya is a PhD candidate in the Department of Gender, Women, and Sexuality Studies at the University of Minnesota, U.S.A., and is involved in queer activism in Eastern India.

Isabelle Clark-Decès was formerly Professor, Department of Anthropology, at Princeton University, in New Jersey, U.S.A. Dr. Clark-Decès's research interests are in South Asia, with a focus on the Tamils of South India.

Sarat Kumar Doley teaches English at the Department of English and Foreign Languages, School of Humanities and Social Sciences, Tezpur University, Assam, India. He has also authored a number of articles in the field of North East Indian literature in English and Tibeto-Burman Linguistics.

Mangesh Kulkarni teaches Political Science at Savitribai Phule Pune University, India. His publications include *Global Masculinities* (2018).

Dickens Leonard teaches at the Centre for Comparative Literature, University of Hyderabad, India. He largely works on caste, religion, and culture.

Chandni Mehta is a doctoral candidate at the Centre for Comparative Politics and Political Theory, Jawaharlal Nehru University, New Delhi, India. Her research interests include gender, labour and sexuality, especially in the context of sex work.

P. Sanal Mohan is Associate Professor at the School of Social Sciences of Mahatma Gandhi University, Kottayam, India. He combines history and ethnography in his research on colonial modernity, Dalit Movements, and Christianity in India.

Silpa Mukherjee is a doctoral candidate in the Film & Media Studies Program at the University of Pittsburgh, in Pennsylvania, U.S.A. Her current research interests include media infrastructures, circulation, and contraband.

Geeta Patel is the Director of UVA in India and Associate Professor at the University of Virginia, U.S.A. Dr. Patel has three degrees in science and a doctorate in interdisciplinary South Asian Studies from Columbia University, New York, U.S.A.

Pranta Pratik Patnaik is Assistant Professor at the Department of Culture and Media Studies, Central University of Rajasthan, India. He has worked on issues of gender, sexuality, and body image in Indian media.

Arunima Paul teaches literature, visual studies, and gender studies at California State University, Los Angeles, USA. Her teaching and research interests include literary and visual studies, popular culture, decolonial, and postcolonial studies.

Sucharita Sarkar is Associate Professor at D.T.S.S College of Commerce, Mumbai, India. Her doctoral thesis investigated mothering narratives – specifically memoirs and momblogs – in contemporary India.

K. Satyanarayana is Professor at the Department of Cultural Studies, EFL University, Hyderabad, India. His areas of interest include Dalit literature, literary history, Indian literatures, and cultural studies.

R. Umamaheshwari is a fellow at Nantes Institute for Advanced Study, France, and an independent journalist and academic researcher. As a former fellow at the Indian Institute of Advanced Study, she has worked on displacements due to developmental projects and on Tamil Jaina history.

PREFACE

The Latin etymology of 'intimacy' imparts the notion of making known (*intimare*) what is innermost (*intimus*) to a close friend (*intima*). Intimacy, thus, conveys an idea of sharing by acknowledging an urge of belonging together, almost inseparably. The paradox of intimacy lies in the fact that it is objective but personal, somatic nonetheless psychological, affective in its dimension yet without having a firm reflective/self-conscious foundation, and most importantly, dependent on 'other' but belonging together in such a manner so that the sharp distinction between the 'self' and the 'other' erases out. The notion of Intimacy thus proves that the self cannot resist from belonging to the other, or to be specific, that the self can only be known through the other, where it seems possible that the innermost qualities can be shared. Here comes the question of choice. Unlike the bond with non-person, intimate bond among human beings depends on, firstly, the palpable possibility of sharing and, secondly, on the mutual consensus and commitment of belonging from both the parties. Is the tangibility of such probability of intimacy purely apolitical? Are the motivations for belonging, through closeness/fidelity, fully impulsive sans politics? What is the politics that drives us from the intimate awareness of belonging-to (externally related) towards/against belonging-with (related internally)?

Initially viewed as the 'sociology of personal life,' intimacy has been recently melded with the complex broader issues related to labour, social justice, commodification, and body shopping. The possibility of finding new ways of belonging together cannot be understood without understanding the complex connection of intimacy with changing notions of nationhood, citizenship, and community. Focusing on the emerging forms of intimacies in contemporary India, our book, *The Politics of Belonging in Contemporary India: Anxiety and Intimacy*, is an endeavour to understand the politics behind the changing notion/nature of belonging. Precisely, these are the questions we are asking: What causes or inhibits intimacy? What restricts or disfigures one's sense of belonging? Moreover, the question can be asked whether transformations in modes of intimacies have, in actuality, paved the way for transversal and emancipatory structures that can politically challenge the hegemonic, traditional Indian concepts of belonging that are restricted by the rigid boundaries of class, caste, religion, region, and normative conformity. This would result in the rise of alternative sociocultural doctrines, new communication technologies and/or transnational media, and thereby giving rise to intimate spaces/intimate settings for intimate encounters. What are the benefits and challenges of unconventional/non-human intimacies? What is/can be the role of power/politics if the contemporary forms of intimate belonging ever attempt for a togetherness of the issues related to marginalised identities like nature/ecology, class, disability, Dalit subalternity, and sexual minority and thereby aim at germinating alternative subcultural praxes? Is there an essential politics behind the fusions of intimacy, commodification, bodies, labour, care, and social justice? How can one apprehend the politics and possibilities of the transformation from naming and relating – like friend, companion, lover, partner, spouse – to polyamorous desires, dissident eroticism, anonymous/unnamed bonding, or even collective belonging in a temporal manner?

Publishing a new book is always an occasion of happiness. However, I feel sad to recall that professor Isabelle Clark-Decès, who was intimately involved with our seminar at IIAS, Shimla, and later on with this book, is no longer with us. With her sudden demise we have lost a passionate scholar who had a genuine sense of belonging with India.

I am thankful for the valuable suggestions that I have received from my friends of Indian Institute of Advanced Study, Shimla. I thank Prof. Chetan Singh, former Director of IIAS, Shimla, for encouraging me in organising a conference on Intimacy and Belonging, and also allowing me to edit a special issue of *Studies in Humanities and Social Sciences* on the 'Anxiety of Intimacy.' I am also indebted to Mr. Prem Chand, the Secretary, IIAS, Shimla, for granting me the required permission. I am very grateful to each of the contributors for their co-operation and patience. Finally, I thank all my friends from Routledge India, and specially Antara, for the interest and involvement with this book.

Kaustav Chakraborty
Darjeeling

INTRODUCTION

The politics of belonging: anxiety and intimacy

Kaustav Chakraborty

> The multitude needs a political project to bring it into existence.
> (Hardt and Negri 2004: 212)

Belonging through intimacy, though often has been exclusively implied as sexual affinity, can be used aptly to refer to the affective bond manifested through a friendly correspondence between the intimate others, like the backward class across the religions, the fair-skinned indigeneity with those of the dark skins, 'sissy' with the 'macho,' paving way for an intimate friendship between the women, queers, Dalits, differently-abled people, religious minorities, environmentalists, all the contested citizens, even without excluding the one from the mainstream who would represent the non-disempowered-ally. An endeavour for a social (sharing intimate moments of companionship), emotional (communicating with one another in crisis), and intellectual (thinking mutually) intimacy might pave way for a recreational intimacy of collaborating each other in areas of mutual concern: 'This advance will . . . change the love-experience . . . reshape it into a relation that is meant to be of one human being to another. . . [where] two solitudes protect and border and salute each other.' (Rilke 1975: 45)

Longing for belongingness

Fabian has aptly observed that, 'if it is true that recognizing others also means remembering them, then we should see relationships between self and other as a struggle for recognition, inter-personal as well as political.' (Fabian 2006: 145). Belonging through intimacy can result into a bond of diverse subcultures of resistance through a belonging, that necessarily does not appropriate/hybridise identity but assist in a performative belonging of togetherness without any premeditative agenda for giving birth to a compromised common identity. It can be founded on a continuum of intimacy that does not seek to threaten the singularity of another at its very inception, while initiating an intense interactions among those inspired by 'collective imaginings'[1] through 'a holding-in-common' (Wilbur 2000: 47) idea of a 'coming community,' with its 'coming politics'[2] of 'wanting to belong, wanting to become, a process that is fuelled by yearning rather than the positioning of identity as a stable state' (Probyn 1996: 19). The significance of this politics of belonging, as an ever shifting (multi)identity, may emerge out of the intimacy based on the 'living union' of the ex-centric-Other through the realisation that 'it is the multiplicity and interconnectedness of our identities that provide the most promising avenue for the destabilization and radical politicalization of these same categories' (Cohen 2005: 45).

The anxiety of intimacy often results from the consciousness of retaining one's 'singular' notion of the self. The awareness that helps in overcoming anxiety about intimacy is that the 'singular' distinctiveness of the self is rather 'singular plural' in two major ways: first, being 'singular' with difference is a 'plural' phenomenon where 'Plurality is the condition of human action because we are all the same, that is, human, in such a way that nobody is ever the same as anyone else who ever lived, lives, or will live' (Arendt 1958: 8); and secondly, it is only through a pluralist interdependent relationship with others that identity as the marker of distinctiveness can be discovered: '[W]e become one whole individual, through and only through the company of others. For our individuality, insofar as it is one – unchangeable and unmistakable – we depend entirely on other people' (Arendt 1994: 358).

'Dialogue' is the first step towards moving beyond anxiety for enabling the self 'to be in the presence of others precisely inasmuch as the Other has become content of our experience. This brings us to the conditions of possibility of intersubjective knowledge.' (Fabian 1983: 91–92). Since 'Difference stands at the beginning of conversation, not in its end' (Gadamer 1989: 113), 'dialogue' assists in 'opening myself to another so that he might speak and reveal my myth . . . Dialogue is a way of knowing myself and of disentangling my own point of view from other viewpoints and from me' (Panikkar 1980: 242). 'We who are a conversation' (Gadamer 1989: 110) is the realisation that empowers one to overcome the anxiety of losing one's own identity through intimacy with an-other for, 'to recognise oneself (or one's own) in the other and find a home abroad – this is the basic movement of spirit whose being consists in this return to itself from otherness' along with the facility 'to recognise otherness or the alien in oneself (or one's own)' (Dallmayr 1989: 92).

Intimacy as the conscious choice of loving others who are equal in their Otherised state of 'statelessness' is the first step towards an assemblage against oppression: 'The moment we choose to love we begin to move towards freedom, to act in ways that liberate ourselves and others' (Hooks 1994: 298). Love, born out of intimacy, then assists in the politics of belonging in the form of a 'thirdness' that empowers one with the capability of listening to the multiple voices of others who seem to be voicing even some parts of the victimised self, and thereby, inviting for a collaborative, intersubjective struggle against the experiences of belittlement. This thirdness 'not to be understood primarily as the intervention of an other, but, rather, requires the "one in the third," the attunement and empathy that make it possible to bridge difference with identification, to infuse observation with compassion' (Benjamin 2002: 50) is also helpful in overcoming the binary between the 'doer' and the 'done to' which, if extended, becomes beneficial for the state to rule by distancing the marginalised people of 'differences' from one another. The politics of belonging as a mode of intimacy among the people in India, equally otherised but differently, is also important in ensuring that the Otherised subject, overcoming the polemical enshacklement often fortified by the particularity of the victimised self, acquires the agency 'to reunite elements that have been divorced and that have come into conflict, [through] interpersonal and inter-cultural communication' (Touraine 2000: 301).

The realisation that even among the differentiated-group identities there are multiple differences, some of which get reduced while some other crop up with time, can motivate one to contemplate upon the notion of what is 'sacred' (what has to be safeguarded) and 'profane' (what needs to be denounced) in order to 'live together while living differently' by forging flexible and need-based intimacies: 'The campaign for acceptance will continue since the decision is never final but only for a fixed duration, and since it is made in a free and fair manner. Considerable negotiation, accommodation, compromise and adjustment is involved. This negotiation and compromise is an important basis for the democratic culture which emerges.' (De Souza 2002: 28).

Marginalised identities and the anxiety of intimacy

The anxiety that one suffers in trying to be intimate with another can be best explained by Irigaray's pertinent observation: 'Mankind [*le peuple des hommes*] wages war everywhere all the time with a perfectly clear conscience. Mankind is traditionally carnivorous, sometimes cannibalistic. So men must kill to eat, must increase their domination of nature in order to live or to survive, must seek on the most distant stars what no longer exists here, must defend by any means the small patch of land they are exploiting here or over there.' (Irigaray 1994: 5). Irigaray, nevertheless, also retains faith on 'those who are persons in their own right to help them [mankind] understand themselves and find their limits' (Ibid.: 5). Kropotkin is one such person who has attempted to assist mankind with his notion of mutual aid: 'the practice of mutual aid and its successive developments have created the very conditions of society life in which man was enabled to develop his arts, knowledge, and intelligence; and that the periods when institutions based on the mutual-aid tendency took their greatest development were also the periods of the greatest progress in arts, industry, and science.' (Kropotkin 1972: 178). Mutual aid and sharing should have been the unifying factors among the differences and disagreements which prevail in India[3]

India gets often projected as the best suited example of successful democracy. Perhaps one needs to rethink how, in recent times, majoritarianism, wrapped up and well propagated as the voice of the democracy, is producing a neo-colonial threat for a wide range of the marginalised inhabitants – queers, Dalits, disables, religious minorities and the people of the North East India. The visibility of the privileged at the cost of the suppressed 'invisibles' that facilitates the 'mainstream' majority to enjoy greater access to freedom of choice and preferences bring out an antithetical image of India that is supposed to be 'shining.' If 'The possibility of intimacy means the promise of democracy' (Giddens 1992: 188) then it is crucial again to bridge the gap between the marginalised but dispersed population in order to strive for an intimate bond that is prerequisite for a democracy to sustain pluralism, nevertheless, through a conscious politics of belonging.

The nation state which is often thought to be the polity of uniting people, can also create a tension/anxiety of intimacy and thus 'signify the source of non-belonging, even produce that non-belonging as a quasi-permanent state' (Butler and Spivak 2010: 4), by censoring some of its indwellers as non-citizens or preclude some others as 'national minorities'[4]. Moreover, if freedom, as observes Arendt, lies in the freedom of exercising it, then it can be further argued that even some of the people who are within the juridical protection of the state, are in fact jostled towards 'statelessness.' Hence, as a counter-nationalist resistance against the conventional national mode of belonging, there needs to be an attempt of post-national belonging through intimacy. This intimacy of 'we' is possible only by and among the people who are on equal footing as expelled/ minoritised inhabitants of the state as well as in their common struggle of challenging the normatised law in order to assert their right to have the right for defiance. This multitude of 'we' can be thus assembled together by people who see themselves as the wretched of the mainstream/majoritarianism – a belonging of the multiple marginalised, having porous borders internally despite their rigid external boundaries of differences.

The anxiety of intimacy is an outcome of the lack of clarity about why to belong with the other. Laclau's reminder that 'a politics of pure difference would be self-defeating' is the prime reason why people of differences as the markers of depravity need to belong with others who are differently marginalised: 'To assert one's own *differential* identity involves . . . the inclusion in that identity of the other, as that from which one delimits oneself. But it is easy to see that a fully achieved differential identity would involve the sanctioning of the existing *status quo* in the relation between groups. For an identity which is purely differential vis-à-vis other groups has to assert the identity of the other at the same time as its own and, as a result, cannot have identity claims in relation to those other groups. Let us suppose that a group has such claims – for instance the demand for equal opportunities in employment and education . . . In so far as these are claims presented as rights that I share as a member of the community with all other groups, they presuppose that I am not simply different from the other but, in some fundamental respects, equal to them' (Laclau 1996: 48). Even if we ignore the plea for counting the opposing other, embracing the other as differently equivalent is important in order to assert the right of the marginalised. Rabindranath Tagore in his *Hey Mor Durbhaga Desh*, translated as *Nemesis*, has also appealed for an intimate belonging, emerging out of amity and intersubjectification: 'Those you trample underfoot, drag you down,/ Further backward they recede, the less you advance./ Shut off the light of knowledge from them/ And a blind wall separates you from your well-being./ You must share with them all, their ignominy.' (Translated by Kshitis Roy; *Mainstream Annual* 1965). Overcoming the anxiety of intimacy by a positive inclination for an intimate belonging of us/we against the 'introverted' I/me, just as one learns to become a multilingual or at least a bilingual, is a mode of de-categorising the *minoritized* as not being a simple stagnant identity but rather multilinear and compound. This multitude of the plebeians, different but equivalent in their marginalisation, can also provide the answer to 'the worrying choice between an illusionary globalization which ignores cultural diversity and the disturbing reality of introverted communities' (Touraine 2000: 12)[5]. Differentiating 'the popular,' as the multitude of 'all defenceless, dispossessed, and aggrieved members' from the privileged, protected and the rightful notion of 'citizenship' as a 'unique historical we,' Vidal has suggested that 'the popular,' 'whatever their racial, ethnic origin or social status, have right to full solidarity' (Vidal 2009: 32). This solidarity can be founded upon an 'amphibious' politics of belonging, that can be 'adopted to both lives or both ways of life' of the marginal individuals with differences and in the course reliably develops each of them into 'more than one cultural tradition and that facilitates communication between them' (Mockus 1994: 37).

Another question that might also arise is why one needs to reconsider intimacy as a mode of belonging when it is often declared with certitude that India is all about unity in diversity. But the premise for such claim, that 'the essence of the concept of India's so-called "unity in diversity" is best constructed at its most basic level in a "functional" sense,' itself shows that the notion of 'living together separately' is based not on intimacy (Hasan and Roy 2005:19). Non-discrimination and equal safeguarding of multicultural, group-differentiated rights need to form the basis of an intimate pluralism which is not mere 'functional,' but instrumental in promoting justice and fairness by its 'tolerant pluralism.' The unity that contemporary India represents, in my opinion, is not intimacy, but integrity. Derived from the Latin in and *tangere* (meaning touched), integrity denotes that, which is uncorrupted, being whole, indivisible and inviolable (Kasulis 2002:25). The marginalised people find themselves confined within integrity's agreement to rules, whereas, intimacy calls for a spontaneous response to the immediate situation out of closeness and concern. As per the integrity orientation, ethics becomes primarily a standardised principle; according to the intimacy code, ethics is nurtured by a morality of love. Integrity's moral request is to be responsibly rational to the other, whereas, intimacy's mandate is to be affectively responsive along with the other[6]. Now the question comes how to be intimate in a culture that injects us with the doses of integrity? One might argue that Indian integrity has prepared us to realise of our differences. Recognising the differences is important. However, from the binary of twoness that splits the existing differences into the polarised opposition of a power struggle shouldn't we aspire for a transformative thirdness of a co-created reality? With our compartmentalised recognition of particularity, we have revealed how imperfect and hostile our ambience is. What is to be done next? Should one become a cynic? Limit our micro-belongings in order to bargain with the rest, on the issues of intimacy? In times like ours, when a Dalit seems to have only the option of death, North East women are destined to be raped by the gun men, queer has to quit academics and learn how to die, or a minority can be killed on the basis of food habits, isn't it a mandate to be intimately together so that the idea of not being the privileged gets the crucial focus of an amplifying intersectional margin? There is pathos in witnessing the very temporary arousal of momentary collective consciousness and that too only in the wake of some unwanted sad incidents, for example the 'kiss of love' or 'hok kalorawb.' Issues that denigrate need to be addressed for annihilation only by having a strong, sustaining, sense of belonging 'together' as an intimate 'communitas.' The contemporary rebel is left with neither utopianism nor cynicism, but rather isolation. Indifference is a euphemism for violence. One may stay remote despite staying near. Even then, the evolving indifference can only be narrowed down by an inquisitive proximity. It's the right time to revisit the model of mutual aid devised by Kropotkin, that focuses on the living being's instinct of sociability as a biological mandate for intimacy and wellbeing. Even our bodies are essentially composite in nature. One's own body is not one entity. The mouth has tons of bacteria and foreign stuff. Human beings are dependent on the animals, and they on little birds and plants. We are not one single entity. In the age of 'genetic citizenship' it is possible to grasp how one is related intimately to more than the presently affiliated identities, since the 'knowledge of one's genetic inheritance traced through the DNA can stand as a proxy for memory by connecting people to their ancestors and reinforcing continuity with them that may be absent in postmodern life' (Finkler 2005: 1065). On the basis of the 'truth' of connectedness and belonging that genetics would gradually reveal, anxiety might get replaced by 'an intimacy that democratically empowers the subject to be free to communicate with all that have been so long distanced under the anxiety of conflict' (Chakraborty 2017:102). Let there be recognition of self as a multiple entity, interconnected into a concerted oneness.

About the book

The Politics of Belonging in Contemporary India: Anxiety and Intimacy is divided into six sections, where an article[7], while focusing on a particular kind of marginalisation, seems to correlate with others who are differently but equally marginalised and thereby engage into a politics of forming 'multitude' of the 'plural singularities.' In the first section, **Intimacy, marginality, and anxiety**, three chapters ponder the anxiety regarding how to be intimate with one who is often projected as the unrelatable Other: the Dalit and the non-Dalit, the native slaves and the colonial missionaries, the human and the non-human 'Nature.' The question of 'Dalit' as a political identity is facing a crisis in the recent times. Dalit Panthers proposed Dalit identity as a pedagogic identity open to social groups subjected to caste and other forms of discrimination and subordination. In the course of history, Dalit identity remained the identity of Scheduled castes and more recently, it was reduced to the identity of specific subcastes in the Scheduled caste list. K. Satyanarayana, in 'Identification, belonging, and the category of Dalit,' argues that 'Dalit' is a category of political identification and belonging rather than a natural, birth-based identity. 'Emotions in the context of caste slavery: exploring the missionary writings on Kerala' by P. Sanal Mohan is an endeavour to understand the emotional world of the slave castes as represented in missionary writings. The idea of community that was impossible in the traditional slave society was articulated through the forms of worship that the missionaries introduced in the fledgling congregations. Such developments in various parts of Kerala are relevant in understanding the everyday life of the slave castes. The oral tradition of the slave castes refers to emotional aspects of life – pain, separation, longing, love – in a substantial manner in the context of oppression by landlords and caste elites. 'Nature and belonging: distance, development, and intimacy' by R. Umamaheshwari is an engagement with the ideas of distance and proximity, with the creation of the illusion of distance, as well as the illusion of proximity, in the contemporary discourse of 'development,' or 'modernity' (within which the idea of 'development' and 'progress' is construed), and within modern political-economic discourses. Umamaheshwari's starting point is a few examples from real-life situations across geographical and socioeconomic spaces in order to engage with what Nature (inclusive of landscapes and general ideas of nature or in the 'Nature' of things) means, comes to mean, and is made to mean. Finally, Umamaheshwari tries to explore some vital issues, like the different manner in which marginalised communities perceive Nature and the debate between mere 'romantic' (within a 'universalised' category of 'romantic') affection and a 'genuine,' intimate association that has been sidelined by the whim of an anthropocentric, corporate, political ideology.

The second section, **Rethinking intimacy, contemporarity vis-à-vis the conventional institutions**, comprises three chapters, from three different perspectives, focusing on the family/home, which has always been considered as the bedrock of intimate belonging. 'Intimacy in Tamil kinship' by Isabelle Clark-Decès, explores intimacy in Tamil kinship and the ethnographic challenges associated with this inquiry. It focuses on two concepts of kinship intimacy. The first is based on the rights of Tamil kin over each other; the second derives from marriages to close kin (the so-called Dravidian kinship system, which often gets viewed as non-normative by the North Indian mainstream), which, this chapter shows, allows parents, siblings, and children to remain in close physical and emotional proximity. Sayan Bhattacharya's 'Reading queerness: same-sex marriages in India' examines the site of queer marriages in India to argue how queer and feminist discourses on marriage often fail to account for the complex ways in which marriage subverts heteronormative norms. The chapter takes up three recent moments of public articulation of queer intimacies in India and the way they have captured the mainstream imaginary in order to rehearse the dominant arguments for and against marriage. Then it seeks to problematise such a binary frame of debate to closely read what work queer marriages perform within the scripts of normative institutions. The third chapter of this section, 'Homes as conversions: literalizing the metaphor of Ghar Wapsi' by Arunima Paul, begins by looking at the ways in which home is delineated in the Hindu Right's characterisation of both an alleged 'Love Jihad' as well as its own counter-campaign of 'Ghar Wapsi.' It considers the ways in which the public and the private (centred around the home) structure the discourse of the Right as well as its liberal critiques – so that conversions are seen to be induced from outside the home. Considering an episode of the popular Hindi prime-time TV series *Savdhaan India/Beware India*, as well as a short story by the writer Shakti Bhatt titled *The Thief* – both of which are set in elite households and use the event of a theft by a domestic help – the chapter mobilises from these texts a quotidian, pluralised, and more ambivalent conception of 'conversion' to bring into view the pedagogic regimes and psychic economies that operate continually within homes and that convert and produce appropriate social subjects. It demonstrates how popular 'true crime' narratives can naturalise conversions into inequitable gendered, classed, and caste-based divisions of physical and emotional labour within the home, and then shows how Bhatt's story lays bare the workings of the same. In doing so, the chapter places conversions and homes not on the exclusive axis of religion but at the intersection of several social vectors – most prominently, that of labour.

In the third section, **Dissident body and belonging**, two chapters engage with disregarded bodies and their attempts to overcome their state of subjugation through assemblage and intersection of multiple marginalisations. In his chapter 'Anti-caste communitas and outcaste experience: space, body, displacement and writing,' Dickens Leonard significantly unpacks how caste affects the body, location, and migration of close to one-fifth of the people in India, by using material made available through recent historical research on indentured labour in the colonial period, by comparing the travel reports of Gandhi and Ambedkar, and by analysing the work of Iyothee Thass (1845–1914), a Tamil-Dalit intellectual who predates Ambedkar and Gandhi, which foregrounds a caste-free imaginary in the vernacular (hitherto understudied). However violent displacement and/or disembodiment be, they exscribe a home 'in-place' and 'in-time,' critically and creatively through writing and practice, conceiving anti-caste values. This is conceptualised as *communitas* of/from the outside. Contemporary critical theory that foregrounds experience as a prerequisite to emancipatory sociopolitical thought is discussed as an inevitable dialogue/discourse, as it emanates from the subaltern-ised Other. Thus, the chapter explores anti-caste communitas as an autonomous embodiment which desires to touch intimately, at least in resistant thought and action. Taking as its primary sources the different renditions of the story of Madurai Veeran, the warrior-hero of Madurai in the *nontinatakam* tradition, as well as in the oral form of the *Madurai Veeran Katha*, Shilpaa Anand, in 'Disability and intimacy in the making of Madurai Veeran,' explores how caste-in-action, disablement, and intimacy intersect to conceptualise bodily difference within a specific Tamil historical geography. Examining different aspects of the Madurai Veeran story, the chapter critiques the 'moral model of disability' as an inadequate theoretical framework with which one needs to combine disablement and concepts of bodily difference as available in different cultural contexts, while arguing for a contextual understanding of the corporeal at the intersections of multiple overlapping bio-social hierarchies.

The fourth section, **Space, vigilance and getting intimate**, is highly relevant in the contemporary Indian scenario where the statist machineries are hyperactive in turning all citizens into codified entities so that intimate moments of private, non-conformist belonging can be under governmental surveillance. 'The modern-day sex worker: the intimate "other" of intimacy and belonging' by Chandni Mehta explores how the consolidation of modern morality through the separation of domains – sex/intimate/private and labour/estranged/public – rests on producing the modern-day 'prostitute' in the immorality of collapsing separations. The 'prostitute' takes the intimacies that belong to the home out into the public domain, makes them indiscriminate, and standardises them through money valuation that is proper only to activities – labour – of the public domain. It is the production of an entire life-world in terms of deception, as 'standing in' for something else, and therefore a life-world brimming with enactments of normative and transgressive intimacies. The chapter explores this aspect at length through a close reading of *The Autobiography of a Sex Worker* by Nalini Jameela, seeing how a subject produced in deception navigates and complicates the question of identity and its firm linkages with intimacy and belonging. It shows that the denial of intimacy and belonging with others, as well as the intimate use of the body to work and survive, produces an intimate relation and belonging with the self by freeing it up from guilt. In socio-anthropological studies, a relationship between private spaces and intimacy is established and reinforced with a claim that the enclosures or boundaries of the private spaces facilitate a sense of belongingness. Parks are primarily seen as public spaces where it is conventionally assumed that no intimacy or belonging can be developed. In his chapter 'Public spaces and private intimacies: the "politics of belonging" in parks,' Pranta Pratik Patnaik argues that marginal spaces like gay cruising parks are not completely rigid enclosures, but rather are filled with openings and spaces for forms of togetherness that are different from those bound by authority and its stabilising mechanisms. These loitering spaces do not expect from the individuals to illuminate the meaning of 'knowing how to act' or 'how to respond' as found in the disciplinary spaces. These spaces are open to a wide variety of behaviours as there is no one given situation, no one set of rules to follow, and no one way to act. Parks thus act as a counter-space to the disciplined spaces which produce disciplined bodies. It is in these spaces that the construction of 'queer' as the 'Other' is subverted. The chapter thus intends to understand how the performance of gender creates a sense of intimacy in the parks which the queers could not find in their homes, community, neighbourhood, and workplace. Focusing on a few case studies, the chapter also argues that parks are not empty containers, but rather are layered with discourses of caste, class, religion, age, and sexual preferences which reveal the politics of belongingness in the parks. Contemporary India, moving far away from the Rajiv Gandhi mode of a panoptical computer network geared towards control, embodies the generic city with a mediatised society that has gone viral. The social media boom in India has provided a technological dimension to public intimacies, transforming the public sphere into the realm of private passions. Notwithstanding the synthetic experience of intimacy in such cases, this unique moment of a viral media landscape offers its solace to queerness when queerness is mostly deemed erroneous and queer intimacies are viewed as abnormal, as 'glitches' in the smooth functioning of the techno-mediatised Indian social economy. Networked surveillance in mediatised India has continued and proliferated in multiple ways in the contemporary information age. Against the official media discourse of mapping out the legal, the peculiar quality of new social media to explode out of the grips of its producers allows it to plot an alternative map of the extra-legal spaces with its own logic of now-viral surveillance. Relying on case studies of queer dating apps that utilise geospatial technology, Silpa Mukherjee's chapter 'Queer intimacies in the time of new media: when Grindr produces alternative cartographies' engages with intimacies (considered as error) and the feedback loop that they create for the official discourse of maximum order and compliance. The popular apps for socialising and gay cruising (Grindr, Blender, PlanetRomeo, OKCupid, GuySpy, etc.) renegotiate the logic of official surveillance, plotting alternative maps of the city which bring to light the sensational, spectacular image of the urban labyrinth left untraced in official survey maps. While this activity of web-based gay cruising shares uncanny similarities with state surveillance mechanisms, it blurs the distinction between categories of technology, law, crime, surveillance, voyeurism, and private intimacies. The delirium of mediatised postmodernity, the hyperlinked logics of commodified experience of the globalising middleclass, and the conflation of intimacy and telematics in a peculiar fashion challenges the ordered logics of love and official control. While the focus of the chapter remains on the queer intimacies mediated by contemporary digital technologies, it refers to spaces of techno-mediatised queerness of the past (viz. cyber cafes, video parlours, single-screen theatres, etc.), searching for traces of the analogue and engaging with the constant remediations shaping the new media world. The body's interaction with changing technology is the central node of inquiry here. The chapter focuses on the proprioceptive body – a body that responds to stimuli between the nerves and fleetingly glances at something and touches something else and thus shifts its attention in an almost plastic way among multiple media objects. Hence it is a body that affectively responds to the official forms of techno surveillance without cognitively assessing it, judging its merits, or forcefully reacting against it.

Textual belongings, the fifth section, consists of two chapters on literary representation of intimacy and the associated inhibitions. 'Intimacy, belonging and masculinity in Bhalachandra Nemade's novel *Kosla (Cocoon)*' by Mangesh Kulkarni provides a psychoanalysis of the novel *Kosla*. Fellow writers and scholars have scrutinized it extensively from various standpoints, giving rise to a sizeable critical corpus over the last five decades. However, the novel has not been interpreted systematically from a psychological perspective. The chapter suggests a possible way of filling this lacuna by drawing on certain key insights available in the work of the distinguished psychoanalyst Sudhir Kakar. It heuristically deploys Kakar's mapping of the modern Indian male psyche and also takes into account the relevant findings that have emerged from recent research on the making of men and masculinities more generally. This twofold investigation seeks to illuminate the complex interweave of intimacy, belonging, and masculinity in the fictional world of *Kosla*. While the chapter focuses on a specific work, it is offered as a modest contribution to the ongoing dialogue between psychoanalysis, critical masculinity studies, and literary theory. A number of North East Indian poets writing in English appear to be engaged in the attempt to create a cultural space for their beloved community, with respect to both the peripheral plurality writhing within the concept of India and the disturbing dominance of the imagined monolithic centre, by writing poems dipped in folktales and myths of immediate cultural origin. Sarat Kumar Doley's 'Hesitant intimacy: North East Indian English poetry vis à-vis the Indian nationhood' scrutinises the duality of the target in terms of the caress with which these myths and legends are held up in the poems and the defiant voice that announces the glory of these ancient myths to the rest of India, presenting an interesting instance of the problems associated with intimacy and belonging within the Indian nation, which in turn, sums up the twin concerns of these poets for the endangered local values and the cultural repression emanating from an imagined centre.

The final section, **Techno intimacies**, has two important chapters on virtual intimacy. In 'Maternal intimacies online: How Indian mombloggers reconfigure self, body, family, and community,' Sucharita Sarkar hypothesises a distinction between – what she has termed – motherhood intimacy and mothering intimacy. This distinction is premised on Adrienne Rich's seminal separation of the oppressive institution of patriarchal motherhood from the potentially empowering experience of mothering. Mothering intimacy between the mother and child is an embodied, private experience that has historically been controlled by patriarchal institutions and reified into publicly enforced motherhood intimacies. The author substantiates this contention by referencing Indian, specifically Hindu, scriptural and contemporary prescriptions of motherhood that subjugate mothers. The chapter asserts that internet-enabled virtual social networks, by destabilising public-private boundaries, have contributed to the emergence of new kinds of maternal intimacies online, intimacies that both resist and replicate the predominant binaries of mothering and motherhood. Through a selective study of a few Indian momblogs, both subcontinental and diasporic, the chapter elucidates how motherhood intimacies and mothering intimacies are mediated and complicated in the blogosphere. Intimacy has conventionally been posed as the antithesis of technology. Orienting its engagements with intimacy through the recent surge of exchanges between people, groups, and communities via technological means, the concluding chapter, 'Routing techno-intimacy: risk, anxiety, and the ambient political' by Geeta Patel, expands the range of technologies to also include statistical collaboratives such as risk pools, identification cards, regulatory practices, and scientific analyses and revisits intimacies between people that are engendered, encouraged, and cemented by routing intimacy through such a plethora of technologies, challenging the presumptions that underlie these commonplace understandings of intimacy.

Belonging through intimacy

In one's private zone one does not remain necessarily alone but with the intimate others. Hence, the question is how to or why to turn the strangers into intimate others through a 'longing-to-belong' (Ferreday 2009: 21). The answer lies in the dream to determinately fight together and 'leave behind the hierarchies and "unfreedoms" of gendered and racially marked identities' (Seidler 1998: 20). Belonging through intimacy is meant for not to negate one's identity but to minimise 'disidentification' – Žižek explains disidentification as tendency to negate the multiplicities by retaining 'false distance toward the actual co-ordinates of the subject's social existence' (Žižek 1998) through interactivity. Belonging 'captures the desire for some sort of attachment' (Probyn 1996: 19) and affect has an important role in the culmination of such desire.

For a meaningful belonging, 'What is important is a holding-in-common of qualities, perspectives, identities or ideas' (Wilbur 2000: 47). Extending this argument one can say that despite having differences in our identities, 'holding-in-common' in terms of perspectives and ideas among the communities of 'unfreedoms' (Seidler 1998: 20) and affect might help in accelerating the politics of belonging which is never in a fixity but always a part of one's prioritised 'shared concern' in the process of becoming. The 'surfaces of the other' as a marginalised being surfaces the 'suffering,' that appeals the self to extend sensitivity to other not to 'order the course and heal the substance of the other, but to feel the feeling of the other' (Lingis 1994: 31). A sense of belonging between subcultures, thus, can be premised upon the hope that 'in the midst of the work of the rational community, there forms the community of those who have nothing in common, of those who have nothingness . . . in common' (Lingis 1994: 13). Jean-Luc Nancy has invited us to reconsider how 'all loves. . . . are superbly singular' (Nancy 1991: 99). Moving beyond the traditional notion of love, predominantly seen as a hybridised encounter/relation, an intimate belonging of love actually remains a singular passage of opening of the one to another, assuring, thereby, singularity of a being in its community.

The politics of belonging is endeavoured at fostering the intimate act of offering help to others, which, according to Derrida's notion of 'hospitality,' is intrinsic to 'the performance of happiness; desire which disturbs the pure narcissistic enjoyment of the Oedipal self and its familiars, and which reaches towards the absolute demand of the other' (Abbinnett 2013:183). Politics of belonging as a mode of exploring intimacy for the recognition of a pluralist identity is closely related to the 'politics of happiness': moving beyond the 'neoliberal economy of pleasure,' happiness as an experience 'can only be approached through the presence of others, both familiar and unfamiliar, to whom we must respond without the expectation of requital. This then is the aporetic fate of humanity: to live between ideological regimes that offer the shelter of collective happiness and the possibility of receiving the spectres that haunt the experience of belonging, plenitude, and love.' (Abbinnett 2013: 185)

The above arguments can be nullified by the single question namely how can an-other perceive the 'lived' experience of an-otherised? If 'lived' experience are marked with the absence of freedom of choice in even altering the experiences but keep on suffering the 'lack,' then one can argue that it is easier to relate the self-'lived' experience of experiencing the 'lack,' howsoever different it might be in form but equal in its degree, for the disables in India with that of the 'not-self' like the queers, Dalits, disempowered women or the North East Indian contested citizens. Moreover, extending the argument provided by Srinivas, it can be said that these diverse marginalised groups reside in 'same cultural universe,' and therefore, unlike someone from the foreign geo-cultural space, it is 'self-in-the-other' that is operational unlike the non-self or non-other position (Srinivas 1996: 656–657). Approving of Srinivas's stand, Sarukkai has also affirmed that, 'For a person steeped in this tradition, this does make a qualitative difference in constructing the other.' (Sarukkai 1997: 1408). Moreover, there are various modes available in this shared 'cultural universe' like the Gandhian *satyagraha* and *ahimsa*, the Upanishadic ideal of *vasudhaiva kutumbakam*, the ideal of collective empathy of the Buddhist *sarvabhutadaya* or the Jaina notion of *syadvada* (interrelation among all things) and *anekantavada* (multifaceted truth), which one can follow in order to acquire a pluralistic understanding of the self vis-à-vis Other(s) and vice versa.

Beyond the traditional linking of opposition/contradiction with difference, pluralism as a guiding trait into our understanding of difference might enable us to treat difference itself as ever-shifting: 'Difference must become the element, the ultimate unity; it must therefore refer to other differences which never identify it but rather differentiate it. Each term in series, being already a difference, must be put into a variable relation with other terms, thereby constituting other series devoid of centre and convergence. Every object, every thing must see its own identity swallowed up in difference, each being no more than a difference between differences. Difference must be shown differing.' (Deleuze 1994: 56). With the acceptance of the self and the other as individuals with differences along with the recognition that 'since differences are what there is, and since every truth is the coming-to-be of that which is not yet' (Badiou 2001:27) differences need to be treated in its more significant facilitating of 'the constitution of a subjectivity in the interrelation to others, which is a form of exposure, availability, and vulnerability. This recognition entails the necessity of containing the other, the suffering, and the enjoyment of others.' (Braidotti 2009:58). Intercultural dialogue among the suffering subjects can pave way for an intimacy. Inert tolerance and passive acceptance of differences do not necessarily enhance intimacy. Rather it often reinforces anxiety. Intersectional communication and a collaborative togetherness alone can enable us to become intimate inhabitants. Touraine has rightly observed: 'The three themes of the Subject, communication and solidarity are inseparable, just as freedom, equality and fraternity were inseparable during the republican phase of democracy. Their interdependence delineates a field of social and political mediations that can re-establish the link between the instrumental world and the symbolic world, and thus prevent civil society from being reduced to a market or an enclosed community.' (Touraine 2000:301).

No consolidated identity is an absolute homogenised one and in that sense any bordering of identity is based on a border crossing. Avar Brah has rightly pointed out that 'border crossings do not occur only across the dominant/dominated dichotomy, but . . . equally, there is traffic within cultural formations of the subordinated groups' (Brah 1996: 209). Combining Brah's observation with that of Clifford's critiquing of our bias for an organic/naturalised culture of a particular group of identity,[8] one may argue that every identity encompasses a double consciousness about subjectivity where destabilising the inside/outside conflict, one's 'intervention is necessarily that of both not quite an insider and not quite an outsider.' As an 'inappropriate other or same who moves about with always at least two gestures: that of affirming "I am like you" while persisting in her[or his] difference and that of reminding "I am different" while unsettling every definition of otherness arrived at' (Minh-ha 1990: 374–375) the essentialised bordering of any excusive identity possibly ends up in framing an outsider-within or an-other as a non-identical-ally. Relating Mockus's plea for an amphibian intersectionality with what Lavie and Swedenburg call 'the borderzone between identity-as-essence and identity-as-conjuncture' (Lavie and Swedenburg 1996:13) one might proceed towards 'soft boundaries' through which the 'amphibian borders' of the diverse identities would crisscross and 'obey partially divergent systems of rules without a loss of intellectual and moral integrity' (Mockus 1994:39). Moreover, this 'borderzone' as a 'third time-space' that moves beyond the older notions of identity without instituting a new fixity of identity by being 'too heterogeneous, mobile, and discontinuous for fixity,' nonetheless, 'remains anchored in the politics of history/location' (Lavie and Swedenburg 1996:14).

Does this plea for overcoming anxiety of intimacy through belonging sound like too much of an impossible utopia? Let me address this by borrowing from Spivak, who while highlighting the importance of a mythopoetic understanding of history 'where history is in the process of becoming' (Butler and Spivak 2010: 115), has insisted upon the need to 'conceive of history as mythopoesis' so that 'we must again and again undo the opposition between philosophy and the practical' (Butler and Spivak 2010:117).

Let me end with a happy note by providing a concrete example of how the contemporary India is slowly but surely venturing to move beyond the age-old anxieties of intimate belonging. September 6, 2018 is historically significant in the politics of belonging in contemporary India. The verdict given by a five-judge Constitution Bench of the Supreme Court that has partially struck down the provisions of Section 377 of the Indian Penal Code has instigated the process of granting approval to consensual same-sex intimacy. The judgement has pointed out how the 158 years old colonial law that criminalised homosexuality in private domain has actually violated Article 14, 15, 19 and 21 of the Indian constitution. The Chief Justice of India has rightly asserted that the majoritarian inhibition or 'mainstream' societal taboos are not the valid lens through which constitution can be explicated. The judgement that decriminalises the queer community in India also provides assurance to all who are engaged with the politics of belonging through intimacy by reinforcing how, securing equality and equal protection within the country, prohibition of prevalent discriminations, guarantying the freedom essential for individuals so that none are deprived of their personal liberties and life are the constitutional safeguards provided to all those who are perceived as the minoritised 'Other' of the proscriptive 'mainstream.'

Notes

1 According to Rosi Braidotti it refers to 'a shared desire for certain transformations to be actualized.' (Braidotti 2009: 51).

2 'The novelty of the coming politics is that it will no longer be a struggle for the conquest or control of the State, but a struggle between the State and the non-State (humanity)' (Agamben 2009: 84).

3 Reflecting on the notion of 'Indianness,' U. R. Ananthamurthy has said: 'The vibrant Indianness emerges only when you don't accord parameters to it. Vaikom Mohammed Basheer writes about Muslims, but he is a very Indian writer. So also with Paul Zachariah, who writes about the lives of Christians. India's plurality has to be continuously explored. Take the popular slogan "unity in diversity." If you overstress diversity, you begin to see unity and viceversa. For instance, when we try to select binding factors in the Indian cultural tapestry, we begin to notice variations everywhere – the Assamese from the Kannadigas, the Bengalis as dissimilar from the Maharashtrians, and so on. On the other hand, when we consciously try to pick up the contradictions, we stumble upon the unifying factors.' ('Interview,' *Times of India* 10 December 1994.)

4 The people who do not succumb to the homogenised national ideology of the state and, therefore, seen as 'illegitimate' residents.

5 Judith Butler has also made similar observations: 'When the chain of equivalence is operational as a political category, it requires that particular identities acknowledge that they share with other such identities the situation of a necessarily incomplete determination. They are fundamentally the set of differences from which they emerge, and this set of differences constitutes the structural features of the domain of political sociality. If any such particular identity seeks to universalise its own situation without recognising that other identities are in an identical structural situation, it will fail to achieve an alliance with the other emerging identities, and will mistakenly identify the meaning and the place of universality itself. The universalisation of the particular seeks to elevate a specific content to a global condition, making an empire of its local meaning.' (Butler et al. 2000: 31).

6 For a detailed study see Kasulis 2002.

7 Chapters 1,2,3,8 and 15 along with portions of the introduction have been published from *Studies in Humanities and Social Sciences,* XX(1): 2015, by the permission of the Secretary, IIAS.

8 '"Cultures" do not hold still for their portraits' (Clifford 1986: 10)

References

Abbinnett, Ross. 2013. *Politics of Happiness: Connecting the Philosophical Ideas of Hegel, Nietzsche and Derrida to the Political Ideologies of Happiness.* New York, London: Bloomsbury.

Agamben, Giorgio. 2009. *The Coming Community*, trans. Michael Hardt. Minneapolis: University of Minnesota Press.

Arendt, Hannah. 1958. *The Human Condition.* Chicago: University of Chicago Press.

Arendt, Hannah. 1994. *Essays in Understanding, 1930–1954,* ed. Jerome Kohn. New York: Harcourt Brace.

Badiou, Alain. 2001. *Ethics: An Essay on the Understanding of Evil*, trans. P. Holworth. London, New York: Verso.

Benjamin, Jessica. 2002. 'The Rhythm of Recognition: Comments on the Work of Louis Sander.' *Psychoanalytic Dialogues*, 12(1): 43–53.

Brah, Avtar. 1996. *Cartographies of Diaspora: Contesting Identities*. London: Routledge.

Braidotti, Rosi. 2009. 'Postsecular Feminist Ethics.' In Elzbieta H. Oleksy (ed.), *Intimate Citizenships: Gender, Sexualities, Politics*, pp. 40–62. New York: Routledge.

Butler, Judith and Gayatri Chakravorty Spivak. 2010. *Who Sings the Nation-State?* London, New York, Kolkata: Seagull Books.

Butler, Judith, Ernesto Laclau and Slavoj Žižek. 2000. *Contingency, Hegemony, Universality: Contemporary Dialogues on the Left*. London, New York: Verso.

Chakraborty, Kaustav. 2017. *Indigeneity, Tales and Alternatives, Revisiting Select Tribal Folktales*. Shimla: Indian Institute of Advanced Study.

Clifford, James. 1986. 'Partial Truths.' In J. Clifford and M. George (eds.), *Writing Culture*. pp. 1–26. Berkeley, CA: University of California Press.

Cohen, Cathy J. 2005. 'Punks, Bulldaggers, and Welfare Queens: The Radical Potential of Queer Politics?' In E. P. Johnson and M. G. Henderson (eds.), *Black Queer Studies: A Critical Anthology*, pp. 21–51. Durham: Duke University Press.

Dallmayr, Fred R. 1989. 'Hermeneutics and Deconstruction: Gadamer and Derrida in Dialogue.' In Diane P. Michelfelder and Richard E. Palmer (eds.), *Dialogue and Deconstructions*, pp. 75–92. Albany, NY: SUNY Press.

Deleuze, Gilles. 1994. *Difference and Repetition*, trans. P. Paton. London: Athlone Press.

De Souza, Peter Ronald. 2002. 'Living Together, Living Differently.' In K.J. Mahale (ed.), *Tolerance: A Golden Pat h to Peaceful Co-existence*, pp. 18–30. New Delhi: Books Indi International.

Fabian, Johannes. 1983. *Time and the Other: How Anthropology Makes Its Subject*. New York: Columbia University Press.

Fabian, Johannes. 2006. 'The Other Revisited: Critical Afterthoughts.' *Anthropological Theory*, 6(2): 139–152.

Ferreday, Debra. 2009. *Online Belongings: Fantasy, Affect and Web Communities*. Oxford: Peter Lang.

Finkler, Kaja. 2005. 'Family, Kinship, Memory and Temporality in the Age of the New Genetics.' *Social Science & Medicine*, 61: 1059–1071.

Gadamer, Hans-George. 1989. 'Destruction and Deconstruction.' In Diane P. Michelfelder and Richard E. Palmer (eds.), *Dialogue and Deconstructions*, pp. 102–113. Albany: State University of New York.

Giddens, Anthony. 1992. *The Transformation of Intimacy: Sexuality, Love and Eroticism in Modern Societies*. Stanford, CA: Stanford University Press.

Hardt, Michael and Antonio Negri. 2004. *Multitude: War and Democracy in the Age of Empire*. New York: The Penguin.

Hasan, Mushirul and Asim Roy (eds.). 2005. *Living Together Separately: Cultural India in History and Politics*. New Delhi: Oxford University Press.

Hooks, Bell. 1994. *Outlaw Culture*. New York, London: Routledge.

Irigaray, Luce. 1994. *Thinking the Difference for a Peaceful Revolution*, trans. Karin Montin. London: The Athlone Press.

Kasulis, Thomas P. 2002. *Intimacy or Integrity: Philosophy and Cultural Difference*. Honolulu: University of Hawaii Press.

Kropotkin, Peter. 1972. *Mutual Aid: A Factor of Evolution*. New York: New York University Press.

Laclau, Ernesto. 1996. *Emancipation(s)*. London, New York: Verso.

Lavie, Smadar and Ted Swedenburg eds. 1996. *Displacement, Diaspora and Geographies of Identity*. Durham, London: Duke University Press.

Lingis, Alphonso. 1994. *The Community of Those Who Have Nothing in Common*. Bloomington, IN: Indiana University Press.

Minh-ha, Trinh T. 1990. 'Not you/Like you: Post-colonial Women and the Interlocking Questions of Identity and Difference.' In G. Anzaldua (ed.), *Making Face, Making Soul*, pp. 371–375. San Francisco: Aunt Lute Foundation Books.

Mockus, Antanas. 1994. 'Anfibios culturales y divorcio entre ley, moral y cultura.' *Analisis Politico*, 21: 37–48.

Nancy, Jean-Luc. 1991. *The Inoperative Community*, ed. Peter Connor, trans. Peter Connor, Lisa Garbus, Michael Holland, and Simona Sawhney. Minneapolis, Oxford: University of Minnesota Press.

Panikkar, Raimundo. 1980. *Myth, Faith, and Hermeneutics: Cross-Cultural Studies*. New York: Paulist Press.

Probyn, E. 1996. *Outside Belongings*. London, New York: Routledge.

Rilke, Rainer Maria. 1975. *Rilke on Love and Other Difficulties: Translations and Considerations of Rainer Maria Rilke*, ed. John I. L. Mood. New York, London: W.W. Norton & Company.

Sarukkai, Sundar. 1997. 'The 'Other' in Anthropology and Philosophy.' *Economic and Political Weekly*, 32(24) (14–20 June):1406–1409.

Seidler, V. 1998. 'Embodied Knowledge and Virtual Space.' In J. Wood (ed.), *The Virtual Embodied: Presence/Practice/Technology*, pp. 15–29. New York: Routledge.

Srinivas, M. N. 1996. 'Indian Anthropologists and the Study of Indian Culture.' *Economic and Political Weekly*, XXXI(11)(March): 656–657.

Touraine, Alain. 2000. *Can We Live Together? Equality and Difference*, trans. David Macey. Cambridge: Polity Press.

Vidal, Hernan. 2009. 'An Aesthetic Approach to Issues of Human Rights.' *Hispanic Issues On Line*, 4: 14–43.

Wilbur, S.P. 2000. 'An Archaeology of Cyberspace: Virtuality, Community, Identity.' In D. Bell and B.M. Kennedy (eds.), *The Cybercultures Reader*, pp. 45–55. New York: Routledge.

Žižek, S. 1998. 'The Cyberspace Real: Cyberspace Between Perversion and Trauma.' www.egs.edu/faculty/Zizek/Zizek-the-cyberspace-real.html. Accessed 4 September 2018.

PART I

Intimacy, marginality, and anxiety

1

IDENTIFICATION, BELONGING, AND THE CATEGORY OF DALIT

K. Satyanarayana

The question of Dalit as a political identity seems to be facing a crisis in the recent times. Is Dalit simply a caste identity which is based on biological differences and therefore, it is natural? Is Dalit a position articulated in the diverse historical and cultural experiences of caste subordination? Dalit Panthers proposed Dalit identity as a pedagogic identity open to social groups subjected to caste and other forms of discrimination and subordination. They pointed out that 'the Dalit is no longer merely an untouchable, and he is a Dalit, but he is also a worker, a landless labourer, a proletarian.' (Joshi 1986: 141). They further claimed that 'the caste nature of the term Dalit is breaking down.' It is important to note that Dalit is not 'merely an untouchable.' Dalit is a political position which is shaped based on a set of identifications in the context of struggles for equality[1]. Sociological caste identity is one of the several identifications in the making of Dalit. Dalit critic Baburao Bagul extended and revised the meaning of Dalit. He discovered the legacy of Western enlightenment, humanism of Buddha and Christ to the category of Dalit and reimagined Dalit as a human figure. He criticised and rejected the Hindu identity that denied humanity and dignity to the untouchables (Bagul 1992: 271–289.). In the course of history, Dalit identity remained the identity of untouchable castes and more recently, it was attributed to the identity of specific subcastes in the Scheduled caste list[2]. I argue in this chapter that 'Dalit' is a category of political identification and belonging, rather than merely a natural, birth-based identity, and that it is built on the multiple legacies of democratic struggles. I turn to two contemporary debates to understand the political significance of Dalit identity: first, the literary discussions on 'Dalit' in contemporary Telugu Dalit literature and second, the public debate on Rohith Vemula's Dalit/caste identity in the recent struggle of the students of University of Hyderabad.

Debate and delineation

The category of 'Dalit' was at the centre of the discussions on Telugu Dalit literature in the early 1990s[3]. Literary critic G. Lakshmi Narasaiah reviewed Dalit literary works and made fresh proposals about the category of Dalit literature in the mainstream forum, *Aadivaaram Andhra Jyothi*, a special Sunday supplement of *Andhra Jyothi* daily. Many Dalit writers and critics responded to Lakshmi Narasaiah's analysis and proposals. These debates and controversies described as 'Dalitavadam' (Dalit critique) continued in small journals and public debates. Dalit poet and critic Satish Chandar contested Lakshmi Narasaiah's construction of Dalit as an omnibus category of SC, ST, BC, and minority social groups. I would like to revisit this debate between Lakshmi Narasaiah and Satish Chandar.

Lakshmi Narasaiah proposed that birth and experience of writers would be an essential condition to define the categories of Dalit and Dalit literature (Satyanarayana 2012). He refuted arguments such as literature is primarily a reflection of social consciousness of writers irrespective of their social origin. He countered views that supported the claim that there is no connection between social existence of the poet and the content of her poetry. He asked a revolutionary Marxist poet Siva Reddy, 'why the poet who responded to several issues in life is not able to respond and write about Dalit issues. There is not a single poem on caste issues in this book of 120 pages.' (Ashcroft et al. 2012: 462). It was argued by some readers that the poet should not be questioned why he/she did not write about caste atrocities but he/she should be judged based on what is written, Lakshmi Narasaiah rejected this theory of literature as self-expression of creative individuals. He rightly rejects this view, arguing that 'a poet is not a dictator' and that the critic is a guide who has the responsibility to evaluate poets with discretion (Ibid.). In other words, literary activity is a self-conscious activity that shaped form, expression, and ideas. He emphasised the social role of the writer and social of function of literature. If we have to identify one key issue in the debate, it is the category of Dalit in Telugu Dalit literature that was formulated by Lakshmi Narasaiah and other interlocutors in the Dalit literary debates.

In a series of polemical essays, Lakshmi Narasaiah argued for a distinctive Dalit identity based on social origin, Ambedkarite ideology and unity of the oppressed castes and minorities. In the 'Preface' to the first published anthology of Dalit poetry, *Chikkanavutunnapata* (1995), G. Lakshmi Narasaiah, the editor declares:

> The truth is that 'the progress' proposed by hitherto existing progressive literature known as people's literature did not recognise the fundamental social reality, the specific problems of the majority people. The well-known writers portrayed abstract oppressed (Amurta peeditulu) and proposed abstract progress (Amurta Abhyudayam) . . . As per this abstract progress, oppressed are those who were subjected to economic oppression and inequality and denial of rights
>
> *(Narasaiah 'Preface')*

Lakshmi Narasaiah defined the new category of Dalit poetry as poetry written by oppressed castes and minority poets. He specified the oppressed castes as S.C., S.T., B.C. poets and the minority poets as Muslim poets. He further proposed that the category of Dalit is an omnibus category of SC, ST, and BC social groups based on their caste identity, as also Muslim minorities based on their religious identity and 'Deeseeya' (indigenous) Marxism, a combination of Ambedkarism and Marxism, would be the ideology of Dalit poets. He observed that the upper-caste writers could only play the role of mediators in Dalit literature (Narasaiah 'Preface'). He counterposed Dalit literature to the Marxist oriented Revolutionary literature and constructed Dalit as a different and distinctive identity in contrast to Hindu, Brahmin, Marxist, and Feminist identities[4]. The Dalit as a collective identity of SC, ST, BC, and Minorities enabled the mobilisation of Dalit writers and consolidated the field of Dalit literature in Telugu. Many Dalit writers and critics identified with the position outlined by Lakshmi Narasaiah. Lakshmi Narasaiah emphasised sameness and ideological unity of SC, ST, BC, and Minorities to construct a unified and singular Dalit identity. While the unity based on caste and religious identities and Ambedkarite ideological leanings provided the foundation to the authentic Dalit identity, the axes of differences based on subcastes, genders, religions, and ideologies posed a challenge to the politics of the authentic Dalit identity. In this debate, the adversaries of the authentic Dalits are not just the Brahmins and upper castes but also Marxists and Feminists. For example, writing about Dalit life from a Marxist perspective is not accepted as part of Dalit literature. Balladeer Gaddar's song 'Dalita Pululamma' (Dalit Tigers), written in the context of Karamchedu Dalit massacre, was criticised for its Marxist perspective. Gaddar, who is from an untouchable caste, wrote 'Dalita Pululamma' from a new perspective in response to the Karamchedu massacre in 1985. Similarly, a small number of Dalits in the Marxist literary organisations began to write about Dalit life after the Karamchedu massacre.

But there were some dissenting voices in this debate. Lakshmi Narasaiah's categorisation of Dalit and Dalit literature was contested by many other writers and critics. They did not accept Lakshmi Narasiah's bounded notion of Dalit literature. The premise of 'pure' Dalit as was challenged. Among others, Dalit poet and critic Satish Chandar contested Lakshmi Narasaiah's idea of Dalit among other issues. I would briefly revisit the debate between Lakshmi Narasaiah and Satish Chandar to understand the complexity of the question of Dalit identity and its multiples legacies.

The ideological battle between Lakshmi Narasaiah and Satish Chandar appeared as a personal dispute as the polemical debate began with Lakshmi Narasaiah's criticism of Satish Chandar's poetry. Lakshmi Narasaiah reviewed Satish Chandar's collection of poetry *Panchama Vedam* and criticised him for his imitation of Revolutionary literature and use of sanskritised Telugu (Satyanarayana 2000:61–64). He described Satish Chandar as a poet with two faces- one revolutionary Marxist and the other Dalit. In reply to Lakshmi Narasaiah, Satish Chandar wrote a series of essays criticising Lakshmi Narasaiah's idea of authentic Dalit[5]. The immediate context of this debate was the wide appreciation of Satish Chandar's poetry as a powerful expression of Dalit identity. K. Srinivas, a well-known Telugu literary critic, observed that the distinctive feature of Satish Chandar's poetry is its representation of a discernible Dalit identity (Srinivas 1995: 79–84). Chandar recalls, 'This appreciation put me in a difficult situation. My fellow Dalit poets wrote articles saying that I was claiming to be an adikavi and Dalit Nannayya (Nannayya is regarded as the father of Telugu literature).' (Satyanarayana and Tharu 2013: 563). Lakshmi Narasaiah analysed the same set of poems when published as a collection and criticised the limitations of Chandar's Dalit poetry and his authentic Dalit identity.

Lakshmi Narasaiah's redefinition of Dalit attracted a lot of criticism. It was pointed out that that the very categories of SC, ST, BC, and minorities are problematic; too broad and vacuous. One of the powerful voices of Dalit poetry, Satish Chandar, who was a Marxist turned to Dalit politics, put forward this view forcefully. He argued that the experiences of the BCs and the SCs are dissimilar. Making a distinction between 'Ooru' (village) and 'wada' (ghetto outside the village), Chandar argued that the problems of those who live in the village (BCs) and the wada (SCs) are quite different. Similarly, he pointed out that the poetry of Muslim minorities does not deal with caste annihilation (Satyanarayana 2000:68–72, 73–80). He along with several others contested the new inclusive category of Dalit as SCs, STs, BCs, and Muslims and the ideology of these Dalit poets as indigenous Marxism (redefined in the light of Ambedkarism).

Satish Chandar questioned the idea of authentic and singular Dalit identity based on mere birth and Ambedkarite ideology. Following Marathi critic Arjun Dangle's view that 'Dalit is not a caste but a realization,' Chandar emphasised conscious identification with the untouchable community, displaying the wounds, social discrimination, humiliation and self-respect as constitutive elements of Dalit identity (Chandar 2015: 303). Satish Chandar claimed the legacy of Marxist ideology as well as Ambedkarite thought (Ibid.: 325). He declared that he is both a Marxist and a Dalit. He contested the exclusive identity based on sociological caste identity and Ambedkarite legacy. Dalit is a position that allows some members of the Scheduled castes to identify with the Dalit identity but also draws on the legacy of Marxist, Ambedkarite, and other ideologies. He was equally critical of the Marxist critics who have reiterated the primacy of the category of 'class' and are unwilling to acknowledge the category of 'caste' as constitutive of the literary imagination and critical analysis. Papineni Sivashankar, a Marxist critic and a short story writer, observed, 'What is there and visible is the consciousness of the middle class and the lower middle class. We have to recognize the power of that consciousness and the special identity questions that it is bringing to the fore.' (Ashcroft et al. 2012: 461). In this comment on Dalit literature, the category of 'Dalit' is described as middleclass; thus, caste identity, which is at the core of the category of Dalit, has been obscured (Ibid.). The elision of caste identity in the construction of 'Dalit' obscures experiences of caste discrimination, social stigma, and violence.

Lakshmi Narasaiah's view of Dalit identity was also challenged by the Feminist critics for its masculine character. In a response to the debate on the *Nishani*, a collection of Dalit poetry, Feminist critics Volga and others observed that Dalit poetry is poetry of struggle. It is the poetry of Dalit men and women. They further said, 'If we have to flourish as Dalit poets and Feminist poets, we have to invent our own voice and style that does not obscure, hurt and prevent the specific identity and distinctive existence (with all the minor aspects) of all the oppressed groups.' (Satyanarayana 2000:119). They strongly objected to the language, which is humiliating, insulting, and abusive to women. Sharing the Feminist anger, Satish Chandar rejected valorisation of abusive, feudal, and patriarchal language as Dalit language and Dalits as uncivilised and patriarchal people[6]. In other words, the masculine Dalit identity as the identity of Dalit poetry is exclusive, sexist, and undemocratic.

In this debate, Satish Chandar asserted his right to lay claim to the ideological legacies of Marxism, Ambedkarism, and Feminism to construct Dalit identity. The bounded and fixed Dalit identity, based on axes of mere sociological caste difference and Ambedkar ideology, is an essentialist identity that does not accommodate differences and negotiations within the Dalit. Chandar conceives a democratic and inclusive Dalit identity.

Rohith Vemula and the claims of contradiction

The controversy surrounding Rohith Vemula's Dalit identity brings several issues to the fore[7]. Is Dalit only a sociological and legal identity based on caste identity? Is Dalit a natural identity based on the patrilineage of a nuclear family? Are caste endogamy and bloodline the basis of Dalit identity? Does 'Dalit' has a social, moral, and political content? Vemula's case poses a problem to the received understanding of Dalit identity and its conflation with caste identity[8].

Vemula was declared as a 'Dalit PhD scholar' when his death was reported. Both Ambedkar Students' Association (ASA) and Vemula mentioned their identities as Scheduled Caste in their memorandums to the University of Hyderabad authorities. Following Vemula's death, the issue of Dalit identity and caste discrimination assumed importance in all the resulting campaigns and debates. The ASA filed a police complaint under the SC/ST Prevention of Atrocities Act against Vice chancellor Appa Rao Podile, Union minister of state Bandaru Dattatreya, Akhil Bharatiya Vidyarthi Parishad leader Susheel Kumar and others. The complaint was accepted on the assumption that Vemula was from a Scheduled Caste. The BJP and several Hindutva organisations, however, began raising doubts over Vemula's caste identity in an apparent bid to derail the debate on caste violence, as also dilute the police case under the SC/ST Act.

An anonymous video released online which shows Vemula's paternal grandmother stating that the late scholar's father, Mani Kumar, and mother, Radhika, were of Vaddera, a Backward caste (BC). Subsequently, the media too began raising doubts about Vemula's identity and the focus shifted to the issue of unscrupulous parties politicising the Dalit identity of Rohith. Another document, an affidavit Radhika submitted to register the birth of her second son, was released where Vemula's mother declares herself a Vaddera. The ASA later released a caste certificate issued by the tahsildar of Guntur that shows Vemula as Mala, a Scheduled caste (SC).

Vemula's father, who had deserted the family more than 20 years ago, was brought in to announce his son's caste identity as Vaddera. The Vaddera association now demanded an enquiry to ascertain Vemula's caste identity[9].

When the character assassination of Vemula reached an unacceptable level, his mother and her two other children declared at a press conference that they belonged to Mala caste. The mother clarified that she was a daughter of migrant Railway labourers from Mala caste and she was informally adopted by a Vaddera family and later married to Mani Kumar. She mentioned her caste as Vaddera in the affidavit register at the birth of her second son, based on the logic of patriarchal law that a married woman inherits her husband's caste. When she separated from Mani Kumar, she moved to a Mala colony with her children. They were subsequently declared themselves as Mala caste by the Tahsildar, Guntur and issued certificates[10].

It is evident now that Rohith Vemula belonged to a single parent family. Rohith was born to parents of intercaste marriage. Rohith's father is a Vaddera, a Backward caste and mother belongs to Mala, a Scheduled caste. After the separation of his parents, Rohith was brought up by his mother who lived among the untouchables in the Mala colony. He adopted his mother's caste identity as his own identity and experienced caste discrimination and prejudice in society. He wrote in his Facebook page that he followed the footsteps of the famous Telugu Dalit poet Jashuva (1895–1971), who claimed his mother's Madiga caste (SC) identity instead of his father's Golla caste (BC). Clearly, he exercised his choice in favour of matrilineage. He identified himself as a Mala and as an untouchable and suffered social stigma and discrimination. He applied for a scheduled caste certificate and got it from the Revenue Department. But he never used his certificate to claim state benefits and concessions for his admission or for his scholarship. He consciously chose to work in the Ambedkar Students' Association and lived as a staunch Ambedkarite. He was one of the five students who were punished by the University by imposing social boycott.

The controversy did not end here. It is repeatedly claimed in mainstream media, Parliament and Telangana state Assembly that Rohith is not a Dalit. Following the logic of patriarchal law, it is argued that Rohith inherited his father's caste and therefore, he is a Vaddera. It is assumed that caste identity is predetermined by birth and patrilineage and therefore, his caste identity is his Dalit identity. It was also contended that Rohith was a Maoist Dalit and therefore he is not an authentic Dalit. In other words, the authentic or pure Dalit is a non-Marxist who is born to parents of the same untouchable caste. Both Christian and Muslim untouchables are not legally eligible to get Scheduled caste status. Following this logic, authentic Dalit is Hindu[11]. It is nothing but the rationale of the *Manusmriti*. Rohith and his mother have no role to declare their caste.

Rohith consciously discarded the inherited savarna caste status based on patrilineage. He identified himself as a Dalit. He believed that the accident of birth does not exhaust possibilities to imagine a new identity. His life and political practice outlined a new set of principles, such as lived social life, experience of social discrimination, political choice, and conscious self-identification to define one's own identity. Rohith wanted to go beyond the imposed identities and questioned the reduction of individual to a number or a thing. He desired to have freedom to choose or reject his given identity and to live as a deracinated individual.

It has been argued that the legal status of a SC person is not a defining aspect of Dalit status and 'the status of SC is nothing more than legal nomenclature and it decides whether or not we avail reservations, and whether or not we avail protection under legislation like the Scheduled Castes and the Scheduled Tribes (Prevention of Atrocities) Act, 1989.' The distinction between the legal status as SC and the political status as Dalit is useful to understand Rohith's politics of self-identification. Rohith is both a SC and Dalit who desired to be a person with no identity. Rohith has a certificate to prove his legal status as a SC, and he has lived experience of discrimination and indignities to claim Dalit status. The general view that the children of an intercaste marriage would take his/her caste from the father was questioned and set aside by the Supreme Court of India in 2012. The court in fact recognised the right of the child to provide evidence of suffering 'deprivations, indignities, humiliations and handicaps like any other member of the community to which his/her mother belonged.'[12]

It is attempted to collapse caste identity and Dalit identity by invoking the patriarchal and Hindu lineage. But Rohith's life story and the struggle for justice opens up the possibilities of the category of Dalit as a democratic and pedagogic identity based on diverse self-identifications and positions of the marginalised castes, genders, and other minorities. The category Dalit is productively employed to consolidate the marginalised untouchable caste groups and its literary cultures. But the fixing of the meaning of Dalit in terms of the unity of caste identities, patrilineage and certain ideologies undermines its emancipator potential. Dalit is an open ended and democratic category to mobilise diverse sections of the marginalised communities to imagine a new human person.

Notes

1 I have benefitted from reading Stuart Hall's essays on the question of identity politics.
2 The Madiga Reservation Porata Samiti criticised that the category of Dalit is occupied by the dominant Scheduled castes like the Malas in Andhra Pradesh.
3 A collection of essays from the debate are edited and published. See Satyanarayana 2000; and also Satyanarayana 2012.
4 Satyanarayana 2000: 217–221. Narasaiah emphasised the Phue-Ambedkarite philosophical outlook, centrality of caste assigned status and values, occupations and graded respect as the constitutive aspects of Dalit perspective, which is different from the Revolutionary Marxist perspective in Andhra Pradesh.
5 Satyanarayana 2000: 68–72, 73–80; *Also See* K. Satyanarayana and Susie Tharu for a summary of Chandar's views559–565.
6 Chandar 297–301. Rejecting the claims of exclusive Dalit language and criticisms of his Brahmanical Telugu, Chandar argued for inventing modern literary expression using all Indian languages including Sanskrit as a common resource. He argued for inventing new literary expression, special language, artistic way of writing poetry.
7 For full details of Rohith Vemula's death and the conditions of caste discrimination in University of Hyderabad, see a report at www.academia.edu/28717795/Report_of_the_Peoples_Tribunal_on_Caste_Discrimination

8 Some of these questions were raised by the Hindutva organisations and certain caste associations.
9 K. Satyanarayana's 'Crossing Caste Lines' recorded some of the local discussions on Rohith's identity in Telugu newspapers at www.thehindubusinessline.com/blink/know/the-politics-over-rohith-vemulas-caste-is-meant-to-thwart-the-identity-he-chose-for-himself/article8163342.ece
10 Sudipto Mandal presented a detailed story of the family in his 'Rohith Vemula: An Unfinished Portrait' at www.hindustantimes.com/static/rohith-vemula-an-unfinished-portrait/
11 BJP leader and Central Minister Venkaiah Naidu writes: 'The Ambedkar Students' Association (ASA), which is a frontal outfit of the ultra-left, is known to have indulged in fascist politics and intimidated political rivals. . . . It needs to be pointed out that the plight of Dalits in general and the activities of the ASA are two distinct issues. Talking against the ASA cannot be construed as talking against Dalits.' See Naidu 2016. at http://indianexpress.com/article/opinion/columns/the-congress-left-bulldozer-jnu-jnu-row-hyderabad-central-university/
12 Rameshbhai Dabhai Naika vs. the State of Gujarat (2012) at https://indiankanoon.org/doc/197038546/

References

Ashcroft, Bill, Ranjini Mendis, Arun Mukherjee and Julie McGonega. (eds.). 2012. *Literature for Our Times: Postcolonial Studies in the Twenty-First Century*. Amsterdam: Rodopi.

Bagul, Baburao. 1992. 'Dalit Literature is But Human Literature.' In Arjun Dangle (ed.), *Poisoned Bread: Modern Marathi Dalit Literature*. Hyderabad: Orient Longman.

Chandar, Satish. 2015. *Nigraha Vaakyam: Sahitya Vimarsha*. Hyderabad: Smiles & Smiles Publications.

Joshi, Barbara R. (ed.). 1986. 'Dalit Panthers Manifesto.' In *Untouchable! Voices of the Dalit Liberation Movement*, pp. 141–147. London: Zed Books.

Naidu, V. 2016. 'The Congress-Left Bulldozer.' *Indian Express* (7 March). http://indianexpress.com/article/opinion/columns/the-congress-left-bulldozer-jnu-jnu-row-hyderabad-central-university/. Accessed 20 September 2016.

Narasaiah, Lakshmi G. and Tripuraneni Srinivas. (eds.). 1995. 'Preface' to *Chikkanavutunna Pata: Dalita Kavitvam*. Vijayawada: Kavitvam Prachuranalu.

Satyanarayana, K. 2012. 'Class, Caste and the Category of Telugu Dalit Literature.' In Bill Ashcroft, Ranjini Mendis, Arun Mukherjee, and Julie McGonega (eds.), *Literature for Our Times: Postcolonial Studies in the Twenty-First Century*. Amsterdam: Rodopi.

Satyanarayana, S.V. 2000. *Dalitavada Vivadalu*. Hyderabad: Vishalandhra Publishing House.

Satyanarayana, K. and Susie Tharu. 2013. *From Those Stubs: Steel Nibs Are Sprouting*. Dossier 2, New Delhi: Harper Collins.

Srinivas, K. 1995. 'Dalita Suryodaya Kavita.' In Satish Chander (ed.), *Panchamavedam*, pp. 79–84. Hyderabad: Navya Prachurana.

2

EMOTIONS IN THE CONTEXT OF CASTE SLAVERY

Exploring the missionary writings on Kerala

P. Sanal Mohan

Introduction

Compared to other parts of India, Kerala had a historically evolved form of caste slavery that made the slave caste men, woman, and children objects of transaction. Anglican Missionaries belonging to the missionary organisations of the Church Missionary Society and the London Missionary Society, based in the native states of Travancore and Cochin in the nineteenth century wrote extensively on slave caste men, women, and children highlighting their sufferings and oppression. Extensively used in nineteenth- and early-twentieth-century writings, the term 'slave castes' denoted the communities such as the Pulayas, Parayas, and Kuravas who were enslaved by the upper castes and exploited as chattel. In the colonial period Kerala was divided into three administrative units viz, the British Malabar, and the native states of Travancore and Cochin. The southern princely state of Travancore had as per 1836 census a slave population of 1,64,864 out of the total population of 1,280,663 (Saradamony 1980: 81). In 1856 the Malabar region had 187,812 slaves out of a total population of 1,602,914 (Logan 1989: 148) while Cochin State had in 1854 more than 50,000 slaves owned by landlords and 6,589 (Day 2006: 65) owned by the government that together constituted one sixth of the total population. In addition to these castes, there were also numerically smaller communities that also would be treated as slave castes. Employed in the wetland paddy fields and dry lands, they provided the necessary labour to the landlords in cultivating their lands in the pre-colonial and colonial times. These landlords, were upper-caste Hindus and traditional Syrian Christians. In addition to them, in certain sources we also come across references to Muslims also owning slaves (Major 2012: 190). Apart from these classes of owners, temples and local governments also owned slaves. In certain cases Churches of traditional Syrian Christians also owned slaves (Kusuman 1973: 40). It was quite common to buy and sell slaves in the open markets and we also come across references to slaves from Kerala entering the Indian Ocean world economy as commodities although we are yet to get detailed historical accounts of such transactions[1]. It is in this larger context that the everyday life of the slave castes came to be observed in the most intimate manner, by the European missionaries who worked in Kerala.

Erasure of emotions enforced by the landlords was one of the major features of caste slavery. For them, the slaves were a property sans emotion. They were not allowed a language to express their emotions. In this chapter the focus is on the emotional world of the slave castes in Kerala from the second half of the nineteenth century through the first half of the twentieth century. For the latter part of the twentieth century I also analyse some writings of Dalit's that could be referred to as vernacular histories in which the emotional aspects of individual and social life appear as a defining feature. Writing of Dalit vernacular histories became a marked phenomenon in Kerala only in the postcolonial period. For understanding the emotional world of the slaves in the nineteenth and early twentieth centuries, I use the missionary writings as source materials. Produced extensively in the course of their interaction with the slave castes in Kerala, the missionary writings constitute the single largest archive on the intimate aspects of the lives of the slave castes that are today referred to as Dalits. Constituting a significant treasure trove of colonial knowledge, the missionary writings foreground the intimate aspects of the lives of the slave castes. Unlike the colonial government officials, the missionaries had close contact with the slave castes that offered them privileged access to the world of the slaves enabling a close observation of their everyday lives[2]. Although the missionaries deployed colonial categories and concepts to analyse the social and cultural world of the slave castes that betrayed their colonial otherness, the information that they provided were sometimes the only source for reconstructing the intimate aspects of the lives of the slaves[3]. While reading the missionary writings on slave castes against the grain we are able to situate them in the particular ideological practical context that enabled their production.

In contemporary studies in the historical experiences and meanings of slavery, the emotional aspects of slavery become very significant[4]. Slavery is signified in the separation of kin, violence and destruction it entailed (Patterson 1982). Needless to say, such an understanding of slavery adds depth to the already accumulated knowledge in the area of slavery studies, which includes the economic structure of the plantation economy in the Atlantic world and the accumulation of capital that trade in slaves made possible. The emotional problems of slavery were very much embedded within its political-economic dimension of labour appropriation and wealth creation[5]. While similar studies are conspicuous by their absence in South Asia, we still have some scholarship in the area of slavery studies. Similarly, only recently have scholars begun to explore the missionary archives to analyse the historical experiences of the slave castes focusing on the intimate aspects of individual and social life. Enfolded in the narrative of the missionaries, the intimate emotional aspects of the lives of the slave caste men, women, and children come to life pronouncing their everyday experience[6]. It is in the study of the everyday life of the slaves that we read about the emotional encounter between the missionaries and the slaves.

Slaves and the missionaries: everyday interaction

Amazed at the family form of the slave castes, the missionaries thought it important to bring them under Protestant Christian discipline. Christian family was thought of as the institutional framework within which the emotional life of the people who joined the missions would find fulfilment. In fact, the family forms prevailing in Kerala among the upper dominant castes such as the Nair were thought of as 'uncivilized,' requiring immediate reform and transformation to install the modern patriarchal family as the norm[7]. One of the central arguments supporting the demand for change in the family form was to provide emotional security to the family as a whole that was not possible in the prevailing matrilineal practices of the Nair. The colonial bureaucracy, the English educated reformists in the community as well as the missionaries who commented on the native customs were all united in their demand for family reforms. A close analysis of the debates in the area of family reforms in the late nineteenth century would show that the rationale for the reorganisation of the family was sought in the emotional economy of society in addition to the economic dimension of it in terms of the inheritance of the family property. While in the case of the Hindu upper castes and some of the lower castes above the slave castes, it was the native states or colonial government that was leading the family reforms. In the case of the slave castes we hardly come across any governmental intervention to reform their family structure or introducing new norms in marriage practices. In the mid-nineteenth century the missionaries who worked among the slave castes had noted the practice of polygamy and polyandry both of which were thought to be against the Christian family norms. It was mandatory for the prospective converts to divorce the wives or husbands whichever the case may be to tread the path of the saviour. The missionaries noted the emotional estrangement that such a policy had created although they could not resolve it as they insisted on Christian family norm of monogamy. Considering the emotional and affective dimension of the slave castes that came under the missionary instruction, such decisions to part with their wives and husbands must have been really painful[8]. In the reports of the Church Missionary Society missionaries we come across a number of similar cases in the Travancore region of Kerala in which the emotional life of the slave castes became the central issue[9]. In many cases the slave caste men and women had the counter argument that their former Gods blessed their marriages and therefore they thought they could continue to remain in their marital status although it contradicted the Christian norm of monogamy.

While this was a case of the people who joined the Protestant Church that imposed its control on the emotional life of the slave castes, there was the age-old practice of the slave transaction that was the most terrible form of emotional estrangement that the slave castes faced in Kerala. Recalled in a heartrending manner in the oral tradition of the slave castes all over Kerala, the piercing pains of the breakups of families foreground the question of emotion in the idiom of the slave castes even before their interface with the European missionaries (John 1998: 33–34). While there are slave transaction documents that have survived from the early medieval period that refer to the particular transaction in slave caste men, women, and children they hardly refer to the emotional aspects of the lives of the people thus separated[10]. In such documents, slaves appear just as any other commodity that, thus transacted, yields a price that has been agreed on by local landlords or their men. None of these documents ever mention the fact that these were men, women, and children with an emotional life. Contrary to this, in the missionary writings – letters, reports, diaries, and other correspondences – slaves emerge as human beings with emotions, history, and expectations of a future[11]. In many cases we read about a possible good life outside the terrible and mortal regime of the upper-caste landlords.

The emotionally distraught condition of the slave castes has been recorded by one of the missionaries in a touching manner:

> [T]hey draw out a miserable existence and are often left in the old age to beg for their support or to perish with hunger. By few are they comforted pitied or relieved; none seeks to remove their distress and no man cares for their souls. These are some of the many woes connected with slavery in this land.[12]

One of the central themes of missionary writings on slave castes had been the sufferings and oppressions that they had to undergo. If we consider the entire body of writings that the Protestant missionaries generated on the slave castes in Kerala, one running theme would be the ontological wounds that the latter had to suffer as a collective. The oppressions and sufferings were part of the structural violence that sustained the system of caste slavery. It is also important to mention here that various forms of punishments including capital punishment used to be meted out to slaves. In all this, what appears as significant is the body of the slaves that appear to have achieved the quality to endure any form of violence. Such a slave body goes along with the social spaces they inhabit which had been marked out in a particular manner challenging the norms of 'civilized' existence. However, it is in this social space that the missionaries intervene with their notions of the sacred making that new idea available to slaves. Its significance lies in the fact that it was for the first time that the space of the slave castes was marked as sacred. The continued visit of the missionary or the mission workers to the abode of the Parayas and Pulayas evinced the possibility of transforming them slowly by persuading them to join the slave schools and chapels for learning scriptures and participating in prayers. Introducing them to the new sociality, the new space of the slave school was a dynamic space that facilitated the transformation of slave castes. It was here that the new elements of a different social organisation as against the one prevailing in the caste society were communicated to them[13].

The interface with Protestant Christianity had a substantial role in developing new practices that went a long way in defining new sense of community among the slave castes. Based on the everyday religious practices, this new sense of community was expressed in the evening prayers at the slave schools as well as readings of scriptures that used to be held there. Emotionally charged as they are, these prayer meetings and scripture reading sessions used to be decisive in deciding the future activities of the community. Missionaries in charge of such congregations have referred to the intimacy that such meetings could create. For example, it has been noted that many people shed tears when they repeated the Lord's Prayer; to the enquiring missionary, they replied that they wept because they could not address any one as 'Our Father' as the practice of slavery made it impossible for them to have a stable family (Hunt: 200). Invoking Peter Burke, I wish to consider tear as powerful mode of communication that very often could be encountered among Dalit Christians.

The regularity with which the slaves met in the chapel made possible new intimacy, which was based on the new ideas of community, based on common worship the missionaries insisted on. In addition to this, it was possible to bring together people for an entirely new purpose other than working for the landlord. Missionaries have noted the great enthusiasm that the slaves had shown great eagerness to assemble for evening reading and prayer sessions, which they thought was due to the social conviviality that the slave castes had imbibed in spite of their terrible experience of separation through slave trade. This was not something unique to the Protestant missions although the reading sessions were unique to them[14]. It has been noted in the context of some of the Catholic missions that regular participation in Holy Mass was thought of as a way to sustain a feeling of community in the fledgling congregation[15]. However, the uniqueness of the Protestant mission was visible in the fact that it encouraged the lay followers to read the scriptures and understand the meaning of the idea of salvation that was central to the teachings of Christianity[16]. The effect of this was felt in the manner in which people experienced the transforming power of the Gospel. The transforming power of the Gospel touched the lives of the individuals, both men and woman, enabling them agential action. It is in such a context that the social space of the individual also underwent transformation, enabling them to move across spaces unlike the situation before they came into contact with the missionaries.

The emotional world of the slaves

In the discourse of the master classes, slaves hardly exist as a people with emotions. In other words, it may be said that the slaves were never thought of as a people with intimacy and bonding. In most slave societies, 'slave family' was a misnomer, as the slaves were never thought of as an independent people capable of leading a stable family life. The masters were interested in the physical reproduction of slaves as it guaranteed reproduction of labour. Du Bois in his *The Souls of Black Folk* refers to the extremely fragile nature of the family relations of the African Americans in the time of slavery that continued to have a debilitating effect on the families even after emancipation. He refers to the manner in which many young blacks 'took up' their wives and their relationship lasting until the master loses interest in either of them (Du Bois 1903: 87). In such an eventuality they could be separated and sold differently to different masters and the couple would never meet again and quite often they would be forced to seek partners as they reach a new plantation.

Surprisingly in the writings of the missionaries based in the native state of Travancore in Kerala we come across similar examples of husband and wife from the slave castes being forcibly separated by the masters and forcing them subsequently to accept partners chosen by the masters. One of the missionaries, John Hawksworth, based in Travancore reported the manner in which a Syrian Christian landlord family forcibly separated their slave women from their husbands and forced them to accept the men whom the landlord chose for them[17]. The example of forced separation noted in the mid-nineteenth century leaves room for us to imagine the practices prevailing as a norm rather than an exception. In another context the same missionary referred to the Pulayas as the lowest among the human race, stunted, black, and filthy. He further noted that they bear all the marks of a people kept through centuries in squalor, misery, and degradation, a monument of man's inhumanity to man, a monument of the cruelty of the Hindu religion. Producing a pitiable image of the slave who suffers the structural violence of society make us understand their emotional life. Miseries and squalor that were accumulated over the centuries have made any new imagination of a future almost impossible for them. In fact, the conditions of the slaves after abolition of slavery in 1855 in Travancore-Cochin and Malabar in 1843 was not fundamentally different as the transaction in slaves continued particularly in the rural areas[18].

The ethnographic research that I have conducted among Dalit Christians in several villages in the Kottayam district of Kerala in 2012–2014 proves beyond any doubt the prevalence of slave transaction as late as the first decade of the twentieth century. While this information tells us a great deal about the practice of slavery even after its abolition in 1855, we have got fragmentary narratives of the people thus separated reflecting on their lives. However, it is possible to speculate on this question following the leads provided by the missionaries. For example, in the case of those who joined the protestant missions since the mid-nineteenth century, the idea of a Christian family was taking shape. The missionaries were extremely clear about the need for educating the slave caste children, both boys and girls, inculcating in them Christian values so that the 'future becomes theirs'[19]. It was also observed that the generation of their parents has been turned into clods through the practice of slavery that has destroyed their mind and body. What comes out quite clearly here is the private life of the slaves. One possible speculation here is to imagine a private life to slaves who were under the control of the landlords who had developed an elaborate system of surveillance that was so hegemonic that it appeared as natural and given. Therefore it's little wonder that on several occasions those who joined the missionary Church were physically assaulted by their relatives as much as by the landlords. In one extreme case we read about the forced burial of a child of parents who had joined the missionary Church by the deceased baby's uncle who was insistent upon, according to the missionary in charge of the station, a 'heathen burial'[20]. The emotionally charged narrative of the child gives way to an ethnographic account of the burial of the 'heathen' Pulayas.

These observations are important, as the missionaries were concerned about the future of the slave castes, and saving their body and mind. Although the document that I quote here is from the first decade of the twentieth century, in fact we come across the missionary concern with the mind and body of the slave castes way back in the mid-nineteenth century itself when they began to interact with the slave castes. While the missionary sources are eloquent about the mind and body of the slaves, we hardly come across Malayalam sources that show any exemplary concern with the slaves. Most sources in Malayalam refer to the slave castes as living like animals that foreclose any possibility of understanding their social world from an alternative perspective that privileges the mind and body of slaves. In the oral tradition of the slave castes they emerge as people with emotions and intimate personal relationships in spite of the structural violence that the upper castes were able to unleash on them. Impending danger of separation of parents and children becomes a major theme in the oral tradition of some of the slave castes[21].

The intimacy of family life was one of the central issues addressed by the missionaries right from the mid-nineteenth century[22]. While narrating the polygamous and polyandrous practices of slave castes, the missionaries expressed their repugnance towards such practices in the strongest possible terms. In many cases the missionaries were also aware of the intimate relations between a husband and his wives and the former's commitment to the latter even as the missionaries insisted on monogamy. In order to overcome the problems raised by the pre-Christian practices it was felt that they should adopt the sacrament of marriage, which would make marriage a permanent and irrevocable relationship[23].

Although interpreted within the framework of patriarchy, the notion of Christian family was important in the context of the slave castes that were gradually coming out of the long shadows cast by slavery. Some missionaries have observed that it was difficult to see a powerful father figure emerging in the slave caste families that joined the mission. What could have made such a situation of the absence of a masculine father figure even as the missionaries wanted the slave castes to acquire manliness? In the prevailing context of upper-caste domination, the superior authority of the upper castes emasculated the entire community of slaves. Therefore, it was felt necessary to infuse the slave caste males with manliness so that they evolve as powerful fathers and husbands. In fact, the need for manliness to be inculcated among the slave caste men was a challenge that the missionaries felt as extremely significant as it was the desideratum for a stable family.

The narratives of 'conversion' are replete with examples of blessings of the marriages of those who are baptised. This, according to the missionary was to bless the marriage according to the principles of Christian sacraments that would make it permanent unlike what they felt as customary marriage practice that was the norm in their pre-Christian past. Ushering in a new temporality, it was an invitation to a different historical and social time when slaves were made part of a new regime of records. I argue this on the basis of the ethnographic researches conducted among Dalit Christian communities in Kerala that with baptism the slave caste entered into a different historical time marked out and decisive. In the vernacular histories of the Dalit Christian communities, the chronological sequences have been fixed by following the dates of baptism entered in the Church records. While I refer to this specific example of historical time it does not mean that the people were not aware of historical time before their encounter with the missionaries. The argument proposed is that through the missionaries and the generation of a new culture of records, many people could trace their families' 'origin' to this particular moment. Some of the family histories of Dalit Christians that I have come across in the course of my ethnographic fieldwork used the Church records effectively to make their narratives chronological and factual[24]. We could probably speculate on a different, modern notion of history, family, and community getting purchased among the slave castes.

I wish to consider here in a little more detailed manner the transformation that the emotional world of the slave castes that had joined the mission had undergone. The missionaries proposed the idea of the extremely interesting state of the minds of the people who were learning with them[25]. It was for the first time that there was any reference to the minds of the slave castes as against the dominant conception prevailing in the traditional caste society that they were never capable of expressing their mind. Thought to be only capable of providing physical labour, the slave castes were quite often referred to in comparison with the draught animals. In absolute contrast to this thinking in the native society, learning with the missionaries offered the slaves chances to express their ideas in relation to whatever was taught to them. We in fact read in the writings of the missionaries how they thought about the slaves. According to the missionaries God almighty has created them bestowing them with inalienable rights as human beings, which was denied to them under the prevailing system of slavery[26]. Therefore, they have to know their creator and worship him. Enslavement prevented the slaves from realising their human essence. Although couched in the language of missionary enlightenment and rationality, these ideas offered new possibilities for slaves to emerge as human beings[27]. It is in this context that we encounter the slaves as people with emotions, affect, and intimate feelings. In many cases where the slaves suffered physical violence due to the cruel punishments inflicted up on them by the landlords, the missionaries who intervened compared their sufferings with that of the sufferings of 'the holy Apostles for the sake of Christ' or in certain cases it was compared with that of the sufferings of Christ himself (Baker Jr. 1862: 57–61). In fact, in most narratives of violence we come across the invocation of the image of the suffering Christ to imbue the sufferings of slaves with new meanings. Capable of producing a different vision of themselves to the slaves, these new ideas provided the slaves a new framework to think of themselves as a community united in emotions. This situation is very well captured in the words of a native missionary:

> Their minds, so long lying fallow, are found to be rich soil for sowing the seeds of Christian truth but its very fertility helps weeds to grow abundantly with the seeds. Their simplicity of character makes them apt to receive our teaching with readings and their warmth of temper makes the zealous for the

> cause they embrace but the same qualities render them liable to be easily led away into error and to take offence at trifles so that much tact and practical wisdom with a great deal of patience and forbearance are required to in managing them.
>
> *(Interview with Yohannan Ayya, see note 31)*

While the fear expressed above was more in relation to the elderly generation of slave castes, the missionaries had a different take on the children. In a way they were claiming the childhood of the slave castes, as the children would be available readily for the civilisational project. Scholars in the area of mission history and anthropology have noted the significance attached to the education of the children, especially the girl children by the missionaries. The CMS Missionaries in Travancore felt that they needed to train girl children properly as they will have to be future wives of the mission workers and responsible future mothers on whom would hinge the mores of a Christian family. This was part of the larger missionary ideology 'to save the girls for brighter and better future.'[28]

Towards this end of educating girl children boarding schools were started in Tiruvalla and the famous missionary, Ms. Baker ran her historic school for girls. The everyday life in the school of Ms. Baker was a matter of pride for the missionaries and one visiting missionary sketched the everyday life in the school showing different activities in which the girl children were engaged. While there was this emphasis on the education of girl children as a matter salvaging future generations, that could not have been achieved without due emphasis on the education of boys. It is in this context that boarding school for boys were established where they would be kept away from the 'evil environment and influence' of their homes. It is quite easy to observe here the language of dominance in which the social and familial background of the slave caste children is referred to. However, in a matter of a generation the missionaries could register appreciable development in the literacy levels of the slave caste Christians, although this literacy was avowedly meant for reading scriptures, even as we know that literacy could have multiple functions. Reflecting on missionary investment in the future of children we find a new notion of childhood coming into being in colonial Kerala through their efforts. It assumes further significance when considered in the context of the slave caste children who would have been working for the landlords even as they are young without any wages in the late nineteenth century when the CMS missionaries had introduced elementary education. Even in the first decades of the twentieth century, most Dalit children irrespective of their religious background would be working for the landlord even before they became 10years old. However, in many places slave caste parents could send their children at least up to class two as the slave schools usually had only up to class two.

In one of the missionary reformist texts published in 1928 we read the amazing story of a Pulaya girl, Aroogi, who undergoes tremendous emotional transformation after she was enrolled in a missionary boarding school. In course of time, as the story progresses, she overcomes the allegedly debilitating habits she had acquired by virtue of her being from the slave castes and starts scaling up in the transformative project of the missionaries (W B. 1928). She becomes the most accomplished student of the boarding who becomes a model to everyone as she excels in the morning prayers and in her case, extempore prayers. She prays for every inmate of the boarding, their teachers, and parents and for those who send money for them from abroad for their wellbeing and upkeep. In the mission boarding school, the slave caste children learn modern habits. This is the moment of modernity for them, which in many ways several thousands of slave castes have undergone. What I wish to argue here is that this resulted in tremendous transformation in their emotions also. In fact, this transformation resulted in the substantial changes in their everyday social conduct, their habits, language, and their being in the world. It was through such a process that they could evolve as modern individuals. Having stated the transformation through the civilising mission I wish to focus on everyday aspects of structural violence to which the slave castes were subjected.

Everyday life of slaves: violence and survival

Like any historical slave society, slaves in the pre-colonial Kerala society were also under the disciplinary regime of the masters. The everyday life of the slave castes was marked by violence let loose by the landlords. Such violence had obvious bearing on their emotional life. It may be noted that in many parts of Kerala violence against Dalits (as the former slave castes are referred to today) continued in a substantial manner even in the 1960's. In the nineteenth and twentieth centuries the upper-caste landlords used instruments of violence to maintain their control over the society and in particularly on the slave castes who tilled their land. Living on the outer dykes of the paddy fields and on the fringes of the farmlands of the landlords, the slave castes had to depend on them for all most everything in life as they did not have access to resources for survival.

I wish to give here a few examples of the violence that defined the life of slaves as well as the masters. I am referring here to the human sacrifice practised in the wetland tracts of the Travancore region of Kerala where the victims used to be from the slave castes. There are innumerable cases in which the spirit of the sacrificial victim returned to haunt the landlord and his family then forced him to worship the malevolent spirit as god. In several cases the landlords forced the slaves under their command to worship such spirits. In most cases it was slave caste men who would be sacrificed, as it takes place in the context of the work, such as rebuilding the bunds of the paddy fields breached in the floods. Usually in such arduous work in the wetland only men would be employed. Yet, we come across cases in the early nineteenth century in which three young girls from the slave caste (Pulayas) were sacrificed in a similar situation of breach of the outer bund of the paddy field, not very far from today's Kottayam town in Kerala.[29]In most cases the landlords out of the fear of the malevolent spirits of the murdered slaves would consecrate their spirits and worship them. There is in fact lot of emotions involved in it as noted by the missionary. In one such case the Pulaya slaves who worshiped such a murdered slave carried his image to the mission compound and explained the whole story to the missionary. In another case the murdered Pulaya slave, Palan used to be worshipped by the Nair landlord family and of late it has become a popular cult drawing on a large number of people across caste divide, which is naively referred to as an example of the religious and social harmony, forgetting the fact that the apotheosis of Palan Pulayan hides the inhuman violence perpetrated on him, by the landlords whom he had served, by taking his life[30].

In the course of our fieldwork we came across an interesting case of a family of Dalit Christians belonging to a Salvation Army Church who narrated to us the horrible story of one of their forefathers who became a sacrificial victim. Yohannan Ayya, the Pastor, who narrated the event, told us how his great-grandfather's brother was sacrificed by a Nair landlord in their village, which is not very far from the famous temple town ofVaikkom[31]. Even after the family became Christian, they kept alive the memory of their ancestor who was sacrificed by the landlord. For them today, revisiting the cruelties of the past is more like conjuring the images of the past, the image of the sacrificial victim who demands a peaceful afterlife. This circumstance is similar to the situation captured in the moving sentence of Michel-Rolph Trouillot in his path-breaking book, *Silencing the Past*. According to Trouillot, 'slavery here is a ghost, both the past and the living presence; and the problem of historical representation is how to represent the ghost' (Trouillot 1995: 146). In the literary representation of the slave castes and subsequently Dalit communities in Kerala, the question of conjuring ghosts becomes a real challenge. In some of the recent novels published in Malayalam, the long dead and gone characters actualise their lives as real flesh and blood human beings as they come back to fulfil their prematurely terminated lives (Vasu 2014). They return with a vengeance, which is quite often a challenge to the domination that the upper caste used to exercise. In many cases the local people worshipped such liminal figures, which were quite often thought to be very powerful malevolent spirits.

With the background of the above discussion we may now turn to certain important aspects of everyday violence as it affected the lives of the former slave castes. Although they were producers of food crops and other agricultural products, they hardly consumed the foods they produced, such as rice, due to structural controls on food products which rendered them scarce commodities. Writings of nineteenth-century missionaries reproduced statements of the slave caste people referring to the fact that they were never allowed to have rice except the meagre quantity that would be distributed to them as their wages at the end of the day. Processing it for daily consumption would not have left with them anything to save for the future except during the harvesting season when they would get more than the usual quantities of raw paddy as their wage. Most slaves would have their evening meal only after processing such hard-earned raw paddy in the night after they returned home from work. It has been noted that the occasion of the preparation of the meals at night was also a time of creativity as men and women used to sing while engaged in the evening household chores. These could also be occasions of drunken bouts and violence. In many local communities where people joined the

Protestant Church, we find that the situation changed substantially, leading to a disciplined life. Missionary sources observed the remarkable changes in the life of the slaves who joined the Churches as they could hear the sounds of people reading scriptures and prayers instead of the inchoate sounds of quarrels. These examples showed the new emotional world slowly developing among the slave castes.

Structural violence in the caste society was better illustrated by the fact that denial of food to the slave caste men and women who produced food and agricultural wealth was the norm. The nineteenth-century missionary writings on slave castes more than any other source analysed this situation and put across the fact that these men and women lived in perpetual hunger and want. The ethnographic fieldwork that we conducted made clear the fact that slave caste men and woman were not allowed to wear proper clothes even in the 1940s. If they managed somehow to buy white cloth, they had to soil it or blacken it with carbon from the bottom of the cooking pots before they could wear it. Over the centuries it has been noted that the slave castes were never allowed to construct houses. Their houses have been compared to something smaller than a large basket erected on the banks of the paddy fields or on the fringes of farmlands. This denial of the basic requirements of life, food, shelter, and clothing was the most important instrument of structural violence in caste society and had a great impact on the emotions of the slave castes. In usual social science practices, the problems discussed here do not figure as a significant research question. However, there is the genre of vernacular history where these issues have been addressed through various texts in which the emotional questions and affect emerge as significant category of analysis. In the next section, I will analyse some of these texts to see how they bring in the question of affect.

Vernacular histories, family history, local history

There is an organic link between the different genres of history attempted by Dalits today and the writing on the emotional and affective dimensions of the slave caste communities in the long nineteenth century. I use the vernacular histories to speak of certain kind of histories that were influenced by the notions of social time that Dalit communities shared. I do not claim it to be unique to them as we would see Christian notions of genealogy and history influenced many such texts written by Dalit Christians (Patric 2014). However, there is a curious mixing of such histories with the notions of the past that were made available by the missionary writings on the social experiences of the slave castes. Therefore, in the vernacular histories that I am referring to there is a desire to make them as accurate as possible. Most of the texts begin from the days when ancestors of Dalits were free and had a social life that was devoid of any external control. Nevertheless, in the context of Kerala, their fall and subsequent enslavement begins somewhere in the sixth century. Henceforth it is history of suffering and oppression, even as they had their own social life. Obviously such a social life would have had complex features. They could also have had occasional joys in life. Arguably, the most significant defining feature of their life was the experience of subordination that they underwent in the form of slavery. In exploring regional histories, the authors of such texts talk about various aspects of slavery: sale and purchase of slaves, the breakup of families, and the emotional violence that they were forced to undergo. In these histories, such long nights of slavery seemingly never had any end. We hardly find anybody in the local society coming up with anti-slavery ideas. Therefore, until the coming of the protestant missionaries in the nineteenth century, we do not come across any efforts at removing the fetters of the slave castes. It is in fact with the missionaries that the world changing events take place, in the case of slave castes. All vernacular histories that we refer to are in agreement with regard to this point. In the context of North Malabar the historian Stanley Patrick refers to the Jesuit missionaries in the late 1930s as the movers and shakers that eventually brought liberation from caste slavery (Patric 2014: 100–109). Similarly, in the case of the local vernacular history of Kunju Kutty Kozhuvanal, we observe the baptisms of Pulayas in the village of Anikkad, which led to their liberation from caste slavery. However, the author is very cautious of the fact that in his village it was the traditional Syrian Christians, a predominantly peasant caste in the late nineteenth century, that began the liberation movement among the slave castes. Kozhuvanal is non-committal about the liberatory potential of such a move as the slave castes continued to be in the subordinated position, as it was Catholic Church dominated by the native Syrian Christian. In the Protestant Churches, in spite of caste segregation there was a possibility to acquire Biblical knowledge, which would have given slaves ideological power, however limited it must have been. It was not the case among the Catholics. However, what is significant from the point of view of emotion is the consistent effort by the enslaved people to overcome estrangement. Comparing these texts would be instructive for a couple of reasons. Both of the texts deal with the Catholic mission among the slave castes. However in the text of Kozhuvanal the Church is Syrian and controlled by those who had been exploiting slave castes for ages (Kozhuvanal 2006). In the North Malabar case, the mission was exclusively addressing the question of slave castes and the missionaries were Italian Catholics. The absence of the local dominant caste in the Church made it a space of freedom for those from the slave castes who joined the mission in North Malabar, whereas in the example provided by Kozhuvanal such a possibility never evolved as the slave castes were dominated by the traditional upper-caste Christians (Kozhuvanal 2006: 11–12). The emotional estrangement continued, and it has been very difficult for Dalits to resolve it even in the first decade of the twentieth century. In the third text of this genre, written by Peter Mathew as narrated by the protagonists, we get interesting history of local Dalit Christian in Malabar who had settled down from the native state of Travancore beginning in the late 1940s. Therefore in this text we get the narratives of life before migration from the southern native state of Travancore as well as the slaves' efforts at developing a new social life in the migrant villages in Malabar. There are narratives of travel to Malabar, efforts to settle down there, and the caste segregation they had to face within the upper-caste–dominated Church. Eventually they move out of that Church and establish a new Church with the help of Fr. Joseph Taffrel, an Italian Jesuit missionary who was originally a missionary of the Chirakkal Mission of North Malabar[32]. This narrative is emotionally charged with people recollecting several events that had a decisive impact on their very survival as a social collective. The elder generation who migrated and worked hard for a new life look at their history from an emotional point of view imbuing their narratives with the days of caste slavery as they had learned from their parents and grandparents. Today all those informants who are above eighty-five years could provide information on the days when caste slavery was very alive in spite of its abolition in the mid-nineteenth century[33]. In this example we find the interplay of caste, Christianity and the longing for liberation that spun the everyday life and emotions of Dalits. However, the significant point of departure is the arrival of a Catholic Jesuit missionary who could turn the terms of the discourse. Today such histories in the vernacular mode are recalled in an emotional manner deploying the categories that were used by the missionaries in the nineteenth century.

Closely following this we may mention the significance of family histories that have been written by Dalit Christians and influenced by Christian notions of history. As a result, family genealogy becomes crucial. However as distinct from the family histories of Syrian Christians in Kerala the few family histories of Dalit Christians in fact refer to the slave experience of their ancestors of for parents. In the case of one family history, Thekkethil family history, their history begins from the days of slavery, when the author's great-great-grandfather was bought from a village named Mathikad near Shertalai in Alleppy district and brought to a village near Kottayam where he and his wife were presented as a gift by a Nair landlord to his niece[34]. The slave couple eventually had children, and the whole family worked for the landlords. The second-generation children also married and had children. In 1862 they were baptised by the Anglican missionaries based in Kottayam who came to their village in Tiruvanchoor. As I argued earlier, with their baptism they enter a different time and history, which the author of the family history tries to follow up in the late twentieth century to write the family history. When we analyse the narrative of the family history, emotional aspects of the social and family life of the slave castes become the central concern of the text. We can also discern the spirit of changing times and their impact on the slave castes. Although they were caught in the vortex of social change, we still encounter 'ordinary lives' in this family history (Pandian 2008: 34–40). The narrative structure follows the missionary genre as it centres on the question of emotions and reveal the affective transformations through which the text had evolved.

While the narrator of the family histories along with the members also have undergone social change, the baptism was paradigmatic as the most significant event that marked the mobility towards the employment in the plantation as a middleman recruiting labour, which was also a significant moment as he could leapfrog from poverty that was rampant. In the course of the narrative we also note the instance of one of the family members moving away from agricultural labour to take up the job of a butcher in the weekend. In the mid-twentieth century, we find the author's children getting a modern education. What I wish to emphasise here is the fact that the emotional changes that were thought to be central to the missionary narratives on slave castes have continued to be significant elements in the narratives of Dalit Christians that are available today through vernacular histories and family histories.

Conclusion

The missionary narratives of intimate aspects of the life of the slave castes in Kerala open up several possibilities for understanding the social and emotional world of both the slave castes as well as the missionaries. As I have argued it was in the narratives of missionaries that for the first time the emotional world of the slaves in Kerala became available to the world at large. Many of these writings on the slave castes were published in the missionary journals that provided it a global reach. Personal and family lives of the slaves were reorganised and specific gender roles in the family became decisive. Yet we find the continuation of several aspects of their social life betraying the elements social life that bequeathed to them from their pre-Christian past. What in fact we find is interesting mix of several practices having a direct bearing in the emotions of the slave castes. In the contemporary studies on Christian missions the new emotional life that came into existence in the context of the missionary labour among the non-European societies assumes significance. Following the experiences of the slave castes in Kerala, it is possible to identify new forms of emotional life evolving in the communities in the context of their becoming free from the control of upper-caste landlords, their tormentors. It is in this context that they began to evolve as modern individuals and the emotional transformation was very decisive in marking changes.

Notes

1 The CMS missionary W. S. Hunt refers to the case of a Pulaya girl who was sold to a European gentleman leaving for Java to accompany his family. However, she escaped and pleaded to the missionary Rev. Ridsdale and his wife for refuge and escaped from her fate of being taken out of Kerala. Although there is information of slaves being taken away from Kerala, we are yet to have a substantial study on this aspect of slavery. For details on Kali see Hunt 1920: 161.

2 Missionaries were the keenest observers of the life and conditions of the slave castes and the information repeatedly occurring on Pulayas and Parayas including census reports and other government documents in Kerala, 'they are regarded as so unclean that they are thought to carry pollution to their fellow creatures by contact and even by approach. They are so wretchedly provided with necessaries of life that the most loathsome things are a feast to them. Their person entirely at the disposal of their masters by who they are bought and sold like cattle and are often worse treated' were originally written by Rev. George Matthan in his *Journal* for the quarter ending December 21, 1850. CMS Archives, University of Birmingham.

3 In the Tamil context Rupa Viswanath has shown the absolutely stunning practice of the Wesleyan missionary Rev. William Goudie who actually painstakingly inspected the faeces of the Pariah families to assess the extent poverty as they had to subsist on a variety of cactus whose red seeds would not be digested. This was to measure the extent famine had made the people (Pariahs) to subsist on cactus. For details see Viswanath 2014: 11.

4 For a critical reflection on the meaning of slavery to the contemporary generation of African- American see Hartman 2008.

5 Mohan 2015: 38–115; for an argument from the history of emotions see, Ray 2003: 124–129

6 Study of emotions has become central to the contemporary concerns of scholars studying history and anthropology of colonial missions. For a detailed discussion see, McLisky et al. 2015; also see Cannel 2006.
7 For a discussion on these issues see Jeffrey 2014: 214–247; for a critical Social Science Perspective on the same questions see Arunima 2003.
8 For details see Mohan 2015: 76–82.
9 For details see the John Hawksworth, Questions by a Missionary Answers by Travancore Slaves Taught in a School of the CM Society dated 19 August, 1853, manuscript true copy of the original C12/07/24.
10 For a reference to early documentation on slavery see, Narayanan 1996: 154.
11 See the extant Journals of the rev. George Matthan from 1846–69, CMS Archives, University of Birmingham
12 John Abbs, 'On Slavery in Travancore' Box No. 3, Folder No. 1 Jacket C, 29 March, p. 3
13 Slave schools were a world changing institution for the slave castes even as it remained as a humble thatch hut, similar to the huts of the slave castes.
14 In fact, the missionaries encouraged the slaves to read the scriptures, and we read from their reports the case of slaves who were capable of reading. We may recall here that in the tradition caste society slave castes were forbidden from reading.
15 For details see Mohan 2015
16 Annual letter of John Hawksworth from Alleppei to the International Secretary of the CMS, 1861 detailing the work among the slave castes, CMS Archives, University of Birmingham
17 For details see the John Hawksworth, Questions by a Missionary Answers by Travancore Slaves Taught in a School of the CM Society dated 19 August 1853, manuscript true copy of the original C12/07/24.
18 My fieldwork among Dalit Christians in Karikkottakkary in Kannur district of Kerala shows that slaves used to be bought and sold in Kerala in the first decade of twentieth century.
19 In fact, towards the end of the nineteenth century, there were lot of discussion on the education of children especially girl children. For example, see Bishop of Kottayam to Mr. Wigram, CMS International Secretariat, London, Document 36, 4 July 1918
20 Journal of Oommen Mammen for the Quarter ending June 30, 1856. Cavioor, 13th Lords Day, CMS Archives, University of Birmingham
21 This is a recurrent theme in the oral tradition of the slave castes and made into a theological category in the discourses of Prathyaksha Raksha Daiva Sabha, a Dalit religious and social movement. For details see, Mohan 2015: 214–265.
22 For details see the John Hawksworth, Questions by a Missionary Answers by Travancore Slaves Taught in a School of the CM Society dated 19 August 1853, manuscript true copy of the original C12/07/24.
23 Ibid.
24 For details see K M Abraham, *Thekkethi Kudumba Charithram* (Family History forthcoming, Kerala Council for Historical Research, Thiruvananthapuram)
25 For details see the John Hawksworth, Questions by a Missionary Answers by Travancore Slaves Taught in a School of the CM Society dated 19 August 1853, manuscript true copy of the original C12/07/24
26 John Abbs, 'On Slavery in Travancore' Box No. 3, Folder No. 1 Jacket C, 29 March, 1847
27 Ibid.
28 See for a similar argument from global missions, Jolly 1991, pp. 27–48
29 Balakrishnan Nair and U. Nare-Beli, *Calcutta Review*, April 1902
30 The Hindu Kerala Edition, Pathanamthitta District, 30 July 2015
31 Interview with Yohannan Ayya at his residence on 2 December 2013 as part of the Social Science Research Council New York funded project, New Directions in the Study of Prayers.
32 Peter Mathew, Interviews with Dalit Christian elders of Kottukappara, Karikkottakkari, and Parkkappara, Manuscript, 2015. pp. 9–53

33 Ibid., pp. 91–107
34 For details see K M Abraham, Thekkethi Kudumba Charithram (Family History forthcoming, Kerala Council for Historical Research, Thiruvananthapuram)

References

Arunima, G. 2003. *There Comes Papa: Colonialism and the Transformation of Matriliny in Kerala, Malabar, c. 1850–1940.* Hyderabad: Orient Blackswan.

Baker Jr., Henry. 1862. *The Hill Arayan's of Travancore and the Progress of Christianity among Them.* London: Werthiem Macintosch & Hunt.

Cannel, Fenella. (ed.) 2006. *Anthropology of Christianity.* Durham: Duke University Press.

Day, Francis. 2006[1863]). *Land of the Perumals: or Cochin its Past and its Present.* New Delhi: Asian Educational Services.

Du Bois, W. E. B. 1903[1996]. *The Souls of Black Folk.* New York: The Modern Library.

Hartman, Saidiya. 2008. *Lose Your Mother: A Journey Along the Atlantic Slave Route.* New York: Faber, Straus and Giroux.

Hunt, W.S. 1920. *The Anglican Church in Travancore and Cochin, 1816–1916.* Vol. I. Kottayam: Church Missionary Society Press.

Jeffrey, Robin. 2014. *The Decline of Nair Dominance: Society and Politics in Travancore 1847–1908.* New Delhi: Manohar.

John, Mariamma. 1998. *Manikkam Pennu.* Changanassery: Manusham.

Jolly, Margaret. 1991. '"To save the Girls for Brighter and Better Lives": Presbyterian Missions and Women in South of Vanuatu: 1848–1870.' *The Journal of Pacific History*, 26(1) (January): 27–48.

Kozhuvanal, Kunjukutty. 2006. *Anickadu Adimajanathayum Lekhu Chartithravum.* Anickadu: Indian Education Development Charitable Society.

Kusuman, K.K. 1973. *Slavery in Travancore.* Trivandrum: Kerala Historical Society.

Logan, William. 1989[1887]. *Malabar.* Madras: Asian Education Services.

Major, Andrea. 2012. *Slavery, Abolitionism and Empire in India 1772–1843.* Liverpool: Liverpool University Press.

McLisky, Claire et al. (eds.). 2015. *Emotions and Christian Missions: Historical Perspectives.* New York: Palgrave Macmillan.

Mohan, P. Sanal. 2015. *Modernity of Slavery: Struggles against Caste Inequality in Colonial Kerala.* New Delhi: Oxford University Press.

Narayanan, M.G.S. 1996. *Perumals of Kerala: Political and Social Conditions of Kerala under the Cera Perumals of Makotai, c. 800 AD–1124 AD.* Calicut: Xavier Press.

Pandian, M.S.S. 2008. "Writing Ordinary Lives." *Economic and Political Weekly*, 43(38): 34–40.

Patric, Stanly. 2014. *Malabarile Dalith Christava Charithravum Varthamanvum.* Kochi: Viani Printings.

Patterson, Orlando. 1982. *Slavery and Social Death: A Comparative Study.* Cambridge, MA: Harvard University Press.

Ray, Rajat Kanta. 2003. *Exploring Emotional History; Gender, Mentality and Literature in the Indian Awakening.* New Delhi: Oxford University Press.

Saradamony, K. 1980. *Emergence of a Slave Caste: Pulayas of Kerala.* New Delhi: People's Publishing House.

Trouillot, Michel-Rolph. 1995. *Silencing the Past: Power and the Production of History.* Boston: Beacon Press.

Vasu, Raju K. 2014. *Chavu thullal Kottayam.* DC Books.

Viswanath, Rupa. 2014. *The Pariah Problem: Caste, Religion and the Social in Modern India.* New York: Columbia University Press.

W. B. 1928. *In A Tapioca Garden: The Story of an Outcaste Girl of Travancore.* London: CMS.

3

NATURE AND BELONGING

Distance, development, and intimacy

R. Umamaheshwari

Some introductory thoughts

I try to engage here with the ideas of distance and proximity – with the creation of the illusion of distance, as well as the illusion of proximity – in the contemporary discourse of 'development,' or 'modernity' (within which the ideas of 'development' and 'progress' as a 'revenue model' are constructed) and within the modern political-economic discourses. My engagement is with what Nature (inclusive of, but not excluding, physiography, landscapes, wildlife, the elements; the general ideas of nature in the 'Nature' of things) means, comes to mean, or is forced to mean, essentially inspired from the everyday, real-life situations, the everyday metaphors of our existence, across geographical and socioeconomic spaces. How is nature, or some aspects of nature, or the natural, perceived by people/communities? Is it perceived similarly by all? Do marginalised communities perceive Nature differently? Or, is it constructed *for* them? How close are we to Nature or how distant is Nature from us? Is this decided by communities, or by a larger idiom, constructed by those who rule the 'developmental' logic? Is intimacy with nature a mere romantic (within a 'universalised' category of 'romantic') whim? Or is it an unfeigned intimacy that can't be sidelined by the whim of an anthropocentric, corporate, political ideology? Can there be intimacy and unbelonging at the same time? Or, is belongingness the quintessence of intimacy?

Most natural spaces are contested today; there is an almost virile male (idea of) nation (in most parts of the globe) in a rush to establish paternity by injecting the seed of authority and dominion over natural resources towards an illusory idea of 'growth,' in spite of *peak oil* and other crises of *climate change* (the two terms used for international agreements and conferences) without changing the ideology of a paternal, exploitative and extractive approach to nature and natural resources.

A telephone conversation in late September 2016, gave me that sense of how a construct has become not just *mainstream* but also the only stream that there is, if one has to live in this world – which seems to be the only singular world – today. This was a Koya (ST) farmer who said to me (over phone), he was planning to buy some land in Hyderabad from the compensation he was about to receive for his own land (nearly 10 acres in the pristine environs of a village not far from the Godavari river) which he had sold for the Polavaram dam, even as he spoke of the kind of corruption that was going on in the compensation process for their land for the Polavaram dam[1]; he was only shown the 'house site' and not the promised land for his land lost, which incidentally is guaranteed by the new Land acquisition Act of 2013[2]. But it did not seem to matter to him – not being compensated for his golden fields/land of corn, maize, paddy, all of these rain-fed. Farming has been rendered an activity that is fairly distant from globally oriented 'skill development' and 'IT' dreams, where Hyderabad and its suburbs are the place to live in. At another level, money is the new intimate; every land can be acquired for money, and in this equation, one has to reconfigure the intimacy that farmers once had with their fields, or tribal communities/adivasis once had with their forests, for which they fought some of the most protracted battles with even the colonial rulers. Of course, some, like the Dongria Kondh from Odisha, still fighting for their Niyamgiri mountain, become a kind of wonder for many.

The state is almost like a design of the new 'intimate' – which is forcing itself into every idea that was/is reflective of the intimacy and belonging (where both intimacy *and* belonging go together) of people to Nature. It has come to a point where slow pace is a luxury for indulgence by the rich, as a break from their routine while the very 'natural' idea of slowness – time taken in agricultural operations, or fishing, for instance – that most poor farmers naturally dealt with, is the new anathema to the constant push by the state to 'diversify or perish' kind of advice given to them, time and again. It is interesting to observe this kind of 'hurry' to 'get ahead' or be left behind kind of advice given to most of the marginalised sections of the country.

> Recent times have witnessed a considerable industry trying to alleviate the pressures of compressed time and accelerated mobility . . . Personal fitness ventures offer a wide range of meditation classes to relax the mind and unwind the body. Urban planners reroute entire roads, block off inner circles, and install speed bumps to decelerate traffic and encourage us to rediscover the joys of urban walking. Travel agencies design detailed packages for all those eager to move beyond the beaten track and avoid the latest hypes of global tourism. . . [However] the slowing down of the global economy in the wake of the financial crises of 2008 has done very little to correct our perception of too much speed and temporal compression. On the contrary, Slowness, as it were, has very different connotations in the realm of economic affairs that it has in the sphere of lifestyle choices. To praise slow markets and slow retail sales would border on the perverse and self-destructive. Many may fault the way in which global capitalism distributes its wealth and produces large arenas of poverty, but neither economic theorists nor populist

> politicians would seriously promote a decelerating of production, distribution, and consumption of financial lending practices, the ensuing sluggishness of economic mobility was thus certainly not what gourmets, health professionals, traffic planners, and new age critics had in mind when applauding the pleasures of deceleration.
>
> *(Koepnick 2014: 1–2)*

At the other end, you have the extremes of 'back to nature' advisories being churned out, most times as another small business, for mostly urban people. It might just be the metaphor of our times, that the thing that is destroyed elsewhere – nature, natural environs, with some of the most intimate relationships between human societies and the flora, fauna and ways of living that exemplified that intimacy – is then recreated in the new city; at least attempts are made to sell that idea. For example, the Telangana government has recently started what is called the *Harita Haram* (Green Garland) programme, to make Telangana green, and is distributing tree saplings free of cost to people to grow more trees in their localities, towns, etc. This comes after destruction of forest habitat through other projects (which may have happened over the last several years, not necessarily under the present government in power, but that has not stopped); similarly, river systems are destroyed elsewhere to bring water to the cities.

Sight, touch, and feel are sensations that are most intimate, but distance is also created in these sensations in violent and conflict-ridden contexts where Nature becomes a distant phenomenon. What is naturally there, and idyllic, is not always beautiful in the typical sense of beauty, either. For example, in a place called Jageshwar in Kumaun region of Uttarakhand, where I once lived, there was 'beauty' of the place: a stream, Deodar trees, scores of Barking Deer, occasional night visits of Leopards, entire star constellations visible on every dark night (satellite TV had only 'arrived' in one rich household at that time) and then there was an ancient temple complex and an ancient caste system. There was beauty in nature sense of the term, and there was violence in sociological context. The lower-caste communities stayed close to the river stream, and some of them in typically beautiful picture-postcard kind of landscapes up in the higher mountains. At one level, they were intimate with the environs and at another, perhaps that intimacy was also their distance from the larger social community, by the roadside, near towns and markets, and of course, the temple complex. There was also contestation over belonging in those spaces, defined by caste.

In southern India, the river Godavari and the villages around reveal the absolute photographic beauty. Many tribal communities/adivasis and fishing communities live closest to Godavari, are intimate with her, and understand perfectly her moods and temperament of each season. At another level, this intimacy makes them the most vulnerable to the distance that is created by the state through structures such as the Polavaram dam (in West Godavari, Andhra Pradesh, or other dams, for that matter, on other rivers elsewhere). There is an almost Cartesian separation between people and nature and nature is considered apart from, outside of, the human society and history.

In many cases, the conflict between human population and wild animals, in places where many wild animals are on the verge of being declared vermin because they are charged with 'destroying' crops, for instance. The former intimacies shared between species, are forcibly destructed through the binary of human versus nature/wildlife, which is evident in policies of the state, that have of late taken over the preservation of the human species with a vengeance within a paradigm of total control, numerisation, surveillance and a universal moral sphere where anything could be declared as 'un-natural' (itself a paradoxical term) and either 'vermin' (because it has gone beyond its 'natural' tendency and begun to destroy the human effort of agriculture) or 'unnatural tendency' (homosexuality, as one instance) through an Act in a modern governmental jargon. Peacock, supposed to be our 'national' bird, was declared 'vermin' in Goa. Dogs are being killed in Kerala with state sanction or with the state looking the other way. Monkeys are declared vermin in Himachal Pradesh. The terminology 'vermin' is an example of how deep the distance between nature and human world is, today.

Intimacies and belongings from different locales, the *Human Project*, etc.

Here I share images and metaphors of everyday existence of one's life (or, our lives, perhaps, if there are some commonalities to all our lives in today's global context, which loves commonalities, which make selling ideas, products easier) which are self-experienced (intimately engaging) and also ones observed, of other selves and spaces over decades, across geographical-cultural locales of India (mountain villages of Kumaun, Himachal Pradesh and hills and forests of Godavari or villages of the Deccan or cities of Delhi, Hyderabad, and others). I am not doing a Wordsworthian nature with a big N. Nor does my analysis fit into the deep ecology discourse. Rather, I seek to problematise ideas of *inside* and *outside*, *here* and *there*, and *intimacy* and *distance* as politically constructed or as constructions whose politics we need to be conscious of; as also of a pattern, a deeper idiom, of our being in, what I perceive as, an increasingly constructed *human project*. This project is the creation, especially, of post-colonial science, and has been in operation through nationalist policies on population, family planning, medicine, education, etc. But of late, the *human project*(as against, and superseding, the *human condition* which is more of a social-historical reality, the understanding of which is ideologically conditioned) is dangerously linked to global capital and has expanded its base; it has in fact intruded into several intimate spaces of private lives of people through technology and consists in keeping the human body as a site for market possibilities, through several experiments carried out overtly or covertly. In this *project*, species other than human are always 'out there' and resources are also 'out there' for exploitation and for currency conversion. Intimacy would kill the currency possibilities. Anthropocentric consumption and commodity overwhelm and in this *human project* many have been rendered dispensable/insignificant. Intimacy to, and belonging in, nature consists in the language people speak, about natural phenomena. The most recent metaphor I received and an older one – which I share here – would urge us to be conscious of these, which are part of people's spoken languages. In recent times I have had the fortune of getting acquainted with some people from Lahaul-Spiti district of Himachal Pradesh. In the course of a conversation around December-January (2016) about cold, and winter, one of them told me, *is baar barf rooth gayi; pata nahin kya hua; bus, rooth gayi.*[This time round, snow is annoyed; wonder what happened; she is just annoyed.]

People in the Godavari region, especially villages in East and West Godavari in Andhra Pradesh and a few villages in Telangana by Godavari, will sometimes foretell the river's flow: *ee saari pedda Godaari raadandi.* [This time big Godavari ('floods') will not come.]

In both cases, snow, and river Godavari, respectively, are feminine. And have an intensely personalised presence for people living in close proximity to each of these natural forces/phenomena. Snow, and the river, can get annoyed. In the language of the people by Godavari, 'she' 'comes' (*ostundi*); she does not 'flood.' Recently, I read somewhere that the Eskimos have more than sixty words for snow (depending on the time, kind, form of snow, etc). People must have similar experience and intimate terms for deserts and forests, as well. In the villages of Godavari, the agricultural seasons have their respective kinds of breezes as well. The winter breeze is not similar to the breeze of the other seasons. The colonial gazetteer, for instance, records one of these which is popularly known as *payiru gáli.*

> Light north-easterly breezes in January and February, the driest months of the year, are followed in March and April by light south and south-east winds which blow during the day but die down at sunset. This south breeze is called by the natives, *payiru gáli*, or the 'crop wind' . . . In December the wind blows from the east during the day and from the north during the night. The latter is called the hill (*konda*) wind.
>
> *(Hemingway 1915: 12)*

The *human project* has an in-built mechanism where nature is for extreme consumption and is commodified. Hence the intricacies of language would not matter. Nature, anyways, as I speak of it, is not about landscapes by themselves, but landscapes are part of the natural world, many of which have had very long-standing interactions with human societies, of varied kinds, and it is in the larger ecological sense that one speaks of it. But I am specifically focusing on spaces with sounds, lights, shades, which are receptacles of meaning for people who live in close proximity to specific natural environs which are today the battle-ground for resource extraction and the deep state. Even so, perspectives on nature and how it is seen vary for different communities. A Kondareddi perspective on a mango or tamarind tree would be different from that of a Kamma or Kapu one[3]. Incidentally, the Kondareddis, and even Koyas of east Godavari consider tamarind a sacred tree, but in some villages elsewhere in AP, the tamarind tree is feared, since they believe it houses ghouls. It may be interesting to understand these differences at some point. The way things in nature are perceived is part of the politics of economics and politics, in general. Several adivasis/tribal communities, Dalits, fisherfolk are being forcibly dislocated from their natural environment that they have consciously (through knowledge systems that they practised across generations) conserved not for simply reasons of beauty in a vacuum, but by ways of utility which are totally different from the greed of capital.

Metaphor of distance – *Verticality,* TV, water taps

When one closely examines the cartography of urban life, the predominant metaphor is that of *verticality*. In this *verticality* of things are constructed illusions of intimacy when reality is just so far, or illusions of distance when the real is so near. The water tap, the moon, and the sunlight and mobile phones may be just a few examples. But the more tangible, visible example is the high-rise apartment. Further up from the ground you see more the mental, physical, and emotional distance from the touch and feel of the ground, the earth, the soil, and the water. These are also amenable to new kinds of purity–pollution discourses. People are 'outside of' and 'sheltered within,' and shielded from, nature. Glasspanes – increasingly used in city buildings – are metaphors of shields between people and nature, just as the sunlight might enter spaces within, but the nearness/the touch and feel of the heat of it, are far/distant. The din of 24x7 TV makes sure that your senses, of hearing, not just the everyday sounds, but also the silence, at times, are numbed. But this numbness and un-feeling are not limited to un-hearing of everyday sounds and birds and insects, but gradually seeps through the system so that, apart from a spectacle, the 'usual' dislocations and displacements of people fail to move anyone beyond a few days. The nature of belonging constructed in cities is to that of a gated community-space, an apartment complex-space, and perhaps, a neighbourhood park-space where, again, the overwhelming, almost pathological 'feeling,' if it can be called that, is how to 'reduce weight,' do the ten rounds, bend, rise, bend, rise and then rush home or to work. The urban space (increasingly expanding, with thousands of smart cities planned), is a cultural and deeply political space, consciously constructed – as a politics – and it is a signifier of increased distance from the ground and earth and water and soil and the wind and the breeze, but by extension, also a signifier of the distance between a seemingly shielded, well-provided for space and the Kondareddis, Koyas, or perhaps the Dongria Kondhs and the Santhals and the largest section of Dalits in the rural spaces, increasingly being dislocated. Perceptions of sharing spaces with animals and birds are nearly the same as perceptions of people that these spaces reinstate. Peacocks are to be declared vermin in Goa, hence ordered to be exterminated; monkeys are vermin in another state: exterminate. Whatever it is that disturbs the assumed (constructed) equilibrium: exterminate, or punish. Programmes such as Operation Green-Hunt (strange that it is called 'Green' 'hunt'), sedition and imprisonment, and torture, are some of the means to straighten the deviant or exterminate them. Of course, the other side is equally true, where the ones 'hunted down' operate on a similar logic of exterminating (at different times) those who turn against them[4].

The malady of living in sanitised, fully serviced apartments (many come with the appendage of a 'no-pet policy' in many cities; and some of them have 'no salesmen policy') vertical and on a notional idea of ownership of the land beneath runs deeper than we imagine. Once these pockets of shielded spaces are created, with a heavy dose ofTV and noise, you only occasionally 'escape' to 'quiet' and 'nature' and 'peace' for a few days to the exotic 'other' space, 'out there,' which may have been once, or perhaps still is (in some cases) a place where tribal/adivasi communities and other Dalits had homes and everyday lives. Today these are eco-resorts (or dam sites, where tourists throng to see the gush of water after torrential rains when the floodgates are opened to avoid disasters), sanitised of the everyday. There, the natural quiet of the everyday becomes re-packaged as 'quiet' and 'Nature' and 'eco' and is serviced to people from cities, sanitised of the people around and the animals and birds, who are then promised lesser spaces in 150 sq. ft; the former in R&R colonies and the latter in city zoos or shrinking National Park spaces. Resettlement homes in a colony called R&R (universally) come with gadgets of urban existence.

In the course of the rise of the city, universities and institutions, are increasingly part of these spaces of urban living, and to me these seem conscious, politically intended; as intended and planned as the verticality and vacuum-isation of senses and sensations[5], so that the longest battle of Dongria Kondhs against the Vedanta company in Niyamgiri and of Koyas and Kondareddis against Polavaram dam on Godavari river, may create no more than a moment's unrest, and perhaps a few days of protest. Most fail to understand the language of Lodu Sikaka and his community when he once said (now famously):

> Niyam raja is our god . . . this mountain is our temple, our god. Because of these mountains, our children live, the rains come, the water comes, the wind blows, the mountains bring water. If they take away these rocks, we will die. Eta Niyamgiri to amaar atma [this Niyam giri is our soul] . . . . Vedanta has no right to touch our Niyamgiri mountain.[6]

What better exposition on human-ecosystem connections can there be than this, coming from people who should have been at the centre of the knowledge system and politics but are today on the fringes, because their language seems to many to be far too idealistic at the best and ridiculously simplistic at the worst to people who look at progress and development only in terms of urban expansion and consistent consumption of products which companies such as Vedanta and others produce for the global market. What Sikaka spoke of, is also spoken of at global conferences on climate change; and government leaders agree that there is indeed something called Climate Change, a term which has recently been incorporated in the Indian Ministry of Environment and Forests (it is now MoE&F and Climate Change). The intimacy of Lodu Sikaka with the mountain-forest is organic, everyday, and not exotic; the 'outside' there is 'inside' – the mountain is where they live and work and is their god, and so they are constantly physically 'in touch' with this god even at a sensual level.

It is interesting to see that in the Sanskritic, which became the universalised, 'Hindu' tradition, the religion necessarily creates a distance between god and human, although bhakti is usually cited as merging that distance to a large extent by making the god an intimate friend, beloved, etc. of the human 'bhakta,' yet the god is still outside, to be invited within the heart of the human devotee through devotion, through friendship, submission, subservience, depending on the way in which the devotee chooses to reach that merger with the divine; same goes for the Sufi tradition. That is a discourse I shall not engage with here, but I wish to point out that in most of the cases where an animal or bird or any form of wildlife is connected to the divine, what happens on the ground seems far away from the iconography which connects human/god with the natural world. For instance, Elephant-god, Monkey-god, Peacock: god's vehicle, Lion: goddess' vehicle, etc. The elephants in most places in India are either ill-treated as procession animals in temple towns or as labourers for forest departments or killed almost everyday by fast moving trains through elephant corridors. Many elephants find themselves attacked when they enter cultivated fields within or around forests. Monkeys have been declared vermin, as I said earlier; so also Peacocks, usually the vehicle for the god Kartikeya/Murugan. Dogs, incidentally, are associated with Bhairava, but the status of dogs in many parts of the country is too well-known to narrate here. Almost every animal has some religious significance. But the actual treatment shows no concern for that *bit* of religion, or their high connections with divinity, ever. The goddess is worshipped almost everywhere in this country, but women are raped almost every other day or restrained from following their dreams in most cases.

What I am trying to say is that in the act of worship itself is the distance, consciously constructed. Once the intimacy is killed, killing, maiming, or raping becomes simpler. The goddess, the different vehicles of gods and goddesses, the animal-gods, are all 'out there' or 'up there,' somewhere far away, very distant, once they are distant, the violence with their real animal/bird forms on the earth/ground seems to effect no sense of horror in people. Praying to distant gods, god-vehicles, and goddesses comes far easier, and hence, the decimation, created after sufficient distance, is equally easy[7].

In case of the Kondareddis, Kondhs, and several other tribal/adivasi communities (or in the case of Dalits living by the sea or rivers) the forest/river is *both* sensual-real and utilitarian (in some cases, utilitarian and hence the feel, the touch, the reverence is both sensual and utilitarian, with no duality there); the utilitarian here, is *not* extreme consumption. It cannot be *extreme consumption* because it is revered, and since it is revered, is divine, its *being* and *presence* is most essential. Hence, there is no space for wanton destruction for greed. It is quite simple. Without being deterministic. The rules of hunting and cultivation are customarily respectful to laws of nature and seasons unlike the blanket bans and reservations of the Forest policies following the colonial legacy, which are signifiers of *extreme Nature*, where reserved forests can make way for plantations by industries (as part of their Corporate Social Responsibility and within the global Carbon Sink market paradigms)[8]. It is the most intimate spaces of marginal communities that are sought to be controlled and manipulated by the state and multinational corporations invoking a different kind of 'development-god' – there is an entire 'religion' in operation here, in the latter case, which is far more entrenched than the regular religious faith of common people.

There is no comprehensive account yet that seeks to analyse the overall attitude towards nature and the interconnectedness of life-systems in the traditional Left and the radical (and presently 'outlawed') Left, so far. In some pockets, the closeness of some Left groups (not necessarily/always Maoist) to people in tribal/adivasi areas, makes it appear that perhaps there is some acceptance of the people's ideas of land, forest, river, etc. But the Left political discourse – in general – remains largely anthropocentric. There is acceptance of people's dislocations from projects that affect their homes and livelihoods, for instance, but the stress is almost always about the human world, and not an entire eco-system; but more importantly, the language of the discourse remains within the dominant paradigm of compensation, R&R, 'development,' even in projects of irreversible ecological destruction, wherein the human world is part of parcel of that destruction, but not the only victim.

Then there is yet another discourse which calls to question protection of wild animal species and conservation, itself, in areas where there is human-animal conflict, without questioning the reasons for that conflict and demanding centrality to the human side of that conflict – in elephant corridors, tiger zones, etc. Both the extreme conservatism, and deep human Rights discourse, seems to reinstate the anthropocentric; keeping Nature or natural spaces as either sacrosanct, and hence distant, or unimportant for the discourse, and hence removed, from human lives.

Another metaphor that comes to my mind is that of the Intensive Care Unit (ICU) of the hospitals where the first thing that is struck off is the cord of intimacy between the family and the patient; what you see through the glass doors of separation is a distant body, under the control of gadgets controlled by the representative of the system (in this case, hospital doctors, nurses, etc). This metaphor could be used for several instances where an artificial distance is not just created, but also maintained and scrutinised by the system and its representatives. Natural resources are similarly being distanced from communities close to them – who are then thrown a few crumbs by way of compensation packages of a lifetime – and then forced to sit by and watch huge machinery on their fields, destroying them, destroying forest land, rivers, and mountains for extracting minerals and resources towards something they say will benefit people in the long run but essentially for consumption elsewhere, 'outside' of their own historically lived spaces.

Water taps are metaphors of distance between a river and the ultimate consumption of a segment of a river's identity, which is H_2O (the formula called water), simply put. The history or the historical relations of the river and the people – who have been dislocated and amputated from the river's history and existence through a single big dam project (or several dam projects) which will then take the water into vertical city-spaces – are of no consequence. Here, in these city-spaces, there is no intimacy, nor belonging, to the idea of a river or river system. The river too, perhaps, does not belong in these spaces as a phenomenon of any significance. Water does. The water tap becomes the Operating System (OS) which must work 24x7, or hell will break lose. At the other end, the same water will be dreaded to the point of being cursed, if a stream or river dares to flow through the streets, of what once were the river's own natural pathways, causing inundation of these vertical spaces which encroached upon the river's natural course, filling them up with sand piles, in order to build spaces distanced from both the river/stream/ lake and the idea of a river as a natural force which 'flows.'

> Taps, which bring water into individual homes, in an apartment in a city – as individuated units, apart from each, and hence '*apart-ment*' . . . denotes the breaking up into several individual units. So the use of water, the flow of it, is also individualised and in a sense invisible to the 'others' (in this complex) . . . what the state, via corporations, brings in through artificial channels into their homes (the way States use the idea of bringing Krishna to Chennai or Godavari to Hyderabad) is not a river but only a segment of a river's identity, which is 'H_2O = water' . . . The river itself, for increasingly urban spaces, is an abstract element or phenomenon, largely invisible; only its uses and its constructs (tanker, drainage systems, pipelines) are visible and hence understood . . . Any damming activity in a far-off, largely invisible space, seems too distant (metaphorically, at least) to the city-dweller. At the other end are gallons of water flowing into industrial complexes or premises or corridors, through similar pipelines, from an abstract distant river . . . Only the end result is visible – in the way it is constructed for us.
>
> *(Umamaheshwari 2016: 37)*

How do you deal with the sacredness supposedly attached to Indian rivers? It does not matter too much. Just as we have dealt with sacredness and destruction of the very thing that was sacred, here too, you go 'elsewhere' to access that sacredness of a river: either the Krishna *pushkaram* or Godavari *pushkaram* (a once-in-twelve-years ritual cleansing supposed to cleanse people of their sins) or the Kumbh and Ganga and you return home to a city (if you are an urban dweller, and most of the friction of intimacy and un-belonging happens in these spaces) and you want the same Godavari or Krishna in your taps at home. By this time, she will become sufficiently desacralised, and turn into H_2O, without the associated sacredness or reverence. Here, the more you pay (in currency terms), the more tankers of water you get, to fill up the overhead tanks for the water you consume in the privacy of your homes.

Of rivers, damming, forests

What is a river all about? A seemingly flat, two-dimensional surface? Or simply water resource? Does a river hold meanings and layers of history in the course she flows or through structures forced on her to divert the natural flow/direction? What about the life within rivers, of species, non-human? These questions would lead you to a river of communities and life histories and an eco-system that urges you to understand that every large river has several smaller rivers, rivulets and streams contributing to that largeness or largesse. A river is not singular, though a river may be named that way; Godavari's identity is closely linked to that of Wainganga's, Wardha's, Pranahita's, Sabari's, and many others, which together make Godavari what she is towards one end of her expanse. At the extreme end, before joining the sea, she becomes two distinct Gautamis. For people living by the river, the river Sabari is distinct, as is Pranahita, or any other. Their intimacy would be with those rivers/streams, rivulets, etc. These aspects belong in a world that is far away from the political river, which is Godavari, which 'wastes into sea' and must be dammed, at several places in Maharashtra, Telangana, Andhra Pradesh and so on. Here, the internal combinations – or linkages – of a river system do not make any sense to the political games. Here the set of questions would be – how much TMC[9] ft of water does this river have? How much can this river be 'utilised' to the last gallon? These questions belong in a world of techno-fixing and policy and power. There are no people here, communities of the riverside, river of the communities, or fish and other species in the river.

Malladi Posi, a fishworker/fisherman from Manturu (East Godavari) had queried me once ironically, 'They won't give us Godavari for Godavari, will they?'

Posi is from the Palli subcaste of fisher community, and he also does part-time ferrying of people from Manturu to Vadapally across the river, villages in the Polavaram dam submergence zone. This seemed to me his pun on the idea of 'land to land' (which is the way people refer to land for land compensation for the project, in these parts) guaranteed for the STs. It also meant he mocked the normative 'compensation language,' which has no consideration for river, which, to fisher communities, is 'land,' a resource they have built their life histories on.

> 'Perhaps we have to go elsewhere, looking for a river, if not Godavari', reflects Sangani Eswara Rao of Kachluru in Tunnur panchayat, East Godavari district. Malladi Posi and Eswara Rao are fishermen, belonging to the Palli caste, from villages along the river Godavari that are threatened by displacement by the Polavaram dam. Posi and Rao's words throw up deeper questions: For whom does the Godavari flow? Just as tribal communities seek land for land, and forest for forest, can these fishermen seek a river for a river in compensation? Is the Godavari meant only for industry or agriculture, not for fishermen/fish workers? Whose river is the Godavari? What about those whose lives and livelihoods depend on 'hunting' fish (*caapala veta*, as they call it. . .)? . . . Should the Polavaram dam see completion, these communities could lose their identity forever . . . There is no mention of fisher communities in the R&R (Rehabilitation and Resettlement) statistics of the Polavaram project; in a strange paradox, they are not counted as part of the population of the 'agency areas'. Although they have fished in these waters for centuries, subtle changes in their settlement patterns were never important enough to be recorded by census officials. When it comes to voting, however, they do seem to count as they have ration cards.
>
> *(Umamaheshwari 2010)*

The attitude towards the fisher communities exemplifies distance and disconnect. The state enumerates them but forgets the essence of people's lived histories. The intimacy of the fisher communities with Godavari is deep.

Sometimes intimacies are also constructed. During the Godavari and Krishna *pushkaram*, the state governed these intimacies constructed from a 'Hindu' ritual idea of river (though many communities *may* partake of these); these constructed intimacies do not ever understand the 'natural' intimacy and belonging-ness of people for whom the river may always be a precious presence, not a commodity, not an exotica either, definitely of 'use' (if they fish), to them, for their livelihoods – so there is the distance maintained between extreme obsessive indulgence in intimacy – and these are communities who actually understand a river's flow as well her moods and seasonal temperament; as they understand the fish cycles or cycle of other aquatic species, whose health is intrinsic to the health of the river and vice versa.

According to Ramaswamy Iyer, 'Apart from the submergence of a certain area, dams and barrages have downstream impacts too: they reduce downstream flows and affect the river regime, its capacity for cleaning itself, its function as a recharger of groundwater, its role as the sustainer of aquatic life and vegetation and downstream communities and their livelihoods, the health of the estuary, and so on.'[10]

At this juncture, let me share two poems here which come from experiential and intimate spaces of two Dalit poets, about two distinct rivers.

Maa aur Nadi

(Omprakash Valmiki, Dalit Hindi Poet)

What a deep relationship it was, between mother and the river
On the river banks was my maternal home
With the Hindon river flowing closely past
One can never forget the cucumbers and musk melons that grew on the river-sands
Just as one can't forget mother's *roti* and vegetables and
the *chutney* ground on the grindstone
the river
is both history and the present
just as mother is[11] (Valmiki 2012: 46)

Godavari

(Yendluri Sudhakar, Dalit Telugu Poet)

When I rest my head on your lap-banks
I feel I am with my mother
When I roll on the sand beds of your body
I feel I am playing on my father's chest (Kallury, Translation. 2008: 185)

Then there is yet another poetry from life which is lived by the fisher communities and other communities along Godavari: this poetry lies in the expression associated with Godavari's 'coming' (not 'flooding'), which is the perspective that truly inheres a soul-connection with a natural phenomenon whose natural identity lies in flowing and the coming in spate of a river is expressed as a natural coming, rather than as a 'disaster' – the latter being a term deeply connected with ideas of 'national' management of natural phenomena, usually in ways more disastrous than the natural phenomenon itself. For the fishermen on Godavari, its flows are intrinsic to their own histories and identities. Fishing zones are culturally and intergenerationally fixed.

The other imaginary of a river is the Anicut over Godavari which is still maintained by the AP state. Sir Arthur Cotton, a government engineer, completed its construction in year 1852. The structure is popular as the Cotton Barrage, at Dowlaiswaram near Rajahmundry in East Godavari, Andhra Pradesh. Cotton continues to be deified in Telangana and Andhra Pradesh to this day, and there are even Sanskrit verses penned on his greatness[12] by those who idolise the dam itself as a structure of great human achievement. Theanicut led the agriculturists to become far more dependent on the structure thus established. The idea of land created here (in the delta) essentially emerged from the idea of the river. With the British colonial rule, some of the rivers became sites of state power and through the enlightenment, Baconian, vision of controlling nature – in this case, usually, floods – engineering experiments became the new modes of establishing, forcibly injecting the seed of paternity over riverspaces. This engineering establishment set such a firm foot on Indian soil, that even today, the structure – especially one that oversees dams, reservoirs, and irrigation projects – apes the colonial construct. They remain paternal and patriarchal.

> In Arthur Cotton's language, 'the river must be restrained from wandering, which, from its having no hard strata in its course, it always does naturally, and all its branches must be provided with artificial embankments to prevent the country being flooded from the river . . . and it is necessary by artificial means, to keep the water constantly at a level which shall command the country, and also by a multitude of channels to lead it to every acre of land . . . The system of works now in progress in the Delta of the Godavery, therefore, are intended to embrace these four objects, viz – to restrain the river; to preserve the land from floods; to supply it constantly with water; and to pervade the tract thoroughly with means of very cheap transit.'
>
> *(Umamaheshwari 2015: 225)*

Discussing the forms in which the present shows signs of certain hangovers from the past, and the process called *ruination* – which could also be used as a metaphor to understand spoiling or reconfiguring of natural landscapes, of the marginalise and poor, usually – Ann Laura Stoler urges on,

> [The] need to refocus on the *connective tissue* that continues to bind human potentials to degraded environments and degraded personhoods to the

> material refuse of imperial projects – to the spaces redefined, to the soils turned toxic, and to the relations severed between people and people, and between people and things. At issue are political lives of imperial debris and the uneven pace with which people can extract themselves from the structures and signs by which remains take hold.
>
> *(Stoler 2013: 8)*

Further,

> The question is pointed: how do imperial formations persist in their material debris, in ruined landscapes and through social ruination of people's lives? . . . It is rather to recognise that these are unfinished histories, not of a victimised past, but of consequential histories of differential futures.
>
> *(Stoler 2013: 10–11)*

I see the anicut on Godavari is an imperial ruin and Polavaram dam an ongoing ruination.

Controlling rivers towards revenue generation has become an immortal legacy of colonial science and technology mission; the distance created then, between: a) people and rivers; b) between rivers' natural flows/as also floods and holding the river waters through an entire mechanism 'releasíng' and closing the gates (by the patriarchal engineering structure, which also leads to conflicts sometimes between states over water sharing on the one hand and unprecedented, human-made floods, on the other) and; c) between natural gravity and forced 'lift.'

I recount an event that occurred in Himachal Pradesh sometime early 2015. The event was reported as a 'freak accident,' but 'freak' it wasn't. In many ways, it could be seen as a kind of institutional murder (the institution in this case, could be the engineering establishment and the entity called the modern-day dam). Several young students from Hyderabad, on their way to Mandi lost their lives in the sudden gush of waters of Beas river; not a single body was found (barring one, many days later, in a decomposed condition, somewhere along the way). The fault was not the river's. But the waters released from the Larji dam, unannounced. Irony it was, that these were young engineering students from AP-Telangana, the state that deifies engineering and dam building projects. Some say the siren was perhaps inaudible to the students out there to have fun, clicking selfies. The idea behind this incident is the damming principle itself, based on controlling flows. The underside of the story was that the everyday this kind of release of dam waters is part of a nexus between the government authorities and sand mining mafia; the force of the water released and stopped leaves a pile of silt, which is then collected in truck loads. Here, river first becomes stored water and then mere sand particles, which then make homes in the cities. Each sequence distances the idea of the river from its end-perception. What was even more pertinent was that following this Larji dam incident, my BSNL mobile phone would send me this SMS everyday, for a long time thereafter: 'We request you to avoid venturing into rivers or entering into river waters, for your own safety and well-being.' This is yet another metaphor of our being in chains of an idea that removes us from what was once an un-oblivious part of people's lives around rivers.

Frames, images, metaphors of other worlds

Finally, I move to some images etched in my memory, which signify kinds of intimacy and examples of distance. Women in the villages of Kumaun (at the time when I lived and worked there for a while) many years ago, used to go in small groups (usually friends went together) to collect fodder and fuel from the forests. Afternoons were times they sat together in the forest, sometimes by a small stream of river, or in a thicket of tall trees giving shade from the Sun, and indulged – in gossip perhaps, or sharing concerns regarding problems at home. Or a love story in the neighbourhood. These were very intimate spaces. Sometimes they bathed together, and lazed about, leaving their animals (if they had any) to graze around. Sometimes there would be sexual plays, too. They were uninhibited here. Many possibilities existed in these spaces. Interestingly, many of the folk songs in Kumaun, I would realise later, sung by women, had the character of the forest guard – *daroga* – who, in the songs, was also an intruder, and the state, in person, fining them for 'destroying' the forests and stealing wood. *He* was the *system*, which created the binary, of forest/Nature as 'outside of' the people. None of these songs ever idealised the forest guard. If there was another male character who found himself in most of the songs of women, it was the bus driver or jeep driver, the medium between the village and the outside world, either bringing in the beloved or taking the beloved far away, or the driver himself being the beloved in some cases. Intimacies always exist alongside a sense of belonging or, on the other hand, the friction caused from un-belonging in an intensely intimate space.

Other moments of intimacy come from a different world, one close to a (belonging to the world of) a river – Godavari. It was when four young boys of a fisher community from Devipatnam, by Godavari river, crossed me across to Singanapally, on a particularly windy summer afternoon, when the river was at her ebb; the nature of their navigation, with a tarpaulin sheet making up for the wind sail of an old boat, with joy and revelry of early teenage years (when the schools were closed for the summer vacations) was another playful moment with the river, whose moods and the nature of flow may have been an intrinsic part of several childhoods, spent in these environs, where the river becomes also a playground and challenges the children to play with her, navigate across, with smiles on their faces as they 'did it.' Here it is difficult to decide who belongs more here, and who is intimate with whom: the river, the children, both to each other or to the space around.

And then there is a completely contrasting moment that I recorded on the same river; where tourist cruises happen on the river, which could be any river, not just Godavari. Here there is an external gaze, a distant, and usually patronising, gaze at the vast expanse of picture-postcard river and villages and the hills around. The river here can be a dumping ground (of plastic coffee cups and soda bottles or leftover food); the people of the place are objects of voyeurism as much as the river is. Would it be of some consequence that most of these tourists belong to upper castes and are usually city-dwellers?

One of the deeply philosophical-political ideas of Nature I also found in the exposition of the Kondareddi woman, Madi Muttem (or Madi Muttamma), from the village Kokkarigudem in East Godavari, AP. She said,

> I am the MPTC[13] (member) for two mandals – Kondamodalu and Tunnur . . . We cannot survive in plain area[14]; this is Agency[15], and hence we have all things we need; in the town, in plain area, you have to *buy* everything – vegetables, edible leaves, fruits, tamarind, etc. *Here*, in the agency, we get all of those *free*. We just need to buy salt, which we get from our village *santa* (the weekly village fairs). *There*, we cannot survive. They say they will build our homes in places which we shall show them; they have not yet shown us anything yet.[16]

Her home lies within the submergence zone of the Polavaram dam, and what she had said to me then addressed sites which were at once personal and political and historically rooted and where she belonged. And the *in-construction* sites that she spoke of were Submergence Zone as a Site, Village as a Site, and an economic construct as a Site[17].

Madi Muttem's was a simple, deep, and profound understanding of the *akkada (there*, distant, where she will never belong, even if forced to) and *ikkada(here*, intimate). The concept of *ikkada*(here) versus *akkada*(there) was the most reflective philosophical point which nearly all the tribal women spoke to me about in the submergence zone. *Ikkada* and *akkada* would occur in a context of contrasts (of being the adivasi person rooted in a historical location versus becoming a state and market project, or in other words, the sacrificial goat for the bogey of public good).

> *Akkada* or *There* is a nameless, disempowering, vague, abstract notion of a place they will be 'thrown into' (*padestaaru – they will throw us*, said many, so they felt they were perceived as things that can be thrown into someplace) and following from there, they will lose their identities and livelihoods. Even if they happened to know the name of the 'RR colony' (in two cases in Polavaram mandal) it was always referred to as 'there', 'that place' (vague, abstract, nameless); no matter how difficult lives were 'here' (their homes by the tamarind and toddy and the forested hills) – it is still their home. . .
>
> *(Umamaheshwari 2014: 17–18)*
>
> Incidentally, the government machinery had the same language – '*ikkada meeru em chestaaru, adavillo undi? Akkada meeku anni sadupayalu untaayi*' ('what will you do *Here*, staying in forests? *There* you will get all facilities').
>
> *(Ibid: 18)*

Shane Phelan has written that

> Nature may be distance, the unreachable referent of our desire or need, but it is never really far at all. What would distance really mean in a world where habit is nature, where nature is cultivated? . . . Instead of eliminating nature in political discourse, I would argue for the mediation of intimate distance . . . The elimination of nature can only further the solipsism of modern Western civilisation, in which the earth becomes 'standing-reserve' for appropriation by humans who have themselves become nothing but resources in a global economy . . . What is needed is a reconceptualisation that heightens respect and care without a return to medieval piety.
>
> *(Phelan 1992: 398–400)*

The world market dogma today is promising cities that are clones of each other; rural spaces are redundant for them, either as idioms of the past and better dead and gone; forests are sites of timber management or entertainment/nature tourism. In some places, rocks and mountains, which sometimes inhere sacredness for some communities (Niyamgiri for the Dongria Kondh of Odisha or the ancient rock-cut caves in northern Tamil Nadu for minorities such as the Tamil Jaina, tamarind and mango trees for the Kondareddi and Koya, among many examples), signify only extraction value for private companies and the state. Human beings and nature are today sites of economic management and currency exchange. In a dam project, while submergence of human habitations is calculated in terms of currency, and policies exist to compensate in monetary terms, the loss of habitat of bird species, amphibians, reptiles, butterflies, wild animals – an entire, distinct earthspace – is non-existent in the vocabulary of compensation. Because the earthspace cannot be compensated for in the same way as the elements of nature cannot be calculated in monetary terms, these too lose their place in the larger history of the universe, which is far more expansive and older than human history.

The distance between the entrance and terminal gats at the airports of big metros; the deity and the devotee in larger temples and; between the ground and the last floor of several skyscrapers, are peculiar metaphors of our times, which also add to the distance between human society and nature/the natural world, and people who still have deep bonds with the natural world, of which they have usually been both partakers, and caretakers, for 'smaller' needs, which never make sense in the bombardment of 8 or 9 per cent growth index.

Notes

1 One of the largest dam projects (multi-purpose, as they all are, now) being constructed on Godavari river in Andhra Pradesh, at the site (which was once a village) Polavaram, is being built with billions of dollar investment to raise a 150 plus feet reservoir for producing 960 MW of electricity, for supplying water (and power) to multinational industries coming up in the south-east Indian coast, which include state and multinational corporations such as Reliance, Cairn Energy, among others, with a token supplementary

benefit of irrigating 7 lakh acres of extra ayacut in the delta region and drinking water for Vishakhapatnam. One of the components is also linking Godavari with Krishna (transferring Godavari waters into Krishna, for use by Krishna river basin farmers/possible future real estate). Three hundred thousand (estimate, official) people from officially 276 (but could be far more, since the estimates are older than a decade that the government has never updated) villages, of which more than 270 are villages in V Schedule/tribal areas will be displaced. More than three thousand hectares of prime forest land (semi-deciduous and semi-evergreen) part of which lies in the Papikonda National Park, with more than 150 bird species, more than 90 wild animal species, including the Gaur, several species of reptiles, including the Golden Gecko, amphibians, an entire habitat of wild grasses, shrubs, etc will also be consumed/submerged in the giant project, which has the singular glory for having violated most of the provisions of the Indian Constitution including the PESA Act (Panchayati Raj extension to the Scheduled Areas) 1/70, inter-state water sharing clause between Odisha, Chhattisgarh, and AP (with cases still pending between the three states on the issue of submergence), Wildlife Protection Act, among a few and is now a National Project. It is one project that saw the support of the Congress government and the present NDA-II government at the centre. Incidentally, Odisha and Chhattisgarh too will lose their farmlands to the dam, once constructed.

2 Right to Fair Compensation and Transparency in Land Acquisition, Rehabilitation and Resettlement Act, 2013

3 Kondareddis and Koyas are Scheduled Tribes (the former categorised as Particularly Vulnerable Tribal Group); Kapus and Kammas are landed upper castes of aristocratic, feudal lineage in Andhra Pradesh-Telangana.

4 However, violence of the state will always be far more ruthless and powerful, in any circumstance, anywhere in the world. The previous line of arguments is not linked directly to the latter half, but I am interested in understanding the language – of 'levelling' the population and living spaces through extermination; of constructing the 'outside,' and hence, a danger to human society.

5 Which comes out in the open, at times, as it has, with the suicide of Rohith Vemula, a Dalit student of the University of Hyderabad, in January 2016, whose scholarship money had been forcibly withheld for seven months by the university. In recent times, however, some of the central universities in bigger metros are gradually becoming visible sites of student resistance, connected with larger issues. But that is not the case with every central university.

6 From the documentary film, Mine: Story of a Sacred Mountain; available at minefilm.com

7 It is perhaps important to note that I am not an atheist, and hence the thinking about different religions, god/non-god concepts, divinity, universal spirit, animism, is a constant engagement and questioning at a personal level, with no resolution yet. One can only say that religion, per se, is complex, so is the idea of divinity, or non-divinity – in any form, across cultures. But the affairs of religion, conducted by mediators, become matters of regular, mundane politics. Since this is a paper on intimacy and nature, this note should make sense.

8 An entire marketing transaction happens on Carbon sinks across the world and most of the so-called 'First world' countries have attempted to dump their responsibility towards reduction of fossil fuels on to increasing Carbon sinks in the so-called Third World nations, and earning brownie points for that. Nature here acts as a simple game of who grows more trees and continues to pollute under transnational agreements to compensate for the destruction already caused. Everything has monetary value here. Hence, of course, Lodu Sikaka, in these contexts, seems like a simpleton.

9 Thousand Million Cubic Feet (28.3 million cubic metres).

10 Personal email communication (year 2010), as quoted in 'Whose river is the Godavari?,' above mentioned.

11 My translation.

12 See, Umamaheshwari 2015: 219. Cotton is referred to, in popular parlance, as 'Delta Shilpi'- architect of the delta.
13 Mandal Parishad Territorial Council, a unit of local self-governance (Gram Panchayat) in the village.
14 That is how people in the V Schedule (tribal) area refer to the non-Scheduled Areas. V Schedule area is locally referred to as Agency, a term that came in with the colonial rule. Emphasis, wherever, mine.
15 Many of them continue to refer to these parts as Agency Areas, as designated during the colonial period. Though sometimes they use Scheduled *prantam* (area) with Agency interchangeably. The opposite of Agency (non-Scheduled area) is Plain area, again in common parlance.
16 Personal communication, on 13th June, 2008, at Kondamodalu.
17 This line of argument comes from my earlier paper (titled 'Self, Other and Constructions of Perpetual Distancing: the "Tribal" Person (Founded on Experiences from the Submergence Zone of the Polavaram Dam in AP-Telangana),' presented at a seminar, *Revisiting Adivasi Autonomy: Self, Home & Habitat*, 19–21 February 2015, at the University of Hyderabad. Parts of the discussion are also in my book (2014), cited.

References

Hemingway, F.R. (I.C.S). 1915. *Madras District Gazetteers: Godavari*. Madras: Superintendent, Government Press.

Kallury, Syamala. 2008. 'Cultural Contexts and the Changing Images of the River Godavari: A Study of Four Poets of Twentieth Century Telugu Literature.' *Indian Literature*, 52(1) (243) (January–February): 180–189. www.jstor.org/stable/23347602. Accessed 14 July 2015.

Koepnick, Lutz. 2014. *On Slowness: Toward an Aesthetic of the Contemporary*. New York: Columbia University Press.

Phelan, Shane. 1992. 'Intimate Distance: The Dislocation of Nature in Modernity.' *The Western Political Quarterly*, 45(2)(June): 385–402. www.jstor.org/stable/448717. Accessed 16 March 2016.

Pouchepadass, Jacques. 1995. 'Colonialism and Environment in India: Comparative Perspective.' *Economic and Political Weekly*, 30(33) (August2019): 2059–2067. www.jstor.org/stable/4403103. Accessed13 October 2011.

Stoler, Ann Laura. (ed.) 2013. *Imperial Debris: On Ruins and Ruination*. Durham, London: Duke University Press.

Umamaheshwari, R. 2010. 'Whose River Is the Godavari?' *Infochange News & Features* (1 October). www.infochangeindia.org.

Umamaheshwari, R. 2014. *When Godavari Comes: People's History of a River (Journeys in the Zone of the Dispossessed)*. New Delhi: Aakar Books.

Umamaheshwari, R. 2015. 'River as a Feminine Presence: Godavari in Andhra Pradesh.' In Ramaswamy R. Iyer (ed.), *Living Rivers, Dying Rivers*. New Delhi: Oxford University Press.

Umamaheshwari, R. 2016. 'Reconfiguring Ideas of Land, River and Forest in the Context of the Indira Sagar Polavaram National Project on Godavari.' In Varsha Bhagat-Ganguly (ed.), *Land Rights in India: Policies, Movements and Challenges*. Routledge South Asia Edition.

Valmiki, Omprakash. 2012. *Shabd Jhoot Nahin Bolte* (Poetry Anthology, Hindi). New Delhi: Anamika Publications and Distributors Ltd.

PART II

Rethinking intimacy, contemporarity vis-à-vis the conventional institutions

4

INTIMACY IN TAMIL KINSHIP

Isabelle Clark-Decès

In the field, anthropologists have many opportunities to witness, if only inadvertently or surreptitiously, acts or practices that usually remain hidden to the outside world. At least this is my experience. Over the 20 years that I have worked in Tamil Nadu I noticed that whenever my informants, my female informants in particular, felt comfortable with me, trusted me, or simply momentarily forgot that I was there, they touched, nursed babies, bathed, or fought with each other in front of me without any apparent sense of embarrassment, shame, or even self-consciousness. Sometimes they invited me to document their personal closeness. Once a young couple in Madurai asked me to take a photograph of the wife dressed in jeans – a garment that at the times she could not have worn anywhere else, but in the privacy of my rented house. The picture of this couple both dressed in jeans and holding hands revealed a bond between them that I had never witnessed before. It also made me feel very close to them. Usually I was the recipient rather than the recorder of love and affection. The one occasion that stands out is the day 'my' cook invited me to eat at her house. When her 30-year-old daughter saw that I was unable to finish the huge quantity of food piled up on my banana leaf, she sat down by my side, pulled the leaf toward her, and proceeded to eat my leftovers. Any scholar of Indian society would know that it is considered extremely rude to offer someone food contaminated with saliva, but that it is not uncommon for spouses or extremely close friends and family to share food from each other's plates. The daughter's show of kinship touched me deeply.

For the most part, though, what I know of the intimate lives of Tamil people came from trying to understand what my informants meant when they said to me that they would rather marry kin than 'outsiders.' It was by attempting to figure out the conceptions of their unique kinship practices – the so-called Dravidian kinship system (Trautmann 1981) – that I came to get a feel for what is intimacy in Tamil kinship.

I began my research on Tamil marriage to kin by attempting to grasp the meanings of the general Tamil equivalent for the English word 'kin.' According to the Tamil lexicon, this term, *contam*, means: 'one's own peculiar right, exclusive property, that which belongs to oneself' (Tamil Lexicon 2007: 1651). My informants shed light on this relatively opaque definition when they explained that each and every Tamil kinship relation comes with rights (*urimai*) that are quasi-legal. 'I've *urimai* in my husband,' they would say or, 'I've *urimai* to ask anything from my mother or father. I've *urimai* to their property.' One of these respondents volunteered that: 'after moving with her in-laws, a newly married girl has *urimai* to proclaim: "This is my house."' In short, in Tamil kinship, what my relatives have is mine. I can help myself to their food, utensils, tools, grooming products and so on. I don't even have to ask, for my claim goes without saying. The reverse is also true, and what I have is theirs. This particularly applies to the patrilineage (*paṅkali*), for each member of this kinship group has a right to a 'share' (*paṅku*) in descent from a common male ancestor and in the ritual cult of a tutelary deity (Arumugam 2011).

When applied to the pragmatics of day-to-day life, this means that with *contam* one is at home, somewhat free from the elaborate codes of conduct regarding appropriate media and appropriate contexts of give-giving activities and commensality. Since these codes, scholars of Indian society have amply documented serve to index relationships of rank, distance, or segmentation (Appadurai 1981, 1985), it is logical to assume that the absence, or at least the reduced presence, of formal codes of transaction among kin expresses relationships of equality, intimacy, and solidarity.

We should not under-estimate the sheer sense of relief the Tamils feel when they are exempted from the intricate and competitive formalities of giving and taking. It is not merely that these formalities carry such critical messages of status that they are sure to offend. It is also the case that in relations of giving and taking one has to ask, one has to wait. Nothing can be taken for granted because one has no right. That the Tamils would rather not be put in a situation in which they have little or no leverage at all is a major reason why families used to prefer, and still prefer, intermarrying. With *contam*, that is with one's own, one does not have to worry about being placed in the types of awkward and socially risky, or even humiliating, situations that are only too common in the public sphere of exchange where one has no right of ownership[1]. With *contam*, one has some control over the relationship, and this advantage allows for a degree of confidence and security.

My informants also volunteered personal reasons for marrying kin. 'We don't want our girls to marry far.' 'We don't want to let go (*pōhaviṭa*) of our love (*pācam*) for them.' 'We don't want to lose the money and jewels.' This last comment has to be understood in light of the fact that when marriage to kin is repeated, jewels, gold, money, land – the usual valuables gifted to daughters at marriage – keep coming back at the next generation. Everyone agreed that no one likes 'to share or divide property (*cottu*) with outsiders.' In sum, these marriages are best because they prevent family relationships (and the couple) from breaking up. Everyone remains *cērntu* –from *cēr*: 'be near,' that is 'together,' 'united' – forever. The social cosmology evoked here is one that lends itself in an especially powerful way to self-segregation, sameness, repetition and, of course, the 'right' to take part in it.

We should not get the impression that the Tamils systematically and indiscriminately 'contam.' They certainly do not marry the people they classify as parents, siblings, or children. Moreover, many castes have (or at least used to have) a marriage rule (*kalyāṅam muṟai)* –or at least a preference – to marry *either* the mother's brother's child *or* the father's sister's child. Thus, in general, the 'right girl' (*muṟai poṅṅu*) or the 'right boy' (*muṟai payan*) is either on the mother's or the father's side[2]. It is important to note that the marriage rule is also a prerogative. The 'right spouses' have rights of ownership (*urimai*); quite simply they are entitled to marry the person whom from their point of view is theirs. This is particularly true of the mother's younger brother[3]. Among the castes that practice uncle niece marriage, this man comes first, before any 'right' boy (Aiyyappan 1934; Clark-Decès 2014). The full extent of his privilege was vividly conveyed by one of my best informants:

> the mother's younger brother has the freedom to come to his sister's house whenever he wishes, ransack the place, elope with her girl and joke about it, if it pleases him. The girl is his.[4]

I now turn to this man. Who is the mother's brother? In a small survey (October–December 2013) that I conducted, four out of ten respondents defined tāymāmā as 'the one who was born with mother.' Two answered that tāymāmā is another mother. A strong indication that the mother's brother is coupled with mother is that both personify the emotion of love (*pācam*), as many women said in answer to a survey conducted by my young assistant Abi:

> 'Ammā *has a lot of love for her daughter. The first love of her first love is for her daughter*' (Padmini, age 40).
> 'Ammā *is like a God. She protects her child from the world until her death. She never loses her love*' (Sridevi, age 25).
> 'Ammā *is the first eye to her children. Until she dies her love remains the same*' (Thangal, age 61).
> 'Ammā *is everything to me. If I don't eat, my mother won't eat either.* Ammā *is the only one who can feel her daughter's feelings*' (Indira, age 28).
> '*Without* Ammā, *we wouldn't be in this world. We wouldn't exist*' (Minakshi, age 33).
> 'Ammā *is the bridge of the family. She has the first place. Without mother, there's no family*' (Celvi, age 44).
> 'Ammā *loves her children until she dies. Mother's affection (pācam) is the best in the world. Nothing compares to her love*' (Arulmori, age 55).

Of course, these are idealised statements made in order to 'inform' the anthropologist of positive cultural stereotypes. They are not necessarily representative of personal experience. In fact, over the many years I have worked in Tamil Nadu I met women and men who did not think that their *own* mother was particularly great. But, in general, 'ammā is a wonderful relation,' as one of the surveyed women put it. I should say 'ammās' because mother's 'big' and 'little' sisters are mothers as well. These periyammās and ciṉṉammās love their sister's children the way they love their own. The same holds true for the mother's brother; he too has, 'immense affection (*pācam*) for his sister's children,' as Kirin Kapadia also notes (1995: 20). As one man explained about his relationship to his nephew in particular, he can feel his feelings and is always willing to help.

What about the father? Does he not worry? Does he not give? He does, of course, but according to the respondents to the survey just mentioned he is not as 'near' or 'close' to his children as their mother's brother is. Besides, his function is different: father is there to raise children, impart knowledge and pass on a profession to them. As the women put it:

> '*Appa educates his children. Without Appa's help we can't grow. Father is the provider of basic things*' (Padmini, age 40).
> '*Appa thinks of our future. He is the only person who thinks of the child's future. He provides for his children*' (Sridevi, age 25).
> '*Appa is a god until the children grow. He helps his child, then he is a friend*' (Thangal, age 61).
> '*Appa is a strict person. If we do something wrong, he beats us*' (Indira, age 28).
> '*Appa is strict. He's the only one who can fulfill our desires and buy us things like a bicycle, for example*' (Minakshi, age 33).
> '*Appa is a friend. He's strict*' (Celvi, age 44).
> '*Appa leads the family. He makes the family. He's like a captain. He leads us*' (Arulmori, age 55).

Appa's disciplinarian role is extended to all 'big' (periyappa) or 'little' (citappa) fathers who see to it that any wayward son (be he his or theirs) is scolded and punished. Hence, when in trouble a boy does not go to his father(s). Instead he confides in his mother's brother, who has a way with him – 'talk to me, what are you worried about?' – and knows better than to report any personal disclosure to exacting appa(s).

Born with mother, the mother's brother loves her sons and daughters the way she does. What characterises motherly 'love' in Tamil society (and I suspect in many other societies as well) is that it transcends the field of mutual exchange. In anthropological terms we might say that this love falls outside the Maussian paradigm of obligatory reciprocity. 'You don't return a gift to mother,' the women quoted above pointed out. It is much the same with the mother's brother: he is a one-sided giver, and a very generous one at that. When his sister's family needs money to help defray the cost of a life-cycle ritual, the mother's brother makes a donation that no matter how substantial – and it is likely to be very substantial – remains unspecified and unreciprocated. The mother's brother, I was told, doesn't have the right to ask for his money back. Thus, from the perspective of a Tamil child, the mother's brother is a special kin, one who gives unconditionally and generously (Mauss 1990). Not that that the child sees this relative very much, for in general the maternal uncle lives away. But when he visits his sister on ceremonial occasions, he is treated with honour and deference (Dumont 1986). Notice the paradox. The maternal uncle is *emotionally* closer to his sister's children than the relatives who live nearby them and with whom they informally 'share' on a daily basis. It is as if the Tamils were saying that in their world, intimacy and distance (physical and social) are positively correlated, so that the more separated two related people are (in terms of geography and rank), the more likely their relationships are to be intimate (as measured by the nature of the confidences shared and the warm context of sharing).

The same positive correlation comes up in the maternal uncle's sexuality with his niece (Dumont 1983). Many of the uncle-niece couples I worked with had met only a few times before marriage, often in the context of festivals, weddings, and puberty ceremonies that are already socially approved opportunities for encountering the other sex, a place to 'discover' the feelings associated with the culturally privileged matrimonial bonds. But some couples had grown up together – if not exactly in the same house, in the same neighbourhood at least – and for them familiarity was a problem. Men, in particular, grumbled that the trouble with marrying a niece is that, 'there isn't mystery,' and a few admitted, 'I had no interest in her. I knew everything about her.' Women did not bring up their feelings, and out of an old-fashioned sense of discretion perhaps I did not ask.

Conclusion

In this chapter, I have explored two concepts of kinship intimacy. The first is based on the right that Tamil kin (especially members of the patrilineage) have to enter each other's households and partake in each other's private lives. Before we assume that we understand this kind of intimacy on grounds that it involves proximity, familiarity, and domesticity, we must remember that there is a mentality of entitlement at work here as well as the potential for power, even violence. Recall this statement: 'I can help myself to what you have, I don't even have to ask, and if you deny me your possessions, I'll forcefully take them.' This kind of intimacy is not exactly about caring or sharing feelings. It is about taking relations and their things for granted, treating them as one's property, which is what *contam* means.

The second concept of intimacy I have discussed in this chapter is encoded in the explanations for kin marriage. The reasons why Tamil families marry kin are subtle, varied, and profound. A yearning to join and re-join, love, convenience, pressure from relatives who hold kinship rights, and the wish for power all certainly factor in. It is just as likely that the elements of compulsion, the inability to separate, and the sheer dread of being outside one's kinship world – one's zone of comfort – push families into intertwinement. But the most important factor, I believe, has to do with the preservation of the primary relationships. Quite simply parents, siblings, and children yearn to stay together and maintain their intimacy (Trawick 1990).

The marriage that enables the birth family to remain close is the uncle-niece marriage. In the attributes that people like and seek in this union, or at least idealise for the benefit of the anthropologist, we see an absolute rejection of engaging intimately with others. With this marriage, 'girls do not marry far.' They stay at home or come back. The family does not have to divide property or even transact with outsiders. They remain 'together.' We even see a condemnation of marriage. For to say, as my informants did, that you marry daughters close by so that they do not leave is in effect to work against the very meaning of marriage, which, throughout India and Tamil Nadu, is to send women away to another family. Whether in theory or in practice there is nothing to indicate that 'the commonest form of close intermarriage' (Good 1996:6) works in favour of marriage itself. This is also evidenced in the conception of the mother's brother who is modelled after mother: a *straight, selfless giver with whom* one can reveal, and be, one's self in complete trust.

Notes

1 As a Dalit (Paṟaiyar) man explained to the anthropologist Robert Deliège: 'Suppose my daughter is married to my sister's son and I pay a visit to her. I reach their house but there is nobody home; the door is locked. But since it is my own sister's house, I can go in, take some food and feel at home. On the other hand, if my daughter is married to a stranger, in the same situation, I have to wait outside their house for their return. I cannot go in, otherwise my daughter would be insulted by her in-laws. They would say that her father only came here to steal food, that he wants to spoil them, that he does not respect them etc. For this reason, it is better to marry close-relatives' (1987: 225–226).

2 Moreover, among the Kallars with whom I worked, the marriage rule or preference does not apply to all boys and girls. Let me make this more concrete by taking the hypothetical case of four married siblings born in the following order: brother, sister, brother, sister. As I proceed, the reader should keep in mind that we must look at Tamil marriages from the point of view of the senior generation. The first brother does the 'right thing' with the first sister by marrying his (preferably) first daughter to her (preferably) first son. The second brother does the same thing with the second sister. Now, let us consider the case of three elder brothers and their younger sister. Here only the first brother is required to do *muṟai* with the sister. If he does not have a daughter, the second brother must offer to do it for him (and so on). But if the elder brother does *muṟai* with the sister, his younger brothers are free to marry their children however they wish. My information here contradicts that of Dumont, who noted that among the Kaḷḷars: 'In principle the obligation is to provide a partner for each *eldest* son of sisters and for each *eldest* daughter of brothers' (1986: 207, his emphasis). As he explained: 'Suppose, for example, that three sisters are born in T and marry respectively into A, B, C. One son of each, and only one, must receive a wife from T. More specifically, he must receive a daughter of one of the three sisters' brothers in T. If there are three brothers, they will provide wives in their own birth order to A, B, and C respectively. If there is only one brother, however, and he has three daughters, he will be obliged to give them in marriage to his sisters' sons in A, B, and C respectively. If there are five brothers and all have daughters, in principle, the last two will have a right to marry their daughters to one of the extra sons of A, B, and C. Not only are other children (brothers' sons, sisters' daughters) involved in other alliances, but once the obligations have been fulfilled, even children of the relevant sex may be married freely' (1986: 207). Dumont further repeats, 'While eldest children's marriages are strictly regulated, younger children's marriages seem free, as a sort of irrelevant addition' (1986: 207). Similarly from the area of Koṅku Brenda Beck notes, 'Once one brother has married a girl of the correct

genealogical specification, then the other brothers have no further claim upon other girls in the same category. Some informants say it should be the eldest brother who makes such a marriage and the younger ones who are "free" to marry elsewhere, but no one would argue over this fine point as long as one of several brothers will consent to take the urimai [*muṟai*] girl' (1972: 238). The men and women I worked with were categorical: only pairs of cross-siblings, especially the first pair, (and not all first-born children of sisters and brothers) are required (or rather entitled) to practice a higher degree of endogamy, and the following unmatched siblings can marry however they want.

3 I was told that the age disparity between a man and his younger sister's daughter would be too great.

4 Up until recently uncle-niece marriage was 'the commonest form of close inter-marriage' in Tamil Nadu, as Anthony Good has also observed (1996: 6; 1980). Such marriages were not merely more frequent, they were given priority over all other kinds of marriages. As David Announssamy, a judge and professor of law in Pondicherry, recalls, 'uncle-niece marriage [used to be] not only normal, it [was] considered the ideal marriage, even *preferred* to cross-cousin marriage' (2003: 69, my translation and italics; see also McCormack 1958; Rao 1973).

References

Aiyyappan, A. 1934. 'Cross-cousin and Uncle-niece Marriages in South India.' In *Congrès International des Sciences Anthropologiques et Ethnosociologiques*. Compte-rendu de la Première Session. Londres: Institut Royal d'Anthropologie.

Announssamy, David. 2003. 'Le mariage entre oncle et nièce dans le Sud de l'Inde.' In Gauthier Bourdeaux and Susy Berthier (eds.), *Etudes en Hommage à Eugène Schaeffer*, pp. 63–75. Paris: Emile Bruylant.

Appadurai, Arjun. 1981. 'Gastro-Politics in Hindu South Asia.' *American Ethnologist*, 8(3): 494–511.

Appadurai, Arjun. 1985. 'Gratitude as a Social Mode in South India.' *Ethos*, 13(3): 236–245.

Arumugam, Indira. 2011. *Kinship as Citizenship: State Formation, Sovereignty and Political Ethics among the Kallars in Central Tamil Nadu*. PhD Thesis. Department of Anthropology of the London School of Economics.

Beck, E. F. Brenda. 1972. *Peasant Society in Koṅku: A Study of Right and Left Subcastes in South India*. Vancouver: University of British Columbia Press.

Clark-Decès, I. 2014. *The Right Spouse. Preferential Marriages in Tamil Nadu*. Stanford, CA: Stanford University Press.

Deliège, Robert. 1987. 'Patrilateral Cross-Cousin Marriage among the Paraiyars of South India.' *Journal of the Anthropological Society of Oxford*, 18(3): 223–236.

Dumont, Louis. 1983. *Affinity as a Value: Marriage Alliance in South India, with Comparative Essays on Australia*. Chicago: University of Chicago Press.

Dumont, Louis. 1986[1957]. *A South Indian Subcaste: Social Organization and Religion of the Pramalai Kallar*. New Delhi: Oxford University Press.

Good, Anthony. 1980. 'Elder Sister's Daughter Marriage in South Asia.' *Journal of Anthropological Research*, 36(4): 474–500.

Good, Anthony. 1996. 'On the Non-existence of "Dravidian Kinship".' *Edinburgh Papers in South Asian Studies*, 6:1–12.

Kapadia, Karin. 1995. *Siva and Her Sisters: Gender, Caste, and Class in Rural South India*. Boulder: Westview Press.

Mauss, Marcel. 1990. *The Gift (The Form and Reason for Exchange in Archaic Societies)*, trans. W.D. Halls. Foreword Mary Douglas. New York: W.W. Norton.

McCormack, William. 1958. 'Sister's Daughter Marriage in a Mysore Village.' *Man in India*, 38(1): 34–48.

Rao, Kodanda M. 1973. 'Rank Difference and Marriage Reciprocity in South India. An Aspect of the Implications of Elder Sister's Daughter Marriage in a Fishing Village in Andhra.' *Contributions to Indian Sociology* (N.S) 7: 16–35.

Tamil Lexicon. 2007. *Tamil Lexicon*. University of Madras, 1924–1936. http://dsal.uchicago.edu/dictionaries/tamil-lex/. Accessed 1 April 2016.

Trautmann, Thomas R. 1981. *Dravidian Kinship*. Cambridge: Cambridge University Press.

Trawick, Margaret. 1990. *Notes on Love in a Tamil Family*. Berkeley, CA: University of California Press.

5

READING QUEERNESS

Same-sex marriages in India

Sayan Bhattacharya

'Seeking 25–40, well placed, animal loving, vegetarian groom for my son 36, 5 11' who works with an NGO caste no bar (though Iyer preferred)' – this advertisement in the matrimonial section of Mid-Day on May 19, 2015 would have passed off as just another matrimonial advertisement in any Indian newspaper. The advertisement placed by a parent specifically lists conditions such as age, professional status as well as eating habits that would make a prospective groom eligible. Most importantly, this ad, like many others in Indian newspapers, demonstrates how the Hindu state is perpetuated by caste endogamy and in that sense, it is not a distinctive event. However, this advertisement is important for a different reason. It marks an important moment in the history of queer articulations in postcolonial India because this was the first ever advertisement placed for a gay wedding in a newspaper. Padma Iyer, mother of gay activist, Harish Iyer placed this ad, for his son's marriage. This advertisement predictably generated a lot of discussion on same-sex weddings in India. While the media and large sections of the queer publics lauded this advertisement as a bold step for the public articulations of queer desires, many also denounced this advertisement as casteist in how it was trying to replicate the way marriages perpetuate caste capital in India.

In July 2013, a photo album went viral in the Indian social media (Karlan 2013). The occasion was an interracial wedding between an American woman and a Hindu woman settled in the US. Shannon and Seema had a wedding that was an amalgam of Hindu rituals (for instance the walk around the fire, the bride being carried to the wedding *mandap* by her brothers) and Christian customs (exchange of rings and a kiss). The photos were lauded because they were supposed to have gone beyond the butch–femme binary. Both Shannon and Seema had long hair and were dressed in so-called feminine attire; therefore it was assumed that this went against mainstream representations of lesbian relationships that always assume one partner playing the 'man' in the relationship. The photographs of the wedding were so widely circulated that soon the couple put up a website which introduces them as follows:

> We are your typical couple. We love each other and we love life. We had no idea that a marriage between Seema and I would go across our nation, let alone the entire world. We created this website to keep the love alive. Love exists in all shapes, sizes and colors. One thing I have learned is that you must always follow your heart, for that is where your passion lives.

Here it would be instructive to go back to Michael Warner's 1999 essay *Beyond Gay Marriage* where he problematises this notion of love as a space of no conflict and politics. He says:

> any politics based on such a sentimental rhetoric of privacy is not only a false idealization of love and coupling; it is an increasingly powerful way of distracting citizens from the real, conflicted, and unequal conditions governing their lives, and it serves to reinforce the privilege of those who already find it easiest to imagine their lives as private.
>
> *(Warner 1999: 269)*

That love is not so benign was proven if one carefully goes through the website. While Seema's caste position goes unmarked in the entire coverage of the wedding, that this particular manifestation of intimacy was rendered possible by the couple's class position is but obvious. The costumes, the jewellery, the décor was all carefully selected. In fact, in an interview on Buzzfeed (29/07/2013), Shannon talks about the wedding and states that, 'We wanted it to be elegant, classy, warm, loving and of course have amazing food, dancing and a lot of fun.' The website that Shannon and Seema created – where they have shared the images from their wedding and where queer people from around the world have commented and have noted how difficult it must have been for an Indian girl to have gotten approval from her family for her desire for same-sex marriage and how love conquers all obstacles – is an advertorial website for Shannon's bootcamp. She tells the audience how both Seema and Shannon were at their prettiest: thanks to the diet and exercise routine at the camp and then goes on to give its contact details. Similarly, details are given for caterers and make-up artists.

On February 20, 2011, two Dalit girls committed suicide in Sonachura in Nandigram, West Bengal. Swapna Mondal, age 23, and Sucheta Mondal, age 19, jointly consumed *Folidol*, a pesticide widely used by farmers in India. In the early hours of the next morning, their bodies were found lying on a stack of hay, hand in hand, a *gamchha* tied around their waists. A packet of sweets and a garland were found beside the dead bodies. Had they exchanged wedding vows before dying together? The sweets and the *gamchha* tied around their waists, reminiscent of how the ends of the clothes of both the bride and the groom are tied together during a Hindu wedding, indeed hints at such a possibility. Swapna left a suicide note for her mother where she clearly stated that the two girls were dying because the community did not accept their love. In fact, Sucheta had been married off against her will. The village community did not even allow the respective families to claim their dead bodies, and after a mandatory waiting period of seven days, the police cremated the dead bodies like they do with other unclaimed bodies.

Exactly a week after their death, a fact-finding team from West Bengal's only LBT (lesbian and bisexual women and transmen) collective, Sappho, arrived in Sonachura. They interviewed the families, local police and the villagers and procured the letter from Swapna's family. Later they came back to the village in November that year to record more footage. The result was a film titled. . .*And the Unclaimed* about the joint suicides of Swapna and Sucheta and the reactions that Swapna's suicide note evokes in queer women far from her class and caste locations. Navaneetha Mokkil points out that often the event through which the lesbian body can become a figure in the imagination of India is through her suicide. 'Suicide becomes the dark act of "coming out," where the couple becomes established through dying together.' She uses data collected by the Alternate Law Forum to show how the spate of lesbian suicides in the state of Kerala, a state in southern India has mobilised queer activism around persons assigned gender female at birth (Mokkil 2011: 392). If we were to map the audience reception to. . .*And the Unclaimed*, we see that the film has been a very effective means of talking about violence faced by lesbian women. Throughout the film we see characters reading Swapna's letter in a wide array of spaces and its content invokes silence and tears.

As the end credits of the film rolls, we hear a humanities professor tell the film-maker, 'Let that cry be there. Let it go on. Let there be a heart wrenching wail in your film.' The act of grieving is extremely political for there are lives that are deemed worth grieving and there are those who are not grieved for. Judith Butler takes the site of post-9/11 America to demonstrate how boundaries of grief are constructed. Those who died in the twin attacks on the World Trade Centre are mourned, but the innumerable lives lost in Afghanistan in the retaliatory strikes by America remain faceless. These lives remain on the borders of public discourse because they cannot be made intelligible (Butler 2004a: XI-XXI). They cannot be represented and hence grieved for because

> Some lives are grievable, and others are not; the differential allocation of grievability that decides what kind of subject is and must be grieved, and which kind of subject must not, operates to produce and maintain certain exclusionary conceptions of who is normatively human: what counts as a livable life and grievable death?

So then when the cinematic text invokes that the tears must stay, it induces an act of public mourning for lives that are always already invisible, that have been deemed unreal. Thus, to mourn for such lives is an attempt at rendering the invisible real. To that extent, both the making and the viewing of. . .*And the Unclaimed* are deeply political acts, rendering real the love and the death of two girls who were disavowed even in death. However, the question is in mourning their lives and their love, why do we not find any mention of the sweets and the garland and the piece of cloth around their waists and what these could mean for the public articulation of their intimate bond? So then, does the hint of marriage vows depoliticise the very act of public grieving? Would the exploration of such a possibility depoliticise queer struggles for recognition?

Yet, this was by no means the first instance of queer women, from subordinate caste or working-class positions – in locations often far away from the advocacy work of queer collectives – marrying. In fact, one of the first widely reported instances of a 'lesbian' wedding dates to 1987, when two policewomen Leela Ramdeo and Urmila Srivastava, from Uttar Pradesh were suspended from their jobs because they married. While many queer women continue to marry and some even live together, there are many who are wrenched apart, who have often embraced death post wedding and their deaths have been the public proclamation of their private loves. For example, *Humjinsi*, one of the first resource books on LGBT rights in India, published in 1999, records how in the Hulipur village of Orissa, two girls – Mamta (19) and Monalisa (24) – married to seal their love. They were in a relationship for five years before they made a Deed of Agreement for Partnership as well as to Remain Life Partners; this deed was a notarised, legal document. But in a heteronormative society, it was soon proven that even such documents hold no value when their respective families separated them, and Mamta and Monalisa consumed poison out of despair. Only Mamta survived (Fernandez 1999: 113). In a recent study with queer women and transmasculine people, the queer feminist collective LABIA notes that many of the respondents had married their partners or wished to marry them even though such marriages mostly fell apart due to external pressures (Shah et al. 2015: 153–154).

However, scholarship around non-normative sexualities in India is yet to fully engage with same-sex marriage as a form of queer intimacy. In a paper drafted in 1997 for a workshop on 'Strategies for furthering lesbian, gay and bisexual rights in India' held in Mumbai, Forum Against Oppression of Women had argued for the expansion of the legal definition of marriage laws to include queer people but they faced stiff resistance from queer activists (Fernandez 1999: 135–140). I deploy these three specific moments to delineate the terms of the debate that one generally witnesses when one thinks of queer marriages in India. Firstly, same-sex marriage is either denounced as an attempt to perpetuate an oppressive heteropatriarchal institution that works at keeping the edifice of one's caste and class privileges intact, say in the case of the Iyer advertisement. Or same-sex marriage is dismissed as a lifestyle choice that is premised on one's purchasing power in the neo-liberal market, say the Shannon-Seema wedding photos.

Both these arguments are deployed to speak against same-sex marriage. While these arguments are politically urgent, I would like to argue in this chapter, that these arguments are not mindful of how marriage is also a very complex, sociocultural institution, imbued with agency for many queer people in India, including those from working-class and subordinate caste positions, say for Swapna and

Sucheta or for Mamta and Monalisa, among many others. By invisibilising these narratives, we stand the risk of not trying to engage with how large swathes of queer people are negotiating their non-normative intimacies. However, a close reading of queer marriage as a phenomenon is not to argue for a need to prove how people with non-normative orientations are also like their normative counterparts and therefore their needs for intimacy are no different. In fact, in her book, *Love's Rite: Same-Sex Marriage in India and the West*, Ruth Vanita speaks on these lines and closely reads Hindu customs and religious, mythological, and cinematic texts to argue that Indian cultures have been tolerant towards such marriages. However, such a project often ends up romanticising marriage as a site of unqualified subversion and agency. Moreover, it tries to look for justification for such choices within religion and this can end up creating hierarchies about which religion is more progressive and which is not. Instead, what I propose is a close reading of contexts within which such decisions about marriage are taken to examine what these decisions mean for how one negotiates one's immediate family, one's community, and the various institutional spaces that one inhabits.

In his critique of same-sex marriage in the United States, Michael Warner writes that marriage is not simply a ritual of validating the intimate relations between two persons and therefore beyond any contestation. He argues that the sentimental rhetoric of a personal need for marking one's love and intimacy through a public declaration elides the ways in which marriage as an institution rests on State sanctioned legitimacy. The ethical meaning of marriage does not involve just two people in love but it means being enclosed within a domain of relationships that the State deems intelligible and worthy of being imbued with rights and privileges – inheritance, insurance, health and so on and the borders of such an institution are secured by foreclosing the possibilities of other intimacies that refuse to be marked ceremoniously. Warner argues:

> As long as people marry, the state will continue to regulate the sexual lives of those who do not marry. It will refuse to recognize our intimate relations, including cohabiting partnerships, as having the same rights or validity as a married couple. It will criminalise our consensual sex. It will stipulate at what age and in what kind of space we can have sex. It will send the police to harass sex workers and cruisers. It will restrict our access to sexually explicit materials. All this and more the state will justify because these sexual relations take place outside of marriage. In the modern era, marriage has become the central legitimating institution by which the state regulates and permeates people's most intimate lives; it is the zone of privacy outside which sex is unprotected.
>
> *(Warner 1999: 267)*

However, Judith Butler points out the social and psychic costs of the lack of state legitimation of one's love that renders Warner's formulation simplistic. Whether it is the non-permission to receive the dead body of one's partner in case she dies, the inability to provide health care benefits for one's partner, or the battle for custody of one's child which one loses as a non-biological parent, there are tangible effects of disenfranchisement that affect non-normative relationships. Butler writes evocatively:

> The sense of delegitimation can make it harder to sustain a bond, a bond that is not real anyway, a bond that does not 'exist', that never had a chance to exist, that was never meant to exist. If you're not real, it can be hard to sustain yourselves over time. Here is where the absence of state legitimation can emerge in the psyche as a pervasive, if not fatal, sense of self-doubt. And if you've actually lost the lover who was never recognized to be your lover, did you really lose that person? Is this a loss, and can it be publicly grieved?
>
> *(Butler 2002: 240)*

On the other hand, to go back to Warner, this imperative for legitimation as a reparative tool ends up creating a hierarchy between those who enter its domain and those who do not. Butler finds ambivalence more useful in trying to think about same-sex marriage. While the domain of legitimacy depends on intensifying and (re)producing zones of illegitimacy in order to foreclose the domain of what is possible, the larger issue is what remains unthinkable is spoken solely as a negative of what is thinkable. So, Butler suggests that instead of taking a stand for or against gay marriage, we critically reflect on how did the terms of the debate come to be defined by this binary. While on one hand, for the sake of social equity, we might defend the need for legitimacy, it is also crucial to maintain a critical perspective on how this legitimacy is ordered. And therefore, to avoid a binary position and maintain a criticality instead, it becomes necessary to understand what constitutes queer life and intimacy (Butler. 2002: 233–234).

Sara Ahmed problematises the formulation of queer life as that which ideally maintains a discomfort with the scripts of heteronormative existence because the emphasis on ideality once again sets up a new script and a new site of legitimacy – to lead ideal queer lives will mean to act in certain ways and not in others. In other words, the ideality of queer life will depend on those who fail to lead such a life. However, not all queer spaces are equally accessible to all. While a queer person will feel discomfort in a heteronormative space, this does not translate into automatic comfort in a queer space (Ahmed 2014: 151–152). For example, a lot of lesbian women or gender variant people may fail to access visible forms of queerness in public whereas they might access the same in private. In other words, the idealisation of 'queer' as a movement against, beyond or away from rules and regulations, norms and normative regimes fails to account for those who may not be able to afford such movement. Ahmed writes:

> The idealization of movement depends upon a prior model of what counts as a queer life, which may exclude others, those who have attachments which are not readable as queer, or indeed those who may lack the (cultural as well

> as economic) capital to support the 'risk' of maintaining anti-normativity as a permanent orientation.
>
> Queer lives do not suspend the attachments that are crucial to the reproduction of heteronormativity, and this does not diminish 'queerness', but intensifies the work it can do. Queer lives remain shaped by that which they fail to reproduce. To turn this around, queer lives shape what gets reproduced: in the very failure to reproduce the norms through how they inhabit them, queer lives produce different effects.
>
> *(Ahmed 2014: 152)*

Thus, 'queer' does not automatically translate as resistance to norms. Ahmed offers a more complex reading of the work 'queer' performs in being imbricated within heteronorms and the dailyness of tensions, frictions, and unease that are engendered through such imbrications.

Following Ahmed, in the remaining part of this chapter, I would like to briefly look at the work that marriage does for the articulation of queer intimacies in India. However, before that it is important to note that when we transpose the debates on same-sex marriage to India, the hierarchisation of the legitimate over the illegitimate is rendered redundant because Indian law does not recognise such marriages. Though Section 377 of the Indian Penal Code that criminalised any sex other than peno-vaginal penetration and thus in effect, was often used to persecute queer people has been read down, Indian law is silent on the legality or the illegality of same-sex marriages. During the hearings for the reading down of Section 377, the Indian government through its additional solicitor general, Tushar Mehta warned the Supreme Court against guaranteeing sexual orientation as a fundamental right of Indian citizens lest such a right extend to same-sex marriages. It reminded the Court that we have the Hindu Marriage Act that governs heterosexual marriages between Hindus and that if the court decides to extend marriage rights to queer people, then the government should be given adequate time to respond. Thus, what is noteworthy here is the state's anxieties about protecting the very foundation of the heteronormative state that is marriage. Marriage between heterosexual individuals leading to birth of future citizens is what keeps the wheels of the nation state running and hence even if a concession can be made for the right of sexual practices in private, such a right cannot become public leading to same-sex marriages. So, in terms of law, be it marriages, live-ins or other forms of relationships, Indian law is silent on all forms of queer intimacies till date. Therefore, rather than looking at queer intimacies in India from the framework of legitimacy and illegitimacy, I argue it will be more useful to read the work these intimacies do on heteronormative attachments.

In this chapter about queer intimacies, I specifically take up the site of same-sex marriages because it is automatically assumed to approximate a heteronormative ideal. As a part of my M.Phil dissertation about lesbian collectivisation in West Bengal, between 2014 and 2015, I completed ethnographic fieldwork and semi-structured interviews with queer women and transmasculine individuals from various class and caste positions. I would spend time with my interlocutors in their domestic spaces, sometimes meet them at work, or accompany them as they navigated various institutions like law, education, and family. Based on these field notes, I wrote an account of how lesbian activisms functioned in Bengal, both as a part of women's movements and as a part of the queer movements in India and the tensions engendered at the intersections of gender, sexuality, and caste. However, for the purpose of this chapter, I take up two sets of interviews with two queer married couples to understand what work marriage does for the enactment of their intimacies and desires. To respect the privacy and the confidentiality of these conversations, I have changed the names of all my interviewees.

My first interviewee, Deepak is 32 and identifies himself as 'male' though he does not intend to go for gender affirmation surgery and does not mind being referred to as a lesbian individual, when talking of his sexual orientation. He works as a sales representative in a car showroom. He has been married to Sudha, 22 for the last two years and they live together in a 600 square feet apartment in South Kolkata. Deepak had fled from his natal family when his father was trying to forcibly marry him off to a man. He took a job in Kolkata, often starved to make ends meet. He has always been in relationships with women. His parents have finally reconciled themselves to this reality. Deepak met Sudha through a mutual acquaintance. Sudha is originally from Bangladesh and she used to live with her maternal grandmother in Chandannagore, a town in West Bengal. Her grandmother was trying to marry her off while Sudha wanted to continue studying. After she met Deepak, she literally packed a few clothes and like in a classic Hindi film narrative, Deepak 'rescued' her from her 'evil' grandmother and they came to Kolkata on Deepak's bike. They started living together.

One-day Sudha challenged him to publicly declare his love for her. To her utter surprise, Deepak took some vermillion kept at the feet of a portrait of a goddess in their bedroom and smeared it on Sudha's hair parting. Next day they went to the Kalighat temple, one of Kolkata's most famous temples and also an internationally renowned tourist spot, for their regular monthly visit and a priest who knew Deepak just happened to say that it was an 'auspicious' day for weddings and before they knew what was happening, they were following the priest in purchasing garlands, conch bangles and other paraphernalia for a Hindu wedding. Deepak states in a matter-of-fact manner that although he looks quite 'girly,' the people all around did not say anything about a 'a girl marrying another girl.' Perhaps they did not realise that Deepak was assigned the female gender at birth. Many stood around them to see the wedding rituals, as happens with most public weddings that regularly occur in Kalighat. After the garlands had been exchanged and the seven oaths taken, Deepak smeared vermillion on Sudha's head and covered it with a handkerchief. Sudha interjects, saying, 'It felt like a dream. I started crying.' While they were on their way back, some beggars followed them asking for alms. Suddenly one of them stood in front of Deepak and shouted out to the rest saying, 'This is not a *dada* but a *didi*! (This person is not male but female!)' And everybody scattered. When they came back to their apartment, Deepak's landlady made Sudha go through all the rituals that a new bride in a Hindu household is expected to go through. The landlady treated Deepak like her own son, despite knowing about Deepak's assigned gender. There was even a reception party.

Deepak tells me proudly that Sudha is known as his wife in the locality and she goes to the local pandal on the last day of Durga *puja* and participates in the Hindu ritual of *sindoor khela* (in which unmarried women and married women smear vermillion on each other). However, Sudha adds that since they have just shifted to a new flat (in the same locality), she applies vermillion only when the domestic help leaves because she is not sure how she will think of her marriage with Deepak. Currently Sudha is studying in a college and Deepak manages the finances of the household. Sudha also gets some money from her parents (who think that Deepak is her flatmate who looks like a Maoist!). Sudha takes care of the house and intends to study law for further education. She also aspires to work in television serials and Deepak has just introduced her to a friend he has in the television industry in Bengal.

Marriage and the family system are the bedrocks of the oppressive structures of heteropatriarchy through which caste and class privilege are sustained and reproduced. So indeed, to see a queer couple living as a married couple, marking all the rituals of a patriarchal institution does seem problematic. Yet, Deepak and Sudha's narrative, I argue, deserves a more complex reading. Our human rights discourse and feminist activist interventions in the realms of law are all negotiating various institutions of the state to reclaim, reform, and reshape institutions in ways that weed out the systemic violence inbuilt in them. Be it the laws on domestic violence on women, divorce and right to property, these are all interventions that aim at reworking institutions like marriage and family to make them equitable and free of violence. This is not to say that institutions should not be questioned but to highlight the limits within which daily politics pans out. So then, while acknowledging that Deepak's choice in life is not a feminist choice, is it still possible to give it a feminist reading, as a politics of reclaiming, and reshaping an oppressive institution? Here it is important to note that Deepak belongs to a scheduled caste while Sudha is a Brahmin. In a country where intercaste marriage often leads to murder, here is a queer couple who has had an intercaste marriage. On the other hand, the way Deepak and Sudha negotiate public spaces, be it their immediate neighbourhood or their respective families, the way they stake claims to heteronormative rituals, while being open about their sexual orientation, could also be read as a politics of resignification.

Deepak thinks of himself as a man but at the same time his maleness is not derived from his biological body. In terms of sexual desire, he thinks of himself as a lesbian. Thus, his very ideas about his identity complicate the way gender is perceived in relation to sexuality and that in itself is a resistance to normative ideals of gendering. On the other hand, Sudha's presence in Deepak's life and their desire for each other affirms Deepak's self-definition of his gender identity. So then, through the normative structures of marriage, that affirmation is realised and thus even though marriage is a normative structure, it is within its very structure, that Deepak and Sudha stage a resignification of norms by interrogating the very limits of who is allowed to enter its domain. This is because individuals are not alone, free of social conditions and thus the autonomy they can exercise is also bound within the social instruments they are a part of (Butler 2004b: 77). So, Deepak and Sudha's marriage can be seen as a challenge to and in relief against the heterosexual coupling and not as a mere perpetuation of heteronormative rituals. Also, their marital life cannot be reduced to an active/passive binary because of the way they are negotiating their marriage is based on mutuality, intimacy, and shared comfort in a space which both are trying to shape into their idea of home.

My third interviewee, Amrita, 32, realised that it was impossible for her to fit into the heteronormative script only after she married a man. She had already conceived, but once her son was born, she chose to divorce her husband. She went back with her son to her natal family while her former husband remarried. At home, she fell in love with her sister's friend, Smita, 28. Soon a relationship bloomed between the two. Smita was also extremely attached to Amrita's son, Avik. However, when Amrita's family discovered that the two were in a relationship, they asked Amrita to leave. Smita brought Amrita and Avik to her home. They lived there for some time. There was not much trouble till Smita's family discovered that Amrita was not just another friend to Smita. The moment they found out, they asked them to leave too. Amrita and Smita were now faced with a new ordeal – house hunting. Smita emphatically asserts, 'Under no circumstances, would I lie to prospective landlords that Amrita was my sister or a cousin.' But the moment, they would say they were friends, they lost their chance in finding 'home' in most places. At times, even if they ended up renting a space, neighbourhood gossip made their lives very difficult and soon they were left house hunting again. Meanwhile, even as Avik was growing up with his two mothers, he also started realising that his family was 'different.' If he went out to play with the neighbourhood kids, he was often accosted with the question, 'Where is your father?' When he would assert that he had two mothers, the jeers would increase. This gradually made him shun company and he was forced to spend his free time at home. Amrita is a content writer while Smita teaches at a private school. When I spoke to them, they had finally succeeded in purchasing a flat after Smita took a housing loan. Their financial situation is precarious but they are happy at least that they have their own house and this constant routine of shifting houses every few months has come to a stop. Recently, they had a get together at home where Amrita and Smita exchanged garlands. Their marriage photos greet you the moment you enter their drawing room. They say that they are now 'officially' a married couple. Meanwhile, Avik is in Class IV. In his official records, he goes by his father's name, but on the wall of his room and in his diaries, he scribbles his name as 'Avik Basu Thakur,' taking the Basu from Amrita's name and Thakur from Smita's.

While, one might question the need for marriage when both Smita and Amrita were already living together, it is important to note how their assertion of giving an 'official' stamp to their relationship is a public proclamation of what is supposed to be private. For example, the petition against Section 377 argued for the right to privacy. It asserts that the State cannot interfere with what two consensual adults are doing in private. However, privacy is also a caste and class privilege. Not everybody can afford privacy. Kothis, hijras, working-class gay men, and transgender sex workers often negotiate their intimacies in public spaces thus problematising the notions of privacy as understood by the petitioners against 377. Coming back to the narratives of Deepak-Sudha and Amrita-Smita, their marriage stakes a claim to the public which is already coded as heteronormative and thus as much as the institution of marriage is oppressive, it is the very site of marriage through which they are staging a queer resistance to heteronormativity. In continuously refusing to recognise each other as friends or cousins in public, they are publicly articulating their intimacy and marriage becomes a way to establish that even more emphatically. The institution of education might not recognise Avik's sense of family but his private refusal of the institution's idea of family through how he scrawls his name on the wall reflects the silent and daily work of queering norms. This is not resistance with a capital R but it is the daily labour of queer love, intimacy, and care within the heteronormative.

Sara Ahmed points out how the ideal of heterosexuality is a zone of comfort for those who can follow it. Here comfort is not only about well-being and satisfaction, but also about ease and easiness, that is an ease in a world for those who follow the rules of heterosexuality. She argues:

> To be comfortable is to be so at ease with one's environment that it is hard to distinguish where one's body ends and the world begins. One fits, and by fitting, the surfaces of bodies disappear from view. The disappearance of the surface is instructive: in feelings of comfort, bodies extend into spaces, and spaces extend into bodies [. . .] Heteronormativity functions as a form of public comfort by allowing bodies to extend into spaces that have already taken their shape.
>
> *(Ahmed 2014: 148)*

However, what about those who fail to find comfort and who feel unsettled? Their discomfort exposes the work that goes into producing shapes that will only fit some and not others. In other words, the more, queer people are closer to spaces shaped by heteronormative structures, the more is their potential in queering such spaces by exposing the constructedness of the space. Although the choices of Deepak and Sudha and Amrita and Smita are not outside the heteronormative script, their discomfort with them works at queering the script. Be it how Avik thinks of his parents at school and at home or how Sudha performs her marriage in public, their discomfort with the predominant script is generative because it works at living norms differently. This discomfort is not about total assimilation within heteronormativity or complete resistance to it. And it is in this doing of norm differently where I locate the marriages and the loves of my interviewees and those of many other queer people in India. To conclude with Ahmed:

> Queer is not, then, about transcendence or freedom from the (hetero)normative. 'Queer' feelings are 'affected' by the repetition of scripts that they fail to

reproduce, and this 'affect' is also a sign of what queer can do, of how it can work by working on the (hetero)normative. The failure to be non-normative is then not the failure of queer to be queer, but a sign of attachments that are the condition of the possibility of queer.

(Ahmed 2014: 155)

References

Ahmed, Sara. 2014. *The Cultural Politics of Emotion: Second Edition*. Edinburgh: Edinburgh University Press.

Butler, Judith. 2002. 'Is Kinship Always Already Heterosexual?' In Wendy Brown and Janet Halley (eds.), *Left Legalism/Left Critique*. Durham, London: Duke University Press.

Butler, Judith. 2004a. *Precarious Life: The Power of Mourning and Violence*. London, New York: Verso.

Butler, Judith. 2004b. *Undoing Gender*. New York, London: Routledge.

Fernandez, Bina. (ed.). 1999. *Humjinsi*. Mumbai: India Centre for Human Rights and Law.

Karlan, Sara. 2013. "The Story behind the Lesbian Indian Wedding that Stole the Internet's Heart." *Buzzfeed*. www.buzzfeed.com/skarlan/the-story-behind-the-lesbian-indian-wedding-that-stole-the-i#.wuMkq22OE. Accessed 17 March 2016.

Mokkil, Navaneetha. 2011. 'Lives Worth Grieving For: Lesbian Narratives from Kerala.' In Samita Sen, Ranjita Biswas and Nandita Dhawan (eds.), *Intimate Others: Marriage and Sexualities in India*. Kolkata: Stree and School of Women's Studies, Jadavpur University.

Shah, Chayanika, Raj Merchant, Shals Mahajan and Smriti Nevatia. 2015. No Outlaws in the Gender Galaxy. New Delhi: Zubaan.

Warner, Michael. 1999. 'Beyond Gay Marriage.' In Wendy Brown and Janet Halley (eds.), *Left Legalism/Left Critique*. Durham, London: Duke University Press.

6

HOMES AS CONVERSIONS

Literalising the metaphor of *Ghar Wapsi*

Arunima Paul

In 2008 right-wing Hindu organisations such as the Vishwa Hindu Parishad and the Bajrang Dal began alleging a slew of abductions of non-Muslim women by Muslim men as evidence of an organised ploy by Muslims to convert non-Muslim women to Islam[1]. Deliberately evoking the global 'war on terror' against 'radical Islam,' these right-wing Hindu organisations gave this alleged ploy the name of 'Love Jihad.' Since then, deliberating on specific cases of interreligious marriage, the judiciary has frequently legitimised this claim by ordering investigations to ascertain the charge of 'Love Jihad.' The cases of Silja Raj and Asghar Nazar in Karnataka in 2007 and the case of Hadiya and Shafin Jahan in Kerala this year are prominent examples of this (PTI 2009; Rajagopal 2017). In case of the latter, the court appeased the woman's father by annulling the marriage and ruled that women in their early twenties were apt to being lured into love and persuaded to convert. Hadiya was thereafter remanded to her father's custody and has been confined to her natal home since. In most of these cases, the court was adjudicating on charges brought by the woman's father against her chosen spouse (Ali 2015)[2]. While the cases received much attention in regional and national media, the findings of the CID investigation denying any existence of a concerted 'Love Jihad' in the state were not given as much attention, and cases of 'Love Jihad' continued to be reported unverified (Punwani 2014; Johnson T.A. 2017).

As a measure to counter the threat of the 'Love Jihad,' the VHP revivified its *Ghar Wapsi* campaign. The campaign invites converts to return to their original, ancestral Hindu fold – targeting in particular states like Odisha, Gujarat, Chhattisgarh, Jharkhand, and Assam. By July 2015, the VHP claimed to have prevented the conversion of 48,651 persons to other religions and as having brought back 33,975 persons to their 'original faith' with their grassroots campaign (Sharma 2015). In characterising the prior Hindu affiliation of converts as a 'familial home' to which they must return, this campaign has renewed reactionary mythologies of home as a space of originary and authentic identity that is being violated with 'inducement' or 'education.' As has been pointed out, by evoking 'return' and not 'reconversion,' the campaign casts the prior act of conversion (out of Hinduism) as a mistake or aberration that is now corrected by the 'return' (Sangari 1999; Menon 2014). *Ghar Wapsi* has been challenged in mainstream media debates in two ways – one line of argument from a liberal standpoint has sought to distinguish between 'real' conversions motivated by genuine self-transformation and a substantive recognition of the new chosen faith, and conversions 'induced' by pragmatic necessities or by 'brainwashing' by devious proselytisers of other religions. With this distinction between 'real' and 'induced,' this liberal line of critique effectively detaches religious identity and practice from pragmatic considerations.

A broad coalition of post-nationalist, leftist, and feminist scholars have taken a different approach by locating this conversion debate within South Asian histories of pluralist and syncretic cultures. They have also pointed to purification (and 'reconversion') campaigns led by upper-caste Hindu elites at certain historical junctures to swell the ranks of Hindus – often by conditionally allowing certain social groups into the Hindu fold (Sangari 1999). Cognisant of this contentious history, scholars have sought to reengage the public protests of Phule, Ambedkar, and Periyar. They have also pointed to the role played by colonial governmentality in creating and consolidating the idea of communal violence as an essential and inevitable problem for South Asia. Thus, if the first critique of *Ghar Wapsi* pivots around a polarisation of the private as the space of the inner-authentic and the public as the world of pragmatic considerations, the second directs itself to the shaping of the debate around religious conversion within the public realm of governmentality, the public life of caste, the realm of arts and letters, formal politics, and social campaigns. However, the characterisation of the site of the familial home has been crucial to larger colonial, metropolitan and nationalist politics – in other words, the private home has been of great public significance. The greatest attention was paid in all these circles to issues affecting middle-class, upper-caste women, even as critiques of caste and gender norms were being launched by non-elite women often left outside the pale of nationalist politics (Nair 1996; Rege 2004; Omvedt 2004). The codification of customary law led to both, a homogenisation of plurality of beliefs and practices as well as a demarcation of the private realm which would be adjudicated by a set of personal laws – that came to be perceived as religious laws (Sangari 1999). If Hindu conjugality in the shape of reformed property laws, age of consent and abolition of sati was crucial to the self-justifying agendas of British middle-class feminists as well as imperialists in the nineteenth century (Agnes 1999; Sarkar 2001), its mythologisation as a place of refuge and essential cultural identity allowed the Indian 'bhadralok' nationalists to 'resolve' the Woman question by sealing off the private-domestic from the sway of bourgeois liberal values transforming public life – thereby preserving gender, caste, and class practices (Chatterjee 1993). This hegemonic construction of home characterises the logics of both, the Hindu Right as well as its liberal opposition today. If the Hindu Right characterises particular interreligious marriages as politically motivated invasions of the private and familial sphere by Muslim men; liberal and leftist critics see 'Love Jihad' itself as the Right's intrusion into the private realm of companionate love where it does not belong. Animated as these debates are by this conception of (familial/conjugal) home as the location of a siloed private sphere, they cordon off from critical consideration the varied and relentless practices through which the familial home incorporates individuals as gendered and caste subjects.

This chapter interrogates the metaphoric idealisation of familial or marital home in the spectre of the 'Love Jihad' raised by the Hindu Right and in its *Ghar Wapsi* campaign. Instead it literalises the metaphor to examine the material and affective ways in which homes are inhabited. It demonstrates how this literalisation can allow us to productively challenge the binaries of the public and the private (or home and the world), sincerity and instrumentality – that structure discourse on the issue of conversion. To do so, this chapter looks at the varied representations of homes in two different texts: an episode of a popular Hindi-language televisual series based on 'true crimes' called *Savdhaan India/Beware India* (episode dated July 2015), and a short story titled 'The Thief' by the late Shakti Bhatt (2007).

In the following analyses, this chapter pivots the discussion about conversions in two ways. Firstly, it moves away from the intensified and contracted temporality of conversions (as brainwashing, elopement) within the imagination of the *Ghar Wapsi* campaigns, and instead explores a quotidian, multifarious, and more ambivalent conception of 'conversion' – as alignment with behaviours mandated by pedagogic regimes that prevail in middle-upper–class homes. These regimes – which often take the shape of respectability, nutrition, education, consumption, forms of work, and leisure – enable homes to play their part in the reproduction of hierarchies of caste, class, and gender. Secondly, home-induced conversions also naturalise the logics for extracting various kinds of intimate labour from a host of domestic workers – by interpellating both home-dwellers and workers into emotional architectures of obligation, pleasure, affection, suspicion, vigilance, and guilt, among others. This chapter shows how the selected short story and TV episode throw light on these 'homely' processes of conversion – by engaging the social narrative of the 'thieving servant' that denigrates domestic workers[3]. Both depict actual or possible thefts by a 'maid-servant' from the household of her upper-middle-class employer. While one uses this potent cultural narrative to provoke anxieties about threats to middle-upper-class conjugality, the other uses it to lay bare the processes of conversion that bolster this narrative.

A materialist view of homes

Home as imagined within Indian popular television is overwhelmingly a middle- or upper-middle-class familial space for caste Hindus. And while it is counterposed as the space of the private against the public as the sphere of work, market relations, political life; the urban upper- and middle-class home is itself in practice often a space of internal variegation. Besides being an abode, a home is also the workplace and source of livelihood for a broad set of domestic workers – maids, cleaners, cooks, guards, nannies, nurses, gardeners, drivers, sweepers. In this sense it straddles and complicates the boundaries between the private and the public. As urban middle- and upper-class women have accessed formal salaried employment, domestic work in their homes has been transferred to paid workers. However, the extraction of domestic physical and psychic labour from the latter remains structured by informal social norms that ensure their social and economic subordination[4]. This also makes the home a site of latent social antagonisms and anxieties. The class narratives that circulate commonly about untrustworthy 'servants' and security of the household can be seen as efforts to manage these antagonisms as well as to normalise inequalities.

Through an analysis of an episode from a true-crime series, this chapter demonstrates how the social narrative of the maid-as-thief foregrounds the social antagonisms whirling within the home. The subsequent section of the chapter offers a close reading of a short story by Shakti Bhatt, to see how the author uses the figure of a young teenaged narrator and her relationship with their domestic help, to develop a critical disaggregation of the space of the home as well as the social narrative of theft. Through these analyses, this chapter probes 'home-grown' attitudes toward domestic labour and cross-class forms of social relationality as non-intuitive and produced through relentless social, symbolic, and epistemological labour that troubles the distinctions between coercive and non-coercive conversions. In doing so, it calls for a critical recognition of the home as a space for politically expedient conversions that have been legitimised and naturalised by various social, legal, and media agencies.

Home-theft plots in true-crime television thrillers

Emerging out of the post-Liberalisation media and cultural landscape, the 'true crime' TV series *Savdhaan India* addresses an urban, middle-class viewing public about a range of criminal agencies and motivations besieging it today[5]. Episodes of the show will frequently figure a young woman-protagonist who deals with a disempowering situation in her personal life by summoning her inner confidence and presence of mind. The episode I discuss here was telecast in July, 2015 and is titled 'Dhongi Mata'/ 'Fake Holy Woman.' It is about how one such protagonist upends a woman named Kaushalya who with the help of an assistant lures unsuspecting women into her den by promising to rid them of their problems with occult rituals, and then poisons them with the aim of usurping their jewellery. The episode begins with one such con that leaves a woman dead. Thereafter, at a temple in Indore, Kaushalya meets Uma – an educated, young married woman and the protagonist for the episode –and pleading her poverty convinces Uma to employ her as a maid. While working as a maid, Kaushalya sets her sights on Uma's jewellery but decides to prey upon Uma's sister Kavya instead after she learns that Kavya is wealthier and is desperate to have a child. Thereafter, Kaushalya pretends to be a holy woman; she then entraps and kills Kavya. A bereaved Uma takes up the mantle of finding the murderer and succeeds in finding the den – where they find Kaushalya laying inside a large chest covered in all her loot, maniacally refusing to part with it. The episode ends with its convention of the journalist/anchor figure, played by actor Sushant Singh, issuing a public warning and moral about people getting led away dangerously by their superstitious beliefs.

This episode maps Indian middle-class domesticity in familiar terms – with already normalised 'settings' and oft-discussed types of 'dramatic impetus.' The normalised setting consists of particularly oriented psychic and physical labour – such as wives concerned with biological reproduction, their display of jewellery as a gendered performance of class as well as *suhag*, or a Hindu woman's sacralised marital status, the household's dependence upon the labour of domestic workers (also a marker of class), and a prevailing sense of threat from the outer world. The plot is propelled by the mistress' lack of vigilance against social inferiors and women's vulnerability to the occult. Two marital homes are threatened by a poor, itinerant, unmarried woman whose desire for jewellery – the drama is at pains to show –is pathological (e.g., uncontrollable shaking of her hand) because the robberies are not conducted out of financial need or for self-sustenance. Rather jewellery is shown to offer her a purely sensual delight. Moreover, in threatening two marital homes, her desire threatens *suhag* and the enormous psychic and material claims it makes on a married woman's labour.

The episode incriminates not just a nomadic working-class woman but also the mistress-protagonist in the chain of events that unfold. The middle-class home's dependence upon domestic workers makes it vulnerable to dangerous intimacies. This class-inflected view structures the dramatisation of the scene in which Kaushalya enters Uma's bedroom to find her sitting surrounded by her jewellery. The scene illustrates an 'undesirable' degree of self-disclosure by the 'mistress' of the house before the coveting 'maid.' Then, Uma goes on to observe and disregard the shaking of Kaushalya's right hand, which the viewer, with her awareness of the genre conventions of 'true-crime,' notes is a serious hermeneutic failure. Ignoring the cue, Uma divulges details of her sister's life to Kaushalya. Thus, while the overt moral of the episode is about the dangers of occult, the implicit one is about the need for vigilance by the mistress of the home in relation to all hired outsiders. Read contrapuntally, this oft-repeated narrative of the 'thieving servant' reveals the anxieties that pervade these relationships within the home. The narrative also shows itself to function as a cultural mechanism of 'conversion' into worldviews that normalise class and gender monopolies that proliferate within the home, over wealth, power, and the labour of others.

Critical disaggregations of the home in Shakti Bhatt's 'The Thief'

Shakti Bhatt's short story 'The Thief' offers a critical examination of the cultural narrative of the 'thieving servant' by juxtaposing this figure with that of the child of the house. With this, the story explores how a home functions as the site of various regimes of education – including and beyond formal education – that reproduce hierarchies of caste, gender, class, and cultural identity. In brief, the narrator (who remains unnamed) tells a story about a domestic help named Narayani who had worked in her family home when she herself was a young teenager. At the time, this Bangalore-based upper-middle-class Christian joint-family was run by the narrator's authoritative grandmother. After an unpleasant experience with their previous cook, the family is relieved to find the eager and diligent Narayani. In the course of the story, the narrator relays to us Narayani's increasing indispensability to the household, her different employment experiences, her familial life, till a series of suspected thefts lead to a crisis in Narayani's tenure at the house. These events unfold alongside a parallel even if subordinate narrative plane where the narrator herself as a growing teenager, negotiates her various parental figures.

The opening passages of the story relate how Narayani's services are hired by the household. These lines also set up the narrative style of the story.

> 'How much for sweeping and mopping?' Grandmother asked, drying her wet, freshly dyed hair with her fingers. 'Everyone here gives 125 rupees but because we have five bedrooms I'll give you 150.'
>
> Narayani, not made uncomfortable by the mention of money, said, 'I'll cook and wash clothes, but I won't clean.'
>
> Grandmother looked meaningfully at me . . . I did not know what Grandmother meant by that look of hers so I imitated it in reply: I pursed my lips, widened my eyes, and raised my eyebrows. Grandmother needn't have asked Narayani why she wouldn't clean – everyone knew that some maids would not clean other people's houses, particularly their bathrooms; they even kept lower-caste maids to clean their own – but she did.
>
> 'No,' was all Narayani said in reply, shaking her head, smiling, hoping she hadn't embarrassed a potential employer. Grandmother ignored her reply.
>
> *(Bhatt 2007: 188–189)*

The scene sets up a tense social encounter, focalising the grandmother's micro-aggressive displaying of power that are spatial, gestural, and verbal. Leisurely drying her hair, she asks and answers her own questions, interrupting Narayani, pointing out the kinds of social hubris she finds unreasonable in her social inferiors. We also see Narayani, a self-confident even if needy seeker of employment, standing outside the gate, negotiate the barbs deftly. She asserts herself as an eager, tactful, and confident worker who takes pride in her abilities. The scene also sets up other significant dynamics, namely, those between the narrator and her pedantic grandparents. More importantly, in focalising these undercurrents and overtures, the narrative provides a dramatic as well as social density to a seemingly quotidian interaction.

The excerpt suggests a narratorial subjectivity that has been initiated into the ways of this inequitable world, and is therefore able to sense the tensions and ruses at play. But she is in many ways still 'unfinished' – so while she is aware of the self-evident truths of this world, she does not yet understand why things that everybody knows are said or asked needlessly. Thus, she puzzles over why her grandmother remarks upon Narayani's refusal to do cleaning when it is a commonly known fact that many maids do not clean homes. She has a child's ear for inconsistencies and kinds of grotesqueness; as well as a child's receptivity to multiple narratives. She focalises her grandmother's response – who mid-speech turns away from Narayani and looks at her, eyebrows raised – a gesture that demands the narrator's participation in a silent pronouncement of judgment upon Narayani – about the 'airs' these maids put on when they refuse to do certain kinds of work. The narrative captures the privilege that allows the grandmother to make the gesture, wherein she can remark upon Narayani's caste-based inflexibility and desire for respectability without any self-implicating irony. Similarly, she can command participation from the young grand-daughter, coaching her implicitly in how to transact class and service relations within the home. Further, the narrator's response of assembling her own facial features into a mimicry of her grandmother's eyebrow-raising enacts at once, the formulation of a pragmatic response by a keen teenager, as well as a critical enunciation of the gesture itself as a non-intuitive, acquired tool in the social and gestural repertoire of the elite. In other words, this can be seen as a moment of an attempted conversion.

The story suggests an equivalence between the narrator – the child raised by the household – and Narayani, the maid, in so far as both are the objects of different pedagogic regimes within this home. The narrator is subject to not merely rigorous home tuitions, but also nutritional regimes (with minimal allowances of instant noodles), enjoys American pop culture and consumerism, and learns her mother-tongue Malayalam. Equally, she is also learning how to interact with the battery of domestic workers employed in the home. In so far as these regimes are geared to raise her to be a future consumer-citizen, they entail processes of conversion, and the everyday, ubiquitous, authoritarian, or pleasurable ways in which they set upon her subjectivity blur the distinctions between coercive and non-coercive, voluntary and involuntary conversions.

A different set of pedagogical regimes gather around the figure of the domestic help who performs various kinds of intimate work for the household, and these reveal the more blatantly coercive aspects of the household. As the cook, Narayani must learn not merely the specific proportions for making tea, the culinary tastes, and the spice levels for the household, but also the larger philosophies of health, nutrition, hygiene, and hospitality they belong to. In the constant monitoring of her obedience to these dictates, there is also the implicit denigration of her own judgment and tastes. Unlike the narrator, what is demanded of her is a partial conversion into the pedagogic regimes of the home – since they are not intended to transform her substantively for inclusion, but rather to produce her as an ideal 'servant.'

As Narayani straightens out the flotsam of teenage consumerism in the narrator's room, she is not to aspire to the same for herself or her own five daughters at home. Patrolling the boundaries between these worlds, the grandmother approves when Narayani's daughter during her sole visit to the house, refuses to accept any snacks or gifts from her thus proving her 'honesty' and good upbringing. Thus, Narayani and her ilk must obey easily and efficiently, defer to the soundness of imposed norms, work surrounded by the material paraphernalia of a globalising middle class but not aspire to the same.

In these terms of admittance and employment offered to the domestic workers, there is also a refusal to see them as also inhabiting the same market-economy, newer worlds of liberalised aspirations and consumer-citizenship. This refusal is bolstered by the social architecture of a classism that reads such desires in the workers as inordinate given their station in life – and creating the potential for 'theft.' This classism also obfuscates the elite's own efforts to extract as much as it can from its workers. Narayani's other employer, an old woman demands massages that go on to the point of leaving Narayani's arms numb. When Narayani protests after being sexually propositioned by the woman's son, she is insulted and fired. Her responsibilities at the narrator's home also go up over time. These excesses are normalised by the overlay of kinship-like modes of address that Narayani adopts toward her employers – so that they become 'like family.' This allows her to take up cleaning and also do various kinds of intimate care work for them. These extractions, which are much in excess of the contractual, do not in the minds of the employers acquire the colour of systematic class theft.

Theft detection as a bid for epistemological authority

Subsequently, in Bhatt's story, several items go missing from the narrator's house – a superfluous vacuum cleaner, some shirts, the narrator's red, heart-shaped keychain, and a precious ring that was a family heirloom. On the one hand, these thefts only confirm the grandmother's notions about the dishonesty of domestic help. On the other hand, they also challenge her sense of total control over the household's affairs. Her efforts to detect which of the workers is the thief, becomes a bid to restore epistemological authority over them. She rules out the gardener, the peon and Narayani – her more trusted employees, from suspicion and instead levels the accusing finger at the cleaning maid. However, the act of levelling the accusation is also an act of definitively altering one's relation with the accused, and making a proclamation about their moral character. In this case, the bid for authority backfires when the cleaning maid responds by bringing back every donation and gift she had received from the family and quitting the job.

The story uses the eventual attribution of thefts to Narayani as a way to explore two different ways in which the intimacy born of domestic work is mobilised by different figures in the family. When the grandmother seeks to verify Narayani's claim that the heart-shaped keychain found upon her was given to her by the narrator, the narrator lies to confirm it – even as this leads to greater parental supervision over her own conduct with 'the servants.' Renewed attention is given to her grooming as a middle-class subject. The narrator lies out of a canny understanding of her grandmother's power and intent, as well as the consequences for Narayani if found guilty. She is also motivated by her affection for the latter and the easy friendship they have come to share. Through her lingerings in the kitchen while Narayani works, the narrator learns about her experience of working in different homes, her daily routine, her turbulent marital life, her determination to put her daughters through school while being the sole breadwinner and her hardships as a worker living 20 km outside the city. Rather than aspiring to epistemological authority, this narrative alliance between the narrator and Narayani, imbues the reader's interpretive posture toward Narayani with an imaginative expansiveness. Speculating upon the theft of the bright-red, heart-shaped keychain – a sanguine icon of youth culture, the reader may sense in the 'thief' desires that go beyond material paucities. In this instance, the theft may have been out of a desire for this (heart-shaped) marker of tender attention, in one who of necessity has had to be the tireless provider for herself and her family. Even the *mangal-sutra* she wears around her neck, she reminds the narrator, she had purchased for herself.

Unable to nail Narayani for the theft of the keychain, the grandmother takes a different tack in the case of the missing ring – one that would force its return without necessitating the firing of Narayani – of whose massages she had become the new beneficiary. Aware of Narayani's failing marriage and her vulnerability at this point to apotropaic beliefs, she tells her that the ring would harm anyone who usurps it, marriages could end. The following day a broken Narayani reveals that her husband has indeed left her and soon after she claims to have found the ring while cleaning the grandmother's bedroom. The scene is narrated as follows:

> The next morning, when Grandmother was teaching me subsets, we heard a shout: 'Amma, look what I found.' Grandmother calmly put her pen down and left the room. In her bedroom, a shiny piece of metal lay on the lower mattress of the bed, near the wooden footboard. Narayani was holding up the mattress with both her hands, *her face engaged in an effort to show extreme surprise and elation*. The afternoon sunlight that filtered through the cotton curtains split the pink diamond into several hundred pieces, and in it I could see traces of striking blue and purple.
>
> *(Bhatt 2007: 202) [emphasis mine]*

The grandmother's calm demeanour at the discovery shows that she is unsurprised by the turn of things – it is only a confirmation of her suspicions. More importantly, this successful manipulation of Narayani's actions completes her bid for epistemological authority – confirming her notions about the nature and scope of Narayani's inner mental and emotional life. It is significant that Narayani's shout had interrupted a pedagogic event – the grandmother had been tutoring the narrator in math. So what lesson is the narrator drawing from the scene now? If the 'discovery' confirms the grandmother's conviction, it also suggests the narrator's altered relationality with Narayani. Her description of the scene conducts a disaggregative reading of Narayani's face which seems to be 'engaged in an effort to show extreme surprise and elation' – detecting a laboured effort beneath the expression. The image of the prismatic shattering of the diamond by light closes the narrative at a moment of indeterminacy. It conveys a reckoning that finds the multidimensionality of reality to be violent, and desires their reconciliation into epistemological certainty. We wonder if the narrator has undergone a conversion by which her interpretive posture toward workers in the home and class hierarchies at large are now more aligned with those of her parental figures.

Conclusion

Defying the Hindu Right's emphasis in 'Love Jihad' on outside threats to the sanctity of 'good' homes, this chapter has demonstrated how homes also participate in the creation and perpetuation of an inequitable world. The TV episode discussed here illustrates how a prime time narrative can obfuscate the structural inequalities that prop up such homes – such as caste, class, and gender based divisions of labour – and naturalise its extensive use poor migrant labour, the physical and emotional labour of women, and its disproportionate benefiting from prevailing and emergent forms of capitalist modernity. However, these inequalities also generate latent anxieties which a story like this stokes in the shape of the theft narrative – and resolves them in ways that once more legitimise the material and psychic effectivities of the familial home. Bhatt's short story makes visible precisely these processes of naturalisation – showing the theft narrative itself to be a part of this. It also explores how as a space of intimacy between elite and non-elite figures, finished and 'unfinished' subjects, there may be forms of mutual recognition that do not seek material subordination and epistemological authority. Through these analyses this chapter has attempted to show that one of the ways of challenging the terms of prevailing debates about 'conversions' and *Ghar Wapsi* would be to demythologise the putative space of home and examine its material and psychic terrains.

Notes

1 The term is known to be used first by the Ram Sena leader Pramod Muttalik in Karnataka in 2005 – and thereafter gained circulation in Western Uttar Pradesh (Gupta 2016).

2 This was illustrated by the unravelling of a case of 'Love Jihad' alleged by the VHP in a village near Meerut in Uttar Pradesh in 2015. The young Hindu woman revealed in court that she had been forced by her father to file a case of rape and forced religious conversion against the Muslim man she had eloped with and married. This led the Allahabad High Court to rule that the administration must make sure that the woman is able to live freely with her partner and husband. See, Mohammad Ali. '"Love Jihad" Couple Move in Together.' *The Hindu*, 22 November 2015. www.thehindu.com/news/national/other-states/love-jihad-couple-move-in-together/article7880921.ece. Accessed 22 September 2017.

3 In this chapter I shall intermittently use the terms 'servant,' 'maid,' or 'maid-servant' with reference to domestic workers to draw attention to the politically loaded lexicon that is used in daily life as well as the chosen stories for this purpose.

4 The recent formulation by the Rajasthan state government of labour laws and minimum pay for domestic help corresponding to strictly calibrated work-hours and load, along with rumblings of similar laws being hashed out at the Centre – constitute more institutional steps in this direction. For details see here: 'Rajasthan Sets Minimum Wage for Domestic Help.' *The Times of India*. TNN. 1 February 2016. http://timesofindia.indiatimes.com/city/jaipur/Rajasthan-sets-minimum-wages-for-domestic-help/articleshow/50799019.cms. Accessed 22 September 2017.

5 This popular show is currently in its seventh season and has aired over 2200 episodes. The show now has editions for different states and cities such as: *Savdhaan India – Maharashtra Fights Back*, *Savdhaan India – Mumbai Fights Back*, *Savdhaan India – Punjab Fights Back* and *Savdhaan India – U.P Fights Back*.

Works cited

Primary texts

Bhatt, Shakti. 2007. 'The Thief.' In Urvashi Butalia (ed.), *Katha: Short Stories by Indian Women*. London, Berkeley, Beirut: Telegram Books.

'Dhongi Mata'/'Fake Holy Woman.' 2015. *Savdhaan India- India Fights Back/Caution India! – India Fights Back*. Prods. Rowdy Rascal Contiloe Pvt. Ltd & Others. Station: Life OK & Star Utsav. Season 23, Episode 1246. Air date: 29 Jul 2015. Television. Available online in some countries at: www.hotstar.com/tv/savdhaan-india/363/dhongi-mata/1000065799.

Secondary texts

Agnes, Flavia. 1999. *Law and Gender Inequality: The Politics of Women's Rights in India*. New Delhi: Oxford University Press.

Ali, Mohammad. '"Love Jihad" Couple Move in Together.' *The Hindu*, 22 November 2015. www.thehindu.com/news/national/other-states/love-jihad-couple-move-in-together/article7880921.ece. Accessed 21 February 2016.

Chatterjee, Partha. 1993. *The Nation and its Fragments: Colonial and Postcolonial Histories*. Princeton: Princeton University Press.

Gupta, Charu. 2016. 'Allegories of "Love Jihad" and Ghar Vapasi: Interlocking the Socio-Religious with the Political.' *Archiv Orientalni*, 84(2): 291–316.

Menon, Madhavi. 'No Fixed Identity.' *The Indian Express*, 26 December 2014. http://indianexpress.com/article/opinion/columns/no-fixed-identity/. Accessed 23 September 2017.

Nair, Janaki. 1996. *Women and Law in Colonial India: A Social History*. New Delhi: Kali for Women.

Omvedt, Gail. 2004. 'Women's Movement: Some Ideological Debates.' In Rajeswari Sunder Rajan and Maitreyee Chaudhuri (eds.), *Feminism in India. Series: Issues in Contemporary Indian Feminism: 2*. New Delhi: Kali for Women & Women Unlimited.

Punwani, Jyoti. 2014. 'Media Doublespeak.' *The Hoot*, 18 September. www.thehoot.org/media-watch/opinion/media-doublespeak-7785. Accessed 23 September 2017.

Rajagopal, Krishnadas. 2017. 'Supreme Court Orders NIA Probe into Kerala Woman's Conversion and Marriage.' *The Hindu*, 16 August. www.thehindu.com/news/national/kerala/supreme-court-orders-nia-probe-into-kerala-womans-conversion-and-marriage/article19501689.ece. Accessed 23 September 2017.

'Rajasthan Sets Minimum Wage for Domestic Help.' *The Times of India*, 1 February 2016. http://timesofindia.indiatimes.com/city/jaipur/Rajasthan-sets-minimum-wages-for-domestic-help/articleshow/50799019.cms. Accessed 22 September 2017.

Rege, Sharmila. 2004. 'Dalit Women Talk Differently: A Critique of 'Difference' and Towards a Dalit Feminist Standpoint Position.' In Rajeswari Sunder Rajan and Maitreyee Chaudhuri (eds.), *Feminism in India. Series: Issues in Contemporary Indian Feminism: 2*, New Delhi: Kali for Women & Women Unlimited.

Sarkar, Tanika. 2001. *Hindu Wife, Hindu Nation: Community, Religion and Cultural Nationalism*. London: Hurst & Co.

Sen, Ilina. 2004. 'Women's Politics in India.' In Rajeswari Sunder Rajan and Maitreyee Chaudhuri (eds.), *Feminism in India. Series: Issues in Contemporary Indian Feminism: 2*, New Delhi: Kali for Women & Women Unlimited.

Sangari, Kumkum. 1999. *Politics of the Possible: Essays on Gender, History, Narrative, Colonial English*. New Delhi: Tulika.

Sharma, Pratul. 2015. 'VHP Claims Huge Success in Ghar Wapsi Campaign.' *New Indian Express*, 5 July. www.newindianexpress.com/thesundaystandard/VHP-Claims-Huge-Success-in-Ghar-Wapsi-Campaign/2015/07/05/article2902434.ece. Accessed 31 October 2015.

T. A., Johnson. 2017. '8 Years Before NIA, CID Probed Love Jihad, Found No Specific Instance.' *The Hindu*, 22 August. http://indianexpress.com/article/india/8-years-before-nia-karnataka-cid-probed-love-jihad-found-no-specific-instance-4807667/. Accessed 22 September 2017.

PART III

Dissident body and belonging

7

ANTI-CASTE COMMUNITAS AND OUTCASTE EXPERIENCE

Space, body, displacement, and writing

Dickens Leonard

Intimacy and belonging seem deceptive in the context of a civilisational violence that schemes with criminal silencing. Indeed, pogroms that immunise and sanitise space and time actually launch intimidation and loss. And caste has been one of the most violent civilisational machinations that have brutally destroyed intimacy and belonging. In this context, Dalits could be understood as an embodiment of shadows that travel.[1] A compartment of bodies, when outcaste – particularly dehumanised and violated – may be usually associated with static immobility, or un-change. But engendered caste gaze is secondary to essential mobility – 'travel' or displacement of those very bodies is precedent to violation and violence. I argue that space and caste are intricately linked, as caste is also about embodied space – it is a spatial location of people into a locked hierarchy.

The caste question with regard to the outcaste – taking a cue from increasing caste violence, Dalit and/or minority lynching, as a continuity in India – is mired within the social category of spatial power relations, bodily (dis)locations and displacements. An outcast, in that sense, is a dislocated and displaced being. Body and shadow, even as metaphor, captures the travails of the most oppressed by caste, whether they are static or mobile[2]. Besides, however violent the displacement and/or disembodiment may be, they imagine a home 'in-place' and 'in-time,' critically and creatively through writing and practice, which constitutes anti-caste values, even when reduced as shadows (Guru 2009, 2011). I would like to conceptualise this as 'communitas'[3] of/from/towards the outside.

This chapter is divided into two sections, and the sections are further divided into three parts each. The first section looks at continuous displacement, migration, and (lived) experience as categories that create anti-caste emancipatory thought in Dalit writing. It demonstrates how historical movement is a prerequisite for emancipatory thought, especially for disenfranchised communities such as Dalits. This is done by exploring the reports on migration of indentured labourers to other parts of the world during the colonial period in order to understand how socially despised communities become silent movers of a 'shadow modernity.' Subsequently, the travel reports of Gandhi and Ambedkar are compared to argue that ideas of space and experience contribute distinctly to emancipatory thoughts on community. The third part explores theoretical ideas on space, experience, and death by reading Ambedkar to understand how writing can contribute to the idea of anti-caste communitas.

The second section is a study on Iyothee Thass's *Indhirar Dhesa Sarithiram* (*IDS*, History of the Indhirar Country). It demonstrates that though 'caste gaze' literally lynches the outcasts, Dalits have historically reversed the gaze and have challenged their reduction to caste-shadow by embarking into writing. Moreover, this section also suggests that marginalised minds and bodies have domesticated local and global space through their labour and have indeed turned it in their favour as 'place.' They find home in time, irrespective of the casteist's shadow and destruction. The section underlines how Dalit and subaltern thought uses interpretation as a method to intertwine ideas of experience and thought, so as to produce a critical and creative idea of casteless-ness.

Outcaste: displacement, indentured labour, and shadow modernity

> An ideal society should be mobile, should be full of channels for conveying a change taking place in one part to other parts . . . There should be *varied and free points of contact* with other modes of association. In other words there must be *social endosmosis*.
>
> – (Dr. B.R. Ambedkar, *Annihilation of Caste*, emphasis mine)

Historical studies on Dalits (Viswanath 2014; Mohan 2015) state that continuous displacements among the outcastes had destroyed an essential notion of human as a unique space – as identity – for pressing historical reasons. A-place-at-home was vulnerable to violence and intimidation, and the human as a unique space was denied. Hence outcastes had to move in and out of places, mostly with their families in large numbers, in search of a home and livelihood. Men and women migrated and worked together. Differences among the marginalised were rejected in the enslaving gaze of both the colonial and local masters. They were reduced to a unified comportment of shadows. Produced only as shadows, they were sought to be distanced. Apparently, the real and the reflected space – body and shadow – became one and the same. In other words, even in travel, the outcaste body as a unique body in presence is rejected, and is reduced to a not-yet-space, which does not embody a unique human presence in relation with the other.

For instance, historian Raj Sekhar Basu studies the migration pattern of the Parayar community, formerly 'untouchables,' in Tamil Nadu during the nineteenth and twentieth centuries in his work *The Nandanar's Children* (2011).[4] He historicises their 'search for fresh pastures' (111) through internal and overseas migration that was accelerated by the colonial governance. He contends, by accounting historical resources that large populations migrated as indentured labourers to Ceylon, Malaya, Burma, Fiji, Mauritius, South Africa, and to some of the French colonies from the early nineteenth century to the late twentieth century. Dalits migrated in large numbers and an essential sense of self was not fixated.

The large number of migrants, who were Tamil coolies, belonged mostly to the 'untouchable' and 'lower' caste backward communities. They travelled to work in the tea estates and plantations. The large-scale migration by these communities was a huge recruitment network that worked across countries and sea routes, which tremendously consolidated the local as well as the colonial configuration of power through violent authority on face value.

Basu notes that people migrated internally to the emergent industrial towns such as Mysore and Madras. Moreover, a large section of Parayars also joined as soldiers in the Madras army since the 1760s and 1770s. They were more popularly known as the 'Queen's Own Sappers and Miners' (Basu 2011: 161). But after the 1857 revolt, Basu mentions that the colonial government's military recruitment policy changed drastically, and it went against the Parayar regiment. The government did not get involved in the religious matters of India, say recruiting 'untouchables.' However, as late as the 1890s, Parayars enjoyed a virtual monopoly of the dangerous yet menial jobs as 'Sappers and Miners' in the Madras army (Basu 2011: 159–161).

Indeed, hardly any historical research is found that is completely devoted to study the links between the army and the mobilisation of the 'lower-caste' groups in pre-independent India. Manas Dutta concurs that though the army played an important role in the lives of the Dalits as a means of immense social and occupational mobility, 'very little work has been done on the role of the "marginalized" or "untouchable" or "labourer castes" in the army' (Dutta 2016: 58). He argues that the Madras army, amongst the three presidency armies, particularly maintained the policy to make the army a viable ladder for social mobilisation for caste groups that were in need (57–71). He points out that the Madras army consisted mainly of low-caste Hindus, untouchables, and converted Christians who were particularly noted for 'the lack of religious prejudices and local attachments' among others (61). This exclusive preferential policy to recruit untouchables as soldiers earned the Parayars an important place in the army.[5] They incorporated themselves in the colonial army not only to explore their physical ability but also to earn maximum respect in the society (Dutta 2016: 62). As Dalits deserted the lands and farms, many more landlords complained bitterly that their 'agrestic slaves' had enlisted as sepoys in the company army. Further, Madras as a colonial town began to grow and the prospect of urban employment increased, particularly to the 'lower castes' (Dutta 2016: 63).

As Madras emerged as a presidential city, Dalits also became menial servants of the British. In this attempt, they escaped agrarian bondage and ritual degradation. Indeed, Parayars and Pallars became butlers, cooks, attendants, keepers of horses, etc. They were employed in Buckingham and Carnatic Mills, Kolar gold mines, the expanding railways, the constructional and transport sectors in and around Madras.

Particularly, British army's military adventures across the globe enabled the Parayars to cross the seas and work as British soldiers. Thus, they travelled all over the world bringing home not only money, but also new ideas, values, and determination (Aloysius 1998: 34–64).

They were also the first to be recruited as manual labourers in the Railways for construction work. In fact, huge deployments were sent to Burma, Uganda, and America; many died and some never returned (Basu 2011). They worked in Kolar Gold Field, tanneries, leather factories, Ice Houses, tea estates, and plantation farms in deplorable conditions during the colonial period. Many worked as cooks and ayahs to British officers and Christian missionaries. Dutta mentions that they worked as 'menial domestic servants' such as – 'butlers, butlers' mates, cook's mates, roundel boys, coach men, palanquin boys, house keepers, grass cutters, dry and wet nurses, water wenches, scavengers, cart drivers, tots, women sweepers, and lamp lighters' (70). They were, perhaps, the foot soldiers of a colonial modernity – probably similar but not congruent to 'conscripts'[6] of civilisation and/or modernity (Diamond 1974; Asad 1992; Scott 2004) – that marched for three centuries in the Indian subcontinent, though worst affected by it. They were neither recognised for their contribution nor given claim over these material spaces of industrial modernity, as social justice and recognition were denied to them historically (Patterson 1982). However, this calls for a separate research all together.

These changes during the colonial period caused an exorbitant change in values and attitudes back home. The Dalits entry into education was largely assisted through the missionaries, the early theosophist society, and the provincial government. The urban educated Dalits took up the cudgels on behalf of their less fortunate brethren by organising themselves through social organisations and movements. This is reflected in the emergence of newspapers and journals, which were one of the favourite media forms of the emerging subalterns. Printing presses seem to have become the centres for discussions, planning, and collective activities. They created the myth-histories of the Subaltern communities appear in the public, and created their own print-world as a social and political space (Aloysius 1998: 98–125).

It is in this context that the Dalits had started a new and autonomous religio-social movement right in the centre of the city of Madras in the early twentieth century (Aloysius 1998: 57). They had expressed the opinion that the emancipation of their community members could be successfully achieved by organising a Buddhist mass movement. The movement had started branches in Bangalore, Royapettah, Pudupet, Adyar, and Mylapore with the help of railway employees and enlisted army personnel, especially from Queen Victoria's own Madras sappers and miners.[7] They also opened branches where the Subaltern groups migrated as indentured labourers in the over port Natal in South Africa and Eticola, Rangoon in Burma. The postal services, railways, and the journal print that were made available by colonial modernity were effectively used to promote unity and carry forward the movement.[8]

I suggest that this shadow modernity – the most oppressed communities' engagement with colonial modernity – which provided opportunities for new employment made travel conditional, and displacement was a prerequisite to search for a-place-at-home and a sense of self.[9] The migration, both internal and overseas, brought about certain changes in the economic conditions of the Parayars in some of the Tamil districts of Madras presidency. However, it did not provide a wide scale improvement in the sociocultural conditions. They remained indigent, socially despised communities who, just like today, received violence from the socially dominant castes. As Rupa Viswanath states there was antagonism and sustained opposition to Dalit welfare. There were united efforts in the 1910s to thwart the demands for civil rights of Madras' first Dalit political representatives (Viswanath 2014: 248).

Despite the long working hours in plantations and health hazards posed by factories to the coolies, some became independent cultivators, as there was overall improvement in their socioeconomic conditions. However, there was constant social opposition from the landed castes (Basu 2011: 164). The migration, or displacement experience, showed visible signs of growing self-respect, thrift, and hopefulness in the community (Basu 2011: 181–182). While travel displaced them significantly, it conditioned them to essentially imagine a-place-at-home, in relation to a sense of respectful-self as a unique space. This history of Dalits' engagement with British colonialism and modernity could be explored more and in detail beyond the frames offered by postcolonial and Subaltern Studies' scholars on colonial modernity. In this context, and on a divergent note, perhaps, this is best synthesised conceptually in two scintillating travels – by Gandhi and Ambedkar.

Gandhi and Ambedkar: space, travel, and thought

Gandhi and Ambedkar travelled for a major part of their lifetime. They embodied different kinds of sociopolitical and cultural thought, which is intrinsically linked to the spaces they belonged to and occupied; even as they animate their post-life now in the country. There are stunning similarities in the travel experiences of these two men, essentially differentiated by the spaces they habituated, as both spent considerable time outside India, before they jumped into politics in India.

M.K. Gandhi and Dr. B.R. Ambedkar travelled abroad and spent their formative years in England, South Africa and America. Gandhi spent 24 years abroad, of which 3 were in England and 21 in South Africa. Ambedkar spent 8 years abroad, mostly for studies, of which 5 were in America and 3 in England. Travel and journey, as experience, played a crucial role in their distinct political practices of their times as they returned to India. Gandhi became Mahatma, whereas Ambedkar became Babasaheb, in contrasting styles (Ambedkar 1993). Wherever Gandhi was, in the words of Jawaharlal Nehru, it was the capital of India, whereas Ambedkar had to apologetically confess to Gandhi that 'I do not have a homeland' (Ambedkar quoted in Guru and Sarukkai 2012: 71).

Their travels were of contrasting styles in the trajectory of their post-life in the country. The places that they started from, travelled to, moved into, mobilised in, worked at and stationed in were culturally constituted spatial phenomena. As both were spatially located and enshrined in foregrounding the nation state, they also became ambiguous and confessional in the journey of the nation state. The spaces that these icons occupy and animate today evoke dichotomous trajectories of cultural practice that reproduce their memory and presence. These practices, I argue, are engendered by violence and violation of their embodiment and memory. Desecration and demolition of, and slipper garlands to somebody's statues; whereas, spatial reprints of somebody's face on rupee notes are intrinsically linked to the reproduction of power relations mapped through spatial memory. To foreground and examine this idea further, let us closely study and understand travel as spatial phenomena by comparing Ambedkar to Gandhi.

Ambedkar's life was marked by multiple sojourns to hierarchical spaces of many a kind. The sense of 'a-place-at-home' was a distant dream for him. He writes in the Columbia University Alumni News, Dec. 1930, that he experienced social equality for the first time in Columbia University. And some of his best friends that he had in life were some of his class mates and professors at Columbia (Ambedkar quoted in Natarajan and Anand 2011: 64). His travels resuscitate memories that embody the violence inscribed in a caste-space that is homeland that was never homely to him. For Ambedkar, a sense of spatial homeliness and camaraderie was only felt outside of 'home.' Though out-of-space as an outcaste at home, he searched for a home-apart nevertheless. Ambedkar's sojourn in the *bastis* of Bombay presidency and elsewhere, so as to mobilise the depressed classes, and eventual conversion to Buddhism, ensured a homeland for his statured presence in his post-life amongst Dalits in India.

It is worthwhile to recount Ambedkar's tragic travel accounts of his life in India. He reminisces about the train travel from Satara to Goregaon to meet his father, along with his brothers. As a 10-year-old, he recounts, they were forced to face the full reality of caste. He writes 'he was forced to learn how caste could force a human being to deny his body's needs and feelings, even so elemental a feeling as thirst' (*ibid*). His experiences in search of lodging at Baroda – a place to live in a city – immediately after he returned from London, forces one to associate experience as a prerequisite to emancipatory sociopolitical thought.

These experiences generally, excruciating as they are, reduce and reject the person embodied in presence, as abominable and inhuman – a mere shadow. Caste as experience is 'un-freedom' as it enslaves and rejects the needs of bodily senses – such as touch, thirst, and taste. Engendered through caste, Ambedkar's sociopolitical thought gave content to emancipatory movements across spaces. Experience sourced through displacement, which produce self-reflective, out-of-space subjects, precedes meaningful, transformatory, political action. However, the conditions that produce out-of-spaces need to be thought critically and contingently.

On the other hand, though on a different note, Gandhi's experience of being discriminated in South Africa gave a radical content to his politics, so as to lead a nationalist movement in India. However, for us, his experiences are markedly different from Ambedkar's, as the space he habituated in Indian subcontinent, and elsewhere, was ontologically distinct. Gandhi, all the while in Africa and India, was supported by rich businessmen and powerful Congress men. Recent works on

Gandhi's 21 years sojourn in South Africa have clearly indicated that his struggles sought to secure separate political rights to Indian traders and merchants who held land in India, distinct from that of the native Black Africans.

In a public meeting at Bombay in 1896, Gandhi delivered an address on the grievances of the South African Indian community, while giving vent to the prevalent prejudices about the native Africans:

> Ours is a continual struggle against a degradation sought to be inflicted upon us by the Europeans, who desire to degrade us to the level of the raw *Kaffir* whose occupation is hunting, and whose sole ambition is to collect a certain number of cattle to buy a wife with and, then, pass his life in indolence and nakedness.
>
> *(Collected Works of Mahatma Gandhi [CWMG] Vol. 1 1999: 410)*

And adds in 1908 on 'my experience in gaol' for *Indian Opinion* that 'the *Kaffirs* are as a rule uncivilised – the convicts even more so. They are troublesome, very dirty and live almost like animals' (*CWMG* Vol. 8 1999: 199). In a petition he drafted in 1899 concerning the designation of an Indian location near the native African settlement, he protested:

> Your petitioner [i.e., Gandhi] has seen the Location intended to be used by the Indians. It would place them, who are undoubtedly infinitely superior to the *Kaffirs*, in close proximity to the latter.
>
> *(CWMG Vol. 3 1999: 76)*

In an open letter to the members of the Natal Legislature in 1894, he wrote: 'the Indian is being dragged down to the position of a raw *Kaffir*' (*CWMG* Vol. 1 1999: 193 and 431). In other words, he protested against Indians being treated like 'raw Kaffirs' – a derogatory word for native Black Africans – in Apartheid South Africa[10].

His experiences of racial discrimination, at the now famous train journey, where he was thrown out of a first-class compartment is as much an issue of racism by the whites, as it is to do with his reluctance to travel with native Africans. He struggled for a non-violent, dignified, partial solution to the treatment of (dominant caste land-holding) Indians in South Africa markedly different from that of native Africans (Reddy 1999). In 1906, he comments on 'the tram case' thus:

> You say that the magistrate's decision is unsatisfactory because it would enable a person, however unclean, to travel by a tram, and that even the Kaffirs would be able to do so. But the magistrate's decision is quite different. The Court declared that the Kaffirs have no legal right to travel by tram. And according to tram regulations, those in an unclean dress or in a drunken state are prohibited from boarding a tram. Thanks to the Court's decision, only clean Indians or coloured people other than Kaffirs, can now travel in the trams.
>
> *(CWMG Vol. 5 1999: 235)*

Hence his *Hind Swaraj* (1908) written during the sea voyage between England and South Africa symbolises diasporic anxiety. Gandhi carried fond memories of a homeland, as he spatio-politically reproduced it abroad. This is the essential difference between Gandhi's spatial sojourn in comparison to that of Ambedkar's. Perhaps, their bodies as spaces are symptomatic of the corporeal homeland they imagined, distinct from each other, in their sojourns. Gandhi's was always in-place, and Ambedkar's constantly out-of-it, and in search.[11]

In studying space as a culturally constructed phenomenon in India, Guru suggests that the dominant social groups historically structure and restructure a given space through spatial hermeneutics of caste. And violence seeks to restructure space in a specific way in the caste society. Hence, Guru invokes Ambedkar to state that caste-based violence is civilisational violence, which reacts to the Dalit struggle that transgresses boundaries, so as to liberate the rigid caste spaces. Dalits pay a heavy price, as violence is defined by the simultaneity of both the 'presence' and 'absence' of the victim of violence (Guru and Sarukkai 2012: 83).

In this civilisational violence, firstly, violence is physical as it annihilates the corporal being – the presence – of Dalits. Secondly, certain groups, such as the untouchables, are eliminated – made absent – from social and culturally active relations. The simultaneous 'absent-presence' thus provides the full definitional conditions for civilisational violence, or so argues Guru. Untouchables, at the zenith of civilisational violence, 'remain untouchable, uncrossable, unseeable, unhearable, unapproachable, and uncommunicable.' As mentioned earlier, they are pushed outside time and space, to embody 'a shock-absorber existence' (Guru and Sarukkai 2012: 83–88). Interestingly, this civilisational violence marks its document on the body, reminding one of Walter Benjamin's seventh thesis on the philosophy of history – 'there has never been a document of culture which is not at one and the same time a document on barbarism' (Benjamin 1969:256).

Guru positively suggests that different spaces yield different concepts, especially when spaces are hierarchically segregated. For Gandhi, self-rule is the main point of contention; however, for Ambedkar, it is self-respect and social justice that acquire central importance. One conceptualisation indicates the limits of other's imagination, due to the experiential space from which it emanates. Guru argues that experience – *anubava/m* – as a category is a primary epistemological resource to produce alternative categories for the politics of emancipation for Ambedkar. Hence, the Ambedkarite movement is an attempt to walkout from constraints, and get a fair chance to enter a new and liberating experience. Guru calls it as an attempt to become 'placeless individuals who then would organize their social protocols with others on an equal basis' (Guru and Sarukkai 2012: 90).

But the process of modernity, as it unleashed in India, only rigidified caste boundaries. Untouchables were seen as mobile dirt, and dirt is considered as mobile untouchability. Guru suggests that there is a spatial dimension to this ontology that continuously produces and reproduces mobile dirt; and thus, untouchability is a particular kind of spatial ontology even in modern urbanisation.[12] For instance, the role of print media in India was ironically significant not in terms of imagining the nation, as Benedict Anderson would passionately argue, but it just consolidated the hold of caste over financial spaces. Guru justifies this observation by stating that the dominant castes wanted 'to recover in tradition the confidence that they were likely to lose in modernity' (Guru and Sarukkai 2012: 93).

Moving from experiential-spatiality to 'ethics of theorizing,' Guru states that experience could be treated as a middle term in between 'social being and social consciousness' (Guru and Sarukkai 2012: 111). Guru does not assign discursive treatment to experience, rather he disputes such an effort.[13] He sees in experience a conceptual possibility for radical, political, and philosophical use. This reference to concrete experience becomes a necessary epistemic resource for the progression of concepts; not a mere journey of concepts that refer other concepts alone. Hence, it is necessary to study the philosophical foundations of emancipatory movements and their idea of experience that are historically produced.

These theoretical principles that look forward to bringing the category of experience to the centre stage also try, rather vigorously, to frame 'the Dalit experience as having the ambition to produce centralizing categories' that would seek 'epistemic departure' from the existing categories due to inadequacy (Guru and Sarukkai 2012: 121). Two premises seem to outlay such an effort. Firstly, the Dalit experience/movement aspires to a more universal, egalitarian alternative as it attempts to produce a discrete 'moral hegemony.' Secondly, social experience is 'an intersubjectifying experience,' where individualities are transcended and transformed – through debate, persuasion, and public exchange of arguments – into collective yet subversive subjects (Guru and Sarukkai 2012: 127).

Anti-caste: lived experience and communitas

The Dalit experience in India, despite gaining material progress partially, has been essentially about what it is to become and emerge as an autonomous embodiment – an intimate longing-to-be-in-the-world. The Dalit body, when violated as an out-of-space subject, bears an ontological wound, and is reduced to a mere shadow. Even today, this rejection of an autonomous space, a-place-at-home, continues to map the power of the socially dominant castes. And in the absence of the Dalit body being recognised as an equal-subject-in-presence – regardless of difference and autonomy – it is excluded/lynched to a space elsewhere through the caste gaze. Genealogically isolated through the loss of heritage and right to pass on their ancestry, the Dalit body becomes a playfield of 'social death' and not social endosmosis. Dalit deaths are a reminder of a phenomenon that reduces the Dalit subject to its shadow.

However, one needs to weave a conceptual terrain to suggest a positional critique of ascribed intimacy, and belonging that is inscribed through birth. One can argue that the Subaltern thought in India that belongs to the anti-caste tradition, uses interpretation as a tool to reconfigure notions of space and time that is open, creative, and resistant. They inaugurate and constitute a millennial anti-caste communitas, of a kind, as creative opposition and history against caste immunitas. This has relevance, as resistance, for the rampant violence and humiliation that oppressively institutionalise the body and mind today in India.

'Communitas' as a concept is immensely useful and is inspired from anti/post-Nazi and Stalinist thought, tracing particularly through Jean-Luc Nancy, Maurice Blanchot, and Roberto Esposito. I ask what could be the Dalit experience of mobile community in India? What is the idea of 'intimate be-longing' (as a longing-to-be) for Dalits, in/toward the wor(l)d? Could there be a counter-look to caste – an oppositional gaze – that treats the 'untouchable-being' itself as an Other? How do the Dalits challenge their reduction as a shadow against caste?

Nancy develops sturdily the thought of being as 'compearance' – to co-appear as the most notable condition for the possibility of the political. He suggests that singular beings exist only in an originary 'sociality,' but 'finite being always presents itself "together," and severally' (Nancy 1991).[14] Communication is at the origin of the community as an originary sociality. It consists of constant exposure to an outside, in the sharing with the others all the limits, the borders of finite beings (Nancy 1994; Agamben 1993). For Nancy, the political would signify a community disposed to sharing. A community that is conscious of its constitutive, communicative experience. Caste perhaps then is the most anti-social, anti-communicative, and anti-communal invention as it sanctions non-fusion as a law.

However, death too disrupts the ontological project of fusion. Hence an 'originary or ontological sociality,' which Nancy calls an 'arche-community,' is understood as spacing or writing about the 'traces' of the community that are 'unrepresentable,' 'unavowable' and 'inoperative' (Gaon 2005). In contrast, for Blanchot, the theme of death is used for the service of the ethical relation to the other. While, caste founds social death; 'Death founds community,' argues Blanchot, 'in the sense that death of the other takes me out of myself and this exposes me to the radical alterity of an outside that thought cannot master' (Blanchot 1988: 12). Vitally, both these reflections on community offer something beyond the traditional model of the social bond. They interrogate community to undo identity and commonality as such. They open the chance of a political to emerge that is otherwise foreclosed. Beyond or before understanding the social bond as a relationship among the previously constituted subjects; they attempt to question, through an ethical-ontological register, the philosophical suppositions of a political community.[15]

Dalit intellectuals seem to conceptualise community as beyond the traditional model of the social bond – caste. They interrogate community to undo caste and Brahminism as such. They open the chance of a political to emerge that is otherwise foreclosed. They question, through an ethical-ontological register, the philosophical suppositions of a caste society through a deconstructive understanding of community. Consequently, this opens – a deconstructive opening indeed – a possibility for a caste-less community. The discussions on community implore that ethics and ontology are fundamentally linked with ideas of community. The attempt to engage with the other, so as to conceive the community as related with the other, has been Nancy's and Blanchot's attempt to theorise the community.

In addition, Esposito's communitas as *munus, communis*, and *itas*, which mean gift, debt, and obligation, respectively, could relate to the Tamil Dalits establishing *sangams* and *sabhas* in the nineteenth and twentieth centuries. Their engagement with Buddhism was about belonging to a community against caste in the vernacular both in the global and local context. In the colonial and nationalist context, it must have enabled them to belong to a world-community and at the same time with their own communities. It inscribes a negation and exscribes an affirmation whereby it becomes both a traditional and an elective community at once. A 'communitas' as a 'totality of persons united not by a property but precisely by an obligation or a debt; not by an addition but a subtraction' (Esposito 2009: 6). This anti-caste communitas is an exposure and it is characterised by the other, by a voiding to alter oneself. The community appeals as it withdraws from caste and Brahminism, by differentiating itself from immunitas. Sophisticatedly, Esposito suggests that community cannot be thought as a corporation or a body, where individuals are found in a larger individual – what a critique of the all-pervasive *Manusha*in *Varnashra Dharma*, where the head, shoulders, thighs, and feet stand for a corporal hierarchy of a people.

These theoretical gestures are intrinsically linked. This could be expanded and extended to understand how the oppressed, importantly the Dalits, in particular contexts view and constitute community – textually – and question the philosophical supposition of the political in caste-*immunitas*.[16] Iyothee Thass's texts are examples that undo the presupposition of the social bond, which is constituted through caste-subjection and immunisation, to reconstruct community through an ethico-ontological communitas with anti-caste values. Experience, as an instituting category, frames this conceptual terrain to understand community (Ansari 2001).

The Tamil intellectual Pandit Iyothee Thass[17] (1845–1914) ran the magazine *Tamizhan* (*T*1907–1914),[18] which revived interest on Buddhism as an anti-caste religion. A man of anti-caste ideas, he was a major leader, intellectual and activist whose life, work, and legacy have regrettably remained neglected by historians until recently.[19] In many ways, a precursor to towering anti-caste figures like Periyar E.V. Ramasamy (1879–1973) and Babasaheb Dr. B.R. Ambedkar (1891–1956), Thass was the first to develop an anti-caste narrative by espousing and writing on Buddhism (Rajangam 2016; Rajesh 2011, 2013). He was a practitioner of *Siddha* medicine, who during the 1881 British-India census, appealed that the *panchamas (ex-untouchables)* were not Hindus and that they must be recorded as original Tamils – *Adi Tamizhar* (Aloysius 2015: 69). He used Tamil literary resources and palm-scripts, so as to field anti-caste, Tamil literature, and folklore-based explanations on Buddhism.

Thass was an intellectual – an expert reader, referee, writer, polyglot, publisher, and organiser; and he initiated a resistant knowledge practice, by using journalism, as a tool to gain inroads into the print public sphere, which was undeniably caste-ridden. Forty-two such Tamil journals – by Dalits – were run from 1850 to 1947 in the Madras presidency (Balasubramaniam 2016, 2017). Such an event in print history is erased in public memory and it calls for a serious enquiry. Particularly the role of academics and history-writing in India must have a critical anti-caste perspective. This revisit would re-evaluate that historical moment of erasure, and could capture the prolific Dalit participation and contribution to emancipatory knowledge practice in print-language (Leonard 2017).

Iyothee Thass and *Indhirar Dhesa Sarithiram*

> *Sasthirathirkotra anubavamum, anubavathirkotra sasthirangalum avargalidam kidaiyavam. They do not have that knowledge which suits their experience, and that experience which suits their knowledge.*
>
> – (Pandithar 2010: 148)

Thass ran the Tamil journal *Oru Paisa Tamizhan* (later *Tamizhan* or *The Tamilian*) from June 19, 1907 to April 29, 1914 – incidentally the year Mohandas Gandhi returned to India from South Africa and Dr. Ambedkar was in the middle of his research in Columbia University, New York. Compared to other radical, anti-race, African-American magazines such as *The Chicago Defender* during the same time, *Tamizhan* ran similar radical contents against caste, health columns, local and international news; and it also had a wide reach among the marginalised (Ayyathurai 2011: 21–22). Thass pioneered the Buddhist movement in the cities where Dalits migrated as coolies, such as Kolar Gold Field, Bangalore, Rangoon, and Durban. He devoted time to start separate *vihars*, worship practices, festivals, libraries, schools, burial places, and marriage customs. These were done to reconstruct Dalit history through a Buddhist framework in the vernacular. Not only did he work for the religious identity of the Dalits, but also for their political, social, and economic needs too (Aloysius 2004, 2007).

Thass reconstructs Tamil Buddhism through a counter-cultural enquiry into religion, history, community, and identity, primarily, against the institutional codes of Brahminism. His attempt at a hermeneutic historiography, subverts, and creates a space outside, or against caste as history. Thass uses the reserves of Tamil language as an archive of history, in the context of an emergent Tamil-print public sphere in Madras Presidency, in the early twentieth century. Defying formal institutionalisation of historical time and space, he attempts an interpretative history and community as practice.

IDS, his serial accounts in 65 parts published between August 1910 and November 1911, in the journal *Tamizhan*, is an attempt to reconstruct a Buddhist history of India (published as a book in 1912, 2nd edition in 1957, and later in 1999 by the Dalit Sahitya Academy). It is a reconstructive social history that politically and culturally counters the established 'story of caste.' It is imperative to study Thass as someone who de-institutes as well as constitutes a *Sarithiram* in Tamil. While it bemoans a genealogy of loss due to civilisational violence, it embarks into civilisational memory as a pre-history of caste, so as to inaugurate an anti-caste millennial communitas.[20]

Thass treats history, or much simply researching the past, as an ethico-ontological pedagogy. Thass, in his preface, states that the intent to publish *IDS* was 'to explain and to remove problems' (*vilakudhal . . . allalai neekudhal*) the stories that were preached as history. He counter-reads stories that were being established as history to reconstruct a counter. He requests 'to research history and reject everything else' (*sarithira aaraichi ininri sagala vatraiyum usaava vendugiren*)[21]. *Villakudhal*, the Tamil word, in fact stands for both interpretation and explanation. In fact, it is instructive to read this practice of research, in the light of Paul Ricoeur's hermeneutic phenomenology, where understanding and explanation are treated as an ontological aspect of interpretation. It seeks to 'bring into language an experience, a way of living in and of being-in-the-world.'[22]

For instance, the title calls for an interesting reading. *Indhirar* in *Indhirar Dhesa Sarithiram* is the Buddha for Thass. *Indhiram*,[23] for him, comes from the word *ainthiram* or *aimpori*(*ainthu* + *thiram* – five + senses) – the five senses – of sight, hearing, smell, taste, and touch. And the one who controlled and conquered the five senses for practicing *aram* – ethical action or conduct is *Ainthirar* also *Indhirar*. Siddhartha, the king of Magadha country who became the Buddha, and preached this method to his followers, was called by that name. *Sangha*s were established in his name to propagate this thought-practice of learning through five senses; these *Sangha*s were called *Indhira Viharangal* – the *Vihars*. The land that teaches, practices, and remembers the *Indhirar* through *Indhira Vizha* was called *Indhiyam*, *Indhiram*, and *Indhiya* where *Indhira Vihars* were constructed. People who lived there and followed the path of *Indhirar* were called *Indhiyargal* – Indians. The word *Indhiyam* is interpreted to generate a variety of new meanings to constitute a resistant concept for understanding nation as space and time. And the land particularly was linked to the idea of practice that trains the five senses (Pandithar 2010: 5).[24]

This mode of thinking questions the idea of community as a given identity and problematises its limits. An originary sociality that is ethico-ontological in principle seem to contest the simple theme of the human as an essential being or the nation as a constructed space in time. Community is underlined as an act – one singular being with another singular being. Finitude exposes itself as a gift and exists as communication in this relationship. *Indhirar Dhesam* and *Aindhirar* co-appears or 'compears' together as space and time – of 'Being Singular Plural' (Nancy 2000).

Thass interprets and explains the verses that were quoted and interpreted from *Arungalai Seppu*, *Manimekalai*, *Tolkappiyam*, *Veeracoliyam*, *Silapadhikaram*, *Valayapathi*, *Kundalakesi*, *Sivaka Sinthamani*, and *Soolamani* – fourth-century AD Tamil texts – through speculative etymology. These were palm-scripts that he personally possessed, and he uses them to derive meaning and describe his idea of India. The formations of the languages signalled a significant shift from the oral to the written word, Thass claims. The three languages Pali, Sanskrit, and Tamil were structured only to spread the Buddhist values far and wide. Through etymological connections, Thass' writings rivet the reader to read India's past as originally Buddhist.[25]

This practice of history is a creative exercise – one of hermeneutic extrapolation. That is through a speculative yet referential etymology. He transfers meaning from one word to another, using available sources, as a deconstructive act, for an alternative construction of community. He neglects and discounts all other available explanations of the word, to derive a new one. This mode of hermeneutics is like what Ricoeur has suggested. On reflecting more on interpretation, Ricoeur argues that reading takes place within a community which displays presuppositions and exigencies. And it is in language that the cosmos, desire, and the imaginary reach expression. Hence this practice of hermeneutics is also an attempt for self-understanding by means of understanding others. Ricoeur categorises interpretation as an existence and an operation of thought, adding that existence then is interpreted existence.[26]

Sarithiram as interpretation: critical/creative communitas

Thass' history research, through the dispersal of meaning in Tamil language, is an act of delimitation as well as limitation. For instance, he explains why India is called *baratha gandam* – the Bharath continent. As *Indhiram*, *Indhiyam*, *A/Indhirar*, and *Indhiyargal* were interpreted to treat the Indian nation geographically by an action principle where the way of the Buddha is practised; the Buddha – the *Aindhirar* – was called as the *Varadhar*, a derivative of the word *barathar*, as he preached *ara varam* – a gift-giver of ethical treatise – to his followers. The land was called North and South Bharath, where *varadhar*'s ethical treatise was preached across lands that spoke, at least, 20 languages – including Chinese, Sinhala to Konkani and Tulu, along with Sanskrit, Pali, and Dravida (Tamil), among others. There are two aspects in this historical reconstruction. The first is reading resistantly a given story (deconstruction), and the other is to constitute an alternative cosmology (reconstruction). Names were particularly used to reinterpret a geography of place as practice, to fundamentally counter the meaning attached to locate the caste of a space in India.

In the subverted story of India, Thass knits a web of referential textuality to reconstruct a narrative through delimitation. Firstly, he rejects that India is caste-Hindu in content. While, one may understand that his exercise is neither an anthropological nor a sociological enquiry; it is but a textual communication. By reconstructing Buddhism, he constitutes a textual imaginary. Thass' practice of history subverts, significantly, the idea of institutional history. He de-institutes the definition of space and time as a quantifiable reference to construct a nation. He constitutes his *Indhirar Dhesam* through locating thought-practice as history. Thass locates as well as dislocates his *Indhiyam*, spatio-temporally, by limiting and delimiting the idea of nation and history.

It is limiting because he works to produce his alternative 'history research' in Tamil, though accessing at least four different languages and resources – Tamil, Sanskrit, Pali, and English. He develops a referential, descriptive, prose-register, which shares space with poetry, compendiums and epic-narratives that are transcribed into journalistic print space. He creates a space for knowledge practice, through en-textualisation, so that it is published and spread across, as Tamil prose, within a limited boundary.

The limitation is, also, fashioned by the attempt to create an alternative history, through reading and referring sources that are in contention with the 'authorized' versions of history and historical practice. It competes with other powerful hermeneutics of caste – that of colonial census, and missionaries namely – Christian, Hindu Vaishnavaite, and Vellala Saivaite cosmologies. Thass' methodology, then, is also an attempt to democratise power and practice it, in his own way, to hegemonise an alterity. In his attempt to reconstruct the history of Buddhism through Tamil print, Thass works with concepts and myths in the language to reconstruct meaning by liberating it from a limited history. Thass, while working within a limitation, delimits temporality and spatiality, and plays with these concepts by rendering them into an anti-caste communitas.

For instance, while researching the history of the *Indhirar Dhesam*, Thass delimits the spatial definition of the idea of nation, and goes beyond to construct it as a community identified by practice. In this, his attempt was not to recreate the history through a linguistic, neither Vedic, nor a temporal description of India. Taking for granted, the Buddhist location of his resources, caste-lessness, he argues, is Buddhist, hence, it predates and is against Brahminism. He considers the idea of India as against something, describing it – pre-empting Ambedkar – as a historical conflict between Brahminism and Buddhism. Hence his delimiting as well as limiting practice of history is an ingenious attempt to describe who Indians are. For Iyothee Thass, it is anyone who is outside and against caste immunitas.

Thass' interpretative methods and evidences involved a fusion of philosophical concepts of Buddhism, Buddhist geographical locations, metaphysical descriptions, and Buddhist literatures that were poetic and fictional. However, his interpretative method also seems to bear the mark of a dialectics between Brahminism and Buddhism as a history of conflict. Temporal linearity and spatial description are creatively explored. For instance, he interprets the Vaishnavite myth of Vamana and Bali to reconstruct a different history. Thass locates Mahabali in historical time and space – in the seventh century CE, at Mahabalipuram, through his references. He rejects the Hindu Vamana-Bali myth – the Vishnu avatar story of victory over the *asura* king, out rightly, and does not even discuss the same in his description. For, Thass, this myth is a content to be re-read to create an alternative history.

Thass states that Mahabali is a Buddhist king from Mahabalipuram, who ruled the southern *Baratha Gandam*, 1,200 years ago. He constructed Buddha-*sangha Vihars* throughout his country and towards his later years, attained *nirvana* on an *ammavasai* (lunar eclipse), in the Tamil month *Puratasi*, at the Vengadam hills (now Thiruppathi). As source references, Thass provides information from rock edicts and plates excavated from Vellur (*T*Vol 2 1999: 40–41). For Thass, this recovery of history/interpretation does not stop here. From this information, he reconstructs the dialectical history of conflict between Brahminism and Buddhism, through the references from the Tamil epic *Manimekalai*.

With reference to the untouchable saints within Saivism and Vaishnavism – the Nayanmars and Alvars – Thass recovers a Buddhist history. He takes two untouchable saints – Thirupaanar, the Alvar, and Nandanar, the Nayanmar. Paanar, Thass clarifies through the references, is the son of Mahabali, a Buddhist Bhikku, who was usurped into Vaishnavism as an Alvar. While Nandan, a Buddhist king, was subsumed into Saivism as a Nayanmar – but both only as untouchable Parayar saints. It is a co-option, explains Thass. He places this co-option in the year 1814, where, in a fight over temple rights and social position, the Brahmins and *Kammalas* (the artisan-craftsmen, sculptors, and metal workers in temples) divided the caste society into right- and left-hand castes[27]. Thass describes, that for want of majority, the Parayars were included into the right-hand castes along with the Brahmins. The Buddhist figures from all castes were co-opted as Alvars and Nayanmars, but for the Kammalas, who were in opposition and were co-opted into the left-hand castes. Thus, Thass explains, there are no Kammala Saiva and Vaishnava saints.

Thass, while mixing his resources to construct a Buddhist history of conflict with Vaishnavite and Saivite Hinduism, also plays with temporality. He links the seventh century with the nineteenth century, back and forth, to do a resistant reading of a myth to make it an alternative imaginary and history. He delimits the concept of time by playing with it imaginatively. He re-converts the Alvar and Nayanmar saints into Buddhism. He recovers them for a Buddhist imaginary. His anti-caste hermeneutics treat folk deities such as Muthan, Muniyan, and Karuppan – as names of figures that had an inherent link with the Buddha. Female folk deities such as Kannagi, Kaali, Neeli, Sintha Devi, and Amman were Buddhist nuns, and they were remembered for their service to the community through festivals (Thass cited in Gowthaman 2004: 139–159). Thass temporally divides the history of the country as a space into seven stages of a language, namely – sound period, script period, grammar period, poetry period – that coincided with the *sangham* period, couplets period, epics period, and lyrical period (*Aadhina Kaalam).* Historical time (Kosseleck 2004) was treated as the time (or the evolution) of a language – here Tamil, as Thass interprets time as language.

His historical project, interestingly, re-converts Jesus Christ, Isaiah, Elijah, David, and Moses – all Semitic figures[28] – as those who preached the *Dhamma* ethics, and who were primarily enlightened Buddhist teachers (*T* Vol. 1 1999: 570). He compared the Dalits with the oppressed Jews. Old Testament, particularly the Genesis chapter, was given a Buddhist re-reading by comparing and using content from *Ashtanga* and *Kundalini* yoga. They explained the meaning of the Biblical miracles (*T* Vol. 1 1999: 567–569). His Buddhist interpretation is one of freedom, imagination, and speculative rendering, while comparing the Biblical verses with the Tamil literary verses.

Thass interpreted the Bible through an experiential hermeneutic, where the Dalits could relate with what he wrote. Even if this could have been a translation from works in English, of this kind, during this period, as there were similar Christian–Buddhist comparisons, Iyothee Thass's exercise with space and time was to create an anti-caste cosmopolitan – a communitas which is primarily a gift and an obligation that belongs to everyone and no one owns it. The hermeneutics, embedded in this act, seeks to achieve multiple possibilities. 'The History' of the most oppressed by the caste system is interpreted, by Thass, as antithetical to, but also, independent of Brahmins, or any caste group that would privilege itself by marginalising the outcaste as its/their other.

Hence, for Thass, I argue that interpretation is resistant creativity. In this imaginative exercise he plays with historiography, especially, with concepts such as space and time. He brings together Buddha, Bali, Nandan, Paanan, along with Moses, Isaiah, and Jesus Christ but also different folk deities as well as Vedic heroes in his creative *sarithiram*. He brings them as a part of Buddhist-Jaina-Siddha civilisational legacy against Brahminism. He reinterprets most of the Indian festivals through a Buddhist lens by working on the words and their meaning. He splits them, plays with them, and creatively make them a meaning against caste and Brahminism[29]. It is simultaneously an active re-reading and writing through affective research. It is linked with the creation of a textual imaginary that shares space with memory, loss, and dislocation along with biographical and creative speculation. In this, it is an attempt, from the 'Dalit-Subaltern' political, to gain inroads into historiography, while, dislocating and transforming the Brahminical caste-Hindu regime and location of knowledge practice.

For instance, Thass does not accept the socio-anthropological constitution and description of the word *Parayar*– that they were meek and weak, or they were untouchable, poor, and socially ostracised. These narratives were scientifically premised on descriptive accuracy and evidential historicity. These were, for him, to be rejected and reinvented. In his history research, *Paraya* as a concept is to be derived and reconstituted to nullify the available category. Hence, he works with the word and interprets it imaginatively. He argues that the word *Parayar* is a derivative of the word *piraiyar* or *pirar* (*others*). He argues, through references, that they were 'Others,' the ancient Buddhists – *purva bouddhargal* (*purvam* means ancient as well as holistic), who did not accept the Brahminical caste differences and therefore were condemned by *vesha Brahmanas* (*deceptive Brahmins*) as untouchable Parayars.

Thass claimed that the 'knowledgeable Dravidian Buddhists' were defeated by the 'crooked machinations of *arya mlechhas*' and were relegated falsely as untouchables (Thass cited in Ravikumar and Azhagarasan 2012: xvii). But he also suggests that Parayars were the ones who spoke the truth – *parai* is to speak. Hence anyone who speaks the truth and exposes falsehood were called as the *Parai-yor*. Thass claimed that they were 'moral leaders of the people who relentlessly intervened and exposed the interloper's trickery, greed, and falsity' (Thass cited in Aloysius 2010: 249). A dialectical hermeneutic as a history of conflict between *vesham* and *purvam* through Brahminism and Buddhism as immunitas versus communitas was creatively woven.

Conclusion

Thass' critical exercise with thought, imagination, and history to create an alterity is closely linked with the idea of a 'political community'[30] in practice, emerging from the Subaltern constituency with their own resources in the early twentieth century. Thass reversed the gaze on caste society from the point of view of the outcastes as a Buddhist – *Pirar* – 'the other' who is pre-caste and primarily caste-less. He did not concede Sanskrit as the language of the Brahmins/Aryans and Tamil as the language of the Dravidian stock, as Caldwell and other Oriental philologists, as well as Dravidian nationalists had argued. For him both Sanskrit and Tamil are sister languages of Buddhist origin with Pali as their common source. Thass interpreted that Pali, the language of the Buddha, remained an oral language, but Sanskrit and Tamil became written languages through Panini and Agastyar to spread the words of Buddha.

Thass perhaps sees Tamil, Sanskrit, and Pali as envisaging an anti-caste 'Vernacular Cosmopolitanism' that conjoins notions of local specificity for a universal enlightenment. Thass profusely uses all these languages – Tamil, Sanskrit, and Pali – to create a Buddhist history of India, while not collaborating with the 'British Discovery.' He just uses the available myths, history, folk-narratives, and literature in Tamil. His effort to read history from within the reserves of Tamil language available to the marginalised community, not only strengthens their agency, but also opens new ways to interpret and understand 'culture' beyond caste, and as part of a collective community of experience.

As someone who organised his community in the name of *Sathi Betha Matra Dravida Mahajana Sabha* (*Casteless Dravida Mahajana Sabha*), Thass gave content to the idea of caste-lessness, Buddhism, and Tamil community. This is a concrete agenda that relied not only on self-identification as an emancipatory process, but also was created on the idea of anti-caste communitas as a cosmic imaginary, in early-twentieth-century Tamil society. It was a Buddhist universal, whose material was the local, limited, finite, every day, and untouched.

The anti-caste 'communitas' of Dalits, in the word, gestures towards an autonomous embodiment, beyond just being restricted as a shadow. It counter-looks caste with an oppositional gaze, with a resistant touch, with an act of annihilation. Its struggle against civilisational violence unravels caste's direct, insidious violence, and its chronic inalienable dishonour. It, hence, fashions a 'genealogy of loss' that integrates experience, understands social inheritances, and anchors the living present with a conscious community through civilisational memory.

This chapter through a variety of writings in English and Tamil, wove a conceptual terrain, so as, to explore anti-caste communitas and outcaste experience in south Asia. It proposed that the subaltern thought uses interpretation as a tool to reconfigure notions of space and time that is open, creative, and resistant; hence a critical way to imagine dignified-life from the given position. It puts forward that Dalits have inaugurated and constituted a millennial communitas, of a kind, as a creative opposition to and history against, which has relevance as resistance, the rampant violence and humiliation that oppressively institutionalise living-deaths in the nation today.

Notes

1 Gopal Guru and Sundar Sarukkai's illustrious book *The Cracked Mirror* (2012)is the inspiration for the phrase shadows that travel. The shadow, as one knows, of socially despised castes were also considered polluting in some parts of the Indian subcontinent. However,

in violence and rape, one may understand that, the phenomenon of shadow pollution is cracked, or conveniently broken. Paradoxically, it eludes that in violation 'untouchable' shadows are not really polluting for the dominant castes, as they remap their ideal shadow or the shadow of purity through violence.

2 Gopal Guru uses Henri Lefebvre's category of experiential space and shadow, so as, to illustrate conceptual links between space, body, travel, and caste. Lefebvre argues that space is actually experienced in its depths, as duplications, echoes, or reverberations. He suggests that space is inscribed in the body and then becomes the body's counterpart, as its 'other' (Lefebvre 1984: 184). In other words, it becomes a mirror image or a shadow. Guru underlines that this category is relevant to understand the shadow of an 'untouchable's' body. He clarifies that an untouchable's body as space doubles up as both corporal substance and its shadow. Thus the real and the reflected – the body and the shadow – become equally powerful in mapping the space, in favour of the socially dominant castes (Guru and Sarukkai 2012: 81).

3 *Communitas*, a Latin loan word, has been theorised in cultural anthropology and social sciences, so as to refer to an unstructured community where people are equal, or to the 'spirit' of community. Victor Turner rendered an anthropological use of this term, in order to capture the interplay between social 'structure' and 'anti-structure.' He conceptualised that liminality and communitas are both components of anti-structure in his third chapter (Turner 1969). However, 'communitas' here is inspired by anti/post-Nazi and Stalinist thought, tracing particularly Nancy, Blanchot, and Esposito.

4 *Nandanar's Children* is one of the very few scholarships in Indian Social History which studies a Dalit community's mobility during the colonial period in India. A chapter titled 'Search for Fresh Pastures: Overseas and Internal Migration Patterns of the Tamil Paraiyans in the 19th and 20th Centuries' brilliantly recounts and captures the colonial 'travels,' or displacement of the Tamil Parayars (Basu 2011: 111–164).

5 The colonial army during the second half of the eighteenth century started to form an army establishment in the South, which served both the Parayars and the British. The Parayars since the 1760s and 1770s had constituted the bulk of the foot soldiers in the company army. They found employment in the following years as military depots started functioning from Madras and Trichinopoly (Dutta 2016: 64). Significantly, in the early decades of the nineteenth century, the recruitment in the British army brought about important changes in the self perceptions of the Parayar soldiers (Basu 2011: 160). Serving the company's army provided the Parayars an opportunity to experience the civic equality enjoyed by other subjects of the company. The performance of military rituals and drills instilled in them the idea of belonging to a martial race. The prestige associated with a military uniform paved way to hope that all forms of caste discrimination, the bonds of exploitation and servitude would be eliminated. Dutta argues that these important changes in their engagement with the British army revolutionised the social and political outlook of most of the untouchable castes in the country (65).

6 The term 'conscript' refers to someone who is compulsorily enrolled or drafted for service. The phrase 'conscripts of civilization' was used by the eminent anthropologist Stanley Diamond. He refers it to the 'primitive' cultures that engage in the 'civilization' project becoming 'conscripts of civilization, not volunteers' (Diamond 1974: 204). This is, however, a unilateral view. Although large populations under colonialism could be understood as conscripts, the case with some – like Dalits – seems to have been complex, critical, voluntary, and engaging. Therefore, though the conditions could be theorised as conscripts, but the content is not congruent and agreeable to the same.

7 During Iyothee Thass' time, Mysore and Kolar Gold Field particularly played a very significant role in not only spreading Buddhism but also to start many educational ventures. Dalits in Kolar Gold Field, particularly M.Y. Murugasen, E. Gurusamy, and A.P. Periyasamy Pulavar started *sangha* activities in Marikuppam, (Kolar Gold Field) by 1907. E.N. Ayyakannu started a library and a Buddhist research centre in Kolar Gold Field. These Subaltern activists became pioneers in caste rejection and self-respect marriages in

the early twentieth century. The Siddhartha Printing Press also played a very major role in this emergence. It could be argued that this Dalit movement paved the way to create content for Periyar's self-respect movement in the mid-twentieth century (Gowthaman 2004: 72).

8 It is in this context that Dalit migrations to South Africa, Burma, Ceylon, Fiji, Mauritius, Singapore, Malaysia, Tanzania, and other lands during the nineteenth and twentieth centuries produced interesting shifts for the community. Apart from that, a caste-less cosmopolis was in the making even through internal migration within the subcontinent. It was in the backdrop of the educated and industriously employed in the Madras city, those who were enlisted in the Bangalore cantonment, the miners of Kolar Gold Field, the railway workers of Hubli, the plantation workers of Mercara, the army men of Secunderabad along with the indentured labourers who migrated to other countries, that Tamil Buddhism, the anti-caste public sphere, and the Dalit print could emerge as a movement in the region (Aloysius 1998: 183).

9 When compared, this is similar and significantly in tune with the experience and condition of Blacks and migration. Paul Gilroy's *The Black Atlantic: Modernity and Double Consciousness* (1993) applies a cultural studies approach and provides a study of African intellectual history and its cultural construction of this condition. Gilroy's theme of 'double consciousness' studies how Blacks, due to the cross-Atlantic migration, strive to be both European and Black. Such a scope is beyond the purview of this chapter. However, Gilroy's book offers insight to understand the Dalits' engagement with colonial modernity. In fact, the term 'double consciousness' as a concept developed by the African-American sociologist and intellectual W. E. B. Du Bois in *The Souls of Black Folk* (1903) to describe the felt contradiction between social values and daily struggle faced by Blacks in the United States. Being Black meant, Du Bois argued, being deprived of a 'true self-consciousness.' Blacks often perceived themselves through the generalised contempt of White America. Being a Black as well as an American raised contradiction between American social ideals, which Blacks shared (Du Bois 1903: 1–14).

10 As more studies are recently done on Gandhi's sojourn in South Africa as a subject for critical research, Joseph Leleyveld's controversial book titled *Great Soul: Mahatma Gandhi and His Struggle with India* documents Gandhi's life in South Africa. Largely research on this period is few but for an early article by Dr. James D. Hunt on 'Gandhi and the Black people of South Africa' in *Gandhi Marg*, New Delhi, April–June 1983 which appears to be an important study on this subject. An article by Les Switzer, 'Gandhi in South Africa: The ambiguities of Satyagraha' in *The Journal of Ethic Studies* 14(1), touches on this subject.

11 It is to be noted that Gandhi's idea of 'ideal Bangi' is an attempt to confine the Dalits into the space of toilet literally. And that is probably the lowest point he stoops down to in his understanding of Dalits, losing his humanity forever. He was in fact far removed from understanding Dalits and Africans. This reflects his ghettoising mentality and pretentious universal tendencies.

Even Gandhi's self-toilet-cleaning public stunts, now reinvigorated as 'Swachh Bharath' by the government of India in 2015, reduces Dalits as mere scavenging bodies, forgetting in the process his own food would have been cultivated by their sweat and blood. Perhaps, Gandhi's infantilising and hegemony over Dalits were in fact attempts to deny a level playing human space to Dalits. This is similar to his de-sexualization and subordination of women, through his asexual experiments. In a discussion with Dr. Gajendran Ayyathurai.

12 Ravichandran Bathran's asks searching questions on the many omissions of 'Dalit' as a concept, and also explores the practice of Indian architecture as an embodiment of caste. He asks why toilets are constructed where they are in India, and argues that 'there has been much discussion on toilets, but their location has never been touched upon or discussed' (Bathran 2016: 31–32). Moreover, he states that 'toilets are built in congested or uncomfortable positions while the bathroom and living room are given good attention.

I call the toilet (a place for filth) an outcaste in architecture, which needs an outcaste (untouchable) to always clean it. The stigmas attached to both are closely related to the caste system' (32).

13 However, in a different context Joan Scott, to criticise the category of experience that was mooted in the context of feminist and race studies, contests that 'experience is at once always already an interpretation and something that needs to be interpreted. What counts as experience is neither self-evident nor straightforward; it is always contested, and always therefore political' (Scott 1991: 797).

14 Nancy was troubled by the Nazist and Stalinist dictatorship that enounced 'socialist communes' in the garb of totalitarian regimes. He raised doubts philosophically about the political nature of communities. He asked, hugely inspired by Heidegger and Derrida, how the community without essence can be presented as such. What might a politics be that does not stem from the will to realise an essence? For details see Nancy 1994.

15 Both Nancy and Blanchot produce a deconstructive understanding of community. They depict that community as 'communality' undoes identity and commonality as such. Consequently, this opens – a deconstructive opening – in an essential way a possibility of politics. Apparently, in the western political thought, community as 'communality' is the pre-originary socius which unsettles the contemporary 'being.' Thus, it is the trace of community, in a Derridean way – an arche-community. Without this politics and community are not possible at all, both Nancy and Blanchot seem to theorise. The discussions on the question of community, as that of ethics and ontology, implore the question of community as fundamentally philosophical. The attempt to engage with the other, so as, to conceive the community as related with the other, has been Nancy's and Blanchot's attempt to theorise community. For contemporary philosophical renditions on community and modernity see Little (2002), Lyotard (1986), and Hall (1997).

16 Esposito also poses the idea of 'immunitas' as a contrary or the reverse of communitas, by foregrounding the opposition between community and immunity. Immunitas derives its meaning from a medical-legal language that suggests self-protection and safeguard. Like one immunises oneself against a danger from outside. However, he underlines that the idea of immunity, which is necessary to protect life, when pushed beyond a limit basically negates it. It at once protects and negates life, in a sense suggesting that protection is negation. Hence he states that protection, when pushed beyond a certain limit, forces life into a sort of prison. It armours life so heavily, in that what one loses is not only freedom, but also the real sense of individual and collective existence. Immunity is posed as opposing the spirit of community, according to Esposito. It limits social circulation and exposure. Through this opposition, Esposito, frames communitas as the constitutively exposed character of existence, and not protection (Campbell and Paparcone 2006: 49–56).

17 Iyothee Thassa Pandithar (1845–1914) was born a Dalit from the Parayar community, nevertheless, he contested the category Parayar throughout his life. He floated alternative, open identities such as *poorva Bouddhar* (*Ancient Buddhist*), *Jaadhi pedha matra Tamizhar/Dravidar* (*Caste-less Tamils/Dravidians*), and *Tamil Bouddhar* (*Tamil Buddhist*). Iyotheethaasa Pandithar (*Pandit*) is also termed as Iyothee Thass and Thass in this chapter.

18 Thass' quotations from the *Tamizhan* archives, including those cited in Gowthaman (2004), and from the book Iyotheethaasa Pandithar's *Indhirar Dhesa Sarithiram* (2010) are translated into English by me. The references from *Tamizhan* archives are taken from Aloysius' three edited volumes (1999 and 2003), and they would be cited as *T* with their corresponding volume number and page numbers in this chapter.

19 Likewise, many such figures seem to have worked similar to Thass during the same period in the vernacular regions. Narayana Guru (1856–1928) from Kerala, Bhima Bhoi (1850–1995) in Orissa, Poikkayil Yohannan (1878–1939) in Kerala, and a little earlier Jyotirao Phule (1827–1920) created a hermeneutic of anti-caste communitas in writing.

20 Thass' *Sarithiram* has a unique tale to tell. His narrative of India is originally a Buddhist nation. The very first part of the *Sarithiram* functions as a political template of Buddhist historical materialism, so to speak, which prefigures his examination in later parts of the

series, of the emergence of *mlechhar* (Aryans), their Saivism and Vaishnavism, the destruction of Buddhist kings such as Nandan and Iranyan, the radical opposition of the lay-Buddhists against the pseudo-Brahmins, and the ascension of Manu Dharma Smriti and its dehumanisation of Indian society to the present.

21 *Sarithirangalai aaraichi seiya vendumaeandri karpanaa kadhaigalai alla . . . sarithira aaraichi-yininri sagalavatraiyum usaava vendugiren* [Research just history, not fantasy stories . . . and research nothing but history] (*T* Vol. 1 1999: 573).

22 Ricoeur, through his seminal works, argues that the attempt to structure time through the use of language, in history as well as in fiction, fulfils a narrative function that ultimately leads back to the question of self. The interrelation of understanding and explanation is, thus, described as an ability to reconstruct the internal dynamic of the text, and to restore to its ability to project itself outside itself in the representation of a world that one could inhabit. Hence interpretation, for Ricoeur, is a dialectic of understanding and explanation at the level of sense immanent to the text. Discourse, thereby, never exists for its own sake, for its own glory. He states that in all its uses it seeks to bring into language an experience, a way of living in and of being-in-the-world which precedes it and which demands to be said (Ricoeur 1983: 154).

23 Thass starts his book with the sentence – *indhiram ennum mozhi ainthiram ennum mozhiyin thiribam* ['the word *indhiram* is a reconstructed from the word *ainthiram*'] (Pandithar 2010: 15), but mozhi also means language, in Tamil, and *Thiripu* may mean, to insert and derive.

24 See, Iyothee Thassa Pandithar, *Indhirar Dhesa Sarithiram*. Chennai: Tamil Kudiarasu Publication, 2010.

25 Language, for Thass, becomes the tool through which the thoughts of Buddha were recorded, preserved, and spread. For this purpose, Pali was used as an oral form, and they were transcribed in Sanskrit and Tamil. These languages – one from the Aryan and the other from the Dravidian family of languages – were not fundamentally opposed to each other, for Thass. *Panchsheel* was transcribed into Tamil and Sanskrit. Figures such as Janagar, Vaamadevar, Nandhi, Romar, Kabilar, and Panini were trained in Sanskrit, whereas Agastyar was trained in Tamil. They spread the thoughts of the Buddha in all the four directions. Language was a tool to access different regions and a community of practice. According to Thass, Janagar went to the North, Agastyar to the South, Thirumoolar to the West, Satta Munivar to the East (Pandithar 2010: 6–7).

26 Ricoeur brings the hermeneutic problem onto the phenomenological method. His theory of hermeneutics is inspired by an ontology of understanding and an epistemology of interpretation that treats language as symbol- a structure of signification which a direct, primary, literal meaning designates; and in addition, another meaning which is indirect, secondary, and figurative which can be apprehended only through the first. Hence interpretation, he claims, unfolds the levels of meaning implied in the literal meaning (Ricoeur 2005: 12–17).

27 Right-hand (*Valangai*) and Left-hand (*Idangai*) refer to a caste-based dual classification and division of communities in South Indian society. It was in vogue, arguably, from the eleventh century to the nineteenth century. The *valangai* faction was made up of castes with an agricultural base, while the *Idangai* was made of castes with a manufacturing base. Reportedly, the right-hand faction was numerically superior and politically organised than the left-hand faction in the nineteenth century (Ghurye 1991: 359).

28 It is to be noted that the Buddha, the Christ, Prophet Muhammad – and other Semitic figures – drawing on the sources from the three religions, are the most compared during the twentieth century discourses on world religion, especially in the context of emergent textualities from/on the 'Orient' (Gwynne 2014).

29 Buddha's birth, monk-hood, Enlightenment (*Nirvana*) and death (*Parinirvana*) were all interpreted to be celebrations on *vaikasi pournami*, *maasi pournami*, *panguni pournami* and *margazhi pournami* – days related with the calendar of the moon (*T* Vol. 2 1999: 355).

30 Political community is generally referred as the republic (*res publica*, in Latin, means a public-legal community in relation to Nation-State). However, in the Subaltern context

of resistance, the 'political' implies a field of struggle where contesting groups vie for hegemony. It is 'the antagonistic dimension that can be given a form of expression that will not destroy the political association' (Mouffe 2005: 52).

Works referred

Agamben, Giorgio. 1993. *The Coming Community*, trans. Michael Hardt. Minneapolis, London: University of Minnesota Press.

Agamben, Giorgio. 1998. *Homo Sacer: Sovereign Power and Bare Life*, trans. Daniel Heller-Roazen. Stanford: Stanford University Press.

Aloysius, G. 1998. *Religion as Emancipatory Identity: A Buddhist Movement among the Tamils under Colonialism*. New Delhi: New Age International.

Aloysius, G. (ed.) 1999. *Iyothee Thassar Cinthanaikal* (Thoughts of Iyothee Thassar). 2 Vols. Palayamkottai: Folklore Resources and Research Center St. Xavier's College.

Aloysius, G. (ed.) 2003. *Iyothee Thassar Cinthanaikal* (Thoughts of Iyothee Thassar). Vol 3. Palayamkottai: Folklore Resources and Research Center St. Xavier's College.

Aloysius, G. 2004. 'Transcendence in Modern Tamil Buddhism: A Note on the Liberative in Popular Religious Perceptions.' In Surendra Jondhale and Johannes Beltz (eds.), *Reconstructing the World: B R Ambedkar and Buddhism in India*, pp. 205–220. New Delhi: Oxford University Press.

Aloysius, G. 2007. *Dalit-Subaltern Emergence in Religio- Cultural Subjectivity*. New Delhi: Critical Quest.

Aloysius, G. 2010. 'Vicissitudes of Subaltern Self-Identification: A Reading of Tamizhan.' In Michael Bergunder et al. (eds.), *Ritual, Caste, and Religion in Colonial South India*, pp. 238–274. Halle: Neue Hallesche Berichte 9.

Aloysius, G. 2015. *Iyothee Thassar and Tamil Buddhist Movement: Religion as Emancipatory Movement*. New Delhi: Critical Quest.

Ambedkar, B.R. 1993. 'Waiting for Visa.' In Vasant Moon (ed.), *Dr. Babasaheb Ambedkar: Writings and Speeches*, pp. 661–691. Vol 12. Bombay: Education Department, Govt. of Maharashtra.

Ambedkar, B.R. *Annihilation of Caste with a Reply to Mahatma Gandhi*. www.ambedkar.org/ambcd/02.Annihilation%20of%20Caste.htm. Accessed 26 June 2017.

Ansari, M.T. (ed.) 2001. *Secularism, Islam and Modernity: Selected Essays of Alam Khundmuri*. New Delhi: Sage.

Asad, Talal. 1992. 'Conscripts of Western Civilization?' In C. Gailey Griner (ed.), *Dialectical Anthropology: Essays in Honour of Stanley Diamond*. Vol. 1. Florida: University Press of Florida.

Ayyathurai, Gajendran. 2011. *Foundations of Anti-Caste Consciousness: Pandit Iyothee Thass, Tamil Buddhism and the Marginalized in South India*. Unpublished PhD Thesis. Columbia University: New York.

Balasubramaniam, J. 2016. 'Migration of the Oppressed and Adi Dravida identity Construction Through Print.' *Contemporary Voice of Dalit*, 8(2): 1–6.

Balasubramaniam, J. 2017. *Suriyodhayam Mudhal Udhaya Sooryan Varai: Dalith Idhalgal, 1869–1943* [*From Suriyodhayam to Udhaya Sooryan: Dalit Journals, 1869–1943*]. Nagercoil: Kalachuvadu.

Basu, Raj Sekhar. 2011. *Nandanar's Children: The Paraiyan's Tryst with Destiny, Tamil Nadu 1850–1956*. New Delhi: Sage.

Bathran, Ravichandran. 2016. 'The Many Omissions of a Concept: Discrimination amongst Scheduled Castes.' *Economic and Political Weekly*, 51(47) (November): 30–34.

Benjamin, Walter. 1969. 'Theses on the Philosophy of History.' In Hannah Arendt (ed.), trans. Harry Zohn. *Illuminations*, pp. 253–264. New York: Schocken.

Blanchot, Maurice. 1988. *The Unavowable Community*, trans. Pierre Jorris. Barrytown: Station Hill.

Campbell, Timothy and Anna Paparcone. 2006. '"Bios," Immunity, and Life: The Thought of Roberto Esposito.' *Diacritics*, 36(2) (Summer): 49–56.

Collected Works of Mahatma Gandhi (Electronic Book). 1999. Vols. 1,3, 5, and 8. New Delhi: Publications Division Government of India.

Diamond, Stanley. 1974. *In Search of the Primitive: A Critique of Civilization*. New Brunswick and London: Transaction Publishers.

Du Bois, W.E.B. 1903. *The Souls of Black Folk: Essays and Sketches*. Chicago: A.C. McClurg and Co.

Dutta, Manas. 2016. 'The Army as a Tool for Social Uplift: The Experience of the Paraiyans in the Madras Presidency Army, 1770–1895.' *Social Scientist*, 44(3–4) (March-April): 57–71.

Esposito, Roberto. 2009. *Communitas*, trans. Timothy Campbell. Stanford: Stanford University Press.

Gaon, Stella. 2005. 'Communities in Question: Sociality and Solidarity in Nancy and Blanchot.' *Journal for Cultural Research*, 9(4) (October): 387–403.

Ghurye, G.S. 1991. *Caste and Race in India*. Bombay: Popular Prakashan.

Gilroy, Paul. 1993. *The Black Atlantic Modernity and Double Consciousness*. London: Verso.

Gowthaman, Raj. 2004. *Ka. Iyotheethassarin Aaivugal* [*K. Iyothee Thass' Research*]. Nagercoil: Kalachuvadu.

Guru, Gopal. (ed.) 2009. *Humiliation: Claims and Context*. New Delhi: Oxford University Press.

Guru, Gopal. 2011. 'The Idea of India: "Derivative", "Desi" and Beyond.' *Economic and Political Weekly*, 46:37.

Guru, Gopal and Sundar Sarukkai. (eds.) 2012. *The Cracked Mirror*. New Delhi: Oxford University Press. Gwynne, Paul. 2014. *Buddha, Jesus and Muhammad: A Comparative Study*. Wiley-Blackwell.

Hall, Stuart. 1997. 'Race: The Floating Signifier?' *Media Education Foundation*. www.mediaed.org/transcripts/Stuart-Hall-Race-the-Floating-Signifier-Transcript.pdf. Accessed 26 June 2017.

Kosseleck, Reinhart. 2004. *Futures Past: On the Semantics of Historical Time*, trans. Keith Tribe. New York: Columbia University Press.

Lefebvre, Henri. 1984. *Production of Space*, trans. Donald Nicholson Smith. Oxford: Blackwell.

Leonard, Dickens. 2017. 'One Step Inside *Tamilian*: On the Anti-Caste Writing of Language.' *Social Scientist*, 45(1–2) (January–February): 19–32.

Little, Adrian. 2002. *The Politics of Community: Theory and Practice*. Edinburgh: Edinburgh University Press.

Lyotard, Jean- François. 1986. *The Postmodern Condition: A Report on Knowledge*, trans. Geoff Benning and Brian Massumi. Manchester: Manchester University Press.

Mohan, P. Sanal. 2015. *Modernity of Slavery: Struggles against Caste Inequality in Colonial Kerala*. New Delhi: Oxford University Press.

Mouffe, Chantal. 2005. *On the Political*. London: Routledge.

Nancy, Jean Luc. 1991. *The Inoperative Community*, ed. Peter Connor, trans. Peter Connor et al. Minneapolis, London: University of Minnesota Press.

Nancy, Jean-Luc. 1994. 'Corpus.' In Juliet Flower MacCannell and Laura Zakarin (eds.), *Thinking Bodies*, trans. Claudette Sartiliot. Stanford: Stanford University Press.

Nancy, Jean-Luc. 2000. *Being Singular Plural*, trans. Robert D. Richardson and Anne E. O'Byrne. Stanford: Stanford University Press.

Natarajan, Srividya and S. Anand. (eds.) 2011. *Bhimayana: Incidents in the life of Bhimrao Ramji Ambedkar*. New Delhi: Navayana.

Pandithar, Iyothee Thassa [Thass]. 2010. *Indhira Dhesa Sarithiram [History of Indhirar Country]*. Chennai: Tamil Kudiarasu Publication.

Patterson, Orlando. 1982. *Slavery and Social Death: A Comparative Study*. Cambridge, MA: Harvard University Press.

Rajangam, Stalin. 2016. *Vaazhum Bouddham [Living Buddhism]*. Nagercoil: Kalachuvadu.

Rajesh, V. 2011. 'Patrons and Networks of Patronage in the publication of Tamil Classics, c1800–1920.' *Social Scientist*, 39(3–4) (March–April): 64–91.

Rajesh, V. 2013. *Reproduction and Reception of Classical Tamil Literature: Textual Culture in Colonial Madras*. New Delhi: Cambridge University Press.

Ravikumar and R. Azhagarasan. (eds.) 2012. *The Oxford India Anthology of Tamil Dalit Writing*. New Delhi: Oxford University Press.

Reddy, E.S. 1999. *Gandhi and African in South Africa*. SARP Seminar.

Ricoeur, Paul. 1983. 'On Interpretation.' In Alan Montefiore (ed.), *Philosophy in France Today*. Cambridge: Cambridge University Press.

Ricoeur, Paul. 2005. *The Conflict of Interpretations*, ed. Don Ihde, trans. Kathleen Mc Laughlin. London, New York: Continuum.

Scott, David. 2004. *Conscripts of Modernity: The Tragedy of Colonial Enlightenment*. Durham: Duke University Press.

Scott, Joan W. 1991. 'The Evidence of Experience.' *Critical Inquiry*, 17(4) (Summer): 773–797.

Turner, Victor. 1969. *Ritual Processes: Structure and Anti-Structure*. New York: Cornell University Press.

Viswanath, Rupa. 2014. *The Pariah Problem: Caste, Religion, and the Social in Modern India*. New York: Columbia University Press.

8

DISABILITY AND INTIMACY IN THE MAKING OF MADURAI VEERAN

Shilpaa Anand

Disability discourses in India appear to be intricately intertwined with intimacy. One aspect of this entanglement is apparent in the familiar yet understudied trope of disability as punishment meted out for certain kinds of intimacies, especially those considered to be transgressive for various reasons. Leprosy serves as one instance. Early discourse of leprosy which designates persons affected with leprosy as ritually impure suggests that one of the reasons for being affected by leprosy may be 'bad actions' such as sexual transgressions or violation of kinship taboos. T.A. Wise's colonial commentary on Hindu systems of medicine documents leprosy being attributed to failure in observing prescriptions of abstinence; a man who 'visits his wife before food is digested' (Wise 1845: 259) could contract leprosy. Just as in the leprosy case, bodies marked with impairments such as facial disfigurement or limb damage or amputation have been interpreted in terms of the transgression those bodies may have participated in. Acid attacks on women serve as a contemporary instance of a similar kind, where the retributive facial disfigurement may be perceived as symbolic of spurned love. The Supreme Court of India, invoking a fairly modern notion of disability as a socio response to impairment, recently ruled that acid attack survivors be given the status of disability so that they may benefit from the same socioeconomic protections offered to other disabled people in the country. These instances enable us to inquire into what appear to be persistent interconnections between intimacy and disability to find out how each is constituted by the other and under what conditions.

Taking the figure of Madurai Veeran[1] as its point of focus, this chapter traces the figure through two Tamil folk traditions, *Nontinatakam* and *Madurai Veeran Kathai*, that developed between the seventeenth and nineteenth centuries. With the aim of investigating the relationship between disablement caused by limb amputations and romantic relations considered to be transgressive, the chapter studies the plot, aesthetics, and sociocultural contexts of these two narrative traditions. Several caste-based communities in contemporary Tamil Nadu identify Madurai Veeran as their chief deity and hero.

Nontinatakam, a satiric performative tradition, is loosely translated as cripple-drama or lame-drama. It is a monologue that narrates the adventures of a layman who is punished with limb amputations by the local king for his thievery and amorous escapades. Though the protagonist of the *nontinatakams* is not named as Madurai Veeran, it is widely believed that the figure of Madurai Veeran significantly influenced the figure of the *nonti* (the lame man)[2] in the *nontinatakams*. The *Madurai Veeran Kathai* is in balladic form, sung in praise of the hero, 'Veeran' of Madurai who was known for his bravery in the face of different kinds of adversity. Madurai Veeran was punished with limb amputations similar to the protagonist of the *nontinatakam* because of his audacity to fall in love with an upper-caste woman, the king's daughter. Studying different aspects of these two forms and their prevalence in the Tamil sociocultural landscape, the chapter examines contextual distinctions related to the conceptualisation of intimacy and bodily difference. The chapter attempts to critically investigate *Nontinatakam*'s common assignation as a morality play as well as the intersectionality of caste and disability in due course of the analysis.

Nontinatakam was performed outdoors before large and mixed audiences in front of temples and other religious shrines by a single actor who would perform with one leg folded and tied up at the back to signify his 'nonti' status. For this reason, the *nontinatakam* is also known as *Orraikal Natakam*, literally, 'drama on one and a half legs.' The solo actor, the narrator-protagonist or the *nonti* as he is often referred to, would begin by introducing himself in terms of region, lineage, caste, and action. He would then narrate, in a comic vein, his adventures related to stealing and thieving in risky situations before describing his romantic encounter with a *devadasi*, which would be described in detail. The tale would turn into a lament as he recalled the way the mother of the *devadasi* cheated him by robbing him of his stolen wealth. Penniless he escapes the house of the *devadasi* and in due course is caught and punished by the king for his thieving and romancing. His alternate arm and leg are severed off, and he is left to die. He survives and travels, undertaking great physical hardship, to the shrine/temple, where he supplicates to the shrine of the deity. His devotion is rewarded, and his limbs are restored. The narrative concludes with a song of elaborate praise for the local deity or local ruler.

Given that *nontinatakam* developed as an independent genre, different performances are known by the different towns, shrines, and deities the play is associated with. Each *nontinatakam* is usually known by the name of the deity and/or the name of the place it emerged from. The earliest known *nontinatakam*, the *Ceytakati Nontinatakam* was performed within the context of Tamil Muslim trading society in the early eighteenth century and one of its chief elements is the praise of the Muslim piety of the ruler of Kilakkarai, Citakkati (Vink 2015). The twentieth-century *nontinatakams* took a turn towards nationalism; one of the two that belong to this period is *Gandhi Carittira Nonti Cintu* (*Nontinatakam* based on the life of Gandhi). It is estimated that there are 44 written *nontinatakams*, available as palm-leaf manuscripts, of which only 15 have been printed; the others still exist in palm manuscript form (Maruthamuthu 1998). The present chapter draws on two *nontinatakams*, *Tinkalur Arulmalai Nontinatakam* (late eighteenth century) and *Tiruppullani Nontinatakam* (nineteenth century).

The *Madurai Veeran Kathai*, also known as the *Maturaiviracuamikatai*, is a folk ballad form that narrates the story of Madurai Veeran, a bandit who became the hero of Madurai in the seventeenth century under the reign of Tirumalai Nayakkar between 1623 and 1659 (Shulman 1985). Sometimes Veeran is mistaken for a member of the Kallar community, which was known as a 'bandit' caste, taking from the word *kallan*, which means 'thief,' as well as a warrior caste known for their professional role as guards of royalty. However, in the story[3] of Madurai Veeran, the hero is not born within this caste but is abandoned by royal parents and later adopted by a couple of the Cakkaliyar caste, a caste that was traditionally involved in leatherwork and shoemaking and was considered to be 'untouchable.' Veeran grows up in the Cakkaliyar household. On duty as a guard of the princess Pommi (the daughter of Pommana Nayakkan) in the forest, he falls in love with her. After his assignment as forest guard ended and Pommi has returned to the palace, Veeran longs for her and steals into the palace one night only to escape with Pommi. The king's army follows and finds the lovers and in the ensuing battle Veeran defeats the army and kills the king.

Madurai Veeran and Pommi move to Tiruchhirapalli where the king welcomes them and Veeran becomes responsible for subduing the bandit caste of Kallar who were known to trouble and rob travellers. Veeran's valiant actions bring him to Madurai where the king Tirumalai Nayakkar appoints him once again to defeat the Kallar. Veeran succeeds and to reward him for his victory, the king sends a troupe of dancing girls. Madurai Veeran falls in love with Vellaiyammal, one of the dancers and tries to abduct her from the Meenakshi temple. He is caught by the guards who mistake him for a member of the Kallars and he is punished with amputations of an arm and a leg. Both Vellaiyamal, his new lover, and Pommi, his wife rush to his side as he is dying. In the interim his true identity becomes known and Tirumalai Nayakkar remorsefully prays to goddess Meenakshi for Veeran's limbs to be restored. His limbs grow back but Veeran has resolved to die as he believes it was ordained by god. He beheads himself at the feet of Meenakshi. Pommi and Vellaiyammal with the consent of the king jump into a pit of fire.

On realising that his death had not been ritualised, the dead Veeran laments to goddess Meenakshi. Instructed by her, he appears in the king, Tirumalai Nayakkar's dream as an untouchable and wanders through the city disrupting people's lives. When Tirumalai Nayakkar presents himself before the deities Siva and Meenakshi seeking redressal of the recent troubles he learns that they have been caused because Madurai Veeran's death was not suitably propitiated. The king then establishes a temple for the worship of Madurai Veeran and the worship of the hero of Madurai, installed at the entrance of several shrines across the city continues to date. Madurai Veeran is considered to be the *kula deivam* (caste deity) of several caste groups, to this day, in the Madurai region including the Kallar who he defeats as per the story.

The hero's courage to transgress various boundaries, of social and sexual norms as well as caste norms, made him synonymous with fearlessness (Shulman 1985). This chapter refers to two other retellings of the Madurai Veeran story, the 1956 film *Madurai Veeran* directed by D. Yoganand as well as the Adundhatiyar historian Ezhil Elangovan's account titled 'The Murder of Madurai Veeran and the Palace of Thirumalai Nayakkar,' published in 2013 in *No Alphabet in Sight: New Dalit Writing from South India*, edited by Satyanarayana and Tharu. The latter, it may be noted, firmly locates Madurai Veeran within Dalit historiography and as an important figure in Dalit cultural politics.

Disability as punishment

Disability studies discourse is critical of the discursive construction of disability as punishment and strongly criticises such conceptualisation as belonging to the religious model or moral model of disability. The conceptualisation of disability in value-laden terms where the presence of blindness, speechlessness, or multiple limbs is recognised as symbolic of divine intervention either as blessing or curse is referred to as the moral model or religious model of disability. Disability historiography posits the moral model as chronologically prior to the medical and social models thereby characterising it as a pre-modern discursive framing of disability (Hamraie 2015; Anand 2016). Disability scholarship on Christian traditions has delineated the history of the west as dominated by the moral model in the medieval and early modern periods. Studies of the bible explicate how divine interventions that heal an individual's body of diseases and deformities also absolve them of their guilt and sin. Charity, within the same discourse, figures as an act of absolution and enhances the status of the charitable person to a position of divinity or super-human capacity.

Contemporary disability studies scholarship in India has identified different ways in which attributing one's disability to past actions has remained a persistent trope of engaging with disability in the Indian context. According to Anita Ghai, disability is comprehended as 'inherent in the mind or body' (Ghai 2015: xix) with two dominant modes of cultural frames, one that conceptualises disability as a 'lack' or 'flaw' and another that associates it with 'deceit, mischief and devilry' (Ibid.). Ghai explains that 'disabled people sometimes are depicted as suffering the wrath of God and being punished for misdeeds that either they or their families have committed – a kind of penance or retribution for past misdeeds' (Ibid.). Similarly, highlighting the dynamics of the 'religious model,' Nilika Mehrotra contends,

> in the South and South-East Asian context, *religious model* has been found to be influential in articulating disability beliefs and practices. According to this model, disability is seen as divine punishment inflicted upon an individual as a result of the sin committed by the disabled person in current or the previous births and explains the source of disability as invested in the supernatural forces.
>
> *(Mehrotra 2013: 40)*

While such association of disability with punishment is recurrent within mythopoetic thought, it is also known to shape everyday discourse and praxis of disability in several non-Western contexts. Mehrotra cites examples from Kenya and China where, much like the Indian context, the discourse of disability is dominated by discussions of causality thus making past actions a significant part of the discussion. Among the Maasai in Kenya, an impairment is viewed 'as a projection on the human body of social or cosmic disorder, a fact of life or misfortune, a curse, a result of sorcery or a consequence of the behaviour of the father or the mother' (Ibid.). Within the more traditional Chinese context where the discourse of disability was also dominated by a narrative of causality, 'having a person with a disability was believed to bring shame and guilt to the family' (Ibid.). Thus, everyday conversations about disability are governed by a focus on explanations for disability rather than on ways of addressing it.

In Anglo-European-American contexts, the discourse of disability is dominated by narratives of addressing or responding to disability. Responses to disability in these contexts are known to have shifted from the 'charity model' or 'moral model' where the response was a combination of pity, fear and charity was meted out to the individual, to that of medicalising disability by making the individual with disability, the entity that had to be treated so that the disability may be removed, decreased or alleviated. Given this historical progression, the contemporary, more desirable responses to disability are framed as the 'social model' response where the action taken is on the physical and social environment of the individual with disability as well and not the individual alone. That all the three approaches to disability are approaches dominated by questions related to 'solving' the issue of disability has not been highlighted in disability studies scholarship. Nevertheless, what has remained at the fore is the progression inherent to this framework, that there is evidence of a shift from a charitable response to a medical redressal to a social-contextual approach. Given the emphasis on progression, responses to disability in all cultural contexts have come to be evaluated on the basis of the progression, rather than in terms of the dominant discursive framework. The discursive dominance of certain narrative frames is, however, a significant constitutive aspect of culturally specific conceptualisation of disability (Devlieger 1995). Delineating this difference of discourse is crucial as misconceptions or conflations accrued in designating both the Anglo-European American West's approach to disability and the approach of certain non-Western contexts to disability as belonging to the so-called religious model or 'moral framework' may be avoided.

Disability-as-punishment is a category that emerges distinctly in different historico-cultural contexts. Given that every emergence of this category is particular to social, historical, geographical, and cultural factors, the present chapter examines this category within the literary and cultural discourses pertaining to Tamil discourse in the seventeenth through nineteenth centuries.

Nontinatakam's place within disability scholarship and the anxiety of conflation

M. Miles, a disability historian who focuses on disability in non-western traditions, particularly the South Asian context, compiled an annotated bibliography of sources in 2008 (*Glimpses of Disability in the Literature and Cultures of East Asia, South Asia, the Middle East & Africa. A Modern and Historical Bibliography*, with some annotation) which lists two entries related to *nontinatakam*. One is Kumur B. Selim's entry in the *Encylopedia of Disability* (2006), which characterises the dramatic form as a 'morality tale traditionally performed as street theatre in South-East India, featuring a rascal who enjoys crime and immorality, before being punished by amputation of a leg and maybe an arm' (Miles 2008). The second reference is to David Shulman's well-known critical work, *The King and the Clown in South Indian Myth and Poetry* (1985), which is annotated as containing commentaries on the prevalence of 'lame' and 'cripple' kings as a popular literary trope. *Nontinatakam* is translated as 'cripple-drama' in the works that Miles refers to. Selim's encyclopaedia entry designates the performance tradition as a morality tale drawing attention to the miracle element in the plot when the limbs of the protagonist are restored as he reaches the temple built for the deity and appeals to be forgiven for his misdeeds. The characterisation of *nontinatakam* as a play that presents the amputations as punishment for his wrongful actions firmly links it to the notion of disability as punishment. Tamil literary scholarship had consistently marked this minor dramatic form as akin to the morality plays of medieval Anglo-European society. More recently, *nontinatakam*'s significance in terms of the moral or religious model of disability has begun to gain popularity among Tamil scholars.

In the *nontinatakam*, the *marukal-marukai* (alternate arm and leg) amputations is imposed as a punishment on the protagonist for the robbery he commits at the king's palace as well as for his romantic involvement with the *devadasi*. But it is important to think of the disablement he experiences in context to see this text in the light of the disability discourse. While the dominant reception of the plot within the disability discourse places it as a linear narrative of 'moral' punishment for his 'immoral' actions of thieving and adultery, a contextual reading of the text within the tradition of Tamil literary culture and as participant in the caste discourse enables a more layered understanding of disablement due to bodily difference.

In the *Tinkalur Arulmalai Nontinatakam* (Maruthamuthu 1998), Pakaletti, the protagonist-narrator appears to be a trickster-bandit whose profession it seems is to steal from the rich. He travels from kingdom to kingdom, travelling as far as Brindavan, stealing the riches of the palaces. In each episode, he invokes the local deity, but most often Murugan of Arulmalai, to assist him in his endeavours. He tricks guards at palaces and other vigilant people by frequently disguising himself as a mendicant traveller. Each episode of thieving is followed by his return to the temple-dancer or *devadasi*'s house where amorous episodes of lovemaking between Pakaletti and the dancer, Kettimutal are accompanied by the dancer's mother robbing Pakaletti's loot. Kettimutal and her mother are presented as scheming and conniving opportunists who take advantage for Pakaletti's penchant for the dancer. Assuming the disguise of a fakir he enters the cavalry barracks of General Hussain, near Mysore. He steals the most physically perfect horse from these barracks when he is chased down by the guards. Pakaletti considers the destiny enforced by Shani, the god Saturn as responsible for his getting caught. While the soldiers who catch him demand his death as punishment, the benevolent general restricts his punishment to severing his right leg and left hand.

The pain that Pakaletti suffers makes him realise that this was his punishment for stealing and he invokes the deity of Arulmalai. As the plot progresses, Pakaletti meets Brahmins travelling from Benaras who are on their way to Tinkalur Arulmalai to visit the deity. Having learnt of the reasons for Pakaletti's amputated condition, they advise him to visit Murukan of Arulmalai and worship him so that his limbs may grow back. They treat his wounds with medicinal herbs and make a crutch out of a tree branch so that he may walk to the shrine. The lame Pakaletti, with crutch, completes his journey to the shrine of Murukan and supplicates before the deity praising his greatness and benevolence. His prayer is answered and his limbs grow back, and he is given the title 'The Nonti of Tinkalur,' literally, 'the lame of Tinkalur.'

On reviewing certain key aspects of this *nontinatakam*, we find that it is Pakaletti's particular action of stealing a horse from the army that brings him the fate of the amputation. The amputations may also be regarded in the context of his horse-riding, something he could not have done with the limb amputations. While the pain of amputation teaches him that he was being punished for his stealing of the horse, there is no moral that is drawn out within the text itself as the play proceeds to give an account of the author in first person and concludes with the 'nonti's' wedding celebration. It may be significant to note here that the protagonist's invocation of various deities before he executes his burglary indicates that certain forms of stealing were considered professional practices and not designated as immoral action as in the Western-Christian tradition. In the *Palani Nontinatakam*, the deities invoked by the protagonist assist him in identifying houses that can be burgled. These include houses that do not feed refugees seeking shelter and houses of people not committed to the worship of god as well as those who terrorise noble citizens (Jayalakshmi and Maruthamuthu 2007). Intriguingly the protagonist is instructed to avoid, among others, 'helpers of poor and needy weaklings' (Jayalakshmi and Maruthamuthu, 49) probably a reference to the Nonti serving as a test case so that people responding to his disabled status could be identified appropriately.

The protagonists of most of the *nontinatakams* appear to belong to the Kallar community of professional burglars (Jayalakshmi and Maruthamuthu 2007). This is explicitly stated in the text of the *Tiruppulani Nontinatakam*, where Coracuran, the hero, introduces himself to the crowd as a member of the Kallar community in the early part of the play. Given these evidences within the texts, it can be argued that thieving within the context of the *nontinatakam* and the Tamil sociocultural context of the time is not to be mistaken for thieving as it is conceptualised within the Western normative sense as an immoral or criminal act that elicits divine or legal punishment but as a way of life ensconced within ethical action. Criminalisation of the Kallar community has been variously attributed to colonial forms of governance that were prevalent at the time (Blackburn 78; Pandian 2005). Comprehending the *nontinatakam* within the frame of the 'moral model' of disability appears to be inadequate in the light of the contextual conceptualisations of acceptable and appropriate actions. 'Nonti' it may be noted is an honorific title presented to Pakaletti. As Martha Rose suggests in her study of bodily conditions in the context of Greek antiquity, individual instances of punishment have to be regarded within specific context and not assumed to be normative or normal (2003). Rose draws attention to different social responses that were elicited by the same kind of impairment to make a case for contextual understanding of impairment where the disablement experienced may be related to the cause of one's impairment and what one's position is in society (2003). Her contention may be extended to be indicating the problem of universalising that appears to be inherent to disability theorising as ensconced in the models approach.

Devlieger points out that, culturally specific notions of bodily difference and disablement may be gleaned by noting the nature of disability discourse and rhetoric in different contexts. He finds that in Songye society, the nature of the discourse related to disability is predominantly focused on causal explanations. Western discourse of disability, in contrast, is centred on addressing the disability. These discourses are related to distinct epistemic frameworks that have distinct ways of making sense of bodily difference. Devlieger's observations enable us to ask whether the designation of *nontinatakam* as part of the moral model discourse is a result of discursive framing that is inherent to Western epistemology.

Costs of intimacy

Intimacy between the *nonti* and the *devadasi* in the *nontinatakams*, and between Vellaiammal and Veeran in the *Madurai Veeran Kathai*, presents itself in various forms through the narratives. Protagonists of the *nontinatakams* describe their erotic encounters with the *devadasi* in explicit detail. In the *Tiruppullani Nontinatakam*, Coracuran, the protagonist, is punished for kidnapping a *devadasi* and is characterised primarily as a womaniser. When the protagonist-narrator recalls to the audience his encounter with the *devadasi*, the sexual attraction in their intimacy is narrated in great detail. Parts of the *nontinatakam* take on the traditional mode of *sringara*, the performative expression of physical beauty and erotic love which was a major part of *devadasi* performative traditions.

The *Tiruccentur Nontinatakam* details the lovemaking between Matappuli (the protagonist) and Citampararatnam (the *devadasi*) by emphasising seduction strategies employed by the *devadasi* while simultaneously underscoring the heartlessness of the *devadasi*'s mother who fulfils the caricature of the recurrent figure of the *vesyamatr*, literally, the mother of the *devadasi* (Shulman 1985: 374).

Intercaste romance seems to be the centre of the *Madurai Veeran Kathai*. Retellings of the *Madurai Veeran Kathai* highlight the mutual love between Veeran who was brought up in a Chakkaliyar (an 'untouchable' caste) household and the daughter of the king. While the *nontinatakams* foreground the transgressive nature of the romantic relations that the heroes have with the *devadasi* and other women, the *Madurai Veeran Kathai* celebrates the risks that Veeran takes which serve to endear him to Pommi and underscore his valiant character to the audience of the story. The

Madurai Veeran Kathai highlights two transgressive romances – one, Veeran's romance and elopement with Pommi, the daughter of the king; two, Veeran's romance with Vellaiammal, the *devadasi* in the king of Madurai, Thirumalai *Nayakkar*'s court. The latter is framed as a transgressive act because most retellings portray Vellaiammal as Thirumalai *Nayakkar*'s favourite danseuse and in some she is also identified as his lover. Narsappan, Pommi's suitor and the king's advisor, enraged by vengeance later tricks Thirumalai *Nayakkar* of Madurai into punishing Veeran by framing the latter's sympathy and infatuation towards the dancer as a transgressive act that amounts to 'stealing' Vellaiammal, the king's favourite dancer.

Yoganand's film *Madurai Veeran* (1956) illustrates the instances of caste hierarchy and untouchability explicitly. Early in the film when Veeran saves the drowning Pommi, she is warned not to inform the king about the true identity of her saviour as that would result in her being excommunicated from the kingdom as she was touched by a lower-caste man. In another instance, she causes great anxiety to the army chief by visiting the *cheri*, that section of the town where the 'untouchable' communities lived. Nevertheless, it must be recalled that Veeran, in the dominant narrative, is after all a man of royal birth and so these transgressions of caste boundaries (Shulman 1985) are in fact not transgressions at all! In the film, the portrayal of the second romance betrays that Vellaiammal had no knowledge of the king's interest in her. She falls in love with Veeran and is shocked to learn subsequently of Thirumalai *Nayakkar*'s romantic interest in her.

Yoganand's film highlights the tragedy of Vellaiammal cinematically with the use of a dramatic monologue in which Vellaiammal, in love with Veeran but forced to be Thirumalai *Nayakkar*'s beloved, contemplates suicide. The dancer's anklets suddenly appear to her as a prisoner's ankle cuffs, her ornate bangles nothing but a poisonous snake and the gold necklace but a noose. She questions the position of the court dancer as the king's prisoner, a mere toy through whom he demonstrates his authority and power. Her liberation then is only possible through a dagger that would end her life. It is at this moment that Veeran comes to her rescue and takes her as *manavi*, literally meaning soulmate but also used to designate wife.

Veeran, in Ezhil Elangovan's non-fictional account is reclaimed as the rescuer of Vellaiammal who is predominantly represented as the court dancer that Veeran falls in love with and abducts. It is most likely that the *nontinatakam*s draw on this episode of Veeran's life for their main storyline. Elangovan's account critiques these characterisations because they serve only to falsely justify Veeran's actions as deserving of brutal retribution.

Elangovan's reclaiming of Madurai Veeran as an important figure of Arunthatiyar history discredits the high caste birth of Veeran by not acknowledging that element of the story. His account focuses on how the dominant narrative circulated by scholars of the palm-leaf manuscripts about Veeran is grounded in caste hierarchy as it charges him with abducting Vellaiammal variously presented as the king, Thirumalai Nayakkar's lover, as a court dancer, a maidservant and as his daughter and by doing so tries to justify the quantum of punishment given to Veeran. He contests each of the several identities that Vellaiammal is cast in by drawing attention to the casteism inherent in these characterisations.

Examining the hypothesis that Vellaiammal, according to some of the manuscripts was a maidservant, Elangovan alleges that maid servants were treated poorly by the royal families and it is unlikely that the king would serve punishment of such a harsh variety to someone who abducted a woman of such low status. Discrediting the accounts of Vellaiammal being a woman of the king's harem Elangovan states that women of the harem would have been in pursuit of the king's wealth and not have found elopement with Veeran attractive given his low economic status. He dismisses the idea that Vellaiammal may have been Thirumalai Nayakkar's daughter because of the difference of region and language evident in the Tamil and Telugu names of Vellaiammal and Thirumalai Chavuri Nainu Ayyalugaru (Thirumalai Naykkar's original name) respectively. However, if Vellaiammal is taken to be a court dancer, he states, the story of Veeran taking Vellaiammal is then an act of rescue and not abduction. The hardships she may have faced due to the pathetic conditions the *devadasi*s lived in cannot be ignored. They were nothing but sexual slaves of upper-caste men. Feminist historians and critics have severally underscored the exploitative nature of the *devadasi* tradition as practised in different parts of India (Anandhi 1991; Nair 1994; Pati 1995; Chakravarti 2010).

*Devadasi*s who were known as '*tevaradiyals*' or 'slaves of the god' in the Tamil region, later came to be known as '*thevadial*' meaning prostitutes, thereby carrying negative connotations that were absent from the previous designation (Anandhi 1991: 739). The *devadasi*s were committed to the temple by a ritual ceremony of marrying the deity of the temple before they attained puberty. Another nuptial ceremony was performed after a *devadasi* attained puberty by which she acquired the status of *nityasumangali*, 'one who is free from widowhood' (Ibid.). A *devadasi* chose her patron hereafter, someone who would also be her sexual partner without having to marry her; the patron was usually a person controlling the temple income, a Brahmin or a non-Brahmin landlord (Anandhi 1991). In the medieval period, the *devadasi*s enjoyed a high status as well as positions of power as they were primarily associated with temples. Part of the temple's wealth was considered to be their property. Anandhi contends that some of the *devadasi*s 'were even entrusted with the temple management as trustees and as administrators of temple funds' (Ibid.). Later, trusteeship of the temples was grabbed by Brahmins and the *devadasi*s lost their high status (Ibid.). A point of interest to us would be the way in which sexual relations that the *devadasi*s could have were prescribed by landed patrons (Anandhi 1991). S. Anandhi provides details of how the *devadasi*s could not maintain sexual relations with the men who surrounded them:

> These men of the *devadasi* community were known as 'melakkarars', 'nayanakarars' and 'nattuvanars', who were either born to *devadasi*s or recruited for temple service as musicians. Among these musicians, the 'cinnamelam' (small drum) group was associated with *devadasi*s dance and music performances. Sexual contact between this group of men and *devadasi*s was prohibited. The

> 'periyamelam' (big drum) group, known as nagaswaram players, provided music for other ceremonies and rituals and thus were not entirely dependent on the *devadasis* tradition. They had to depend on the landed classes for patronage. This again prohibited any sexual contact between *devadasis* and these musicians. In short, it was not a free flow of *devadasis*' desire which marked out the system, but its almost exclusive control by the landed patrons.
>
> *(Ibid.)*

Vellaiammal's desire for Veeran is also a prohibited desire as he was after all a *dalapati* or chief of the king's army, not a landed patron or a Brahmin controlling a temple's wealth. The tragedy of not being able to possess the one she desired and loved is at the heart of the *Madurai Veeran Kathai* tradition. Her sacrifice of giving up her lover is however, overwhelmed by the story of Veeran's sacrifice for the safety and security of the kingdom.

The disability of *marukal-marukai* amputations

Disability studies discourse is dominated by studies that resist portrayals of disability as an unfavourable or undesirable condition given the academic discourse's commitment to the 'movement framework' or a rights-based approach. The very emphasis of the social model framework is to reject social constructions of disability as undesirable and reform processes that constitute disability negatively. Given this predominance, drawing attention to the story of Madurai Veeran where disability emerges as an undesirable condition, would be an unpopular move in the scholarly climes of disability research. Retaining its attention on the fact that disability and disablement may be conceptualised differently in different cultural contexts, it might be significant to examine closely the contours of the emergence of disability caused by alternate limb amputations as an unfavourable condition. Being located at the intersections of two other conceptual axes of caste and intimacy, it is imperative that disability be studied here as constituted by and constituting the other two conceptual discourses and not independently. What follows is a review the *marukal-marukai* amputation as manifest in the lives of the different protagonists as well as its social configuration given the literary and cultural responses their stories attract.

If Veeran is a Kallar then the retribution of *marukal-marukai* imposes severe limitations on the profession of burgling or of keeping guard (*kaval*), both identified as occupations of the Kallar at different times and in different accounts of Veeran. It may be recalled that thieving was located within a social system that did not problematise it within moral or legal domains. This would be true of all the *nontinatakams*. Given that the nontinakam best fits the description of popular culture, the *marukal-marukai* amputation has a performative significance that cannot be overlooked – the performer is known to have tied one leg behind his back to perform the nonti. *Nontinatakam* is located within Cirrilaikiyam, or minor literary traditions, in the context of Tamil literary history. The performative form belongs in the literary category of *Cintu*. Aesthetically, it is identified as belonging to the category of *ellal* or ridicule. Was being nonti or lame then constitutive of the comic element of the time? What exactly was the object of ridicule? What was laughable – elements of the plot, the ribaldry of the narrative, or the performance that may have bordered on slapstick and clownery? If it was indeed the plot, then was it that a thief had been amputated and could not thieve anymore? Or was it that a thief was being in turn robbed by the *dasi*[4] and her mother's cunning? Or was it that a womaniser had been amputated, thus sounding the doom of all his cavorting? If not the plot, then were the comic elements dependent on individual performers and their rendition of the tale – the buffoonery of hobbling while narrating a tragic-comic tale? The script of the play throws up several moments that may have unmistakably caused the laughter – the descriptions of the *nonti* stealing into the houses and palaces to steal their riches; the thief being robbed by the *dasi* and her mother; the preparation of the magic potion that makes the *nonti* unconscious and his subsequent waking up to the fact of being robbed; a reversal of fortunes as the *nonti* and the *dasi* stealthily robbed each other in turn.

The *nontinatakam* tradition frames disability as undesirable in another way as well, if we consider the fact that the play may be read as a miracle play. Every nontinakam concludes with the amputated limb's of the protagonist being restored by the local deity, thus bringing glory to the deity who performed this miraculous act. The story of the nonti then stands as a 'narrative prosthetic' (Mitchell and Snyder 2000) that only consolidates the desire for a whole body. David Mitchell and Sharon Snyder argue that disability's persistent presence in literary and cultural texts serves as a corrective narrative that is forwarded to 'resolve or correct – to "prostheticize" [. . .] – a deviance marked as improper to a social context' (Mitchell and Snyder 2000: 53). The protagonist's *nonti* status is improper considering that the social context portrayed in the *nontinatakams* is one that does not accommodate, if one could call them, at the risk of sounding anachronistic, orthopaedic disabilities such as those of the nonti. The deity, be it Murugan as in the *Tinkalur Arulmalai Nontinatakam*, or Thirumal as in the *Tiruppullani Nontinatakam*, or Meenakshi if we consider the *Madurai Veeran Kathai* resolve the disablement experienced by the *nontis* with the boon of limbs. The corporeal restoration of the *nonti* also corrects the social disablement of the *nontis* evident in the fact that his condition of *marukal-marukai* amputations is a cause of textual and metatextual mirth symbolic of social derision.

The audience response to the *nonti's* limping on stage seems to be offset by other roles that the *nonti's* disabled status serves. Take for instance, the Brahmin pilgrims in the *Tinkalur Arulmalai Nontinatakam* who don't ignore the *nonti* writhing in pain but fashion a tree branch into a crutch for him and take him along with them on their pilgrimage to visit the deity of Arulmalai. Here, we can say, drawing on Ato Quayson's typology of disability representation (2007), the *nonti's* disability works as test of the Brahmins' ethical action. The pilgrimage assumes a symbolic significance fitting the familiar trope of 'journey as destination.' Thus the spiritual fulfilment the pilgrims attain is not by reaching the destination of the temple but by performing ethical actions along their long journey. The interaction between the nonti and the Brahmins is reminiscent of the Jaina tradition of *nirvicikitsa* as well, where one's response to the sight of disability enables the Jaina a higher spiritual status. Not responding with disgust to another's disfigured status facilitates the Jaina's overcoming of disgust as an affective state thereby taking the individual closer to the achievement of detachment from worldly emotions, a desirable spiritual state (Miles 2000).

Social contexts portrayed in the texts studied, cannot be adequately assessed by viewing responses to limb amputations as reactions to impaired conditions alone. Let's take the case of the figure ofVeeran as a member of the 'untouchable' or Chakkaliyar/Arunthatiyar community to see his amputated body as a marker of caste-based violence. The *marukal-marukai* amputations serve as retribution for aspiring to transgress one's caste boundary. What is being punished here is the 'audacity' of a lower-caste man to aspire to romance a princess and to take the king's lover as his own. The corporal punishment of wounds, torture, and amputation serve their metaphorical purpose of reminding the transgressor and all other potential transgressors to the cost of violating caste boundaries. The loss of an arm and a leg would not only limit the Chakkaliyar's professional activity of leatherwork and other manual labour but it would also result in him bleeding to death. *Marukal-marukai* amputations here are euphemisms for a painful and violent death. Elangovan's account stresses the death ofVeeran as a crime, as 'murder' (2011) of a lower-caste man by powerful upper-caste people.

In the tradition of the Madurai Veeran Kathai, it is the tragic vein of literary representation that brings to the fore his impaired body as symbolic of the so-called 'downfall of the hero' brought about unfairly by the king, Thirumalai *Nayakkar*. Veeran's subsequent death from the amputations is presented as martyrdom, as a sacrifice he makes for the members of his community. Yoganand's film presents this sacrificial figure ofVeeran as meeting an unjust end. Pommi and Vellaiammal's mourning of his death, in the text of the film, is framed within the melodramatic form thus accentuating his death as sacrifice and heroism. The public spectacle of his bleeding amputations leads the spectators to become awe-struck – the amputations then appear to facilitate his heroic status.

The theme of sacrifice runs through the different retellings. Shulman's summary of the *Madurai Veeran Kathai* tells us that Veeran's ghostly presence haunts Thirumalai *Nayakkar* after Veeran has died from the amputations. Veeran's death was not propitiated according to custom and he returns to demand an explanation. Driven to account for his failure in appropriately propitiating Veeran's death, Thirumalai *Nayakkar* seeks goddess Meenakshi's forgiveness and asks for the restoration of Veeran to life. Upon returning to the world of the living, Veeran decides to give up his life in an attempt to take rightful responsibility for his transgressive actions. His sacrifice is thus celebrated. Elangovan's recovery history ofVeeran characterises his sacrifice as one that symbolises his fight against casteist violence meted out to the Arundhatiyar. Elangovan's primary contention is with the writers of the palm-leaf manuscripts who he accuses of neglecting Veeran's role in ending casteist violence in the kingdom of Thirumalai *Nayakkar* and not duly acknowledging the heroic role played by Veeran in ending ritualistic human sacrifices of Arunthatiyar men, women, and children by the king's builders (2011).

Apart from being symbolic of Veeran's sacrifice, can the *marukal-marukai* amputations not be read as symbolic of punishable intimacies? Veeran's amputations, it may be noted, mark the end of Vellaiammal's desire as well. They punish his body but also her daring to desire his body. What is undesirable is not just Veeran's physically amputated condition but the impositions those amputations simultaneously place on Vellaiammal's desirability. The disability experienced as a result of the amputations is not configured as an individual person's experience of corporeal disablement but is reflective of how disablement within the Tamil context of these cultural texts works as at the level of interconnected body selves.

Conclusion

Adopting a disability studies approach to *Nontinatakam* and *Madurai Veeran Kathai*, two literary-cultural traditions that have been extensively studied as part of folk culture, Tamil history and more recently within Dalit studies, this chapter has argued for a contextual understanding of bodily differences and their worlds of signification. Motivated by the question, 'how do different historic-cultural contexts frame disablement,' this chapter has attempted to explicate how two Tamil cultural traditions based on the figure of Madurai Veeran have framed the disability of *marukal-marukai* amputations. Finding that the discourse of cross-caste intimacy is deeply intertwined with disabling retribution, the chapter has sounded the limitations of disability studies approaches to categories of 'undesirable disability' or disability-as-punishment. While acknowledging the anxiety inherent in engaging with the trope of disability-as-punishment, the chapter seeks to enliven close reading of instances of disability-as-punishment, as a way of moving closer to understanding how corporeality is conceptualised differently in relation to other social axes such as caste and sexuality.

Notes

1 A note on spellings: This chapter uses the spelling 'Madurai Veeran' as the English transliteration of the Tamil name while it acknowledges other existing spellings, such as 'Maturaiviran' as used by David Schulman and others. Similarly, the spelling 'nontinatakam' is used here in order to adopt a standard use across the chapter while other spellings such as 'nondinatakam' and split usage such as 'nonti natakam' are also acknowledged in English transliteration. The transliteration Pommi is used while Bommi may also be prevalent in usage.

2 The language of disability used in this chapter, especially words used for disability have been used descriptively and not evaluatively, unless specified. Well aware of the debates on the language of disability in the field of disability studies, certain terms that are rejected by the larger discourse such as 'lame' have been retained to capture their descriptive essence in context.

3 The story summarised in this chapter primarily draws on David Shulman's account in *The King and the Clown in South Indian Myth and Poetry*.

4 *Dasi* is used synonymously with *devadasi*.

References

Anand, Shilpaa. 2016. 'The Models Approach in Disability Scholarship: An Assessment of its Failings.' In N. Ghosh (ed.), *Interrogating Disability in India: Theory and Practice*, pp. x, 198. New Delhi: Springer India.

Anandhi, S. 1991. 'Representing Devadasis: "Dasigal Mosavalai" as a Radical Text.' *Economic and Political Weekly*, 26(11/12): 739–746.

Blackburn, Stuart H. 1978. 'The Kallars: A Tamil "Criminal Tribe" Reconsidered.' *South Asia: Journal of South Asian Studies*, 1(1): 38–51. doi: 10.1080/00856407808722957.

Chakravarti, Uma. 2010. 'Whatever Happened to the Vedic Dasi? Orientalism, Nationalism and a Script for the Past.' In K. Sangari and S. Vaid (eds.), *Recasting Women: Essays in Colonial History*, pp. 27–28. New Delhi: Zubaan.

Devlieger, Patrick. 1995. 'Why Disabled? The Cultural Understanding of Physical Disability in an African Society.' In B. Ingstad and S. R. Whyte (eds.), *Disability and Culture*, pp. x, 307. Los Angeles: University of California Press.

Elangovan, Ezhil. 2011. 'The Murder of Madurai Veeran and the Palace of Thirumalai Nayakkar.' In K. S. A. S. Tharu (ed.), *No Alphabet in Sight: New Dalit writing from South India (Dossier 1: Tamil and Malayalam)*, pp. 129–139. New Delhi: Penguin.

Ghai, Anita. 2015. *Rethinking Disability in India*. New Delhi: Routledge.

Hamraie, Aimi. 2015. 'Historical Epistemology as Disability Studies Methodology: From the Models Framework to Foucault's Archaeology of Cure'. *Foucault Studies*, 19(27): 108–134.

Jayalakshmi, R. and Muthu M. Marutha. 2007. *Tiruppullani Nonti Natakam*. Chennai: Institute of Asian Studies.

Maruthamuthu, M. (ed.). 1998. *Redemption through Grace*. Chennai: Institute of Asian Studies.

Mehrotra, Nilika. 2013. *Disability, Gender and State Policy: Exploring Margins*. Jaipur: Rawat Publications.

Miles, M. 2000. 'Disability on a Different Model: Glimpses of an Asian Heritage.' *Disability and Society*, 15(4): 603–618.

Miles, M. 2008. Glimpses of Disability in the Literature and Cultures of East Asia, South Asia, the Middle East & Africa. A Modern and Historical Bibliography, with Some Annotation (Annotated Bibliography). Independent Living Institute (ILI) Library Retrieved 8 August 2016, from Independent Living Institute www.independentliving.org/docs7/miles200807.html.

Mitchell, David. T. and Sharon. L. Snyder. 2000. *Narrative Prosthesis: Disability and the Dependencies of Discourse*. Ann Arbor: The University of Michigan Press.

Nair, Janaki. 1994. 'The Devadasi, Dharma and the State.' *Economic and Political Weekly*, 29(50): 3157–3167.

Pandian, Anand. 2005. Securing the Rural Citizen: The Anti-Kallar Movement of 1896. *Indian Economic & Social History Review*, *42*(01): 1–39.

Pati, Biswamoy. 1995. 'Of Devadasis, "Tradition" and Politics.' *Economic and Political Weekly*, 30(43): 2728–2728.

Quayson, Ato. 2007. *Aesthetic Nervousness: Disability and the Crisis of Representation*. New York: Columbia University Press.

Rose, Martha L. 2003. *The Staff of Oedipus: Transforming Disability in Ancient Greece*. Ann Arbor: The University of Michigan Press.

Selim, Kumur B. 2006. 'Nonti Natakam.' In G. Albrecht (ed.), *Encyclopedia of Disability* (Vol. 5). Thousand Oaks: Sage.

Shulman, David D. 1985. *The King and the Clown in South Indian Myth and Poetry*. Princeton: Princeton University Press.

Vink, Markus P.M. 2015. *Encounters of the Opposite Coast: The Dutch East India Company and the Nayaka State of Madurai in the Seventeenth Century*. Liden: Brill.

Wise, T. A. 1845. *Commentary on the Hindu System of Medicine*. Calcutta: Thacker and Co.

Yoganand, D. 1956. Mathurai Veeran [Feature Film]. In L. Chettiar (Producer): Krishna Pictures.

PART IV

Space, vigilance, and getting intimate

9

THE MODERN-DAY SEX WORKER

The intimate 'Other' of intimacy and belonging

Chandni Mehta

From the devil of the sacred realm to the evil of moral society

Georges Bataille, in his work *Eroticism*, argues that sex and death became the first objects of taboos when man invented tools and began to work (Bataille 2012: 30–31, 40–51). Sex involved bodily 'continuity' and fusion, while work required bodily 'discontinuity'; to enable work, sex came to be regulated through taboos (*Ibid.*, 40–51).[1] Insofar as taboos on sex were for making work possible, the desire that taboos induced towards sex/bodily continuity also became a desire for freedom from work/bodily discontinuity. What was tabooed became sacred, induced awe, and produced 'inner feelings' towards it (*Ibid.*: 68). The ritual sanction on periodic and organised transgression of taboos, through animal sacrifice, orgies, sacred prostitution, etc., drew out these desires into a convulsive play, making it possible to 'experience' sex/bodily continuity (Bataille 2012). To this extent, the act of consummation in marriage was also a sanctioned and organised transgression, although one that would inevitably lose its erotic and transgressive character with repetition and habit (*Ibid.*: 109–111, 134). The sacred prostitute, however, played out religiously sanctioned transgression every day, and hers was a life consecrated to erotic experience (*Ibid.*). Contrary to the simplistic characterisation of primitive and ancient sexual life in terms of promiscuity and absence of shame, Bataille points out that a sense of shame, real or pretended, was a sign of acknowledging the taboo and inviting transgression. The religious prostitute or the courtesan were not very different from other women insofar as they held a reserve, maintained the principle of first-time contact, played out enticement only to follow it with first-time denial and build-up of sexual pursuit. But unlike other women, they practised this ritually, artfully, the play of taboo and transgression (*Ibid.*: 133).

Work with tools became routine and 'profane' while sex as object of taboo and transgression became ritualised and 'sacred' (*Ibid.*: 68, 114–115). Thus, the coupled play of taboo and transgression created a dialectical relationship, as it were, between work/bodily discontinuity and sex/bodily continuity, and created a subjective/human experience of sex even as it objectively appeared animal-like. Bataille points out that in early religious societies, there was not a complete separation of the animal and the human and both populated the sacred realm (*Ibid.*: 136–137). Thus, erotic practices belonged to the sacred realm as its rebellious dimension.

The progression from religious societies to a moral ordering of the world took place through different contextualised histories, but it was exemplified by the emergence of 'Christian morality' (*Ibid.*: 136). Christianity transformed the sacred realm into the divine realm by cleansing it of animal depictions and creating God in man's image (*Ibid.*: 136–137). Christian morality redirected and sublimated the desire for bodily continuity towards the experience of divine community among men via their personal unions with a common God (*Ibid.*: 118). Freedom as salvation of the soul, was turned away from sex and against the earlier experience of freedom (from bodily discontinuity) in convulsive and deathly plays of bodily continuity. The distinctively human activity of work, which had been profane vis-à-vis the sacred realm in religious societies, was turned towards the divine world (*Ibid.*: 117–128). While the taboo on sex continued, its transgression was no longer sanctioned, which in turn weakened the power of taboos and the desire for transgression. Sex was exorcised of its eroticism and reduced 'back' to its animal nature (Bataille 2012: 128; Federici 2013: 37–38, 163–206; Foucault 2014). In this it was recast as the central object of moral, medical and penal regulation, whereby it could be humanised through guilt and disciplinary correction(Foucault 1992, 2014), and redeemed only in procreative sex in which bodily fusion was life affirming and led to individuation through childbirth. Even a 'fallen woman' could redeem herself if she evinced guilt and repentance.

It is this Christian morality that gets smuggled into the very political economic and scientific developments in Western Europe that were undermining divine authority and mounting attacks on the Church. The salvation and liberation of the soul in God's divine kingdom was challenged by the search for freedom in this world, in mankind's future. There was an unprecedented elevation and centrality of labour, and scientification and regulation of sex, in pursuing this secular promise of freedom. The moral-divine community gave way to the moral community of the nation. As the secular translations of Christian morality in political economy and disciplinary regimes travelled through colonial rule, they made the colonies an experimental site and part of these developments (Stoler 1995; Federici 2013) through contestations and collaborations, transforming and universalising Christian morality as modern morality.

Modern/national morality, through political economic and scientific-governmental discourses, entailed a co-constitutive separation[2] and hierarchisation of the domains of labour and sex, man and woman, public and private, as well as a linking of these domains through conjugal procreative sex and housework

(Fortunati 1995; Federici 2013). At the core of these separations was the moral separation and hierarchy of human potential (for freedom) and animal temptations (of necessity). The modern promise of transformation and freedom of all men from animal existence was freeing up the immutability of older status-based hierarchies. Yet, the promise of transformation meant that hierarchy itself was not abolished and constantly required separations.[3] Thus, modern morality works through incessantly producing separations, the most fundamental being the division between men/labour, as de facto moral/human, and women/sex, as immoral/animal, and further within/between women/sex, individually and socially, into the potential for moralisation and humanisation and the tendency for immorality and animality – '*stridharma*' and '*strisvabhav*' (Sangari 1999: 351). Woman can be moralised by linking separations of labour and sex, public and private, through housework and procreation (and therein perpetuating and maintaining separations) as wife and mother. She can also become immoral by collapsing modern separations and therein rejecting the modern responsibility of transformation as 'prostitute.' 'Objective' specifications of (im)morality of woman/sex were created by legal and medical regimes and the sociologisation of (im)morality drew upon emerging distinctions of race, class and caste, just as these were also getting consolidated and contested around the question of (im)morality of 'their' women (Andrews and Bushnell 1898; Jeffreys 1987; Jha and Sharma 2016; Jordan 2006). Through pauperisation (Bannerjee 1998; Levine 2003), racialisation, pathologisation, criminalisation (Ballhatchet 1980; Levine 2003; Tambe 2009a) and casteist associations, the modern-day prostitute was produced in animal existence. However, all of these were indexed around questions of procreation, monetisation and mobility of woman/sex, thus producing the prostitute as not only animal existence, but also a thriving in animality, flaunting it in the public domain, and perpetuating it through illegitimate procreation. Animating the prostitute in an indifference to humanisation (Bataille 2012: 136–138), an enticement of men away from work, value and freedom, and a temptation of sex/woman into shamelessness. In the next few passages I will try to unpack these developments.

Money, mobility, and (im)morality

Monetisation of exchange and relations of production, and the emergence of the public realm where 'value' is endowed, played a critical role in the modern separation of life into labour and nature (Federici 2013: 29–30, 61–100). They had the fundamental effects of freeing up and enabling an unprecedented movement of commodities, including the most essential commodity for capital accumulation – labour power- by enabling abstraction and exchange through standardisation (Fortunati 1995; Marx 2010). Exchange of labour power in the public realm necessitated the privatisation of the labouring body – this is what characterised the double-edged freedom of the labourer – freeing his body from servitude by privatising it while freeing up his labour for waged exploitation through the public realm.[4] The maximisation of labour exploitation by 'freeing' the labourer from the labour of his own reproduction and production/procreation, and the maximisation of surplus accumulation by making reproduction and production/procreation of labour power/labourer 'free' (as in gratis) – both were achieved by the feminisation, privatisation and non-monetisation of housework (Fortunati 1995), through the creation of the modern family.[5] Thus, labour power/labourer constitutively draws on and excludes housework from the domain and measure of labour. The non-monetisation and privatisation of housework by immobilising the movement of women/sex into the value endowing public domain, 'naturalized' housework/women/sex (Fortunati 1995; Costa 2012a, 2012b; Federici 2012: 74–80; Federici 2013), recasting them in proximity to the body, proximity to animal functions, and inalienability, making them appear as pre-capitalist continuation of natural activities and roles under capitalism. But non-monetisation and privatisation also create a domain and measures for the intimate moral regulation and valuation[6] of housework/women/sex as the most critical and ambivalent elements of capitalist modernity. This was particularly salient in the history of colonial rule post 1857, when the impetus of separation and hierarchisation between the ruler and the ruled was pursued for decades by creating a sexual spectre out of diverse native practices and forms of life of women by pauperising and discursively reducing them to sex/animality (Nair 1996; Anagol 2005; Agrawal 2008) and the widespread distress migration of women to emerging urban centres (Ghosh 2008; Levine 2003). This came to be contested by mobilising the 'inner domain' of the family (Chatterjee 1993) and intimate moral spheres of regulation around women/sex (Sangari 1999), thus consolidating the shift to modern morality by contesting the morality of colonial rule.

Monetization and the emergence of the public realm, which separate out production from reproduction, also become inversely operating, and eventually independent and intimate, tools (as non-monetization/sacrifice and privatization) of moral regulation and valuation of sex/woman. The less monetized and the more distant from the public realm, the more is the moral value of woman/sex.[7] Thus, over and above naturalisation, there is a moralisation of woman/sex, recasting them in terms of duty and responsibility, as pre-capitalist continuation of traditional roles and activities in capitalist modernity. However, it is procreation (of male child) and motherhood that are the definitive instance and process when woman/sex produces value as per its reigning form and meaning – surplus and extricable from the body, directed towards the public realm, promising progress and freedom. However, unlike other value-bearing commodities, the offspring is not for exchange but derives promissory economic value as potential labour power, which accrues to the mother as supreme moral value. The production of sex/woman in dual nature and mutually antagonistic potentials, makes her responsible for her own regulation by disavowal of monetisation and public realm, and avowal of sacrifice in housework and procreation.[8] However, while doing so, woman/sex must remain under multiple registers of patriarchal regulation – 'the domestication of fertility' (Menon 2012: 75), starting in the family to the caste/community to the nation state – for the moral valuation of woman/sex gets its stamp only by the name of the husband and the name of the father to the woman's child. The name of the husband/father, at once a universal standard and a specific stamp for moral valuation, creates and circumscribes intimate and private circuits of moral valuation.

Creating the moral separation of man/labour and woman/sex, and creating the potential of woman/sex to be moralised by maintaining and linking these separations – both of these rest on, producing the modern-day 'prostitute' as the monetisation and movement of sex/woman, as collapse of separations, as the contamination of sex/woman by the indiscriminating and public touch of money and men. The stigmatisation of the prostitute by the very money payment and publicness to which she is reduced and which subsists her enables and reveals the moral function of money and mobility in (an inverse) relation to sex/women (Kosambi 2000; Ramabai 2000a, 2000b). At the same time, the fact that payment to the prostitute does not acquire the status of wage for labour and the movement of the prostitute in the public domain is not the free movement of labour reveals the natural function of money and mobility to configure labour in alienation, extrication, and exchange. If the morality of the wife/mother lies in not charging anything, indeed sacrificing, for the use value she reproduces and procreates and the exchange values that it enables; if the de facto morality of the labourer/man lies in creating exchange value; then the immorality of the prostitute lies in charging the client while potentially depleting his use and exchange value (perhaps even gaining a child for her needs at the cost of devaluing the child amidst and into prostitution), transforming the payment which the client makes into theft in the hands of the prostitute and prostitution into dishonest work (*The News Minute*; Phoenix 2001; Qureshi 2006). Scholarship shows that sex workers can indeed feel guilty or choose to not charge when they enjoy their work with a client (Sunder Rajan 2011: 135; Bernstein 2007: 101–102), eliciting the uneasy proximity between money and sex. If privatisation allows the valuation of wife/mother by name of the husband/father; if public domain allows the valuation of labour/man by monetisation; then public-ness of the prostitute invisiblises her housework in general and stamps her procreation in particular with illegitimacy by rendering the father un-identifiable among her many clients and denying the child the name of the father. Taken together, the very monetisation and public-ness to which the prostitute is reduced and in which she is sustained, come to signal her wilful thriving and revelling in immorality/animality, the abdication of her duty and responsibility towards conjugal family and motherhood, and her indifference to humanisation.

Legal and medical discourses serve modern morality in producing the prostitute in immorality through 'objective' translations (Srinivasan 1987, 2006). Thus, the legal discourse on trafficking criminalises living off the earnings of a prostitute (potentially criminalising her natal/conjugal family and motherhood).[9] The racialised medical discourse from venereal diseases to HIV-AIDS produces the prostitute in depletion of value – in degeneration, morbidity, and even fatalism. The movement of the prostitute[10] is criminalised as either trafficking or soliciting,[11] restricted by creating 'red-light areas,' pathologised as spread of contagion, and medically racialised as threat of miscegenation (Soofi 2012; Swarankar 2008; Tambe 2006, 2011; Vijayakumar 2015).

We have seen how the progression from early religious society to moral ordering of society separates and hierarchises human potential and animal tendency, and seeks to shun the latter by creating intimate and inner domains of moral regulation and transformation, therein generating norms of intimacy and belonging. Three aspects of moralisation/humanisation of sex/woman that we discussed – non-monetisation, privatisation, and procreation – create the norms of self-denial and sacrifice, fidelity and health, and endurance and preservation, respectively. We have also seen that this moral ordering of society rests fundamentally on producing the modern-day prostitute as the animal tendency of woman/sex, as the intimate other of intimacy and belonging, by reducing her to cold cash transaction and theft; dangerous movement in the public/indiscriminate realm – pure deception and irresponsibility which threatens fidelity and health; illegitimate procreation from monetised and indiscriminate sex (in which 'the father' becomes indistinguishable from/among clients) – which cannot claim lineage, identity or commitment (Daggers and Neal 2006; Dutta 2010; Chatterjee 2008). By making the intimate and the private into the alienated, standardised, indiscriminatory and public, the prostitute can neither claim intimacy and belonging of the private domain, nor the recognition/value of the public domain. Her predicament is not that she is not paid for her work, but that her earning becomes theft. Her predicament is not that she has to be hidden, but that she has to be exposed as deception, that she has to be in public without identification (Zelizer 2000; Sahni et al. 2008; Mies 1994; Maciszewski 2006; Kotiswaran 2011). Her predicament is not that she is shamed, but that the absence of shame and guilt is what criminalises her and makes her threatening. Her predicament is not that she is banished, but that she must be proximate without being intimate. Her predicament is not that she cannot produce a child if she wants, but that she must produce a child without becoming a mother. How does the prostitute inhabit these impossible predicaments – this is the question I will now pursue through a close reading of the second autobiography of Nalini Jameela, 'a wife, mother, successful business woman and social activist – as well as a sex worker – at different stages of her life' (Jameela 2007). We have seen how the modern moral regime makes regulation and transformation matters of responsibility to oneself, creating intimate and inner domains whereby moral regulation and transformation and individual subjectivity become co-constitutive. Writing one's history, of the individual or the nation, the autobiographical stance – creating a narratable past through the unity of motives, authenticity, and true nature – is crucial in claiming morality, subjecthood, futurity, and freedom. Erasing the Vedic *dasi* from the history of the nation by imbuing her diverse practices with immorality, configured the moral Hindu woman in this history as well as in contemporary reality by the prevailing terms and conditions of claiming individual and national morality (Chakravarti 1989). However, this erasure through (im)moralisation also produced the descendants of the Vedic *dasi* in modern-day prostitution, in lacking the claim to subjecthood and freedom themselves and undermining that of the nation as well (Jordan 2003; Kannabiran and Kannabiran 2003; Pande 2008). Indeed, the erasure created a spectral presence of the modern-day prostitute, as what immorality may look and thrive like.

Refracting the autobiographical 'I'

When Nalini Jameela came out with her first autobiography in Kerala in 2005, it became an instant bestseller, its success attributable to several possible factors from 'sexual curiosity to political solidarity' (Maruthur 2010: 99). But it was also staunchly opposed by many sections, leading literary figures of Kerala society called it a 'prurient money-spinner' (Jameela 2007: xi), middle-class reformist feminists saw it as a neo-liberal celebration of women's objectification, and still others as a 'craving for fame' that was indifferent to the victimisation of sex workers (*Ibid.*, 175). Jameela rejected the first autobiography, but for a different reason – her amanuensis had assumed an authoritative role at the cost of her participation and stylistic inputs (*Ibid.*, 179). In a rare gesture, Jameela sought to reclaim her autobiography by writing a second one, *The Autobiography of a Sex Worker*, within six months of the first (Maruthur 2010: 100). In its introduction, she recounts her troubles in beginning to write, including the loss of a client when he happened to read her very first jottings, which mentioned her age – seven years more than what she had told him (Jameela 2007: viii)! The setbacks apart, she also found the support of several activist friends who didn't assume authoritative or patronising roles and with whom she had 'very equal relationships,' making it possible for her to interact freely, 'reactivate' her memories, and write in her 'own style' (*Ibid.*, 179).

> [E]ven when the first version came out, many thought that I – and my story – were not true. They thought this was fiction, that I wasn't a real person . . . The story was that the person who helped me with the first version 'created' me, and then, because I am a woman, the 'feminists' stole me from him. Whichever way you see it, in this story, I'm like a puppet who dances to others' tunes!
>
> (*Ibid.*, 178)

We can begin to unpack this by pursuing Uday Kumar's discussion of 'autobiographical agency' (Kumar 2016: 16). Kumar suggests that we explore connections between the two opposite meanings of 'agent' – agent as one who 'acts or exerts power' and agent as 'one who acts for another, a deputy, steward, factor, substitute, representative or emissary,' i.e. between the 'real originators' and the 'authorized performers' of action (*Ibid.*, 15–16). Further, Kumar writes,

> [R]ather than extend the scope of *autos*to cover the author's originary self, it might be useful to explore structures of authorization in autobiographies. Under what authority does one gain the right to speak about one's life, write one's autobiography?
>
> (*Ibid.*, 16)

In an interview appended to the second autobiography, Jameela says, 'Let me also tell you that the struggle to get this story written the way I wanted it written, and to get it into the public eye, has been as intense as any in my whole life' (Jameela 2007: 179). One way of opening up this statement is to see how Jameela's various struggles in life, and her struggles with autobiographical writing and its reception, involve struggles over the two meanings of 'agent,' what may be called autobiographical struggles in a double sense, and to that extent are 'anecdotal' (Kumar 2016: 41) of each other. My reason for invoking the question of autobiographical struggle is not because I seek to show the agency of the sex worker or deny it, but because the modern sex worker subject, especially the contemporary sex worker subject is produced *by* incessantly trapping her in struggles for an 'I.' The trouble then is not only that the scope of the auto- may be extended to cover the author's 'originary self,' whereby Jameela's autobiography, precisely because it is the autobiography of a sex worker, has to be an extraordinary, if not anomalous, story. The trouble here is also that the 'structures of authorization' over-determine as well as immobilise the auto- of the sex worker. By authorising multiple antagonistic identity scripts, the 'originary self'/the autobiographical 'I'/the 'truth' of the sex worker is over-determined as deception as well as denied in victimhood. This obtains from the specificity of the lower-class, lower-caste sex worker as a marginal subject – a marginal subject who is most intimate with the centre insofar as sex is constituted as the most intimate domain in morally ordered modern society, and threatens to expose it since this intimacy, in its political economic and disciplinary use, is denied and violently pushed back on her as stigma. Thus the challenge here is to explore *how* these over-determining and immobilising structures of authorisation are navigated, and what kind of subject formation takes place in this process.

Navnitha Mokkil Maruthar's work on Jameela's autobiographies teases out some of these structures of authorisation and the 'staging of infractions' within these structures. Maruthar shows how the 1990s saw a shift in the state's 'modes of address' in a neo-liberal developmental context and within the public health discourse on AIDS (Maruthur 2010: 97–109). These targeted the sex worker as an entrepreneurial economic agent in her familial setting and as a safe-sex practitioner, who takes 'responsibility for the well being of herself, her family and the social body,' through self-disciplining and participation rather than as passive beneficiary or political actor (*Ibid.*, 117). Maruthar shows that while Jameela draws on some of the categories of the state's new modes of address and aligns with the safe-sex discourse, she also unsettles the neat separations of the domestic woman and the sex worker in the state's public health discourse by 'writing in an "elaborate domestic" into the narrative of the life of a "public woman"' (*Ibid.*, 125). Further, by calling out the hypocrisy of the state through her narratives of police violence and making political demands on the state in terms of rights and citizenship, justice, and social change, Jameela claims a political subjectivity in excess of the governmental frame (*Ibid.*, 129–133). Lastly, Maruthar goes on to show how Jameela exceeds the language of law and entitlements to make an 'appeal to the public for a new imagination of the sex worker and her position within the social' (*Ibid.*, 137). The literary form of the autobiography allows Jameela a 'self-exploration' which is not possible within the rights discourse and the state discourse, but '[s]ince the "auto" or the

"I" she sets out to plot is not contained or stable, the form of the autobiography is reconfigured and pulls at its seams as she narrates her story' (*Ibid.*, 100). Kumar suggests that

> Instead of seeing the autobiographical act as a movement from the inner domain to the outer, we may see it as located from the outset in a public, exhibitionary space . . . A focus on exteriority may help us see autobiographical utterances as performances. By this I do not mean to suggest a distinction between inner selves and their outer dissimulations; we need to consider the inner world itself as inscribed on the surface of things, as produced through actions and utterances in a field of mutual exposure and unevenly shared visibility.
>
> *(Kumar 2016: 20–21)*

Maruthar's foregrounding of the public in exploring structures of authorisation, and Kumar's insights in this regard get pushed to their limits if we delineate the specificity of the lower-class, lower-caste 'public woman's' relation to the public domain as an over-determining and immobilising structure of authorisation. I mentioned earlier the specificity of the sex worker subject's marginality owing to her unique intimacy with the centre. This intimacy and its denial are also played out spatially for the sex worker's political economic and disciplinary functions are themselves significantly spatial.[12] The sex worker must create intimacy in the public domain but do so on the sly, creating her tenuous secret economic geography in the public domain, but which is shared intimately, just as it is denied, by respectable characters.[13]

The word 'prostitute,' derives from Latin 'prostitut' – 'exposed publicly, offered for sale,' from verb 'prostituere,' from 'pro-' – 'before' + 'statuere' – 'cause to stand, establish, set up, place.' The 'prostitute' is by definition in a state of exposure and this exposure necessarily has a monetary dimension. Moral stigma, poverty, fear of contagion and criminalisation require the sex worker to be secretive in her work even while having to be public, especially in contexts such as of Kerala, where the absence of brothels and red-light areas means that sex workers have to solicit on the streets and go with clients to lodges or work out of short-stay Company houses. The author-protagonist Jameela has to clock her work to avoid increased police harassment during shift of duty, constantly be on the move from one town to another, and deploy tropes of conjugality and domesticity to navigate the public domain – standing outside cinema halls before and after show timings, as if waiting for her husband and children; in case of a client with money, attiring respectably in matching saree and blouse and *mangalsutra*, carrying a suitcase to book a lodge as a married couple; when the hotels are near temples, walking out purposefully early in the mornings as if going to the temple. Even inside the relative privacy of Company houses in Jameela's early career, sex workers and managers maintained respectable hours of work and brokers created appearances of respectable business in order to merge with the neighbourhood rhythm. 'The local people knew the truth, but in those days there was a special co-existence amongst us' – a secretive neighbourliness, we could say. In fact, growing intimacy of the state with sex workers through identification and medicalisation came along with heightened exposure to police violence and neighbourhood hostility, pushing them into private retreat as well as intensifying their public assertion. Jameela argues that sex workers' groups do not include privileged sex workers because 'they are able to shield themselves from public view and so don't have to endure much suffering,' while the lowest class of sex workers get associated with criminality and face the state intimately and routinely (Jameela 2007: 147–148).

The work of maintaining and suffering the secret of sex work continues for Jameela even after leaving sex work, in the 'private' domain, in her second marriage with a client. As the secret gets disclosed in her conjugal family, Jameela has to manage another secret of her brother-in-law seeking to sexually exploit her through her past secret. When Jameela produces a baby, the condition on which her client, Koyakka, marries her and promises her shelter for life, a curious charge of illegitimacy is levelled against the newborn by her father. While the charge of illegitimacy here is of the child being born *haram* ('outside of faith'), for Koyakka is Muslim, there is a contextual undercurrent of Jameela's sex work in these developments. Jameela ends the marriage and takes to sex work again, only to find it more difficult with increasing harassment by police and thugs, lack of shelter and the need for a caregiver for the baby every time she left for work. Soon leaving the unviable sex work upon her third marriage with a client, Shahul Hameed, who promises to keep the secret of her sex work and father her daughter, Zeenat, as his own, Jameela charts 12years as 'proud housewife and trader' (*Ibid.*, 60). When the marriage, business and her health begin to fall apart, Jameela is unwilling to make any community-mediated claims or settlements with Shahul through five years of intense hardship with her dependent daughter, struggling with homelessness and ill-health. This is guided by her resolve to not let Shahul take advantage of the secret of her daughter's real father as much as her reluctance to make claims on a relationship that was forged in a 'moment's attraction' and Jameela pretending to be a Muslim on Shahul's insistence but not formally converting (*Ibid.*, 77). In fact, Nalini takes the name Jameela after living with Shahul for some time. Well after this marriage ends and Jameela returns to sex work, an old client in the police catches her in a conversation and calls her Nalini, whereupon she takes the name Nalini Jameela.

We see how forging situational identities becomes a professional requirement for a lower-class, lower-caste 'public woman,' and how these overlap and underwrite her 'private' relationships, even relationships that pre-date her sex work, such as Jameela's relationship with her mother and with her daughter from her first marriage to support whom she first takes to sex work, as well as any appearance in the public domain (an aspect that I will discuss shortly). Caught in these multiple binds, the lower-class, lower-caste 'public woman' 'stands to be exposed' in multiple senses. But by virtue of the very same stigmatised sex work, the 'public woman' holds many an intimate secret of respectable society and state – of respectable men – clients and police, and fragile dominant womanhood – and can threaten to expose them. Jameela's work makes her intimately aware that if her work involves others, then so does the secret of her work, that a secret by its very nature is shared, that it takes two to create a secret (for a secret to be held even by a single individual, requires the subject to be split into a relation with itself). If masks are necessary for her professional survival then so is masking necessary for the social and moral survival of her clients and of respectable society at large. For instance, Jameela's brother's threatening reflex on seeing her with another sex worker, Rosa *chechi*, gave away his own secret of being Rosa *chechi*'s client! Jameela's autobiography throws up diverse situational instances of deploying secrets to turn situations of power in her favour. After her experience of police brutality upon being turned over to the police by her very first client – a senior police officer, she is quick to figure out the power dynamics of the police station and tactfully make a few clients in the police. She keeps them in 'good humour,' and, when need be, pulls the strings of intimacy with one policeman-client to prevent an assault by another officer and bail herself out, to silence clients in the police, or to trick them into inaction by fear of embarrassment.

That Jameela's experiences reveal to her the links and slips between the exposed and the hidden in the public domain, that in fact the secret is the currency of the public domain, is suddenly revealed to the reader when she narrates her second visit to the office of the sex worker's organisation, Jwalamukhi. By the second visit itself, she is impatient to talk about 'how they'd hit back.' Picking up a recurrent problem of the gathered sex workers, of having to pay lawyers for getting bailed, Jameela states in no minced words that approaching a lawyer meant that the sex worker herself believed that she had committed some offence. Instead, if any two sex workers from the organisation could offer bail each time a sex worker got arrested, and argue that no offence was committed, then there would be no need for a lawyer.

> 'If you think it's an offence, you're sure to be punished . . . How are we offenders? In what sense? If sex is the offence then there's one more person who must be punished. How come that fellow is never punished? Isn't he an offender too?' Then the question shifted to how a *man* could be caught.
>
> *(Ibid., 85)*

Jameela's experiences of tactfully deploying secrets, organically reveal to her how secrecy is the instrument that over-determines and immobilises the sex worker in all kinds of deception – criminality, contagion, theft, immorality – and shields respectable society from its own perversions. This organic understanding now directly informs her activism – calling out the hypocrisy of society, from police and 'respectable' clients to fellow progressive 'respectable' women activists in various other struggles, and demanding the acceptance of sex workers. This passage from Jameela's contingent and tactful struggles to her sustained and tactful activism is not automatic, even though it is organic. Chancing upon the sex workers' rights organisation, Jwalamukhi, where she could see her work as acceptable (indeed it is upon her interactions with Jwalamukhi that Jameela takes the firm decision to stay on in sex work), is critical in this passage. Jameela's very first intervention, the one within the organisation itself, arguing for bailing each other out, is premised on sex workers' acceptance of themselves and of each other as sex workers. The possibility of being with herself and being with others simultaneously is what anchors her to the organisation and characterises the sense of community and autonomy that she develops in it. This is also what made the organisation a political community with 'no insistence on what "line" to take' (*Ibid.*, 110). It is Jameela's broken narrative of narrow escapes from near-death situations and the 'departure' of friends that creates the most palpable pangs of a community for itself. Uninvestigated murders shrouded in the silent indifference of respectable witnesses, inexplicable suicides, bodies wrecked by police brutality and local gangs – Jameela writes how the pangs of helplessness and abandonment lead to the decision to claim and collectively cremate the body of a deceased sex worker activist and friend and not let the body be 'disposed of as an unclaimed corpse in the public cemetery' (*Ibid.*, 101). Jameela's secret life as a 'public woman' casts shadows of deception over her 'private' relationships and any appearance in the public, forcing her to be constantly on the move to alter the public itself in which she appears. Her acceptance as a sex worker in Jwalamukhi changes her daughter's 'lurking feeling that her Amma was doing something wrong' and gives her the self-confidence that she too would be accepted (*Ibid.*, 116–117). It also critically turns around the sense in which Jameela is a 'public woman' – experiencing the transformation of Jwalamukhi from a label of mockery to a symbol of self-confidence, rallying to police stations and making significant advances in checking violence of police and local gangs, speaking at protest gatherings and national and international symposiums, making documentary films, and writing her autobiographies. All these narratives are propelled by assertions in the public sphere and a refusal to be stigmatised or victimised in exposure. Yet, insofar as Jameela continues to do sex work along with her activism, these public assertions do not once and for all turn around her standing as a 'public woman,' both within activist forums and outside it. The shadow of suspicion and the attempts to patronise continue to loom large, in collaborations and solidarities with progressive activists and the constant search for a space of work and rest continues even into activism, the rich and the poor alike in refusing to share their neighbourhood space with sex workers' organisation.[14] On the one hand, Jameela's autobiographical exposure is derided in some quarters by folding it back into her monetised exposure as a 'public woman,' on the other hand, Jameela's very first jottings for her autobiography, run against her professional requirement of forging situational identities, costing her a client and an income. In a 2016 interview to *Azhimugam.com*, Jameela mentions that when she put out an advertisement on Facebook asking for monetary help for publishing her most recent book, she received calls offering her help in exchange for 'beautiful girls' or even 'getting her.'[15] The charge that Jameela parrots the language of certain feminists follows her from her very first public address in a symposium to her autobiographical acts precisely because she continues to be a sex worker. Jameela insists that while the organisation gave a critical strength to her acceptance and assertion of her work, her own engagement with the organisation was always contingent on its equal acceptance of her and the criticality of her experiences in shaping its politics. By recasting her autobiographical exposure as the deceptive and perverted exposure of a 'public woman,' as capable of doing anything for money and fame, respectable masculinity is sought to be fortified, and by showcasing her as a victim to expose patriarchy, respectable femininity is sought to be asserted and safeguarded.

Here, Jameela's short discussion about abusive language becomes useful. Jameela writes how 'pungent tongues' are the 'sole defensive weapons' of the weak – from homeless women beggars to sex workers to vulnerable migrant couples – because they 'effectively repel any assailant who has some sense of honour left in him' (*Ibid.*, 151). Contrary to the production of sex workers, and sex workers alone, in pervasive foul-mouthing and obscene utterances, Jameela argues how most sex workers, including herself, are not exceptionally foul-mouthed. Jameela's autobiographical struggle, her struggle to speak and write in her own voice in an over-determined and immobilising field, is also a struggle against marginalisation in discourse (where discursive power is denied to the limits of producing a 'rain of uncouth words') while retaining the intimate threat of discourse from the margins. This makes Jameela's autobiographical narrative and activism straddle between an exposure of respectable society by exposing her own experiences, and a demand on society to own up to its secrets and accept the multiplicity of desires and identities, including sex work and sex workers by herself owning all her experiences, her multiple identities, as collections of a multifaceted life.

> One should never be one-dimensional . . . It's like saying that one can do only one thing . . . I look after my family, I also do social work, and when in financial need, as someone in my situation often is, I do sex work. There are people who say that I'm not true to one vocation, and that somehow doing many things is linked to a craving for fame . . . When people choose to do many things, many of the things they do are often for the benefit of others.
>
> *(Ibid., 175–176)*

Jameela warns that she might write a sequel, 'As long as one's life continues to offer fruitful experiences that may cast light on other people's lives and sorrows, one should share what one can. For that reason, I will keep on telling you the story of my life' (*Ibid.*, 179). She also mentions that if she had the chance to re-write her second autobiography, she would appeal to her community (of sex workers), 'exhorting them to be less reticent, to enter public life, and be of service to the public,' as well as address girls from other communities, 'who are young and know little of life,' on how to avoid traps of sex rackets (*Ibid.*, 178). Jameela's desire for autobiography is also a desire for forging conversational intimacies and social belonging. But what is perhaps the most unsettling demand that her autobiography makes is to accept the possibility of a woman disavowing sacrifice, asserting sex as a 'woman's need,' and still managing to be a good mother! In Jameela's words, 'There's no need for sacrifices; all things can be done' (*Ibid.*,156).

Jameela's frustration with sex work, her desire for domesticity, her abandoning of both her marriages, and her five most difficult years of struggle with illness, coalesced around questions of identity and its firm linkages with the politics of homelessness and shelter.[16] After the most trying phase of her life, in which she moved from one mosque to another in search of shelter, took rounds of her relatives' houses, Jwalamukhi provided her a nourishing anchorage. A different kind of belonging emerges around the same time when she settles down in Bangladesh Colony, where Jameela and her daughter, Zeenat, 'had no reason to hide our name or our roots.'

> Kids from that area don't get jobs in decent places, people don't treat them well . . . But I have never felt so secure anywhere. Since we are all 'gone cases', outsiders don't bother us, and all of us insiders get on very well with a lot of mutual cooperation and affection.
>
> *(Ibid., 118)*

While Jwalamukhi made it possible for her to intervene in the public sphere, visiblise herself and assert with other sex workers, Bangladesh Colony became a place of rest and of not caring about the acceptance of the respectable public sphere.

'Freeing' from guilt: memory and body

I will now try to pursue the discussion of subject formation at a more intimate level of experience.

> I have always drawn strength from my memories in troubled times. After the first shock when trouble descends, I take a moment to reflect on all the challenges I have survived. If I could go through all that, I tell myself, why be scared now?
>
> *(Ibid., 169)*

Abolitionist feminists have argued that the 'harm' suffered by sex workers is too immense to be contained in human memory, that a sex worker's experience renders her broken and she can never be whole, therein dissolving the ground of agency (Kotiswaran 2012: 25–26). Perhaps what distinguishes this sense of memory from Jameela's is that it conceives memory as a container, where memories are accumulated and lend themselves to memorialisation, to creating a unified subject. Jameela's moments of dislocation, from her body and its memories, by the shocks of danger, do run against any linear and progressive trajectory of memory work and subject formation. But they also necessitate a ready and dynamic memory work of recollecting her into action, rendering rather cinematic memories, which have a surface and motional quality bordering on a corporeal/dimensional and dynamic quality. Her recurrent recollections train her into sizing down and sharpening her experiences through her memory work, turning them into 'anecdotes' (Kumar 2016: 41), rather than monumentalising them. 'The anecdote speaks' of itself, independent of the author of the self-narrative, even if it originated in the personal experience of the author' (*Ibid.*). By developing an 'anecdotal' relation with her own memories, by invoking them to 'speak' to her, the dislocations of Jameela from her memories and her body in moments of danger and manoeuvring identities, get transformed into situations in which her freed up memories propel her to act in unexpected and situational ways. Her memory is like a resource that is harnessed instead of she being harnessed in them. Hers is not the confessional mode in which memory work binds the individual to itself in guilt and disciplines it into conformity. It may not be incorrect to say that what holds Jameela together through incessant battles for survival and manoeuvres of identity, and what makes their narrativisation possible, is her refusal to be bound to herself in guilt.

Growing up in a lower-middle-class family of the Ezhava caste, Jameela deciphers and creates visual and bodily clues of authority, control, influence, meekness, silencing, and helplessness. These are gendered clues and are collated by observing her aunt and mother and linked to whether one is working and earning money. '[T]o be one's own boss, one had to work. No one had been able to bully us when Mother was working' (Jameela 2007: 5). Pulled out of school at the age of nine, Jameela decides to work at the tile factory. Her narratives of daily-wage labour, domestic work and sex work are significantly sartorial, corporeal and display a visceral sense of danger, flexing into action the moment she smells trouble. These are gendered experiences of danger, which intuit her gender. They alienate her from her body and bind her to it in multiple ways – in 'strange thrill,' in shame, but ultimately in a skilled apparatus relation. Writing of her hurried journeys back home from work at the tile factory every evening, Jameela recalls, 'There was tension in that flight and also a strange thrill. As if each day some victory was renewed in life; as if it were an achievement, valiant and glorious' (*Ibid.*, 10–11). Her sense of achievement welds with her sense of being a 'very important person' each time she bought provisions for the house with her wages. When Jameela takes to domestic work thinking that she would 'be able to eat plenty of food,' she is sexually abused and made to believe that she has done something wrong. By the time she starts working in a clay mine, she develops a firm and working relation with her body, freeing it up from guilt. Through several narratives of working her way out of near-death situations, Jameela exhibits a bodily intelligence and an athletic mind, an almost creaturely readiness in the routinised anticipation of hostility. While speaking of the persistence of violence and struggle for survival across meaningless distinctions of dignified and undignified work, Jameela evokes one such creaturely metaphor,

> They (men in homes where women work as domestic workers) are like snakes that lie in wait for the frogs, absolutely still – the frogs hop around, unaware, and are swallowed by the snakes in a flash!
>
> (*Ibid.*, 174)

Not only does Jameela's narrative suggest that her advanced and skilled use of her body like an apparatus is possible by its freeing up from guilt, she also states it in so many words,

> I often see young sex workers who are beautiful, but bowed and bent because they bear the huge burden of guilt. These are the young women who are most vulnerable to exploitation. I tell them, 'Once you get into this, it is important to pick yourself up. Stop pitying yourself, hold your head high; tell yourself, 'This is where I am' and get a hold on your situation if you don't want to be exploited.
>
> *(Ibid., 170)*

While there is nothing natural and certain about the sex worker subject freeing herself up from the burden of guilt, it is nonetheless a possibility embedded in the lives of women, especially in the lives of lower-class, lower-caste women. Not only is the postcolonial history of moral regulation through guilt and shame, enmeshed with the consolidation of dominant caste, upper-class womanhood, they are carved out of the spectre of lower-caste lower-class women in immorality, shamelessness, poverty, migration, criminality, pathology, and deception. While the burden of moral, political-economic, and governmental regulation has been borne far more by lower-class, lower-caste women, it has also sharpened other possibilities of subaltern lives and worlds. A radically different and intimate relation with the working and survivalist body is revealed as one such possibility by Jameela's autobiography. We will pursue the shoring up of this possibility and its dynamic trajectory with Jameela chancing into sex work.

Jameela writes that after the death of her first husband, when she needs to raise money in order to have any claims over her children in her conjugal family, a friend hints at the option of 'go(ing) along with a man.' When Jameela didn't follow the hint, her friend hints further – going along with moneyed men who 'need women.' Jameela instantly understands that 'this had to do with using the woman the way the husband does' (*Ibid.*, 23). In this coded interaction between two women friends, the transactional experience of sex, whether in housework or in sex work, whether in the hidden economics of housework or the criminalised economy of sex work, are indistinguishable. Jameela's nonchalant use of the phrase 'using the woman' and her matter-of-fact characterisation of her own sex work in terms of her 'body' being 'used' compel a fundamental rethinking of objectification. Further, just as Jameela appears unconcerned with making any moral distinctions between marital sex and sex with a client, she discerns a critical monetary distinction between the two. She is only too amused and pleased by the thought that she would be getting handsomely paid for her company and sex, 'Something earth-shaking was going to happen. Someone was going to spend fifty rupees on me!' (*Ibid.*, 24). It is this monetary distinction, that remains critical in cataloguing and separating the numerous instances of the use of her body – (a) the husband and the 'husbands' (brokers/'ropers') who use without paying, who are useful for accessing shelter and for producing and fathering children but who extort money and labour and abandon the sex worker with disease and the burden of child rearing; (b) the lower-class clients who mildly use and pay, who are not 'obnoxious' in their demands but among whom one has to be selective; (c) the middle-class clients who make full use of their pay – set on getting their money's worth, but with whom a hotel of choice, shelter for the night and at least a pretension of dignified behaviour is assured; (d) the better-off clients, especially the young ones, who 'like to bulldoze' and pay, and (e) the thugs who use for free.

Not only did the instrumental framing of her friend's suggestion resonate with her own experience of marital sex, Jameela's transactional relations with clients twice turned into marriages. More importantly, Jameela's narrative shows how it is the imperative of motherhood that guides her in and out of sex work and marriages. Marx in his discussion of alienation has famously argued that under capitalism, the worker feels most human when he is engaged in his most animal functions like eating, sleeping, and procreating, and feels most inhuman/animal-like when he is engaged in what ought to distinguish him as human, i.e. his labouring activity. What capitalist modernity obscures is that these 'animal' functions involve the 'work' of women, and become the primary site of routine alienation for women in the way factory work becomes for men. The meaningful distinction then emerges when payment is offered for some of this work and it is brought into the indiscriminating public realm. What is most important is that this very distinguishing function of payment is to stigmatise the work and discipline other women rather than recognise and visibilise it as work, but for Jameela, this payment has the function of what can be called an *economic pleasure*. Narratives of sex workers within and outside the scholarship on sex work, are characteristically inflected by the pleasure of charging for that which is assumed to be free. It is a particular kind of experience of economic independence and dignity – inflected by the pleasure of snubbing indifference at the stigma that is stamped on the payment. It becomes the most intimate pleasure of the sex worker with herself, one that no one can share with her.

Notes

1 To keep the discussion focused, I have only discussed Bataille's arguments regarding sexual experience. However, for Bataille, sexual experiences and near-death experiences, especially those created and intensified by taboo and transgression, were fundamentally the same. They were characterised by the experience of individual annihilation and visceral continuity, which ceased to be subjective experience upon death and became objective reality of fusion with natural cycles over ages, till the point of getting individuated again through reproduction. Thus, Bataille shows how work and the appearance of life/reproduction involve individuation while sex and death involve individual annihilation and fusion. However, while in early religious societies, experiences of both individuation and individual annihilation through bodily continuity were sanctioned; in a morally ordered society, the latter is shunned.

2 For an illuminating discussion on the concept of 'separations' as the violence of western modernity, Gandhi's critique of 'separations,' and the moral-political implications of these for the subaltern *veshya,* see Skaria (2006). For more on this, see Tambe (2009b): 21–38.

3 Friedrich Nietzsche's formulation of morality as the 'self-division of man,' in which 'man treats himself not as *individuum* but as *dividuum*,' illuminates the multiple and incessant divisions of the self and the social through which modern morality and its promise of transformation played out (Nietzsche 1994).

4 Different formulations of modern-day sex work turn on this critical question of abstraction of labour power from the labouring body and ownership of the latter. Thus, Karl Marx excludes prostitution from labour but invokes it to critique alienation of labour under capitalism (Marx 2012); Friedrich Engels saw prostitution as waged labour and marriage as sexual slavery of the wife under capitalism (Engels 2010); and abolitionist feminists see sex work as sexual slavery (Dworkin 1993; Pateman 2014).

5 Other critical factors in the creation of the modern family being the perpetuation of private property and maintaining purity of lineage and identity (Menon 2012).

6 For a discussion of the family as an intimate sphere of political-economic regulation and its rethinking as a regulatory site *between* reproduction and production, see Humphries (2009).

7 What I'm referring to here is a continuum in which monetised exchange and publicness are in an inverse and co-constitutive relation to the morality of woman/sex. When I say non-monetisation and privatisation as wife/mother and monetisation and publicness as prostitute, I am referring to the two poles of the continuum so as to clarify their inverse functions of moralising and stigmatising woman/sex, respectively. In reality, of course, these neat separations are rarely to be found but I would argue that the inverse and co-constitutive relation nonetheless operates even in enmeshed situations. Thus, even the female labourer who does not engage in the monetised exchange of woman/sex (as which prostitution is framed), because of her movement outside the home in the public domain, gets cast with the suspicion of immorality, as being promiscuous and disposed to prostituting herself, resulting in demands of sexual favour or instances of sexual abuse. On the other hand, for the work she does do, she gets discriminately paid or paid only upon supplementing her work with what her movement outside the home indicates – providing sex. Thus, money doesn't perform the direct function of valuation of labour, rather it performs the function of devaluing the woman/sex who seeks money and hence goes out of the home, whereby she may be sexually abused with greater impunity. Thus it also performs the function of reminding her the primacy of conjugal work – unpaid and privatised – in her valuation, albeit a moral valuation.

Secondly, I must emphasise here that monetisation (or its absence) refers strictly to monetised exchange. Hence, the passing on of money or goods to the houseworker for housework, dowry in marriage, offering of gift or *nazrana* in courtesan culture – none of these are to be seen as monetised exchange, indeed not letting them take the form of money exchange is absolutely crucial for the specific functions they perform, such as naturalisation (Fortunati 1995) and moralisation in the case of housework, and maintaining distinction (as opposed to standardisation by money exchange) and respectability of service in the case of gifts in courtesan culture (Feldman and Gordon 2006).

8 Amrita Nandy writes how 'women across classes – especially as mothers – are expected to show relentless allegiance towards care work. Those who come close to this archetype are promised a social pedestal, *albeit they are not supposed to seek it but serve selflessly*' (Nandy 2016, emphasis mine).

9 Government of India.1956. 'Immoral Traffic (Prevention) Act, 1956.' www.hrln.org/hrln/child-rights/laws-in-place/1715-the-immoral-traffic-prevention-act-1956.html. Accessed 11 May 2017.

10 Ratna Kapur explores the politics of border control and shows how controlling the cross-border migration of poor women in search of work becomes a key site for enacting the scripts of nation, sexuality and family (Kapur 2005). Also see Kempadoo et al. 2012 and Agustin 2007.

11 Government of India.1956. 'Immoral Traffic (Prevention) Act 1956.' www.hrln.org/hrln/child-rights/laws-in-place/1715-the-immoral-traffic-prevention-act-1956.html. Accessed 11 May 2017.

12 For spatial politics of sex work, see Legg 2009; Shah 2014; Bernstein 2007; Hoang 2015.
13 While the discussion here is based on my reading of Nalini Jameela's autobiography, I was struck by how closely and unintentionally my discussion was guided by Svati Shah's ethnography of *nakas* – street corners in Mumbai where men and women stand in anticipation and search of daily-wage labour (Shah 2014). Like her respondents at the *naka*, Shah also knows the secret of the *naka* being used covertly for soliciting clients for sex work. However, like her respondents, Shah too feigns ignorance, partial knowledge or by-the-way curiosity about the secret, thereby exploring the public space of the *naka* and the politics among its users, through the workings of its/their secrets (Shah 2014).
14 For a discussion of the discomforts that creep into solidarities between sex workers' organisations and feminist, labour, Dalit, LGBTI movements, see Vijayakumar et al. 2015.
15 www.thenewsminute.com/article/malayalee-men-are-sex-thieves-says-author-and-sex-worker-nalini-jameela-41515 Accessed 22 October 2017.
16 For detailed discussion of this question, see Oldenberg 1990; Shah 2014.

References

Agrawal, A. 2008. *Chaste Wives and Prostitute Sisters: Patriarchy and Prostitution among the Bedias of India*. New Delhi: Routledge.

Agustin, L. 2007. *Sex at the Margins: Migration, Labour Markets and the Rescue Industry*. London: Zed Books.

Anagol, P. 2005. *The Emergence of Feminism in India, 1850–1920*. Hampshire: Ashgate.

Andrews, K. and E. Bushnell. 1898. *The Queen's Daughters in India*. London: Mogar and Scott.

Ballhatchet, K. 1980. *Race, Sex and Class under the Raj: Imperial Attitudes and Policies and their Critics, 1793–1905*. New York: St. Martin's Press.

Bannerjee, S. 1998. *Dangerous Outcast: The Prostitute in Nineteenth Century Bengal*. Calcutta: Seagull Books.

Bataille, G. 2012. *Eroticism*. London: Penguin.

Bernstein, E. 2007. *Temporarily Yours: Intimacy, Authenticity and the Commerce of Sex*. Chicago: Chicago University Press.

Chakravarti, U. 1989. 'Whatever Happened to the Vedic Dasi: Orientalism, Nationalism, and a Script for the Past.' In K. Sangari and S. Vaid (eds.), *Recasting Women: Essays in Colonial History*, pp. 27–87. New Delhi: Kali for Women.

Chatterjee, G. 2008. 'The Veshya, the Ganika and the Tawaif: Representations of Prostitutes and Courtesans in Indian Language, Literature and Cinema.' In R. Sahni, V. K. Shankar, and H. Apte (eds.), *Prostitution and Beyond: An Analysis of Sex Work in India*, pp. 279–300. Los Angeles: Sage.

Chatterjee, P. 1993. *The Nation and Its Fragments: Colonial and Postcolonial Histories*. Boston: Princeton University Press.

Costa, M. D. 2012a. 'On the General Strike.' In C. Barbagallo and S. Federici (eds.), *'Care Work' and the Commons*, pp. 70–73. New Delhi: Phoneme Publishers and Distributors (Pvt.) Ltd.

Costa, M. D. 2012b. 'Women and the Subversion of the Community.' In C. Barbagallo and S. Federici (eds.), *'Care Work' and the Commons*, pp. 23–69. New Delhi: Phoneme Publishers and Distributors (Pvt.) Ltd.

Daggers, J. and D. Neal (eds.). 2006. *Sex, Gender, and Religion: Josephine Butler Revisited*. New York: Peter Lang.

Dutta, M.K. 2010. *Babuder Andarmahal Theke: The Life, Passion and Inner Conflicts of Fixed Partners of the Sex Workers*. Kolkata: Durbar Prakashani.

Dworkin, A. 1993. 'Prostitution and Male Supremacy.' *Michigan Journal of Gender and Law*, 1(1): 1–13.

Engels, F. 2010. *The Origin of the Family, Private Property and the State*. London: Penguin.
Federici, S. 2012. 'Wages Against Housework.' In C. Barbagallo and S. Federici (eds.), *'Care Work' and the Commons*, pp. 74–87. New Delhi: Phoneme Publishers and Distributors (Pvt.) Ltd.
Federici, S. 2013. *Caliban and the Witch: Women, the Body, and Primitive Accumulation*. New Delhi: Phoneme.
Feldman, M., and B. Gordon. (eds.). 2006. *The Courtesan's Arts: Cross Cultural Perspectives*. New York: Oxford University Press.
Fortunati, L. 1995. *The Arcane of Reproduction: Housework, Prostitution, Labor and Capital*. Brooklyn: Autonomedia.
Foucault, M. 1992. *The Use of Pleasure: The History of Sexuality. Volume 2*. England: Penguin.
Foucault, M. 2014. *The History of Sexuality: An Introduction. Volume 1*. New York: Spark Publishing.
Ghosh, D. 2008. *Sex and the Family in Colonial India: The Making of Empire*. New Delhi: Cambridge University Press.
Government of India. 1956. 'Immoral Traffic (Prevention) Act, 1956.' www.hrln.org/hrln/child-rights/laws-in-place/1715-the-immoral-traffic-prevention-act-1956.html. Accessed 11 May 2017.
Hoang, K.K. 2015. *Dealing in Desire: Asian Ascendancy, Western Decline, and the Hidden Currencies of Global Sex Work*. Los Angeles: University of California Press.
Humphries, J. 2009. 'The Origin of the Family: Born Out of Scarcity Not Wealth.' In J. Sayers, M. Evans and N. Redclift (eds.), *Engels Revisited: New Feminist Essays*. New York: Routledge.
Jameela, N. 2007. *The Autobiography of a Sex Worker*. New Delhi: Westland Ltd.
Jeffreys, S. (ed.). 1987. *The Sexuality Debates*. New York: Routledge & Kegan Paul.
Jha, D. and T. Sharma. 2016. 'Caste and Prostitution in India: Politics of Shame and of Exclusion.' *Sociology and Criminology-Open Access*, 4(1).
Jordan, J. 2006. '"Trophies of the Saviour": Josephine Butler's Biographical Sketches of Prostitutes.' In J. Daggers and D. Neal (eds.), *Sex, Gender, and Religion: Josephine Butler Revisited*, pp. 21–36. New York: Peter Lang.
Jordan, K. K. 2003. *From Sacred Servant to Profane Prostitute: A History of the Changing Legal Status of the Devadasis in India, 1857–1947*. New Delhi: Manohar.
Kannabiran, K., and V. Kannabiran. 2003. *Muvalur Ramamirthammal's Web of Deceit: Devadasi Reform in Colonial India*. New Delhi: Kali for Women.
Kapur, R. 2005. *Erotic Justice: Law and the New Politics of Postcolonialism*. Britain: Glasshouse Press.
Kempadoo, K., J. Sanghera, and B. Pattnaik. 2012. *Trafficking and Prostitution Reconsidered: New Perspectives on Migration, Sex Work, and Human Rights*. Oxford: Routledge.
Kosambi, N. (ed.). 2000. *Pandita Ramabai through her own Words: Selected Works*. New Delhi: Oxford University Press.
Kotiswaran, P. (ed.). 2011. *Sex Work*. New Delhi: Women Unlimited.
Kotiswaran, P. 2012. *Dangerous Sex, Invisible Labour*. New Delhi: Oxford University Press.
Kumar, Uday. 2016. *Writing the First Person: Literature, History and Autobiography in Modern Kerala*. New Delhi: Permanent Black.
Legg, S. 2009. 'Governing Prostitution in Colonial Delhi: From Cantonment Regulations to International Hygiene (1864–1939).' *Social History*, 34(4).
Levine, P. 2003. *Prostitution, Race and Politics: Policing Venereal Disease in the British Empire*. New York: Routledge.
Maciszewski, A. 2006. 'Tawa' if, Tourism, and Tales: The Problematics of Twenty-First Century Musical Patronage for North India's Courtesans.' In *The Courtesan's Arts: Cross Cultural Perspectives*, pp. 332–352. New York: Oxford University Press.

Maruthur, N.M. 2010. 'Sexual Figures of Kerala: Cultural Practices, Regionality and the Politics of Sexuality.' Unpublished PhD dissertation, University of Chicago.

Marx, K. 2010. *Capital*. New Delhi: Leftword Books.

Marx, K. 2012. *Economic and Philosophic Manuscripts of 1844*. New York: Dover Publications, Inc.

Menon, N. 2012. *Seeing Like a Feminist*. New Delhi: Zubaan.

Mies, M. 1994. *Patriarchy and Accumulation on a World Scale: Women in the International Division of Labour*. Trowbridge: Redwood Books.

Nair, J. 1996. 'The Devadasi, Dharma and the State.' In Ratna Kapur (ed.), *Feminist Terrains in Legal Domains: Interdisciplinary Essays on Women and Law in Colonial India*. New Delhi: Sage.

Nandy, Amrita. 2016. *Motherhood and Choice: Uncommon Mothers, Childfree Women*. New Delhi: Zubaan Books.

Nietzsche, F. 1994. *Human, All Too Human*. London: Penguin.

Oldenberg, V. 1990. *Lifestyle as Resistance: The Case of the Courtesans of Lucknow*. Lucknow: The Upper India Publishing House Ltd.

Pande, R. 2008. 'Ritualized Prostitution: Devdasis to Jogins – A Few Case Studies.' In R. Sahni, V. K. Shankar and H. Apte (eds.), *Prostitution and Beyond An Analysis of Sex Work in India*, pp. 101–117. New Delhi: Sage.

Pateman, C. 2014. *The Sexual Contract*. New York: John Wiley & Sons.

Phoenix, J. 2001. *Making Sense of Prostitution*. New York: Palgrave.

Qureshi, R. B. 2006. 'Female Agency and Partilineal Constraints: Situating Courtesans in Twentieth-Century India.' In M. Feldman and B. Gordon (eds.), *The Courtesan's Arts: Cross Cultural Perspectives*, pp. 312–331. New York: Oxford University Press.

Ramabai, P. 2000a. 'A Short History of Kripa Sadan, or Home of Mercy.' In N. Kosambi (ed.), *Pandita Ramabai through Her Own Words: Selected Works*, pp. 278–294. New Delhi: Oxford University Press.

Ramabai, P. 2000b. 'Famine Experiences.' In *Pandita Ramabai through Her Own Words: Selected Works*, pp. 247–260. New Delhi: Oxford University Press.

Rajan, R.S. 2011. 'The Prostitution Question(s): (female) Agency, Sexuality and Work.' In P. Kotiswaran (ed.), *Sex Work*, pp. 118–153. New Delhi: Women Unlimited.

Sahni, R., V.K. Shankar and H. Apte (eds.). 2008. *Prostitution and Beyond: An Analysis of Sex Work in India*. New Delhi: Sage.

Sangari, K. 1999. *Politics of the Possible: Essays on Gender, History, Narrative and Colonial English*. New Delhi: Tulika.

Shah, S.P. 2014. *Street Corner Secrets: Sex, Work, and Migration in the City of Mumbai*. Durham: Duke University Press.

Skaria, A. 2006. 'Only One Word, Properly Altered Gandhi and the Question of the Prostitute.' *Economic & Political Weekly*, 41(49).

Soofi, M.A. 2012. *Nobody Can Love You More: Life in Delhi's Red Light District*. New Delhi: Penguin.

Srinivasan, A. 1987. 'Reform and Revival: The Devadasi and Her Dance.' *Economic and Political Weekly*, 22(51): 2225–2228.

Srinivasan, D. M. 2006. 'Royalty's Courtesans and God's Mortal Wives: Keepers of Culture in Precolonial India.' In M. Feldman and B. Gordon (eds.), *The Courtesan's Arts: Cross-Cultural Perspectives*, pp. 161–181. New York: Oxford University Press.

Stoler, L.A. 1995. *Race and the Education of Desire: Foucault's History of Sexuality and the Colonial Order of Things*. London: Duke University Press.

Swarankar, R. 2008. 'Ethnographic Study of Community-Based Sex Work among Nats.' In R. Sahni, V. K. Shankar and H. Apte (eds.), *Prostitution and Beyond An Analysis of Sex Work in India*, pp. 118–125. New Delhi: Sage.

Tambe, A. 2006. 'Brothels as families: Reflections on the History of Bombay's Kothas.' *International Feminist Journal of Politics*, 8(2).

Tambe, A. 2009a. *Codes of Misconduct – Regulating Prostitution in Late Colonial Bombay*. New Delhi: Zubaan.

Tambe, A. 2009b. 'Gandhi's "Fallen" Sisters.' *Social Scientist*, 37(1–2): 21–38.

Tambe, A. 2011. 'An Elusive Ingenue: A Transnational Feminist Analysis of European Prostitution in Colonial Bombay.' In P. Kotiswaran (ed.), *Sex Work*, pp. 3–26. New Delhi: Women Unlimited.

The News Minute. www.thenewsminute.com/article/malayalee-men-are-sex-thieves-says-author-and-sex-worker-nalini-jameela-41515. Accessed 22 October 2017.

Vijayakumar, G. 2015. '"There was an uproar": Reading The Arcane of Reproduction Through Sex Work in India.' *Viewpoint Magazine*. www.viewpointmag.com/2015/10/31/there-was-an-uproar-reading-the-arcane-of-reproduction-through-sex-work-in-india/. Accessed 20 October 2017.

Vijayakumar, G., S. Chacko and S. Panchanadeswaran. 2015. 'As Human Beings and As Workers': Sex Worker Unionization in Karnataka, India.' *Global Labour Journal*, 6(1). DOI:http://dx.doi.org/10.15173/glj.v6i1.2297. Accessed 20 October 2017.

Zelizer, Viviana A. 2000. 'The Purchase of Intimacy.' *Law and Social Inquiry*, 25(3): 817–848.

10

PUBLIC SPACES AND PRIVATE INTIMACIES

The 'Politics of Belonging' in parks

Pranta Pratik Patnaik

Mobile bodies and gendered spaces: an introduction

The relationship between body, space, and gender identity can be examined through the culture and politics of everyday life. The discussion on moving bodies in gendered spaces has quite often been discussed in academia mostly in terms of restrictions on the mobility of women in public spaces (Phadke 2013). Female bodies are seen as lived entities that constitute the narrative of a social structure, which is patriarchal and compulsorily heteronormative. The body becomes a site of spatial orientation as well as a medium of communication with others. Streets become unfriendly and hostile spaces for women. There is a need to reclaim these spaces as it is in the spaces that gender is performed and the construction of identity is facilitated and re-shaped.

Mostly ethnographies on body and space do not theorise the body, per se, but utilise it as a spatial metaphor and representational space. Even though the body is considered as a tool in the production of cultural forms (Bourdieu 1977; Douglas 1971; Mauss1979), it is treated as an empty vessel without any consciousness, emotion or intention. Douglas, Mauss, Bourdieu, and others are more concerned with the body as a metaphor for social and cultural conceptualisation than with the organism itself, and the effect of cultural influences on it and its operations. Any adequate analysis of body, therefore, needs to consider it as 'a material, physical and biological phenomenon which is irreducible to immediate social processes or classifications' (Shilling 1993:10). However, this should not imply that I am advocating for a biological determinism, which reduces the complexity of human psychological and social life to the biological make-up of individuals and groups. Such an essentialist argument reduces the complexity of life to a fixed and pre-given biological component of individuals (Low 2003).

Earlier discussions on the relevance of body began with the Cartesian dualism of mind and body, where the latter is considered as a constraining force which ideally should be brought under the control of the former. In order to overcome the dualism between the mind and body, we need to understand how the body is constructed through sign, symbols, and discursive practices (Turner 1984). The concept of the self is often used to avoid the assumed split between the body and mind. While defining the self, we construct the 'Others' who help us in defining particular ways of imagining about ourselves and performing self-identity. This self was referred to as the 'looking glass self' by C.H.Cooley. Self-identity is, thus, an expression and manifestation of our internalisation of how we are perceived, positioned, and responded to by others.

The fact that bodies are always 'made social' points to the social and cultural processes which enact upon the thoughts, actions, and habits of individuals. They exist within a network of ties, obligations, and duties as prescribed by the society. At this point, I would like to invoke Foucault's concepts of positivity and productivity to describe the role power plays in producing, what he termed as 'docile bodies' (Foucault 1973, 1977). According to him, disciplinary power does not prohibit or constrain rather works through the ways in which norms and regulatory ideals of the society are incorporated into an individual's internal forms of self-monitoring and self-regulation. This is achieved not through any imposition or force but through their self-internalisation of particular body techniques and practices where disciplinary power works through the acceptance and active participation of its subjects thereby creating spaces to perform their identities.

Theoretically, this chapter draws on Henri Lefebvre's theory of the production of space and Judith Butler's theory on performativity in order to unravel the intersections between body, space, and identity. Henri Lefebvre (1991) talked about three moments in the production of space: spatial practice, representation of space and representational space. Spatial practice refers to the way how we perceive our surroundings and ourselves as we negotiate their use. Representations of space are the signs, symbols, codes, and ideas associated with institutional knowledge; representational spaces denote qualitative, fluid, relational spaces that are produced and modified over time. Although Lefebvre's discussion of space is based on the mutual constitution of bodies and space, his analysis is silent about the gendered bodies having multiple sexual identities and practices. By taking resort to Judith Butler's theory of performativity, my aim is to fill the gap of Lefebvre's theoretical work, as well as that of a queer theory, by exploring a queer theorisation of social space. Butler's analysis of identity as performance parallels Lefebvre's productive view of space. Identities and spaces are simultaneously constituted through representation and discourse thereby creating productive bodies, which constitute performative spaces. The performative acts of social space and gendered/sexed bodies offer the possibility for moments of "truth" wherein sexuality and space can be performed differently (Ilcan 1998). It needs to be understood that by bringing these theorists together, in this chapter my goal is not to reduce one to the other; there are clear differences in theoretical orientation and subject matter. What I am suggesting is that Lefebvre's and Butler's proposals echo one another. Despite their differences, these projects are underscored by critical accounts of the social reality that, when placed alongside one another facilitates a productive rethinking on the interrelationship between sexuality and social space. Thus, space and sexuality are inevitably intertwined and sexuality cannot be confined to narrow definitions of the sexed body as it permeates all material and representational practices. Queerness, both as performative attributes of individual bodies and as products of spatial practices, are inseparable components of space (Conlon 2004). The agency of the queer bodies is considerably diminished in heteropatriarchal spatial discourses and practices.

The argument that spaces limit the mobility, therefore, needs to be re-evaluated through the lens of human agency, where creative strategies are employed to dismantle the hegemonic spaces through emotional investment (Baydar 2012). In this context, the body then needs to be seen as having multiple identities that are no longer secured or confined to certain fixed social space. It has been argued that spaces speak of regulation and control – control of desire, passion, and need in order to maintain the social order but one cannot deny the fact that identities are neither stable nor unified across time and space. Consequently, the body is not a singular bounded entity rather what Anne Marie Mol (2002) terms as the 'body multiple,' which stresses on what bodies can do and become. Since bodily identities are fluid identities which changes according to contexts, the spaces in which these identities are performed are also not a unified, homogenous, and neutral entity. It can be better understood as an ongoing and continuous production process where individuals perform their identities. Such deliberations represent a context of uncertainties where there is no fixity of the identity and space. It is against this backdrop that I seek to understand three key research questions – In what ways do the social structures exert their power in the regulation of bodies? How does the 'agency' of the bodies subvert or challenge the disciplinary social structures? What could be the possible limitations to the performativity of such agencies? These queries relate to the sociological debate between structures vs. agency, where it becomes difficult to determine who is more powerful between the two. This chapter exemplifies the interplay of structures and human agency. By human agency is meant the individual capacity to act, to subvert, to resist and to interrogate the rigid social structures. As Shilling (1993) argues, that the body is always an unfinished entity. It is not simply defined by a fixed human nature but also has the potential to change, subvert, and transform the particular set of historical circumstances within which they are socialised. The body is, no doubt, affected by discourse but we also need to recognise of how the body reacts back and affects the discourse. The key argument here is to understand human agency through the notion of everyday politics. In an attempt to answer the above-mentioned questions, this chapter limits itself to an understanding of public parks as an 'embodied space,' that is, as a point of intersection between body, space, and identity where the creation of place is made possible through spatial orientation, movement, and language. The concept of embodied space underscores the importance of the body as a physical and biological entity, lived experiences, a centre of agency and a location for speaking or expressing desires. In contrast to disciplinary spaces, which confines people to act, behave, or work in particular ways, this chapter focuses on 'marginal' spaces of gender practices and habitable relations like gay cruising parks in Delhi, a North Indian city and capital of India.

Gay cruising parks in Delhi – mapping the field

The capital city of India, Delhi, offers several public spaces that are being used by the sexual 'minorities' to seek pleasure and companionship. At the outset, it needs to be mentioned that the public parks in Delhi are marked by both homosexual affirmations and heteronormative assertions. These parks have become spaces of cruising for those who do not find a place for sexual pleasure and for those who cannot afford the gay dating apps in their mobile phones. Even if they have access to gay dating apps, they meet in these parks as some of them do not have a 'place for sex.' They do not feel comfortable taking someone from the park to their homes or even hostels (in case of students) in order to avoid any questions from family members, friends, and neighbours. There is a kind of mixture of familiarity and strangeness when they meet someone for the first time in the public parks. There are several such parks in Delhi, where one could find the gay intimacy. This study takes an in-depth plunge into the research on these spaces by looking into the tussle between human agency and social structures.

The park is a symbolic reminder of the rigidity of social structure, which is partly subverted by the queer population who visit the park. This section deals with the 'field,' not only the physical field, i.e. the park, but also the psychic field in terms of the role of the researcher and their relation with the participants. My regular visit to several parks in Delhi within a span of four years led me to develop an observational account of these public spaces. I was accompanying one of my friends for his research work and developed a keen interest in understanding the nuances of sexuality and space. Apart from the intermittent visits to the park, gradually I started investing my time in parks during the evenings and late nights. I confined myself to study the 'SA' park (pseudonym), one of the gay cruising parks in Delhi. Though this chapter uses the term 'gay cruising parks,' it should be noted that these parks were not exclusively cruising areas. There were families who visited the park for outings as well. Furthermore, the queer population who visited the park did not always identify themselves as gay. There were other words which were used by them in the parks, like *koti*, *hijra*, and *chhaka*, a sort of local way of addressing each other. This exemplifies how the terms 'gay' or 'LGBT' are part of a donor category, which most of the people did not necessarily identify with. One evening I asked someone – *Are you gay or bisexual?* He replied – *Is it necessary for your research to categorise me? Can't I be both or neither?* It made me realise how our academic lenses in a way curb our ways of understanding human behaviour. Consequently, I allowed my participants to define and express themselves not only in terms of their sexual preferences but also from the perspective of their life-world experiences.

The SA park needs to be seen in terms of temporality and spatiality simultaneously. Initially, the periods of observation of this park were on an average three hours in duration, with variation in time of day and night, days of the week. While the number of people in the park does not remain constant, it was difficult to know where they disappear after few weeks or months. There is again a new set of people who visit the park. Gradually I increased the duration of my loitering in and around the park mostly from evening to late night as I observed that this was the time when the park was more crowded with queer people. While the number of people ebbed and flowed, there were 2–3 groups I observed most frequently in the park comprising of five or six men who ranged in age from their early 20s to late 50s. At night I saw many of the people that I had seen in the park during the day hanging out in the surrounding area. This group spent their time hustling for money, food, and drink; soliciting other men; and relaxing on the park benches. The activities of these individuals were harder to track at night as they appeared and disappeared deftly and were rarely stationary for very long. This might have been due to the presence of large crowds of people in the surrounding area at night, especially at weekends and also the noticeable level of police surveillance of the area at night.

The New Delhi Municipal Council posts the opening and closing hours of the park at each entrance alongside a lengthy list of prohibitions restricting smoking, spitting, public display of affection, plucking of flowers, gambling, and cooking. During the evening, it is crowded with men, women, and children. After 7:30 p.m., the families leave the park. Few couples still hang around in the park. By 8:30 p.m. groups of men throng around in the park waiting for their chance to open up a conversation with someone or to meet their lovers. As it becomes dark, men start choosing their partners for the night. If a conversation goes right, they go to any of the decided places to fulfil their desire. In case they do not choose anyone or are not picked up by anyone, they move out of the park towards the nearby McDonald's restaurant, which provides another space for the upper-middle-class gays. The gays in front of the McDonald's rarely come to the park, as they consider it to be a dirty place full of '*hijras*' (eunuchs), low-class guys, thieves, and drug peddlers. They have named the park as the '*mandi*' (a slang for the place where bodies are for sale) indicating that it is not classy or elite and essentially depicts a low-class culture. Thus, queer spaces for cruising are divided along the class lines. After 9:30 p.m., there will be no one in the park as the police drive them away from the park. Space comes under surveillance after a particular time. Those 'unlucky birds' who could not make it for the day proceed towards their home/destination but with a hope that the next day it will be their day.

The park is located amidst the busy streets, shopping complex with a cinema hall in front of it. It has four entrances, two on the right and other two on the left, which makes the park a space in which people either pass through or fill conveying a message about themselves and their cultural status by dress, accessories, posture, and speech. I initiated conversation randomly with the queer people in the park, telling them about my research on sexuality and space. Most of them were not able to understand why I am doing this research. Few thought this research will endanger this park and it would be known to everybody and as such, they can never visit the park for cruising. They reposed their trust in me when I expressed my desire to know about their lives, their relation to the park. On the condition of anonymity, they narrated their life stories, their desires, and the hardships they undergo by not being acceptable in society. The structured, open-ended interview questions became irrelevant as they started telling about themselves. The psychic field – my relation with them – moved from being a stranger to a level of intimacy. They found a friend in me. Someone told me that they found an 'agony uncle' in me, someone with whom they can share anything. I initially took them as respondents for my research, but gradually they became active participants for this work. A few of them were initially curious to know about my sexuality and whether I was looking for a sexual partner in the park. I was approached by few with great flattery, even with a hint that I pay them for a sexual favour. Later they realised that I was visiting the park for my research and not to have any physical relation. Consequently, a few lost interest in talking to me in the park. I was able to have deep conversational interviews with 38 participants through random and snowball sampling. All of them belonged to a low-middle-class family. Though it is difficult to identify the category of the middle class in India, the participants preferred to define themselves in this category in terms of their income and occupation. Within the park itself, there is a segregation of spaces. The corners of the park were occupied by the *hijras* (eunuchs), mostly in the rear portion of the park. The elderly gays rarely walk in the park. They prefer to sit on the benches or the lawns. The young and the middle-age persons took rounds of walk on the pathways within the park. The participants found it difficult to converse in English; therefore most of the conversations took place in Hindi. All the participants felt that SA park has given them a space to explore their identities without any fear of judgment. They felt more comfortable in the public park than in their homes. Most of the conversation with my participants revolved around the issue of the rigidity of private spaces like home, neighbourhood, places of study and work as compared to the 'freedom' they feel in the park. This sets the background to discuss the flaws involved in the dichotomy between public and private spaces and to explore how public spaces can be felt to be private zones. The key argument is that parks offer a space to replace the public/private distinction through a critical understanding of the everyday through the eyes of the queer people visiting the park.

Bodily practices and politics of the everyday

Historically speaking, the definition of what constitutes the public or private is quite essential for distribution of power and resources. It has helped us in many ways to understand the existing power relationships in the society, especially in terms of gender discrimination. However, the public/private distinction has been argued to be misleading as it fails to take into account a 'prospect of heterogeneity' (Prokhovnik 1999: 33). There are 'liminal' spaces, as Victor Turner and Foucault point out, which does not adhere to the conventional definition of public and private. The SA park is one such liminal space as it exhibits the feature of being public but instilling a feeling of private simultaneously among the queer.

Firoz (name changed), a 21-year-old Muslim guy, belongs to Chandni Chowk area in Delhi. He is medium built, extremely fair, with an average height. He comes to the park every evening after finishing his daily work and leaves at night by 9 p.m., either after having a brief sexual encounter behind the bushes in the dark or after several rounds of walking in the park. The way he walks, swaying his waist, and talks – with a smile and a glimmer in his eyes – attract the men who are present there to satisfy their desire. At a very young age, he had to work in a household garment factory as a tailor. He mastered this skill from his father. He could not complete his formal education in a college under Delhi University due to some economic constraints. He identified himself as gay when he was in school. He has been visiting the park for the last 10years. On being asked why he visits the park regularly, he replied that he comes to this park to get 'fresh' air. I probed further and asked him why only this park, whereas there was another park just opposite the road. '*Es park mein ek apna pan sa lagtaa hain*' (A feeling of belongingness comes for this park), came the prompt reply. The presumed privacy of the home is challenged when a public place like park provides the context where the queer body feels at home and where gender performance can be managed in a heteropatriarchal society.

He told me about the different categories of people who visit the park and how the park has changed over years:

> Earlier there used to be a decent crowd that came to the park for cruising. Nowadays all the professional guys are coming. (Professional guys are those who are willing to sleep with another man for a handsome amount of money in return). There is more police vigilance these days. Some thieves are also roaming in this park. They trap a guy, go with him, and take away all the valuables at knife point. I am very cautious due to this reason. I generally hang around with those guys whom I have chatted with earlier and are known to me. There are some guys who are also from Chandni Chowk area, so I prefer to talk to them mostly. Most of my neighbours are also here and I am not shy in front of them being a gay as they are also like me. But once we leave this park, and if accidentally we meet in Chandni Chowk area, then we don't recognise each other and behave as if we have never met.

The fluid boundaries between the public and the private intersect in complicated ways with the fluid boundaries of gendered performance as the queer bodies need to sacrifice their queerness off stage. He even advised me that I should not recognise him if I see him while travelling on the Metro train.

Mr. Tarun (name changed), a 50-year-old man, is a doctor by profession who roams with a 25-year-old guy in the park every day after their daily routine. Tarun's wife stays in Meerut with their children and occasionally visits Delhi. Tarun claims to maintain a balanced dual life by not transgressing the societal boundaries:

> I do all my duties as a husband and as a father. I have never shied away from my responsibilities towards them. So I am honest with them. This is another part of my life. This park is my home as this is where I met my boyfriend and

> we fell in love with each other and he is my lover. I am not hurting anyone, so why should I have the feeling of guilt? Even he (his lover) is married and his wife is also expecting a baby.

Even though disciplinary regimes like family/household aims to separate the outside (the undisciplined, the marginal) from the inside (ordered), to dominate social spacing, and to regulate who is to be put in operation, they fail to eliminate the outside. The outside always remains an unordered space of spontaneity, unpredictability, and indeterminability, something Grosz (1994) describes as a 'space of multiplicity,' capable of creating sociable relations, producing new views on living life, and challenging hegemonic borders. It, therefore, becomes imperative to examine how through bodily practices in their everyday lives in the park, the queer body subverts the structural practices.

It needs to be mentioned here that the introduction of the concept of everyday implies an understanding of history in terms of processes and as a product of people's daily appropriations. This chapter takes a critical understanding of the 'everyday' through the work of Michael E, Gardiner, which perceives the everyday as 'polydimensional,' highlighting the ambivalences and empowering potentials through our practices. A critical notion of everyday is concerned with questions like who and what is being excluded and what forms of exclusions prevail in the society? The answer to these questions opens up ways of theorising how everyday life is a site of power relations and a continually politically contested field. It is thus a site of emancipatory moments and counter-hegemonic struggles. I would like to invoke the concept of 'spaces of habit' (Grosz 1994) and counter spaces to understand the everyday politics of the queer, which constitutes a strategy of resistance for them.

Frequently visited by the sexual 'minorities' of the city, the SA park can be called as spaces of habits which include their gestures, dress, speech, and mannerisms that they use to occupy, negotiate, or modify such 'marginal' spaces. In such spaces, people tend to act in their own way leading to a somewhat flexible behaviour pattern of manners and styles that has a degree of familiarity or offers a space of comfort to them. A study of such 'closet' spaces is essential as it uncovers how any kind of bodily performativity in these spaces both constrains as well as defines the body and constructs the personal identity.

While leaving home for the park, Firoz puts a fancy dazzling t-shirt and tight hugging jeans in his bag, which he changes in a public bathroom before entering the park.

> This park has a different dress code. Looking at me, he said if you come dressed like this nobody will notice you. Even though you are not that fair and smart to get noticed, so you should try to get attention by your dress. Since I am extremely fair, all colours suit my skin and this tight hugging jean is the best way to show what you have to offer. If you want a guy, make eye contact and then give a smile. If the other person is interested a same gesture

> will be reciprocated. If that does not happen, initiate a conversation by asking him – what's the time? And then you have to take the lead in making a conversation with him. If they leave the conversation midway or refuse to tell you the time or give a light, then you should understand that they are not interested. Don't sit on these railings in the park. It invites danger. Policemen will identify you as a gay and will drive you out of this park. Other guys will think that you are easily available. So always keep walking and if you like a guy then just brush aside his body in a way as if it happened accidentally.

Apart from the dress codes and movement of bodies, there is a kind of voyeurism that exists in these spaces. The existence of heterosexual and queer gaze is quite prevalent in the SA park. The eye contact and a smile that is reciprocated among the gays in the park is considered to be a sign that one is interested in the other. I came to know that scratching the middle finger on the palm while shaking hand is considered to be an invitation for sexual relation. The elderly gay men sitting on the benches or near the bush make a 'smooching' sound to invite the other person for mutual masturbation.

All these mannerisms in the park followed by the gays make these as 'spaces of habits.' However, such habits are not common to all the gays and it differs from person to person but generally, they all indulge in certain bodily practices in the park producing their own counter spaces. These counter spaces are to be understood as spaces of resistance to the dominant order arising precisely from their subordinate, peripheral or marginalised positioning. In this park, practices where the private is made public and the queer bodies formulate a domestic scene under the protection of concrete representations of gay identity questions the presumed social and sexual order of public space. The very act of loitering and cruising in the park reflects a kind of politics of resistance that the gays are indulged. They could not have walked, talked, or dressed in a similar manner in their home or locality as they do in the parks. It gives them a feeling of freedom and a sense of satisfaction of 'doing what they had always wanted to do,' as one of the participants put it.

At this juncture, one can think of Michel Foucault's concept of 'heterotopia,' which he suggests are spaces that are different from the entire emplacement that they reflect. There is a connection as well as a complex relationship with other sites, few resemblances, and more differences; they are connected in such a way as to 'suspend, neutralise, or invert the set of relations designated, reflected, or represented by them' (1998:178). It is above all a liminal space, a break from normality. It is in these liminal spaces that liberating trajectories emerge through the negative critique of normative discursive and material practices by attending to alternative subjects, sexualities, and spaces that are largely silenced by the latter. Parks offer a space of alternative belonging, which challenges the disciplinary spatial regimes that command bodies and prescribe fixed habits. Hence, heteropatriarchal constructions and regulation of space are always already an incomplete project.

However, the park as space is not a given stage where actors perform rather is constituted through, a product of permeated social relations. There is even the construction of the 'Other,' which takes place in this park, which is discussed in the next section.

Encountering the societal–structural limits

In the previous section, we discussed the existence of agency of the body in performing their sexuality in the parks. However, one cannot turn a blind eye to the multiple hierarchies that still exists in such spaces along the lines of religion, age, class, sexual positions (top, bottom, versatile), looks, etc.

Firoz and Tarun were always against the eunuchs who visited the park. The eunuchs were considered to be ugly, dirty, and unhygienic people. Moreover, they were poor than the gays who visited these parks. They were often considered to be more interested in soliciting money from others in the park. While I thought of including the eunuchs who visited the park in my study, the participants told me that I cannot find anything for my research from them. One evening while I was talking to one of the eunuchs, Firoz crossed us but pretended not to recognise me. I was given a hint that my conversation with the eunuchs in the park was not appropriate. Most of them prefer to stay away from the eunuchs in the park. Firoz was also quite particular about the religion of the guys with whom he wanted to have a fair chance of an affair. One evening, a guy introduced himself to Firoz as Sameer, to which he asked – *Hindu wala Sameer yaa Musalman wala Sameer?* (Do you belong to the Hindu or Muslim Community?) Firoz has a kind of bitterness for the Hindus, as he had lost his close relatives in the Gujarat riots that took the lives of many Muslims in the state.

Apart from religion, age was also one of the factors that created hierarchies of space and in conversations in the park. Mr. Avadhesh Kumar, a 60-year-old man and a retired government employee, comes to the park every weekend from Shalimar Bagh by bus. A feeble old man, Mr. Kumar is always made fun by the younger group of people in the park. *Ab es umar mein tumhe jawani chaddhi hain* (At this age, you are looking for sexual relations). He lamented that persons of his age are in a double dilemma since he was forced to consummate a heterosexual marriage because of the pressure from his parents and relatives but yet still has an eagerness to stay with a young guy. His age is the biggest obstacle for him to find guys in the park, yet he comes to the park every weekend with a hope to meet someone. He recalls:

> When I was young and visited this park, I was the queen in the park. Everyone looked at me and wanted to talk to me. I was fair like milk with dark hair. Now people don't look at me. I don't find anyone in the park. I go to the public toilets to seek sexual pleasure seeing someone peeing, exchanging glances with guys hoping that someone might be interested in giving me either a hand job or blowjob. Public toilets become private areas, isn't it?

There are several such instances that I came across in the park where the able bodies become disabled due to aging, looks, facial features, baldness, bulging belly, etc. The pressure of looking good, well dressed, and having sharp features is built up in this park. This kind of situation has also developed in the gay dating sites where people want to be connected with good-looking guys having a muscular body, which I have discussed elsewhere (Patnaik 2013).

It should be noted that it is not that all the gays visit this park to seek sexual pleasure. Few just come to roam around and silently move out of the park. In case they find someone, they stick to those partners but there are some who are at an advantageous position due to their good looks. Jeetu is a 26-year-old Sikh jaat guy who quite often visits the park for '*masti*' (pleasure), as he puts it. His father does not take care of the household; his stepmother ill-treats him; his sister runs the family through the salary that she gets as a school teacher. Jeetu's inability to handle the responsibility to run the family despite being the male member haunts him. This has led him to booze many times. In such an inebriated state, he speaks a lot about his problems. Being muscular and tall, fitting the idea of a 'perfect' hunk, he has many choosers in the park. He is more interested in being picked up by the wealthy guys who can pay for his booze, clothes, and other accessories. Age is not a matter for him, rather what matters is the class position of the person with whom he roams around. He had been to various fashion shows and parties where wealthy men take him as an 'escort.' He claims that he is not gay but does all these for money and always under the influence of alcohol. What worries him most is that after a certain age, he will not be even looked at by the same wealthy persons who are paying for his expenditures.

All these instances of defining the eunuchs in the park as the disruptive miscreants, choosing one's partner on the basis of religion, age, and class, points out that an attempt is made to produce the social space of the park along patriarchal and narrowly defined social parameters of hierarchy.

Despite the playing out of rigid social hierarchies and surveillance, the queer bodies take a risk in performing their gender in the park. One pertinent question that comes to mind is – Why do they take such risk? Why are they not afraid of being seen by someone familiar or known to them? The answer to this question can be answered partially through the notion of 'pleasure seeking bodies,' which can be labelled as what Lisa Blackman (2008) calls as a 'somatically felt body,' that has 'aliveness or vitality that is literally felt or sensed but cannot necessarily be articulated, reduced to physiological processes or to the effect of social structures' (Blackman 2008: 30). The somatically felt body recognises the potential of the body to think and feel. The key concept to understand the somatically felt body is affected, which refers to a realm of feeling that is not self-contained and separate but rather enhanced and produced through the relations between the self and other. Such a realm of connectivity blurs the boundaries between self and other. The feeling body enlarges the scope for performativity, according to Butler (1990), where the individuals do not simply internalise the positions that they are invited to inhabit, in terms of cultural norms of masculinity and femininity, rather struggle with the contradictions. These struggles might produce resistance to gendered norms and might even lead to the formation of what Foucault termed as 'reverse discourses' through which people experience their embodied subjectivities. According to Bruno Latour (2005), a French Sociologist, giving prior importance to the feelings and emotions in understanding the body poses challenges to the valid existence of the 'social' in determining the bodies. He advocates for a complete rejection of the concept of social dimensions of the bodies opening up questions for future research in this area.

Moving bodies, queering the space: concluding remarks

This chapter began with an alternative perspective on the relationship between space, belonging and intimacy through a case study of the parks in Delhi. It claims that parks are not just spaces of movement but they become so through movement of bodies. Bodies exist between discourses and institutions and at the same time, we must remember that desire is also an important dimension in the constitution of bodies. The practices of marginalised queer bodies point to alternative understandings of space based on fluid and porous boundaries between such dualities as materiality/representation, inside/outside and private/public. They all focus on strategies that counter-hegemonic spatial practices and engage with the crucial question of how to think space differently. Both Butler and Lefebvre argue that the notion of authentic spaces and sexual identities are fictional and hegemonic conceptions of social reality are tentative. If we take these claims seriously, practice these politics and extend these observations to other public spaces I propose that everyday life may be filled with possibilities for performative bodies and productive spaces, which would interrogate the boundaries that have been naturalised and consequently would break down their rigidities. During my recent revisit to the park, I found tremendous changes in the park. There has been a huge national flag that can be seen in the park. Gates have been built at the four entrance/exit points, which were open earlier. After 9:00 p.m., the gates are locked. A small open museum dedicated to Mahatma Gandhi has come up inside the park due to which one has to buy a ticket of Rs.50 to enter the park. The gentrification of the park, however, has not deterred the gay people from visiting the park. After the park gets closed, they sit outside on the railings on the pavement, near the metro stations and engage in looking for partners. Their practice of everyday politics to subvert the heteronormative space to a 'homonormative' one through cruising and loitering in the park enables one to think about the possibilities for change in the society. To conclude, I would like to end with a quote from Jeremy Seabrook's work, 'Love in a Different Climate' where he claims that 'by definition, those who frequent it (the cruising park) are self-selecting: by doing so, they become known to others and are compelled into some form of self-recognition, even though many still feel shame and anxiety about their sexual needs. . . . Cruising is more about (expressing one's) sexuality and less about sex' (Seabrook 1999: 3).

References

Baydar, Gulsum. 2012. 'Sexualised Productions of Space.' *Gender, Place and Culture*, 19(6): 699–706.

Blackman, Lisa. 2008. *The Body. The Key Concepts*. Oxford, New York: Berg Publishers.

Bourdieu, P. 1977. *Outline of a Theory of Practice*. Cambridge: Cambridge University Press.

Butler, J. 1990. *Gender Trouble: Feminism and the Subversion of Identity*. London, New York: Routledge.

Conlon, Deirdre. 2004. 'Productive Bodies, Performative Spaces: Everyday Life in Christopher Park.' *Sexualities*, 7(4): 462–479.

Douglas, M. 1971. 'Do Dogs Laugh? A Cross-Cultural Approach to Body Symbolism.' *Journal of Psychosomatic Research*, 15: 387–390.

Foucault, M. 1973. *The Birth of the Clinic*. London: Tavistock.

Foucault, M. 1977. *Discipline and Punish*. London: AllenLane.

Foucault, M. 1998. 'Different Spaces.' In J.D. Faubion (ed.), *Aesthetics, Method, and Epistemology: Essential Works of Foucault*. Vol. 2, pp. 175–185. London: Penguin.

Grosz, E. 1994. *Volatile Bodies: Towards a Corporeal Feminism*. Bloomington, IN: Indiana University Press.

Ilcan, Suzan M. 1998. 'Occupying the Margins on Spacing Gender and Gendering Space.' *Space and Culture*, 1(5): 5–26.

Latour, Bruno. 2005. *Reassembling the Social: An Introduction to Actor Network Theory*. Oxford, New York: Oxford University Press.

Lefebvre, H. 1991. *The Production of Space*, trans. Donald Nicholson-Smith. Oxford: Blackwell.

Low, S.M. 2003. 'Embodied Space(s): Anthropological Theories of Body, Space and Culture.' *Space and Culture*, 6(1): 9–18.

Mauss, M. 1979. *Sociology and Psychology*. London: Routledge and Kegan Paul.

Mol, Anne M. 2002. *The Body Multiple: Ontology in Medical Practice*. London, New York: Duke University Press.

Phadke, Shilpa. 2013. 'Unfriendly Bodies, Hostile Cities. Reflections on Loitering and Gendered Public Space.' *Economic and Political Weekly*, XLVIII(39): 50–60.

Patnaik, Pranta Pratik. 2013. 'Bearly Indian: "Fat" Gay Men's Negotiation of Embodiment, Culture, and Masculinity.' In Rohit K. Dasgupta and Moti Gokulsing (eds.), *Masculintiy and its Challenges in India: Essays on Changing Perceptions*, pp. 93–105. Jefferson, NC: McFarland & Co. Publishers.

Prokhovnik, R. 1999. *Rational Woman. A Feminist Critique of the Dichotomy*. London, New York: Routledge.

Seabrook, Jeremy. 1999. *Love in a Different Climate. Men Who have Sex with Men in India*. London, New York: Verso.

Shilling, C. 1993. *The Body and Social Theory*. London, Thousand Oaks, CA, New Delhi: Sage.

Turner, B.S. 1984. *The Body and Society*. London: Basil Blackwell.

11

QUEER INTIMACIES IN THE TIME OF NEW MEDIA

When Grindr produces alternative cartographies

Silpa Mukherjee

The digital turn in the country substituted the imagination of the village with the generic cityscape which shares a unique multisensory, synesthetic relation with the world of gadgets: latest apps, games, social networks on the internet, hyperlinks and pop-ups, contemporary film culture, and the existing world of mobile telephony, lamp-post stickers, and television. This generic space with zero concern for specificities of identity transforms older spaces for proliferating desire; the fuzzy delirium of the virtual, the screens of the gadgets, and the spectacular, hyperstimulous malls are preferred to the Euclidian spaces of the park and the cinema hall. In an age saturated with electronic information that encodes or recodes lived experience in a different logic, these seamless spaces of love destabilise the classic binaries of public-private, plan-counterplan, and order-chaos. From the Rajiv Gandhi mode of a panoptical computer network geared towards control, the contemporary mediatised India is the generic city with a society gone viral.[1] Relying on case studies of apps, this chapter engages with the logic of desires (as error) and the feedback loop for the official discourse of maximum order and compliance signalled by the welter of media noises. The popular app for socialising and gay cruising, Grindr, renegotiates the logic of official surveillance, plotting alternative maps of the city which bring to light the sensational spectacular image of the urban labyrinth left untraced in official survey maps. The delirium of mediatised postmodernity, the hyperlinked logics of commodified experience of the globalising middle-class warp and conflate desires and telematics in a peculiar fashion which challenges the ordered logics of love and official control.[2]

James Donald explores an alternative archive of urban images as generated in mass media and its mediatory role in the first half of the twentieth century in America and Europe. He notes: 'They provided the mediating pedagogy between the reality of the metropolis and its imaginary place in mental life' (Donald 1999: 73). To provide an example, he traces the growth of the cinemas in the low brow ghettos in the early days to the explosion of the cinemas (their conversion into picture palaces) and their proliferation to the suburbs (often quite affluent). Cinema thus offered the total experience of 'going out' (consolidation of the suburbs with the close proximity of luxurious environment, department stores, air conditioning, stage shows with the theatres) as opposed to 'staying in' (mediated through the privatised experience of the new techno media infiltrating the homes). A similarity is chalked out between film spectatorship and urban experience, both being marked by 'distraction, diffusion and anonymity' and thus the geography of film exhibition helped reclaim cinema's entertainment value from primarily the working-class audience to an expanding number of 'cultivated and unaffected' people, even for the popular genre films (Donald 1999). Similar to this networked design of the city by U.S. planners in the 1930s, technological networks proliferated in the postcolonial cities of India in the 1980s. Low-cost media technology blurred the boundaries between producers and consumers of media and technology, culture, and everyday life for urban populations. Ravi Sundaram calls it the 'pirate city,' to capture the nuances of the media condition caused by the simultaneous operation of legal and sometimes extra-legal media infrastructures (Sundaram 2010 'Introduction'). The manic desire for technology, leads to an explosion of the consumption of technology which erases distinctions between technology, surveillance, entertainment, intimacies, and crime (Prakash 2010). The unauthorised and extra-legal proliferation of the video market in the 1980s in India ushered in the notion of the global for the first time in Indian homes, markets, and offices; making the global accessible to the not so privileged sections of the society. Piracy continues to dominate the zone owing to the existence of hackers, peer to peer networks which provide a platform for user generated media sharing and the endless buyers of cheap pirated media. This chaotic, 'no-limits' condition of media piracy is described by Sundaram as disruptive of contemporary media property, working through both bazaars and markets, both enabling and disrupting creativity, evading the issue of classic commons and at the same time extending access to subaltern groups in the Third World (Sundaram 2013). About Nigerian video culture, Brian Larkin points out the role of viral media in creating globalisation and postcolonial cultural production at a time when the global economy has distanced itself from Nigeria, piracy brings to the Nigerian population their fair share of Indian and Hollywood dramas. Larkin writes: 'Instead of being marginalised by official distribution networks, Nigerian consumers can now participate in the immediacy of an international consumer culture- but only through the mediating capacity of piracy.' (Larkin 2004: 297). Along with this neo-urbanisation, the turn of the century also witnessed the changing mediascape in India. The specific markers of a city; parks, open spaces, bazaars, single screen old theatres were transformed radically in favour of new technocratic infrastructure; the seamlessness and fuzzy delirium of the high-rise buildings, suburban highways, flyovers, shopping malls with its multiplex cinemas. The mediatised cities have now become what Mark Auge refers to as the 'non-places' as opposed to sociological notion of place as the receptacle for culture localised in space and time (Auge 1995: 34). In such neo-urbanised mediascapes, human desires are warped.

The Deleuzian question of how to react to, in spaces which we-no-longer-know-how-to-describe arises at this juncture. New media disrupts the space of the known world with its sensory-motor schemata in place. The architecture of a city that one was familiar with, the Euclidian spaces and the hodological spaces integrally associated with the cityscape is longer available to regulate the movements of the individual whose body was disciplined in a certain way (Deleuze 1997: 128–129). The body is thus left in a new space (media frenzy and overabundance of media induced affects), rendered catatonic with a sense of motor helplessness. It becomes a storehouse of infinite amounts of data that its senses (which as Deleuze notes, 'no longer a-motor extension which is-established, but rather a dreamlike connection through the intermediary of the liberated sense organs') cannot fully perceive and assimilate (Ibid.: 4). The body that assumes the schizo's walk now, the old sensory-motor co-ordinates being disrupted behaves in a fashion similar to an insect caught in a condition of rupture of boundaries or contours between the figure and the ground, which Rosalind Krauss points out in Caillois's work: 'In Caillois' early essay the boundary condition is precisely what breaks down in what he describes as a form of insectoid psychosis, when the animal is unable to keep its distinction between itself and its leafy milieu intact . . . Caillois compares this condition to that reported by schizophrenics who feel themselves dispossessed and even devoured by the space around them. In the grip of this, he writes, "The individual breaks the boundary of his skin and occupies the other side of his senses. He tries to look at himself from any point whatever of space . . . He is similar, not similar to anything, just similar. He invents spaces of which he is the convulsive possession."' (Bois and Krauss 1997: 75). The body thus shut out into a pure mediascape perceives a seamless continuity of itself into the landscape. The morphed landscape now is nothing but Rem Koolhaas's 'junkspace'; the 'body double of space . . . A fuzzy empire of blur, it fuses . . . public and private . . . to offer a seamless patchwork of the permanently disjointed. Instead of development it offers entropy . . . Because it is endless, it always leaks somewhere in the Junkspace.' (Koolhaas 2002: 177). In this case the Deleuzian time image produces an array of pure images, released from the motor perceptions into pure 'op-signs' and 'son-signs.' The body starts to display queerness, sometimes collapsing the distinctions between fantasy and the real where the body too fails to discern the 'reality' of the sense perception. Deleuze notes, 'Visual description replaces the motor action. We run in fact into a principle of indeterminability, of indiscernibility:we no longer know what is imaginary or real, physical or mental, in the situation, not because they are confused, but because we do not have to know and there is no longer even a place from which to ask. It is as if the real and the imaginary were running after each other, as if each was being reflected in the other, around a point of indiscernibility.' (Deleuze 1997: 7).

Scott Bukatman notes that technological supersession leading to progress and modernity are accompanied by continuing anxieties of a previous technological oeuvre (Bukatman 1993). He lays down three parallel advances affecting globalised cities: advanced industrialisation, economic exhaustion, and cultural ambivalence. According to Bukatman, technology brings in disruption and crisis of culture, which leads to a dystopia where citizens are trapped by the techno-political system. 'The citizen trapped in this new subject position which interfaces with the global realms of data circulation, occupies and intersects the cyberspaces of contemporary existence . . . the new terminal identity' (Ibid.: 9). The new terminal identity is located in the dominant 'invisible spaces . . . as the city of the modernist era is replaced by the non-place urban realm and the outer space is superseded by cyberspace.' (Ibid.). Such terminal identities are marked as bodies which face bewilderment and sense of dislocation at the warped world space of media.

This brings us to the inevitable question as to what causes the apparent unease of the body with the new techno-media era. Deleuze proposes that the new machine economy with its motto of '100% error free performance' is a control society which organises space according to certain principles of signification. Those bodies that fail to accommodate their movements do not receive representation in the control society of perfected subjects. Their bodies are silenced, condemned as 'abject.' As Gregory Flaxman explicates, 'Deleuze never ceases to insist that representation begins by grafting order onto "the delicate milieus of overlapping perspectives, of communicating distances, divergences and disparities, of heterogeneous potentials and intensities" . . . representation swindles us of the very experience of difference, especially the difference of space, and for this reason the more apt question with which we might begin is this: how can we understand space in the context of Deleuze's desire to deterritorialise the ground (Abgrund) of representation and, thence, the regulated and regular determination of all perception?' (Flaxman 2005: 176). However, the new regime of techno media being an enforced territory of model citizens, the seething tension beneath the surface of perfect subjects often clamours to be given vent to. This is known as the technological 'glitch,' that disrupts the smooth functioning of the network and is exposed in the form of 'noise.' As Mark Nunes suggests, 'Error reveals not only a system's failure, but also its operational logic . . . When error communicates, it does so as noise: abject information and aberrant signal within an otherwise orderly system of communication . . . Noise is errant signal . . . in feedback systems, then the spurious information of noise- from the pops and glitches of transmission error to the hacks and jams of counter-agents-functions as a kind of information that exceeds programmatic control by widening the gap between the actual and the possible, rather than narrowing the deviation between the intended and the actual.' (Nunes 2011: 3, 13).

Expression of queer desires becomes error in the control society of mediatised India, media explosion performing the dual role of proliferating queerness and also expressing it through the media channels as noise, completing the feedback loop of the official order. Piracy works as the counterfoil to state sponsored discourse around computer education for the youth in the Rajiv Gandhi era which sought to deploy imported technology on a modernised, nationalist model. That kind of computer network was also devised to work as a tool for official surveillance for the nation. But the internet in its morally corrupting tendencies really made its presence felt in the decade succeeding globalisation and the opening up of the economy in 1991, as a parcel of the landscape of taboo swept in by cable television,

Miss India contests, Coke, and music videos. However, the state has been a failure in monitoring, predicting, or controlling the growth of cyberspaces. Since users have circumvented the machinations of the state in almost every way possible, Nishant Shah points out that the cyber laws in India were taken to a new level of policing of these technologies with the rhetoric of 'responsible usage' and 'ethical consumption' of the webspaces: 'The State adopted a policy of disavowal with regards to the Internet . . . it decided to put the onus on the individual user and transferred its attention to fights over the radio spectrum and the threats to national security that the new technologies posited.' (Shah 2007: 34). Networked surveillance in mediatised India has continued and proliferated in multiple ways in contemporary information age via the new digital identification proofs. Michel de Certeau and Henri Lefebvre point out monumental structures are symbols of the state's desire to control human agglomeration by transformation of an urban fact into a concept city (Lefebvre 1997). Both point out the difference between the concept city (panoramic with Euclidian transparency) and the lived city (migrational and metaphoric, the labyrinthine arrangement of space). Certeau suggests that the polar existence of the urban life balances the rigidity of the panoptic vision of the concept city and the things that were excluded in the urbanistic project are brought back in the proliferation of the urban life in ways that are beyond the administrative control of the transparent city (Certeau 1988). Spatial practices which involve 'everyday practices, lived space, the disquieting familiarity of the city' undo the collective administration of the 'disciplinary' society (Ibid.). Despite the impossibility of producing neat Euclidian cartography of the nebulous space from which all signifiers marking its specificities of being a place has been erased by mediatisation, the official discourse of extreme transparency produces a map and coerces its model citizens to walk along the lines marked out in black and white. Bodies that are queer refuse to walk on grids.

They 'disidentify' with the gridded pattern of movement. However they do not become what José Esteban Muñoz calls 'bad subjects' outright by 'working on and against the dominant ideology' (Muñoz 1999: 11–12). Instead, they take detours within the officially cartographed space and generate residual and lived spaces from within, thus undoing the administration's every attempt to regiment bodies in spaces. They appropriate spaces when they walk the city streets. About walking on the city street, de Certeau suggests that if the cityscape is like a map with an ensemble of routes to be traversed, the walker actualises some of them through detours, crossing, and improvisation of walking privilege thus 'transforming every spatial signifier into something else' and in selecting certain routes over others, the walker manages to avoid the fixed possibilities of the constructed order of the planned city (Certeau 1988). In the process, he creates a 'rhetoric of walking' in 'condemning certain places to disappearance,' others into 'illegitimate, rare or accidental' (Ibid.). In a mediatised landscape both the obsessive desire to control every corner of the city and the constant exploration of new detours rely on modes of media surveillance.

Official surveillance disguises itself in spectacles functioning as benign but effective modes of control.[3] It deploys technologies of mass media in offering a plurality to confound the subject with a plethora of choices at the altar of spectacles just as media's offer of channel selections (constant flow of images, sounds, and narratives providing the illusion of cultural abundance and promise of diversity) which guarantees the freedom of the subject in making a choice within the culture. Within this blip culture bombardment of stimuli which paradoxically prevents cognitive reception of information, the official is often unwittingly challenged by the media developments that have gone viral.[4] The viral media is appropriated by queer subcultures and the condition defies certain authorities in unexpected forms.

When queerness is officially deemed erroneous and queer desires are declared as criminal, as 'glitches' in the smooth functioning of the techno-mediatised Indian social economy, the viral media landscape offers its own solace to queerness. The logic of surveillance through media gets used up for a different purpose than that it was originally intended for. As the official surveillance increasingly attempts to track down individuals according to set patterns of demographical groups, choices and behaviours, media surveillance goes out of control. It opens up new spaces, queer spaces which work to complete the feedback loop of the official order of surveillance. Against the official media discourse of mapping out the legal, the peculiar quality of new media to explode out of the grips of its producers plots an alternative map of the extra-legal spaces with its own logic of now viral surveillance. This also warps the older spaces of proliferating desires, conventional spaces of gay cruising which were earlier earmarked as criminal spaces in every city or small town in India, certain parks, pubs with gay nights, some restaurants, bus stops, some single screen theatres of ill repute and so on.

To provide a contemporary archaeology of Grindr, it became a popular gay cruising app towards the end of first decade of the twenty-first century, when app driven technology transformed urban governance along with absolute metamorphosis of the mediatised sensory apparatus. Collateral with the burgeoning market of cheap smartphones with haptic interfaces and larger display screens, and the rise of geosocial networking, corporate owned applications which allowed developers to pull consumer information like product reviews into third-party applications gave birth to mobile based social networking apps like Grindr. It is interesting to note that gay cruising as an act has gone to the through successive stages of technological development which include the darkened space of the theatre to the smaller, cosier setting of the video parlour. Unlike the theatre which simply promised the space for community viewing and thus scope for bodily intimacies to flourish, the video parlour had to offer the collective joy and adventure associated with record and tape hunting, the subterranean status of the video parlour rendered the desire and hunt for video with the unspoken moniker of gay cruising. About gay cruising's interconnectedness with videophilia, Lucas Hilderbrand notes: 'Videophilia has become a lifeline for millions of people who don't belong . . . Film has also provided both escapism and identification for queer audiences. Dark movie theaters were also, historically, one of the most active places for same-sex cruising and public sex. Video facilitated access to classic or gay texts for those isolated in the hinterlands, but it has also killed off the theater as a charged space of consummated desires.' (Hilderbrand

2009). In suburban India, video parlours too operated as proxy space for gay cruising, often tucked in one corner of the bazaar. The global dot com boom snowballed into the subcontinent and introduced the world of the cyberspace, second-self identities and the online chat rooms and dating websites to Indians. While there were continuities from the earlier decade, the early 2000s sought to create a sharp divide between the virtual and the visceral layers of intimacy and sexuality. Thus, it was also the decade of endless role playing on the web; the act of 'coming out' was still largely limited to the virtual. The web of desires could mutate into a network of anonymous users who would enact their queer selves or simply playact queer characters on virtual chat rooms (the physical space of the cybercafé still had to play a role in the proliferation of desires at this stage). PlanetRomeo is one such queer dating website which allowed users to create profiles and cruise online without the danger of risking their identity in an offline or official space. Post dot-com, the crackdown on the second self of the erstwhile cyberspace led to the dispersion of Web2.0 programmes which insist on ID-centric profiles. Web2.0 networks resonate with the Deleuzian logic of the control society, as Steven Shaviro points out: 'Once we have all been connected, there is no longer any need for the Panopticon's rigid, relentless, centralized gaze. The new forces of control are flexible, slack, and distributed. In a totally networked world, where every point communicates directly with every other point, power is no longer faceless and invisible. Instead, it works in plain sight. Its smiley face is always there to greet us. We are fully aware that its eyes are looking at us; it even encourages us to stare back.' (Shaviro 2003: 31). Although profiling of users is primarily a mode of corporate business and governmental surveillance, Grindr is the curious app which allows users to access profiles of other users along with their geographical locations, not precise but by mentioning the distance between the two users. There are other filters of preferences which curate the interface of the app for a particular user making use of algorithms whose exact functioning is not quite perceptible. The algorithmic anxiety working behind Grindr however often poses the threat of exposing the real time and exact location of the user rendering him vulnerable in climates that are hostile to queers. Despite the threat of exposure and imminent legal censure, the intimate space provided by Grindr throws a challenge at the notions of legal and moral cohesion on the issue of propriety and the approved sexual acts. As Nishant Shah writes: 'It also hints at the shifting paradigms of authority and power – as bodies more powerful and pervasive than the geographically restricted nation state emerge – and become the new policing and governing bodies in a world defined, understood and consumed through the deployment of cyberspatial technologies.' (Shah 2007: 40).

Gay cruising is now seemingly invisible, but constantly happening at a virtual space similar to the background apps running in one's gadgets. The physical act of waiting and soliciting partners has been reduced to the prosthetic network of androids making the act of cruising as spectacular and as overwhelming as the delirious screens in the user's hands. Steven Shaviro resorts to a McLuhanism in reflecting on internet as an even cooler medium than television, a haptic space that is intrinsically dependent on user participation: 'In this way, the hand becomes an extension of the eye: I reach right into the screen and travel through its iconic, hyperlinked space. Cyberspace is what Deleuze and Guattari call a "haptic" space, as opposed to an optical one: a space of "pure connection," accessible only to "close-range vision," and having to be navigated "step by step . . . One never sees from a distance in a space of this kind, nor does one see it from a distance. (1987: 492–493)" No panoramic view is possible, for the space is always folding, dividing, expanding, and contracting.' (Shaviro 2003: 7). Grindr produces an alternative map of the city, a map marking the geographical location of the criminal bodies by using its own surveillance technique (mostly Google maps) to locate its users. Ramon Raichert, in an essay on online courtship, writes 'The cartographies of the online dating communities transform flirting and dating into spatial information. Satellite photography not only offers realistic visual graphic quality, but also a kinesthetic sensation of movement through the shown virtual spaces (zooming).' (Degim, Johnson, and Tao Fu 2015: 39). The app thus aids these queer bodies freed out of the sensory-motor schema of the older order of control to move in a certain schizoid manner resembling that of the user of the geospatial technologies like Google Earth on certain portals like Ogleearth.com, GoogleEarthHacks.com, and Juicygeography.co.uk in which the body moves as if under the influence of intoxicants. Just as the user manipulates Google Earth, which was initially designed as surveillance mechanism, for his own pleasure, transforming it into 'digital peep-boxes' that can turn 'looking into ogling, uncertainty into paranoia, and pleasure into intense exhilaration,' the queer peripatetic bodies which were disciplined according to the needs of the control society make use of new media technology to alter the same structures of panoptic dominance to 'cause subjectivity to vanish to the point of complete self forgetting . . . Singing and dancing, man expresses his sense of belonging to a higher community; he has forgotten how to walk and talk and is on the brink of flying and dancing, up and away into the air above' (Kingsbury and Jones III 2011: 172).

At this point it is important to speculate on the material infrastructure of the media economy that goes beyond what they were set up for. In the process, the infrastructure entangles people and objects in complex hybrids of networks which mutate, and displaces the virtual and visceral personas. The signature of the mobile telephony based social networking apps is the rhetoric of user participation which aids the functioning of corporate business by inconspicuously but constantly updating the total network in which one programme which collects user information for its own functioning serves as the database for other programmes. The allure of the 'free' communication ensnares the community of users, who are further blinkered by the offer of personalised interfaces (supported by additional profile information, or Grindr Xtra, which is a premium account that guarantees matches with the cream of the available users against a payment of a subscription fee). Grindr hinges on to existing technologies of geo location, messaging, media sharing, remediates them all and caters to the queer community with an offer of tactile immersion; an intimacy which is at best synthetic and at the same time can be referred to as an 'extimacy' (intimacy that is public in nature). The intimacy is synthetic but at same time acutely visceral; the proprioceptive body of the user of Grindr is the key player here, a body that responds to stimuli between the nerves and fleetingly glances at something and touches something else and thus shifts its attention in an almost plastic way between multiple media objects. As Mark B. N. Hansen suggests, with digital data's loss of material specificity, the body assumes a firmer role of the selective processor of information (the digital image no longer remains as the surface appearance but is extended to become the entire process by which information is made perceivable through embodiment) and its scope of perceptual and affective possibilities now becomes the connect with the medial interface (Hansen 2004: 8, 21). The new medial interface yields the framing function to the body, rendering the process flexible and the body's position supreme in its proprioceptive role. The haptic sensorium created by Grindr's interface is seminal for the understanding of this intimacy as both synthetic and visceral at the same time. Hence it is a body that affectively responds to the official forms of techno surveillance without cognitively assessing it, judging its merits, or forcefully reacting against it.

State power constantly deludes its subjects with its spectacular offer of rights, liberties and spaces in a way that it simultaneously ensures the inscription of the individuals' bodies within the state order making it impossible for the subjects to break free from the sovereign power (Agamben 1998: 72). In trying to posit sex as a political issue, Foucault writes, 'The right to life, to one's body, to health, to happiness, to the satisfaction of needs and beyond all the oppressions or alienation the right to rediscover what one is and all that one can be, this right-which the classical juridical system was utterly incapable of comprehending-was the political response to all these new procedures of power.' (Foucault 1978:145). Thought in this light of the Foucauldian logic of networks of repressive power inversely producing discourses about the object of repression, media surveillance in contemporary India performs a similar role in controlling and proliferating queer desires in a tacit, underhand fashion. Judith Butler points out that it is the juridical unconscious that disciplines bodies, forcing them to make invisible certain characteristics which would otherwise not allow them to fit themselves into stable and officially acceptable identities (Butler 1990: 2, 7). New media technologies work to keep the juridical unconscious at work, and at the same time it allows the queer desires to flourish in hitherto unimagined ways. Meanwhile it warps the spaces of desire and tangles desires with telematics in ways that often bypass the vigilance of the control society.

Notes

1 The Rajiv Gandhi model of computer network is engaged with in great detail in Sundaram 2010. *Introduction*.

2 Telematic Culture 'consists of a set of behaviours, ideas, media, values, and objectives that are significantly unlike those that have shaped society since the Enlightenment . . . It involves the technology of interaction among human beings and between the human mind and artificial systems of intelligence and perception.' From Ascott 2003: 232–246.

3 The notion of insatiable addiction to spectacles is borrowed from Debord's *Society of Spectacle*

4 The concept of 'blip culture' is borrowed from Alvin Toffler's *The Third Wave*.

Bibliography

Ascott, Roy. 2003. *Telematic Embrace: Visionary Theories of Art, Technology and Consciousness.* Berkeley, CA: University of California Press.

Agamben, Giorgio. 1998. *Homo Sacer: Sovereign Power and Bare Life.* Stanford, CA: Stanford University Press.

Auge, Marc. 1995. *Non-Places: Introduction to an Anthropology of Supermodernity,* trans. John Howe. London, New York: Verso.

Bois, Yve-Alain and Rosalind Krauss. 1997. *Formless: A User's Guide,* New York: Zone Books.

Bukatman, Scott. 1993. 'Introduction.' In *Terminal Identity: The Virtual Subject in Postmodern Science Fiction,* pp. 1–22. Durham: Duke University Press.

Butler, Judith. 1990. *Gender Trouble.* New York: Routledge.

Certeau, Michel de. 1988. 'Walking the City.' In *The Practice of Everyday Life,* pp. 91–110. Berkeley, CA, London: University of California Press.

Debord, Guy. 1983. *Society of Spectacle.* Detroit: Black and Red.

Degim, Alev, James Johnson and Tao Fu (eds.). 2015. *Online Courtship: Interpersonal Interactions Across Borders.* Amsterdam: Institute of Network Cultures.

Deleuze, Gilles. 1997. *Cinema 2: The Time-Image,* Minneapolis: University of Minnesota Press.

Donald, James. 1999. 'Light in Dark Spaces: Cinema and the City.' Chapter 3 In *Imagining the Modern City,* 63–92. Minneapolis: University of Minnesota Press.

Flaxman, Gregory. 2005. 'Transcendental Aesthetics: Deleuze's Philosophy of Space.' In Ian Buchanan and Gregg Lambert (eds.), *Deleuze and Space,* pp. 176–188. Edinburgh: Edinburgh University Press.

Foucault, Michel. 1978. *The History of Sexuality,* Vol 1: An Introduction, trans. Robert Hurley. New York: Pantheon Books.

Hansen, Mark B. N. 2004. *New Philosophy for New Media.* Cambridge, MA, London, England: MIT Press.

Hilderbrand, Lucas. 2009. 'Cinematic Promiscuity: Cinephilia after Videophilia.' *Framework: The Journal of Cinema and Media,* 50(1/2) (Spring &Fall): 214–217. www.jstor.org/stable/41552555. Accessed 15 March 2016.

Jacobs, Katrien, Marije Janssen and Matteo Pasquinelli (eds.). 2007. *C'Lick Me: Netporn Studies Reader.* Amsterdam: Institute of Network Cultures.

Kingsbury, Paul and John Paul Jones III. 2011. 'Google Earth as Dionysusphere.' *New Geographies* (Issue 4 'Scales of the Earth'): 171–175.

Koolhaas, Rem. Spring 2002. 'Junkspace.' *October* (100): 175–190.

Larkin, Brian. 2004. 'Degraded Images, Distorted Sounds: Nigerian Video and the Infrastructure of Piracy.' *Public Culture,* 16(2): 289–314.

Lefebvre, Henri. 1997. 'The Production of Space (Extract).' In Neil Leach (ed.) *Rethinking Architecture: A Reader in Cultural Theory,* pp. 138–146. London, New York: Routledge.

Muñoz, José Esteban. 1999. *Disidentifactions: Queers of Colour and the Performance of Politics.* London: University of Minnesota Press.

Nunes, Mark. 2011. *Error: Glitch, Noise and Jam in New Media Cultures.* New York, London: Continuum.

Prakash, Gyan. 2010. 'Introduction: Imaging the Modern City, Darkly.' In Gyan Prakash (ed.) *Noir Urbanisms: Dystopic Images of the Modern City,* pp. 1–14. Princeton, NJ: Princeton University Press.

Shah, Nishant. 2007. 'PlayBlog: Pornography, Performance and Cyberspace.' In Katrien Jacobs, Marije Janssen, and Matteo Pasquinelli (eds.), *C'Lick Me: Netporn Studies Reader.* Amsterdam: Institute of Network Cultures.

Shaviro, Steven. 2003. *Connected, or What It Means to Live in the Network Society.* Minneapolis, London: University of Minnesota Press.

Sundaram, Ravi. 2010. *Pirate Modernity: Delhi's Media Urbanism*. London, New York: Routledge.

Sundaram, Ravi. 2013.'Revisiting the Pirate Kingdom.' In Ravi Sundaram (ed.), *No Limits: Media Studies from India*, pp. 114–164. New Delhi: Oxford University Press.

Toffler, Alvin. 1981. The Third Wave. New York: Bantam Books.

PART V

Textual belongings

12

INTIMACY, BELONGING, AND MASCULINITY IN BHALACHANDRA NEMADE'S NOVEL *KOSLA* (*COCOON*)

Mangesh Kulkarni

> *I'm not alone in abysmal sorrow,*
> *I'm not alone in loss of aim – there are men and men.*[1]
>
> (Shakti Chattopadhyaya 1974: 301)

Introduction

The renowned writer Bhalachandra Nemade (b. 1938) received the 2014 Jnanpith Award for his contribution to Marathi literature. His published work spans diverse fields like fiction, poetry, literary criticism, and sociolinguistics.[2] But Nemade is best known as a novelist, and successive generations of readers have hailed his very first novel, *Kosla* (1963), as a masterpiece[3]. A bildungsroman with an obvious autobiographical backdrop, it has only a rudimentary storyline that can be summarised in a single sentence: Pandurang Sangvikar, the only son of a prosperous middle-caste farmer[4], leaves his native village (Sangvi) in North Maharashtra to join the reputed Fergusson College in Pune where he spends several years during the 1950s fitfully pursuing a BA programme, has to repeat the final examination, returns home feeling utterly disoriented, and finds himself drowning in 'the idiocy of rural life'[5]. What turns the dross of such seemingly unpromising material into aesthetic gold is Nemade's virtuoso deployment of narrative strategies that enable the reader to dive deep into the protagonist's inner world and to see the human world afresh through his eyes.

As the very title of the novel (*Cocoon*) indicates, a concern with intimacy and belonging is central to the existential Weltanschauung eloquently embodied in the novel. Much has been said about the intertextual and social matrices in which *Kosla* is embedded. Critics have also commented extensively on the novel's distinctive style comprising a variety of registers ranging from the colloquial to the lyrical

(Bhand 1979). But there is little systematic discussion of the psychodynamics structuring the novel. The present chapter probes this relatively neglected dimension of the opus[6] by focusing on the fictional suture where two of its key motifs – the precariousness of intimacy and the (im)possibility of belonging – are braided into discourses of masculinity.[7] To this end, it heuristically employs certain psychoanalytical concepts that are central to Sudhir Kakar's pioneering work on the constitution of the masculine self in India.

The oedipal dynamics

As is well-known, the concept of the Oedipus complex gained currency in the early twentieth century through the seminal writings of Sigmund Freud (1856–1939). The psychoanalyst Robert Young (2005: 3–4) has explained its crux as follows:

> Children from about three to six years have intense loving feelings towards one parent and seek to possess that parent exclusively, while having strong negative feelings towards the other parent. Boys love their mothers and hate their fathers. At the unconscious level, these feelings are sexual towards the desired parent and murderous towards the same-sex parent. [. . .] The intense Oedipal feelings get reprised in adolescence, when teenagers are typically rebellious . . . and make trouble . . . for their parents.

According to Freud, 'It is only in the male child that we find the fateful combination of love for one parent and simultaneous hatred for the other as a rival.' (Cited in Colman 2009: 524). He considered it to be one of the most profound and universal elements of the human psyche.

The Freudian claim to the universality of the Oedipus complex has been contested by psychologists like Sudhir Kakar (b. 1938). In *The Inner World*, a treatise inspired by Erik Erikson's psychoanalytical theory of individual development, Kakar provides a perceptive account of childhood and society in India.[8] He underscores the unusual intensity and ambivalence of the mother-son relationship in the Hindu family (Kakar 1992: 52–139). Further, he argues that boys raised in such a family rely on their fathers to a much greater extent than their Western counterparts in the endeavour to acquire a masculine identity by overcoming maternal dominance. Hence they feel the necessity of an oedipal alliance more acutely than the hostility of the Oedipus complex. Kakar holds that the son's ambivalent attitude towards the mother, who is seen both as a nurturing benefactress (the good mother) and a threatening seductress (the bad mother), eventually leads to a lasting identification with her. However, the subliminal fear of the 'bad mother' is not completely erased and typically surfaces as an anxiety focused on the threatening sexuality of older or mature women. Another consequence of such upbringing, argues Kakar, is a permeable ego formation which generates trusting friendliness and eagerness to develop attachments. To him, this explains the intimacy and vitality evident in Indian social relations.

In a recent paper, Kakar (n.d.: 4) has reaffirmed his position on the oedipal dynamics as follows:

> First experienced as an ally and a protector the father rarely emerges as a rival in myths and folklore. Where it does occur, the rivalry in popular Indian myths and most of the case histories, is not so much that of Oedipus, where the power of the myth derives from the son's guilt over a fantasized and eventually unconscious parricide. The Indian context stresses more the father's envy of what belongs to the son – especially the mother – and thus the son's persecution anxiety as a primary motivation in the father-son relationship
>
> *(Kakar n.d.: 4)*

> If there is anger against the father, then it is due to his failure in not fulfilling the little boy's need for an oedipal alliance, that is for the father's firm support, solidarity and emotional availability at a stage of life where the wishes and fears related to maternal enthrallment, later banished into the unconscious, were at their peak.
>
> *(Kakar n.d.: 5)*

The psychodrama which unfolds in *Kosla* bears out Kakar's contention as to the son's persecution anxiety vis-à-vis his father. An intense form of such anxiety runs like a red thread through the textual fabric of the novel.

Indeed, in a speech delivered nearly three and a half decades after the book was first published, Nemade (1997) himself made a pointed reference to the novel's foregrounding of the father-son conflict.[9] There are certain overt explanations of this conflict stemming from the contrary temperaments and tastes of the protagonist and his father. Being a sensitive lad given to literary and artistic pursuits, Pandurang is always up against his father's boorishness and philistinism. Besides, he has been often at the receiving end of the latter's unrelenting verbal abuse and corporal chastisement: 'My whole childhood passed in awe of my Father. He used to be wicked and cruel etc.' (Nemade 2014: 20).

But what does one make of extreme emotional responses of the sort cited below?

> For one thing, his build is like a true Father's, terrifically sturdy and solid. At Pola, the bull-festival, grown-up men's games are held, *kabaddi* etc. For fun, you see. Then his bare body seems obscene to me.
>
> *(Nemade 2014: 20)*

> Then I waited, expecting Father to say something about the cigarettes. Of course he will bring it up. Then I shall burst, say anything I feel like. (. . .) I'd say, I'm just waiting for the moment when you croak finally.
>
> *(Nemade 2014: 176)*

> Unfortunately, our ancestors were not gifted with sterility. That's why this turn and return – all because of manly sires!
>
> (*Nemade 2014: 239*)

The roots of such visceral disgust and rage might be traced to the father's callous disregard of the infant Pandurang's oneirically expressed plea for an oedipal alliance:

> Ever since my childhood on and off I would have terrific dreams of a set pattern. Mother says that having risen in my sleep I used to chatter a great deal about matters-not-to-be-spoken-about-again. Then even Father's arms would ache from slapping me on my cheeks. Mother would weep. When I came to, though, I would fall asleep quite drained out.
>
> (*Nemade 2014: 25*)

These traumatic episodes can be seen as triggering a persecution complex of the sort adumbrated by Kakar.

Maternal enthralment and gynophobia

Kosla also testifies to Sudhir Kakar's nuanced characterisation of the mother-son relationship. Kakar considers maternal enthralment to be a key aspect of the Hindu male psyche and explains it as follows:

> In clinical psychoanalytic work . . . one often comes across the existence of what I have called 'maternal enthrallment': the wish to get away from the mother together with the dread of separation, the wish to destroy the engulfing mother who also ensures the child's survival and, finally, incestuous desire coexisting with the terror inspired by an overwhelming female sexuality. [It] is the largely unconscious underside of the overt and ubiquitous idealization of the mother by the Hindu son, which will influence his later relationships and unconscious attitudes towards women.
>
> (*Kakar n.d.: 1*)

Kosla reveals various strands of the mother-son bond sketched above.

Pandurang's mother represents the prototypical Indian housewife of her generation and class, who willy-nilly performs arduous domestic chores, copes with the stratagems of the mother-in-law, and provides endless succour to her son. She is his only source of solace in childhood. His sentiments towards her find an echo in the following poem culled from *Melody*, Nemade's collection of poetry, which was first published in 1970:

> You are just mine, mother dear
> Do not lay more than one egg
> You hold my navel spellbound
> There are two hair whorls on my head

> And your wealth-line is etched only on my palm
> It is all yours. Let none beside me slurp your milk
> Your breasts are only mine to suckle.
> *(Nemade 1980: 15)*[10]

While Pandurang's mother remains supportive of her 'wayward' son, his relocation to Pune marks a seemingly final cutting of the 'umbilical cord,' which he expresses as follows:

> Another calamity would descend upon me regularly. My Mother's letters. She'd write, I think of you very much. Besides, your four sisters too remember you. But I miss you most of all. Then I would send off a long reply. But, truth to tell, gradually, Mother's memory became fainter. And here novel things kept happening. So naturally one neglected old things. *But having written a long, long letter I'd go to Madras Cafe and stuff myself on something or other.*
> *(Nemade 2014: 47, emphasis added)*

Despite the bluffness of this assertion of independence, the italicised sentence indicates that it is tinged with a subliminal disquiet originating in his separation from the 'good mother' (perceived as a nurturing benefactress), which triggers the incongruous activity of eating voraciously.

Many episodes in *Kosla* signal Pandurang's unmistakable anxiety aroused by the threatening sexuality of an older or mature woman who symbolises the 'bad mother' perceived as an ominous seductress. Thus, he is greatly repelled by the supposed immodesty of urban women: 'The very first day when I went out for a walk in a nice part of town, I thought, There seem to be quite a few prostitutes in Poona' (Nemade 2014: 47). Specifically, he finds his Maushi (mother's sister) guilty of unladylike deportment: 'Everybody in Poona dresses up, it's true. But it's not nice for one's own Mauvshi to dress up and strut about. Maushi tarts herself up every day and goes out promenading' (Nemade 2014: 47). He complains about his Maush's misdemeanour to her husband (who is his local guardian) only to be rebuffed by the latter.

Pandurang breezily justifies these negative views about women: 'I was new to Poona. I was bound to speak like that' (Nemade 2014: 47). But his misogyny cannot be explained entirely in terms of the culture shock experienced by a country bumpkin in an alien social environment. Thus, many years later, this is how he responds to the mild advances of a bold and sensuous collegemate, Bundi (a nickname alluding to her rubicund complexion), presumably in a restaurant (Nemade 2014: 268):

> I was watching all her shenanigans. I lit a fresh cigarette.
> She said softly in my ear, Now enough of that. Then holding the cigarette carefully, I inflicted a nice little burn on her hand.
> Rubbing at the ash stuck to it with her other hand, she said Shhh . . . Brute!
> All those around us were of course watching all this. I thought, Now she's sure to hit me. But wordlessly she picked up the key from the table and went away.

Pandurang's bad mother syndrome turns into gynophobia. He disdains the opportunities for companionate intimacy, which are available in the vibrant milieu of a coeducational college campus: 'I came across so many girls, but I didn't misbehave, ever. But even as entertainment I found girls a nuisance, generally' (Nemade 2014: 147). The sole female friend he cares for is Rami, a soft-spoken, sickly classmate suffering from a lung disease, and their friendship turns out to be ephemeral. He is loath to explore merely instrumental avenues of sexual gratification. Thus, he recoils when a windfall occasion for hooking up transpires. The prospect of an arranged marriage is also repugnant to Pandurang, and he resists his mother's efforts to find a suitable bride for him. Consequently, his libidinal longing finds expression only in fantasy, voyeurism and onanism.

Homosociality and homoeroticism

Pandurang is unable to sustain meaningful relationships with women; but he is no recluse. He has a fairly large circle of friends and acquaintances. He is also trusting and makes determined, if infructuous efforts to take up collective responsibilities so as to win social esteem. However, his peer attachments are largely circumscribed within a homosocial compass. It is hardly surprising that many of Pandurang's interactions with boys and men are unpleasant, such as the exploitation of his generosity by certain unscrupulous college friends; and some are abhorrent, such as a nightmarish childhood experience of bullying by a schoolmate. But there are also a few instances of true camaraderie. For example, he forms a strong bond with his fellow student Suresh and spends a lot of time with him, especially as both stay in the same hostel and have common interests.

Scholars in the field of Critical Masculinity Studies have noted that male friendship typically involves 'doing things together' rather than emotional intimacy and sharing, and that it often has strong misogynist overtones (Messner 2004: 253–265). To an extent, this is true of the friendship between Pandurang and Suresh. Their favourite pastime is exploring the hills in and around Pune. The novel contains extended and vivid descriptions of these excursions. The two young men also like to stay away from and poke fun at female batchmates. But *contra* Messner, they share deeply held thoughts and intimate existential preoccupations that buttress their bond. Thus, they have mordantly witty conversations through which utopian yearnings are articulated by critiquing contemporary life from the standpoint of an imagined society in the distant future.

During a nocturnal hiking excursion, Pandurang and Suresh experience a moment of intense communion and reach the very edge of homoerotic desire which is voiced, but not consummated:

> I have never found a girl that would really please me.
> Not me either.
> If you'd been a girl, I would not have let you go.
> Do kiss my hand.
> Give it here.

> Yuck! No, not that one. Give your right hand.
> That's just it. Suresh is always pursuing the other extreme. He would dampen the heat of the moment just like that. He fills again a state of great emptiness that has come about.
>
> *(Nemade 2014: 214)*

It is no coincidence that their friendship breaks up when one night Suresh makes a racket in a vain attempt to expose the suspected homosexual assignation of two hostel mates, in the process disturbing Pandurang's sleep and nearly driving him round the bend. The psychodynamics of this rupture seems to be driven by the logic of displacement which typically involves 'redirection of emotional feelings from their original object to a substitute object related to the original one by a chain of associations' (Colman 2009: 216).

At this juncture it is necessary to note that Suresh's active participation in ragging – a malady that plagues educational institutions around the world – is a major reason for the widening rift between the two friends before they fall out. Pandurang detests and opposes such sadistic behaviour, and provides a perspicuous account of its aetiology (Nemade 2014: 155). This is of a piece with his compassionate concern for the gratuitous and egregious suffering of humans as well as animals. He frequently brings such a concern to bear on the quandary of girls and women trapped in the cage of a patriarchal society. It finds a particularly poignant expression in the passage containing Pandurang's response to the untimely death of his younger sister, Mani (Nemade 2014: 163–174).[11] These instances of sensitivity to an oppressive gender order, which stand out in the narrative structure of *Kosla*, have led certain critics to find a feminist sensibility in the novel (Gurjarpadhye-Khandeparkar 2014: 172–185), and to project it as a critique of patriarchy (Patil 2015). In light of the foregoing discussion, it seems problematic to characterise the novel as an embodiment of feminism. However, it does disclose the ugly reality of and fault lines within hegemonic masculinity.[12]

Coda

This reading[13] of *Kosla* is anchored in a hermeneutic perspective which holds that a novel, 'under a single criterion of acceptable interpretation, which allows the author's work to stand on its own without disappearing, can provoke a rich variety of interpretations that reward the reader in different ways' (Goldman 2002: 25). It explains some of the reasons why Pandurang Sangvikar's autobiographical narrative is reminiscent of a statement made by Jean-Baptiste Clamence, the anti-hero of Albert Camus's novelette, *The Fall*: 'The portrait I hold out to my contemporaries becomes a mirror' (Camus 1973: 102). Pandurang, a soul lost in the labyrinth of patriarchal masculinity, has acquired an abiding place in the republic of Marathi letters and in the hearts of innumerable readers who share his predicament and see him as an intimate stranger. In turn, he may see each of these readers, the 'ninety-nine out of a hundred' people to whom *Kosla* is dedicated (Nemade 2014: xv), in a fraternal spirit a la Baudelaire (1982: 29): 'Double-faced reader, – kinsman, – brother mine!'

Notes

1 These lines culled from Shakti Chattopadhyaya's 'Four Sonnets' were translated from the Bengali by Manish Nandy.

2 Nemade's Marathi publications include six novels, two collections of poetry and a compilation of critical essays. Besides, he has published works in English on themes such as nativism, the medieval saint-poet Tukaram, and the influence of English on Marathi.

3 Written in white heat during a fortnight and published in 1963, *Kosla* has gained wide and enduring recognition. In a survey co-sponsored by the All India Radio in 1997, the novel was accorded the second place – next to the novel *Yayati* by V. S. Khandekar (1898–1976), winner of the Jnanpith award in 1974 – among the top ten Marathi literary works published after Independence (Nemade 1997). *Kosla* has been translated into English and eight Indian languages.

4 Nemade himself belongs to the Lewa/Lewa Patil (also spelled as Leva/Leva Patil) community described by the renowned anthropologist Irawati Karve as an agricultural caste living in Khandesh (North Maharashtra). While providing evidence pointing to a central or northern Indian origin for the Lewas, she notes that they 'are now completely Marathised. . . [and] are a very industrious and progressive community and are making their influence felt in the educational, professional and public life of the Maratha country' (Karve 1968: 31–32).

5 Marx and Engels (1966: 46) famously used this phrase to invoke the isolation, stupor, and apathy of rural life.

6 The English extracts cited here are drawn from Sudhakar Marathe's translation of *Kosla* (Nemade 2014), which was first published by Macmillan (India) in 1997.

7 The term 'masculinity' is used to connote 'a place in gender relations, the practices through which men and women engage that place in gender, and the effects of these practices in bodily experience, personality and culture' (Connell 2005: 71). Masculinity assumes multiple forms through its imbrication with class, caste, race, and sexuality. For a review of literature on masculinities in India and Maharashtra respectively, see Kulkarni (2014) and Kulkarni (2011).

The second most populous and third largest state in the Indian federation, Maharashtra reveals a gender scenario that is replete with contradictions. Since the mid-nineteenth century, it has witnessed significant reform initiatives aimed at women's empowerment. But traditional patriarchy remains deeply entrenched, especially in the demographically large rural sector, and its bastions include the extended family commonly found in the prosperous farming community of the type (see footnote no. 4) from which Nemade (and his *alter ego*, Pandurang Sangvikar) hails. Not surprisingly, the sex ratio (females per thousand males) in the state is as low as 925, which is well below the national average of 933. During the decade in which *Kosla* is set, it had declined from 941 in 1951 to 935 in 1961 (Census of India 1961: 3).

8 Kakar's seminal book was first published in 1978.

9 Nemade's speech was occasioned by a recent survey (mentioned in footnote no. 3) of Marathi readers who placed *Kosla* just below V. S. Khandekar's *Yayati* (1959). He highlights the father-son conflict as a significant commonality between the two novels and cites it as a probable reason for their popularity. There is a delicious irony here. In their younger days, Nemade and his confreres had staged a rebellion against many writers of the preceding generation, and Khandekar was one of their prominent targets.

10 This is my rough-and-ready translation of the original Marathi poem.

11 The passage has been justly applauded as a *tour de force* for its fine-grained interarticulation of existential angst and social critique. The renowned litterateur Vilas Sarang

translated it into English for the pioneering Penguin anthology of new writing in India (Nemade 1974: 119–126).

12 R.W. Connell (2005: 77) cogently defines hegemonic masculinity 'as the configuration of gender practice which embodies the currently accepted answer to the problem of the legitimacy of patriarchy, which guarantees (or is taken to guarantee) the dominant position of men and the subordination of women.'

13 This chapter is a revised version of a paper presented at an International Seminar on 'Intimacy and Belonging in Contemporary India,' organised by Dr. Kaustav Chakraborty under the aegis of the Indian Institute of Advanced Study (Shimla) during 4–6 April 2016. Dr. Sudhir Kakar, doyen of Indian Psychology, responded to my presentation during the seminar and subsequently shared one of his recent papers on 'Maternal Enthrallment.' The well-known Marathi literary critic Pushpatai Bhave offered helpful comments. Dr. Sudhakar Marathe, distinguished scholar and translator of *Kosla*, subjected the penultimate draft to a searching scrutiny and made extremely valuable suggestions. He also drew to my attention a relevant seminar paper authored by Dr. Z. N. Patil (former Professor of English) who kindly sent me the published version. I thank each of them with utmost sincerity. The responsibility for any remaining errors is exclusively mine.

References

Baudelaire, Charles. 1982. *Selected Poems: Baudelaire,* trans. Joanna Richardson. Harmondsworth: Penguin.

Bhand, Baba. (ed.) 1979. *Koslabaddal.* Aurangabad: Dhara Prakashan.

Camus, Albert. 1973. *The Fall,* trans. Justin O'Brien. Harmondsworth: Penguin.

Census of India. 1961. www.pib.nic.in/archive/docs/DVD_41/ACC%20NO%20822-BR/HOM-1961-03-28-4571.pdf. Accessed 5 November 2017.

Chattopadhyaya, Shakti. 1974. 'Four Sonnets.' Trans. Manish Nandy. In Adil Jussawala (ed.), *New Writing in India.* Harmondsworth: Penguin.

Colman, Andrew. 2009. *A Dictionary of Psychology.* Oxford: Oxford University Press.

Connell, R.W. 2005. *Masculinities.* Crows Nest: Allen & Unwin.

Goldman, Alan. 2002. '*The Sun Also Rises*: Incompatible Interpretations.' In Michael Krausz (ed.), *Is There a Single Right Interpretation?* University Park: Pennsylvania State University Press.

Gurjarpadhye-Khandeparkar, Prachi. 2014. 'Reinventing the Self: Nativist Cultural Imagination of *Kosla.*' *Indian Literature*, 282, July–August, 172–185.

Kakar, Sudhir. 1992. *The Inner World: A Psycho-analytic Study of Childhood and Society in India.* New Delhi: Oxford University Press.

Kakar, Sudhir. n.d. 'Maternal Enthrallment' (typescript received from Kakar on 22/4/2016).

Karve, I. 1968. *Maharashtra – Land and Its People.* Bombay: Directorate of Government Printing, Stationery and Publications, Maharashtra State.

Kulkarni, Mangesh. 2011. 'Understanding Masculinities in Maharashtra.' In *Samajhdar Jodidar: Enhancing Male Participation for Improving Gender Equality in Maharashtra.* New Delhi: Centre for Health and Social Justice.

Kulkarni, Mangesh. 2014. 'Critical Masculinity Studies in India.' In Rohit K. Dasgupta and K. Moti Gokulsing (eds.), *Masculinity and Its Challenges in India: Essays on Changing Perceptions.* Jefferson, NC: McFarland & Company Publishers.

Marx, Karl and Friedrich Engels. 1966. *Manifesto of the Communist Party.* Moscow: Progress Publishers.

Messner, Michael. 2004. 'Friendship, Intimacy, and Sexuality.' In Stephen Whitehead and Frank J. Barrett (eds.), *The Masculinities Reader.* Cambridge: Polity Press.

Nemade, Bhalachandra. 1963. *Kosla.* Pune: Deshmukh Prakashan.

Nemade, Bhalachandra. 1974. 'Mani's Dying.' Trans. Vilas Sarang. In Adil Jussawala (ed.), *New Writing in India*. Harmondsworth: Penguin.
Nemade, Bhalachandra. 1980. *Melody*. Mumbai: Pras.
Nemade, Bhalachandra. 1997. 'Ya Katritun Mihi Sutawe.' *Maharashtra Times*, 26 October.
Nemade, Bhalachandra. 2014. *Cocoon,* trans. Sudhakar Marathe. Mumbai: Popular Prakashan.
Patil, Z. N. 2015. 'Contextualising Patriarchy in *Kosla*.' *Yashashri*, VIII(3–4): 19–31.
Young, Robert. 2005. *Oedipus Complex*. Delhi: Worldview Publications.

13

HESITANT INTIMACY

North East Indian English poetry vis-à-vis the Indian nationhood

Sarat Kumar Doley

The contested nation

Ernest Renan, in 'What Is a Nation?,' a lecture delivered at the Sorbonne on March 11, 1882, said, 'Man is a slave neither of his race nor his language, nor of his religion, nor of the course of rivers nor of the direction taken by mountain chains. A large aggregate of men, healthy in mind and warm of heart, creates the kind of moral conscience which we call a nation.' (Renan 1990: 21) If what Renan said is to be taken seriously, then the ethnically conscious, and at times separatist, expressions by poets writing in English from the northeast of India would pose a sizable challenge to Indian nationhood. Alternatively, both the geographical and the cultural circumference of the idea of nationhood in the northeast expressed in such writings may shrink smaller and smaller. It is, of course, a mistake to circumscribe the variety and diversity that exist in the poetry of the region and represent them as one single political voice. But then, for the sake of coming to terms with their regional concept of nationhood, since they do exhibit signs of unification up against the idea of nationhood in circulation, and their reaction to the so-called imposed Indian nationhood embedded in these writings, the various forms of diversity and differences are momentarily overlooked in this discussion. They may very well choose to differ in many ways, but here.

One additional limitation of this chapter is that it is not a comprehensive study of the kinds of poetry written in English by poets from the northeast of India. It exclusively looks at some of the problems raised, along with some possible solutions suggested, in relation to the notion of Indian nationhood by some poets writing in English from the northeast. As the number of poets in the region is growing by the day, I am sure more strands of analysis exist.

So, twisting itself in the narrative coils of folk myths and legends, the poetic in much of North East Indian English poetry veers towards the Yeatsian in content as, more often than not, it seeks to confront the so-called narcissism of the mainstream narrative in the centre from the very site of real or imagined peripheral negligence. Invoking the legends in the folktales and myths of immediately local origin, it appears to be engaged in the attempt to create a cultural space for itself both in the context of the competing plurality in the margin and the persistent dominance of the imagined monolithic singularity in the centre. First, it does it by a passionate poetic indulgence in the elaborate narration of the myths and legends to help rescue them from extinction and oblivion. Second, it assumes a defiant political voice to the centre to announce the existence of a rich cultural heritage bespeaking its ancient glory in the fate of its marginalisation. More importantly, this twin concerns in North East Indian English poetry should be read both as loud instances of the aggressive but intimate negotiation with the rest of the nation for reception on equal terms, and as tacit expressions of the undeniable inner truth of their willingness to meaningfully belong to the Indian nationhood.

Versing culture, voicing consciousness

One of the more politically implicit strands in North East Indian English poetry (Hazarika 1997) is its expression of the communal hatred and distrust for intimacy that exist in the region in the form of insider–outsider binaries. These binaries sometimes took a violent shape in the region in the recent past. For instance, in the xenophobic outrage of 1986, a large number of non-tribals were peremptorily evacuated from Shillong city. The immediate cause of this ethnic tension was the issue of trade licence by the state government to the non-tribal traders. The matter remained a major cause of the festering communal division in Shillong for many years following that incident. The non-local traders kept complaining about the harassment inflicted on them by local bodies and the persistent delay in the renewal of trade licences. They proclaimed that they had been doing business in Shillong city for ages together and nobody could stop them from doing legitimate business there. The problem of issuing the renewed licences to non-local traders persisted in the Iewduh market or Burrabazar in the heart of the city of Shillong. As this part of Shillong falls under the jurisdiction of the Dorbar of the Syiem of Myllieum, the Autonomous Khasi Hills District Council cannot issue trade licences here without the recommendation of the Syiem. Because of this tussle between the powerful local body and the non-local traders, the ethnic tension continues to simmer in Shillong city. The tension between the communities often gears up during the festive seasons as at this time religious and communal feelings are at their apex. In October, 1992, during such an occasion, a communal riot broke out in Shillong and 26 people were killed. Since then, the communal gulf between the local tribal community and the non-tribal communities from outside the northeast has widened and that rupture often flares up in the form of conflicts between groups in Shillong.

By inviting the conflicting communal interests to the platform of consensus and mutual belonging, Kynpham Singh Nongkynrih, one of the leading poets from the region, moves beyond the mere recording of these events in his sonnet 'Sundori.' It is worthwhile to mention here that Kynpham Singh Nongkynrih, born in the wettest place on the planet, Cherrapunji in Meghlaya, in 1964, has published several collections of poetry both in Khasi and English. He was awarded the first Veer Shankar Shah- Raghunath Shah National Award for literature in 2008 and the first North-East Poetry Award in 2004. He teaches at the Department of English in North-Eastern Hill University, Shillong. 'Sundori,' one of his most well-known sonnets, opens with an account of such rare communal conflicts that shamed the history of Shillong city in the recent past. In the opening lines, the poet addresses his beloved who belongs to the community with which the poet's own community is in conflict:

> Yesterday one of my people
> Killed one of your people
> And one of your people
> Killed one of my people.
> (Nongkynrih 2009: 207)

The violence inflicted upon each other on a certain day has made the perennial subterranean hatred and suspicion between the interested communal groups go explicit. It was not that the entire populace got physically involved in that bloody conflict. There were sections in both the communities with a communal agenda that served their topical political interests which was responsible for such conflicts, as per the poet. These stray communal forces ignited more hatred by drawing in communal fear and lop-sided interest and as a result, the rupture began to grow wider and deeper:

> Today they have both sworn
> To kill on sight.
> (Nongkynrih 2009: 207)

A private quarrel involving individuals from different communal roots has the potential to be magnified into a violently larger communal conflict that may result in the loss of many innocent lives. Repeating the lines twice, the poet expresses his disgust for the conflicts by describing the incidents of killing nonchalantly. Continuing the strand of harmonious co-existence despite the differences, it offhandedly raises the problems inherent in the idea of Indian nationhood and its confused and troubled acceptance in the region.

Another strand in North East Indian English poetry, a bit similar to the strand already mentioned with reference to its political pitch and yet different from it in its more inward-looking nature, is its reflection of the political desire to place the cultural excellence and difference of the region on a visible space. Desmond Kharmawphlang, another Khasi poet writing in English, usually glorifies the traditional cultural artefacts and folklore in his poetry in a way that the poet in him often gets subsumed by the folklorist. One example of such poetry is 'Tyrchiang,' one of his shorter poems, where he eulogises the traditional Khasi art of Khiew Ranei or terracotta pottery. Tyrchiang refers to the Tyrchiang village near Lyrnai, originally famous for earthen ware, by the NH44 of the Shillong-Jowai road in West Jainita Hills in Meghalaya. The art of terracotta pottery practised in this part of the world has a long history. But the decline of local demand for terracotta pots among the Khasi, Jaintia, and Garo tribes is putting this fine art into danger. The art of terracotta pottery has mythological significance for the poet. There are 'coils of mythology' created with 'dough of clay' for-

> the pact made with gods
> on mud.
> (Kharmawphlang 2009: 144)

Besides the use of the terracotta pots in the preparation of certain local delicacies, they are used in religious rituals. The Doloi or the chief of Nartiang uses the earthen ware made in Lyrnai village in some important religious functions. The Chief of Nartiang orders them in large quantity as the ritual remains incomplete without these pots. People following the traditional animist religion use the terracotta pots to keep a piece of the ruptured umbilical cord of the newborn baby preserved for a later ritual performed during the welcoming ceremony of the newborn. The locals believe that the traditions and practices of the past are given earthen shape by the potters. They re-live the traditions of their tribal past and become intimate once again with their cultural root. The craft of the potters provides aesthetic pleasure and the rootedness of that craft in the cultural traditions of their tribal life bestows them immense cultural significance. 'Myths construct themselves' in the hands of the potters at Tyrchiang giving a shape to their imagination. Their art offers them personal pleasure, and the rootedness of their art enables them to create 'the metaphors of substance.' Because of this rootedness in the cultural traditions of their community, the potters are clear-sighted, self-sufficient, and blissful. Unlike the poet, they are not lost in the maze of cultural confusion. The poet, on the other hand, is ashamed that he has been uprooted by modernity and city life:

> Tyrchiang, the wind among your
> pines, shames me with its
> simplicity
> (Kharmawphlang 2009:145)

The reason for his shame is that he is no longer a part of his cultural root at Tyrchiang. His values have been shaped by the practices of an increasingly dominant and culturally foreign ethos emanating from institutions dictated from a hegemonic axis. Yet the poet is unable to transport himself completely to the new ways of life as his ancestral roots necessarily bind him to the traditional cultural values. So, he finds himself in an awkward situation as he is neither here nor there-

> . . . I whose roots draw
> deep from books to prop up
> my tribal bones.
> (Kharmawphlang 2009: 145)

Yet another strand in North East Indian English poetry is exemplified by Esther Syiem, another significant poet writing in English from the northeast of India. Writing poems dipped in the folktales and myths of Khasi origin (Nigel Jenkins 1993; Rafy 1920; Syiem 2009), she appears to be engaged in an attempt to create a cultural space for her beloved Khasi community both in respect to the peripheral plurality writhing within the concept of Indian nationhood and the disturbing dominance of the imagined monolithic Indian core. The duality of concern in terms of the defiant voice in her poems that announces the ancient glory of the Khasi myths and legends and the caress with which these myths are held up for the general reader sums up her poetry. In contrast to the two strands already mentioned, her poems explicitly and more aggressively reflect on some serious complications embedded in the formation of the Indian nationhood. This aggression or defiance is not a violent dismissal of an opponent as such but an attempt at a showcasing of her relatively unknown cultural heritage against the backdrop of a perceived epistemological violence emanating from the core, different from the second strand in its political explicitness. Underneath the angry voice of a revolutionary runs deep an affectionate complaint and this complaint is in sooth a covert appeal for a respectful space. The anger on the surface is in reality a camouflage for the safeguard of the core values of a dear culture ignored and on the verge of extinction.

In one of her more well-known poems, 'To the Rest of India from Another Indian,' this anomalous mix of the defiance and the wish for intimate belonging expresses itself to the fullest. The native culture of the poet in terms of the myths and legends located at the geographical and intellectual periphery is defined against the better-known cultural items of the Indian centre. The poem begins referring to a few legends from the two celebrated Indian epics: the 'Ramayana' and the 'Mahabharata.' The poet triggers the mood of defiance at the very beginning of the poem by not subscribing to these legends. She stresses them as cultural items situated more within the boundary of a separate cultural identity or nationhood than within her own. The mythical characters of Rama, Sita, and Arjuna may very well have cultural significance for the rest of the Indians, but the poet does not subscribe to their authority. She is suspicious of the cultural encroachment and hegemonic occupation intended by the migrant and dominant centre at the core of Indian nationhood. It is not just her political rights under threat but also the rich cultural items in the form of these marginalised myths. Yet, she refuses to acknowledge the supremacy of the cultural paraphernalia of the occupant centre by denying their power over her perception. In contrast, she happily upholds the numerous mythical characters found in the oral traditions of her community as an alternative.

She begins her poem with a proud announcement by drawing a distinct borderline between the well-known cultural heritage of the centre and the yet unknown myths and legends of her own peripheral locality. The centre may take pride in the fact that it has a cultural heritage rich and long, but the poet refuses to succumb to the glory of that wealth. Her approach to her lesser known cultural items is as confident and proud as the centre. She unequivocally announces,

> We have
> no Rama
> no Sita
> no Arjuna
> ours are
> differently named.
> (Syiem 2017: 9)

The poet treats her local myths and legends with the same symbolic cultural signification as the centre treats its mythical characters. Although the symbolic images of the poet's native culture may not have the same range and fame of the more widely familiar mythical characters like Rama, Sita, and Arjuna for the centre, they have parallel significance and meaning for the poet and her community.

The two Indian epics narrate two wars fought between the forces of evil and the messengers of virtue ending with a predetermined victory for the latter. These two wars and the religious meanings associated with them have served as moral guide for centuries together in the centre. The participant characters of the wars and the motives driving these characters in various capacities and moral situations have served as exemplars of the best and the worst in the centre. So, the ancient glories represented by them are stored in the memory of the centre enlightening its present and showing it a road map for the future. What happened in Lanka and Kurukshetra has assisted in the understanding and description of the perennial spiritual life of the centre. But, speaking from the margin, the poet does not share the symbolic significance of these wars. She is part of a different course of history. The values and ethics at the heart of the ethos of her community reside in the moral and psychological struggles of another kind. She writes,

> ours were in camouflage
> up the stony tracks of the antelope
> down impossible ravines and
> through impassable jungles.
> (Syiem 2017: 9)

The unrecorded battles fought in the oral history of the poet's community had woven a separate series of myths. These battles may not have received the same quantity of attention and fame accrued to the battles in Lanka and Kurukshetra, but they have enormous moral and ethical significance for her community. The poet emphasises on the geographical differences between the battlefields. The mythological battles fought in the poet's country occurred in the hills and the glory of the wars and their symbolic vitality were created through difficult mountain ranges. The emphasis on the geographical dissimilarity of the battles point out to the fact of the varied conditions of life leading to disparate myth creations.

From the subject of myths and legends the poet moves to the issue cultural practices and sarcastically mentions the site of worship so very important to the cultural pride of the centre. The poet writes,

> We've no temples,
> none to be purified
> with litanies and
> incense to leaven
> crimes of the night.
> (Syiem 2017: 9)

The cultural significance of the temple is immense to the centre. But the poet finds it rather a place to wash one's hands from crimes. As per the poet, the site of the temple operates as the conscience of the centre. The corporeal functions of the centre run without disturbance if only the conscience is properly taken care of. The poet alleges that the site of the temple is created by the centre to escape from the pangs of conscience. The poet muses mockingly on the fact that a minor ritual performed by the centre inside the temple may get them out of guilt and pain of repentance following hundreds of crimes. Chanting of some sacred lines from a holy book may wash away the crimes from the hands of a criminal. The poet takes pride in the fact that such bigotry does not exist in her community as there is no such place of worship in her country. The intention of the poet here appears to be the conclusion that the centre cannot boast of the existence of such spiritual cultural institutions because these institutions do not function as they are meant to be. The poet rather rejoices on the fact that her community has not developed such dubious institutions. The poet carries along the derogatory tone when she writes,

> No one river too sacred
> to purify impurities.
> (Syiem 2017: 9)

Her direct oppositional tribal stance against the Hindu centre is oriented towards the Holy river in the Hindu scripts. Since this river has magical powers because of its original incarnation as the Goddess that resides in the loop of Lord Shiva's hair, as described in the Hindu scriptures, one drop of it may change the fortune of a believer. A life full of sins and wrong-doing may be relieved of its impurity with the touch of this sacred river. Such holy rivers do not exist in the poet's community. There is a tone of sarcasm in the way that the poet mentions the sense of possession often shown by the centre. The poet takes up to expose the shallowness in the pride that the centre associates itself with in the form of the abundance of cultural paraphernalia it has been privilege to for ages together. The obvious purpose of the poet in enlisting the cultural differences with reference to myths and legends is to stress the border that divides the imagined centre from the margin. As the poet emphasises,

none of our gods
bear god-names like yours.
(Syiem 2017: 9)

The poet refers to a number of Khasi myths and legends showcasing the abundance of these myths gripping the cultural discourse of her community,

Earth-gods and sky-deities
nymphs and elfin dwarves
that winnow souls and scale bamboo leaves
rinsed intestines in running streams.
(Syiem 2017: 10)

These references bring into light the political purpose in writing about them in the other mythological poems by the poet. In her more popular poems like 'U Ksuid Tynjang,' 'Just One More Field,' 'The Hill of Woman's Death,' 'Only for the Bird-brained,' 'Memoirs of a Dismantled Lover,' 'The Fable of the Mustard Seed,' and 'Suburban Friends,' the poet elaborately incorporates Khasi myths and legends as part of the poet's struggle to gravitate national cultural attention towards her provincial cultural identity-

LumShyllong and SajerNangli
and how we swallowed our written script,
stones that eat and rivers that fly,
talking tigers and tiger-men.
(Syiem 2017:10)

These poems may be understood here as fervent attempts at communication between the poet's ardent self and the alien audience in the centre for the legitimate realisation of the poet's sense of belonging to the larger national identity, sometimes expressed in wounded tones. The poet is confident too of the cultural wealth of her community. Glorifying the rich oral traditions of her culture she writes,

And our translucent caves let me tell you
that rig our underground world
stitch in the ancestor
who sanctified the speaking tongue.
(Syiem 2017:10)

This passionate mix of the love for Khasi myths and the concern for Khasi space in the Indian cultural maze gets itself served with plenty of pride in a poem 'U Ksuid Tynjang.' A spirit from Khasi folklore is the focus of the poem. This spirit, infamous for his cruelty, was a monster suffering an incurable itching disease. It hunkers down to be scratched cajoling, threatening, demanding, willing pliant fingers to scratch the itch on his back. He would cast a spell over people losing their way in the woods, trapped them in the thick forest and made them itch his body till skin peels off the scratcher's finger-tips, nails break off on nerveless hide, blood erupts to flow all night, and till scratcher turns to legend in the next dawn. Whoever dared to disobey his orders would be dealt with cruel punishment as they would be tickled to death. But this monster loses his life in the hands of a couple of teenagers. Losing their way in the woods where the monster lived, Ka Thei and Ka Duh with their brother, as they were returning home from a fair, were trapped by the evil spell of the monster. But they managed to free their brother as the monster was asleep. With the blessings from the god of Shillong, Ka Duh killed the monster with a big knife. But the monster took a different form of life after his death. He became the notorious Tynjang creeper that troubles hunters in the forest and destroys plants cultivated by peasants. As per Khasi folklore, this monster needs to be frightened off by fire even today. Otherwise it still holds the power to tickle people to death.

Another reference in the poem draws the reader's attention to yet another poem by Syiem, 'Just One More Field My Child,' which tells the mythological story. It describes the sorrowful fate of the innocent mother who falls prey to the idiosyncrasy of destiny. The poem narrates with plenty of sympathy the pain and agony of the mother whose baby turned to a stone. The woman kept her baby on a giant stone as it was asleep. She was working in the field nearby as the baby started crying. The bay cries because of the swallowing stone. The baby keeps on crying for a while, and the mother, unaware of the situation, tries to console her baby from the field, promising to feed it after a little more work. The baby stops crying and the mother goes back to the stone upon which the baby was kept. To her pain, she finds the baby missing and finally gets to know that the giant stone swallowed up her baby. The poem expresses the tragic intensity of the legend through the child's complaints and the mother's realisation of the cruel reality,

> Mei, don't keep me on hold any longer
> Don't you know that my feet are clamped in its jaws?
> (Syiem 2003: 176)
> The poet makes a reference to another Khasi legend-
> Icons that died for a love
> that endorsed a freedom
> uninhibited, as our wild mountain herbs.
>
> (Syiem 2003: 176)

This legend is elaborately described in a poem entitled 'The Hill of Woman's Death' by the poet. This poem recounts the myth of the beautiful girl whose suitor dies an unexpected death. As per the legend, there was a beautiful girl whose fame reached far and wide. Young men seeking her hand in marriage came from all corners of the world. As the girl could not decide the right person for marriage, the father of the girl organised a race among the suitors of the girl. The young men gathered in the house of the girl hoping to win the race and marry her. Although the beautiful girl did not have relationship with anyone among the suitors, she kept a soft corner for a valiant young man. She wanted that young man to win the race. The suitors started running and the girl's heart was on her mouth. She was very happy as the suitor for whom she had affectionate feeling won the race. But unfortunately, the winner suitor dies immediately after the race. As the suitor was about to cheer the moment of victory, his lungs burst because of the excessive labour. The beautiful girl was stupefied and went into deep pain. She decided not to marry anybody. She mourned the loss of her valiant suitor in the hills,

> Father, I know you decreed this form me.
> My destiny you wrote
> on these grassy steps.
>
> (Syiem 2003:178)

This consciousness or the effort to arouse a consciousness on the issue of the cultural divide is to resist the hegemonic occupation of the dominant cultural norms emanating from the centre. In the face of a real or imagined imminence of a cultural coup, the poet enumerates the ancient cultural glory of her community and projects it as an attempt at a contest with the rich and powerful centre. In a way, the poet is virtually on the last mission to prevent this cultural invasion of the dominant centre on her ever-receding cultural heritage situated in the periphery.

Intimacy through mutual recognitions

Ernest Renan concluded his speech at the Sorbonne, 'Wait a while, gentlemen; let the reign of the transcendants pass; bear the scorn of the powerful with patience. It may be that, after many fruitless gropings, people will revert to our more modest empirical solutions. The best way of being in the future is, in certain periods, to know how to resign oneself to being out of fashion.' (Renan 1990: 21). The truth is that the present concept of Indian nationhood has not been accepted without questioning by the poets. The sociocultural differences that exist force the unitary idea of nationhood to be re-examined and reconstituted. But the process for an uninhibited intimacy has never started. Instead, the multiple voices in the periphery that do not share the sociocultural features of the centre have been either ignored or crushed. So, the poets in the region deeply lament the resentment that leads to disturbance of various kinds in the region.

It appears that the solutions to this impasse have been looked at from two levels. At one level, poets like Robin Ngangom decide to look inward. The conflict outside has been described as shaping up to be more frightening as a result of the conflicts inside. Definitely all is not well within northeast India. These inner conflicts are not about the opposite pulls of honest and sincere duty, the pangs of sacrifice and the glory of martyrdom. The conflicts within have degenerated into contradictions between bestiality and humanity, material exhibition and moral austerity, corruption, and honesty. In the majority of the cases the dark forces are eroding the foundation of humanity. Robin Ngangom's 'When You Do Not Return' attempts at an interpretation of the expression of an inner decay that the poet makes responsible for the troubles in the land. It takes up the themes of moral degradation and sociopolitical turmoil in his native land. The poet creates an imaginary situation in which a speaker addresses an absent persona whose non-existence in the land has resulted in moral degradation and sociopolitical turmoil. Without providing any explicit reference, the poet recounts the troubled periods in the history of contemporary Manipur. But the indirect references provided in the poem hint at 'native hills,' regret the 'sunless kingdom,' and grieve the situation in which

> gunfire reverberates
> in the hills, and bullets sprout from
> windows instead of geraniums.
> (Ngangom 2009: 198)

These indirect but meaningful references in the poem testify to the fact that it is an appraisal of the moral and sociopolitical situation in the contemporary times in Manipur. Manipur has been the breeding ground of insurgency in the northeast for many years as it has been described as the 'sick man of the North east' in Indian political discourse. The sociopolitical discontents of the people inhabiting that beautiful land in the easternmost part of India often took the shape of violent protests. These protests gave rise to not less than 17 insurgent groups in Manipur. The poet laments the fact that the revolutionary ideals of the youth in the past has deadened into unprincipled terror-mongering. Both the youths in the insurgent groups and the common youths in the streets of his native land have been led astray. The-

> messianic young men betray principles
> and there's no fire in their eyes.
> (Ngangom 2009: 198)

The main cause of the revolution is forgotten, and only they know the truth of their continuous fight. The youths in the streets are left with no ideals to follow and they have degenerated into a sloganeering crowd. They follow a self-proclaiming, self-righteous, and arrogant demagogue of a leader who may use them as he pleases. For easy material gains, the youths in the land of the poet have surrendered to sycophancy as

> In the streets students shout themselves
> hoarse for newly-arrived patriots.
> (Ngangom 2009: 198)

Since violence and bloodshed have become a routine in the poet's native hills,

> . . . The barbwire
> of the day encloses us as we enter the era
> of the assassin.
> (Ngangom 2009: 198)

The world has entered the era of the killers and everybody is counting his days. The inevitable is knocking at the doors of the people as if the Judgment day has arrived. In this age of the killers, only those who kill will survive. So, the poet regrets the fact that only the stories of sorrow and violence, decay and bloodshed could be sent to the imagined persona as an appraisal of the lives of the people inhabiting the hills. The poet wishes that these stories of pain might change its mind and it might think about returning to its native hills. Only its return may potentially bring back peace that has left the poet's country.

At another level, some poets believe that the solution exists out there. They often end their poems with an implicit, as well as explicit, indication that there is a scope for peaceful intimacy if a condition of mutual curiosity, respect, and compromise is created. These poets clearly set the rules for appeasement and settlement. Kynpham Singh Nongkynrih's sonnet 'Sundori' concludes with a call for harmonious and peaceful co-existence. He invites his 'Beloved Sundori' for a reconciliation and asks,

> Shall we meet by the Umkrah River
> And empty this madness
> Into its angry summer floods?
> (Nongkynrih 2009: 207)

The poet anticipates that this small step of affection taken at the personal level will create a ripple effect. It will surely help alleviate the anger and the communal hatred that separated the people by setting an example for them. The poet sends his message of love and peace to his beloved 'Through a fearful night breeze' as the violence and animosity between the communal groups in Shillong was then at its peak.

Putting into focus the cultural richness of her community as a display intended for the centre, poets like Esther Syiem is in the mood of a settlement. Since the marginalised status of the poet's community is undeserving and injustice, she hopes for a better deal. In the final few lines of the poem 'To the Rest of India from Another Indian,' for example, the poet complainingly inquires of the centre whether it is in the mood for an alliance and assimilation:

> Would you then, even care to enter, tongue-twistingly,
> into the spoils of our speaking-wealth?
> (Syiem 2017: 10)

Through these lines, the poet makes it clear that there is no dearth of effort from the margin for a bond of intimacy with the centre. Historically speaking, it is the centre that refuses to bestow them a patient hearing. The confrontational mood that disturbs the contemporary ambience may be easily mitigated if that due is paid to the margin. The sense of belonging has been hijacked for the lack of this tryst. There must be an aggressive effort for the construction of trust between the so-called centre and the margin. Only then a climate of peace will arrive for the nourishment of intimacy.

The following lines from 'To the Indians from Another Indian' by Esther Syiem unequivocally express the poet's solution of the complications that have started to show up-

> But if you should
> twist your tongues around ours
> as we learnt to twist ours around yours,
> you'll get a taste of
> webbed legends.
>
> (Syiem 2017: 10)

The poet implies that the animosity and distance that separate the imagined centre and the so-called margin is created by the centre itself. The centre has kept itself out of touch as it has not been sufficiently curious and pliant. It has been bragging its supremacy by refusing to allow the minority to merge into it. So the less populous section has been marginalised and placed at a location of disadvantage. Subsequently, the margin is now refusing to be interpreted and dictated by the centre. There is a constant rise of the rebellious in the atmosphere as the margin is now beginning to define the centre. This confrontational situation may be resolved by an assimilation and alliance. As the margin has been pliant and accommodative to the cultural items of the centre, the centre must also change its approach. It must help create a space for practice and growth to the revolutionary voices rising in the margin. Respecting the voices of dissent, it must learn to be humble and receptive of the cultural richness at the margin. The poet asks for a historically denied relationship of equality between her community and the centre. The poet pleads the centre for an attention to the myths and legends of her culture. Only then, she thinks, the centre may intimately discover, though a dialogic politics of belonging, the rich cultural heritage of her community.

References

Hazarika, Sanjoy. 1997. 'Kallika: The Unveiling of Literature from India's North East.' *The Book Review*, xxi(4): 23–24.

Kharmawphlang, Desmond, L. 2009. 'Tyrchiang.' In Robin S. Ngangom and Kynpham S Nongkynrih (eds.), *Dancing Earth: An Anthology of Poetry from North-East India*, pp. 144–145. New Delhi: Penguin.

Ngangom, R. 'When You Do Not Return.' In Robin S. Ngangom and Kynpham S. Nongkynrih (eds.), *Dancing Earth: An Anthology of Poetry from North-East India*, p. 198. New Delhi: Penguin.

Nigel Jenkins, 'Thomas Jones and the Lost Book of the Khasis.' *The New Welsh Review*, 2I(1993): 56–82.

Nongkynrih, Kynpham S. 2009. 'Sundori.' In Robin S. Ngangom and Kynpham S. Nongkynrih (eds.), *Dancing Earth: An Anthology of Poetry from North-East India*, 207. New Delhi: Penguin.

Rafy, Mrs. 1920. *Folk-Tales of the Khasis*. London: Palgrave Macmillan.

Renan, Ernest. 1990. 'What is a Nation?' In Homi K. Bhaba (ed.), *Nation and Narration*, pp. 8–21. London: Routledge.

Syiem, Esther. 2003. 'Poems.' *Anthology of Contemporary Poetry from the North East. NEHU*, 176–181.

Syiem, Esther. 2009. 'U Ksuid Tynjang.' *Kavya Bharati*, 61.

Syiem, Esther. 2017. 'To the Rest of the Indians from Another Indian.' *Many Sides of Many Stories. Writers' Workshop*, 9–10.

PART VI
Techno intimacies

14

MATERNAL INTIMACIES ONLINE

How Indian mom bloggers reconfigure self, body, family, and community

Sucharita Sarkar

Introduction

This study is a comparative analysis of historical and contemporary representations of motherhood intimacy (obtained through extensive secondary research) with online emergences of networked maternal intimacies in momblogs. For the latter, I have undertaken a close reading of selective blog posts chosen from a purposive sampling of Indian momblogs, curated from my primary research of over 130 such blogs conducted for my ongoing doctoral dissertation. Purposive sampling allowed me to focus on specific blog posts that manifested the theoretical concepts I wish to explore in this chapter. The deployment of these interdisciplinary theoretical concepts, such as motherhood intimacy, mothering intimacy, motherline, scalable socialities, and networked intimacies are grounded in, and indebted to, existing scholarship in motherhood history, feminist motherhood studies and new media studies.

The embodied intimacies of mothering

Motherhood scholars, following Adrienne Rich, differentiate between motherhood and mothering: 'The term *motherhood* refers to the patriarchal institution of motherhood that is male-defined and controlled and is deeply oppressive to women, while the word *mothering* refers to women's experiences of mothering that are female-defined and centered and potentially empowering to women' (O'Reilly 2008: 3; emphases mine). Mothering – from conception to parturition to nurturing – is an experience that is deeply intimate. Numerous religious, historical, and psychoanalytical sources attest – and the prevalence of mother-goddess cults indicates – that the mother-child relationship has often been theorised and sacralised as the primary intimacy from which other social relationships are derived and perpetuated. In the *Rig Veda*, Aditi, whose name is mentioned over eighty times, is worshipped as the primal mother, giving birth to gods and kings (Bose 2010: 18). Her embodied maternity is emphasised by depicting her in the 'uttana-pada' posture – crouching with legs spread up and wide – that is common during childbirth (*Rig Veda* 10.72.1–5, quoted in Doniger 2011: 127). Later scriptural discourse, however, invisibilises the physicality of the maternal body, and focuses more on the symbolic significance of motherhood.

The biological facts of conception, pregnancy, birthing, and breastfeeding make mothering an embodied, intimate experience between mother and child. The long period of nurturing and care – especially in a society where the mother is culturally expected to be the primary caregiver – intertwines the identities of mother and child into a complex and intimate dyad. The physical and sensory closeness involved in mothering makes it an embodied and intersubjective engagement. Feminist scholar Mielle Chandler writes: 'It is my position that "mother" is best understood as a verb, as something one does, a practice which creates one's identity as intertwined, interconnected and in-relation' (Chandler 2007: 531). She also emphasises the 'context-specific' plurality of mothering subjectivities, a plurality that is erased by the abstraction of motherhood as a sociocultural role (Chandler 2007: 531).

The closeness between mother and child, and the dependence of the child on the mother shapes the psyche and development of the child in complex ways. Psychologists theorise that this shaping happens differently in male children and female children. Sudhir Kakar writes that 'for the analyst, the story of a man's relationship with women inevitably begins [. . .] with his mother' (Kakar 1990: 86). He further states that 'sexual fantasies' are imaginative choices a man makes 'to maintain an idealised relationship with the maternal body' (Kakar 1990: 132). In contrast to this idealising tendency of sons, daughters' relationships with their mothers are more ambivalent, and simultaneously powerful and painful. One of the reasons for this, of course, is the resemblance between their bodies and experiences. Daughters experience the constant and contradictory pulls of identification and differentiation, often leading to a perception of 'overwhelming enmeshment' (Boyd 1989: 292). It is this enmeshed and embodied dyadic intimacy that is sought to be controlled by patriarchal ideologies through the institutionalisation of motherhood for their own purposes, which include the perpetuation of patrilineality.

Cultural constructions of motherhood intimacy

Scriptural and mythical motherhood intimacies

Since, as of yet, the reproductive powers of mothers are indispensable for the continuation of the human species and human relations, patriarchal social systems have inevitably, and understandably, attempted to control it. Adrienne Rich describes motherhood as 'a condition which had been wrested from the mothers themselves to buttress the power of the fathers' (Rich 1986: 62). Each stage of the mothering experience – conception, gestation, parturition, and post-parturition – has been ritualised, regularised, and scrutinised through scripture and custom. Sukumari Bhattacharji lists a spectrum of rituals in various Hindu scriptures that attempts to control mothers – the *Atharvaveda*'s prayers for a male child spoken by the father prior to conception, the *pumsavana* ritual described in the *Hiranyakeshin Grhyasutra* for pregnant women to perform in order to ensure a male child, the post-birth rites for sons such as *varsavardhana* for long life of the son – most of these are discharged by the father while the mother is passive, and 'nowhere in the scriptures is there a prayer for the long life of . . . the prospective mother' (Bhattacharji 2010: 45). The 'woman was the field, and the man sowed the seed in her'; the *Manusmriti* categorised the seed as 'superior' and stated that child always inherits the 'quality of the seed' (Bhattacharji 2010: 57). Thus, there prevailed the paradox of intense scrutiny of the mothering process along with near-complete denial of any maternal autonomy or voice. The intimate bonds between mother and child were systemically disrupted by patriarchal institutions and replaced with the binds of motherhood.

Prescriptive and essentialised motherhood demanded that all women become mothers, especially mothers of sons. Barren women could be 'discarded after ten years' and a mother who bears only daughters could be 'discarded after twelve years' (Bhattacharji 2010: 47). The unabashed son-preference that prevailed in Hindu society had a distorting effect on mothering intimacies, especially on the intimate relation between mother and daughter. Most scriptural references glorify mothers of sons and denigrate daughters. The *Brahmavairatapurana* states that the 'life of a woman who has no son is useless,' while the *Manusmriti* considers the daughter to be the 'ultimate object of pity' (Bose 2010: 78–79). Through the strategic deification of son-bearing, obedient mothers, patriarchal institutions ensured complicity of mothers in the perpetuation of women's subordination. The cultural valorisation of the mother–son dyad exists simultaneously with the invisibilising of the mother–daughter dyad, which takes place through a persistent positioning of the daughter as *parayi* (belonging to others) rather than *apni* (belonging to oneself); this positioning is facilitated through the custom of virilocal marriages (Johri 2013).

The simultaneous glorification and disempowerment of women was aided by the prevalence of mother-goddess worship, where the 'idea of the goddess functions as a philosophical and social archetype' from where 'models of conduct have emerged to dominate women's lives' (Bose 2010: 13). Mandakranta Bose further states: 'Hindu thought forges links between goddesses and women, and invests women with mystical authority even as it locks them within subservient social roles [. . .] It is through such ambiguities and paradoxes that the Hindu tradition projects its conception of women' (Bose 2010: 10). By centralising the life-giving, domesticated, and nurturing aspect of consort goddesses like Parvati and Lakshmi, and by banishing deviant goddesses like Kali to the margins, Hindu Brahmanical narratives seek to construct the ideal mother as docile and chaste. This divine ideal of maternal love and sacrifice is enhanced by the representations of mythical motherhood intimacies of Kaushalya–Rama, Sita–Luv/Kush, Devaki–Krishna, Renuka–Parshuram, and many others. The mother–daughter dyad, however, is strikingly absent.

Contemporary Hindutva prescriptions of motherhood

Contemporary cultural constructs of motherhood in Hindutva discourse reinforce the stereotype of the devoted and sacrificing mother. The surveillance and training of the mother begins during the stage of pregnancy itself. The Gita Press manual on *How to Lead a Household Life* advises that 'pregnant mothers should listen to the stories of God and His devotees, should think of them and see their photographs in order to give birth to noble and excellent offspring' (Ramsukhdas 2012: 43). The Handbook of the Rashtra Sevika Samiti centralises women in the familial-social-national structure of the Hindu rashtra: 'Woman is a common bond of affection and attachment in a family, in her capacity as a daughter, a sister, a wife and a mother,' and she has to be trained in the 'correct and coordinating outlook regarding her duties towards the family and society and create a deep sense of devotion and pride for nation, religion and culture' (quoted in K. Menon 2012: 162). The 'bond of affection and attachment' and familial intimacy is sought to be homogenised and controlled by external agents for their own political ends.

It can be argued that any individual mothering intimacy, by its own necessarily flawed experiences, will undermine any imposed ideal of perfect motherhood intimacy. As Chandler states, 'No matter how hard one tries to hyperconform, to simulate the perfect mother, the baby will always disrupt the simulation' (Chandler 2007: 538). However, maternal feminists emphasise the need to create and circulate a counter-narrative comprising mothers' own voices to challenge the subjugation imposed by constructed ideals of motherhood. This is because the imposed construct of motherhood intimacy suppresses any kind of non-normative maternal practice or disobedient emotion; devalues mother-daughter intimacy; and creates an oppressive pressure on mothers to choose motherhood over selfhood.

Maternal intimacies and the internet

Pre-internet oral narratives of intimacy

Discussing maternal rage, the 'moments of murderous anger at our children,' one of the many tabooed emotions that infuse mothering intimacies, Adrienne Rich comments, 'The words are being spoken now, are being written down; the taboos are being broken, the masks of motherhood are cracking through' (Rich 1986: 24–25). Rich was writing this a few decades before blogging and social media became a convenient and popular mode of communication among mothers (and others). In Indian contexts, oral and folk narratives are rich sites where mothering subjectivities have been articulated, especially the mother-daughter intimacies marginalised in mainstream patriarchal discourse, for instance, in this Maharashtrian folk song which describes mother-daughter intimacy: 'The moon has gone/ behind the attic;/ sweet is the talk/ between mother and daughter' (Tharu and Lalitha 1991: 137). The covertness of the mother-daughter bond that can only be expressed in the dark, at night, is indicative of its suppression by patriarchal institutions, yet the very existence of such oral counter-narratives also validates the tenacity of such intimacies. As Ira Raja and Kay Souter write in their Introduction to an anthology of mother-daughter stories, 'mother-daughter intimacy proves more resilient than familial and social structures would seem to allow' (2010: xiv).

Theorising intimacies on the internet

Yet, it is the growing popularity of the Internet as social media, that has radically transformed the definitions, borders, and practices of intimate relations, including the domain of maternal intimacies. Social media have been defined as 'scalable sociality'; explicating this term from an anthropological perspective, Miller et al. write:

> We can envisage two key scales. The first is the scale from the most private to the most public. The second is the scale from the smallest group to the largest groups. At one end of both of these scales we still see private dyadic conversation and at the other end we still see fully public broadcasting. What is it that is being scaled? The core to the study of social science is the way in which people associate with each other to form social relations and societies. This is called sociality. The best way to define what is popularly called social media but also includes prior media is thus to describe the new situation as increasingly 'scalable sociality.'
>
> *(Miller et al. 2016: 1)*

This perspective is useful in both situating social media relationships within a tradition of sociality, while also highlighting the unique flexibility of social media communication. It is this flexible or scalable sociality that breaks down the private/ public binary in several ways and allows for new kinds of intimacies to evolve in the digital space. Social media platforms like Facebook and WhatsApp have rescaled the boundaries of familial intimacy from the local to the global, offering ways 'to be separate and together, providing connections to support familial intimacy in terms of knowing [. . .] loving [. . .] and caring,' hence emerging as valuable tools for maintaining and strengthening mother-child bonding, especially in the contexts of families dispersed through migration and globalisation (Valentine 2006: 387).

While various social media platforms like Facebook and WhatsApp have re-mapped the terrains of intimate relations in significant, and significantly different yet imbricated ways, my focus in this chapter will be only on momblogs. Valentine states, 'The Internet is not just a tool for maintaining and sustaining existing familial relationships; it can also facilitate the creation of new intimacies' (Valentine 2006: 378). The attempt here is to explore the geometries of the new maternal intimacies as created and experienced in blogs written for mothers by mothers. Momblogs are communities of mothers for mothers: they 'capture maternal experiences, give mothers a voice, and foster conversation and participation in a community' (Friedman 2013: 11). Here, I will define intimacy by 'three necessary and sufficient conditions: self-revealing behavior, positive involvement with the other, and shared understandings' (Barton 2009: 578). Mombloggers strategically reveal aspects of their selves and invite the reader into a zone of privacy, and the evidences of self-disclosure, positive response, and mutual understanding, mark personal blogging as an intimate activity. I must, however, emphasise that the maternal intimacies interrogated in this chapter belong to privileged and mainstream intersections – urban, educated, heterosexual, predominantly Hindu, uppercaste and middleclass, with easy access to computer mediated communication, and that I have excluded mothering experiences on the other side of the digital divide.

The blogosphere, or mamasphere as it is also called, is what the interlinked network of mom bloggers is collectively known as. It is marked not only by multiplicity, but by relationality: it lives 'at the intersection of mother and other, of conversation and memoir, of audience and author' (Friedman 2013: 87). This relationality – textually evident in the comments, shares, and hyperlinks received by the blog posts – creates a 'networked intimacy,' although the lack of temporality in blogging leads to a deferred or asynchronous intimacy (Lejeune, quoted in Serfaty 2004: 61). The blogger can connect or separate from the reader by manipulating her online identity as both mirror (for self-representation) and veil (for identity-protection) (Serfaty 2004). Serfaty also suggests that online intimacy is transformed by the mediation of the computer screen, which shields the blogger from the gaze of others and allows them the space to say things that might be tabooed in scrutinised offline relationships (Serfaty 2004: 13). Some of the over 150 contributors to the group blog *Indian Moms Connect*, for example, choose not to use their real names or to post their profile pictures, preferring pseudonyms like 'D's Mom,' 'modernmom2012,' or 'Simply Me' ('Writers and Contributors':*n.d; n.pag*).

The anonymity offered by the internet allows the blogger immense transformational and transgressive potential and also a creative freedom to shape the intimacy with the reader by having agential control over the creation of an online second self. The blogger's authorial control over her blog – for instance, she can choose to moderate the comments by her readers, choose to link to other blogs of her choice and choose to post on subjects of her choice at a time and pace of her own convenience – allows for the creation of a networked intimacy where the momblogger often has much more autonomy than in the offline world of familial intimacies. The very fact that the momblogger can select and alter the scale of sociality on online platforms like blogs gives her more agency than is usually possible in offline interactions.

Anonymity, however, is a diminishing trend in contemporary social media, at least in the sphere of maternal intimacies. One main reason for this is the increasing use of polymedia, that is, of multiple social media platforms that may have overlapping content and/or audiences. Such interconnected and cross-media communication – where the blogger may write a post on her blog and then tweet about it or link it to her Facebook profile – both expands the hyperlinked networks of online intimacy and makes them more persistent and circular. Differentiating offline intimate groups from online encounters, Carolli prefers the term 'collaboration' rather than 'community': stating that the internet 'acts as a terrain where the public/private distinction is deconstructed' through collaborative and potentially radical encounters with the 'other,' these encounters are 'informed by a postmodern sense of irony, fragmentation, and multiplicity' (Carroli 1997: 359).

Carolli states that, 'one conceptual framework for the collaborative and generative possibilities of the Internet and notions of collaboration is provided by Gilles Deleuze and Felix Guattari's notion of rhizomatics,' as rhizomes connect any point to any other point through lines of stratification as well as lines of flight (Carroli 1997: 360). Since the rhizome is by nature anti-genealogy, my argument is that the blogosphere can be positioned as anti-family, where family is defined as a patriarchal institution with codified and controlled norms of entry, interaction, and exit. Hence, the possibilities of multitudinous and fragmented intimacies offered by the blogosphere are radically different from the linear and predetermined familial intimacies witnessed in families.

The reason why mothers read and write blogs can be explained through Anthony Giddens' theory of 'pure relationships' (1992). In this late modern age, technology has disembedded social relations from local contexts of physical and temporal closeness and redistributed them across a different matrix of time and space. This has led to traditional kinship relations (with their attendant obligations) being replaced by 'pure relationships.' Valentine defines such relationships as those which are 'entered into for their own sake in the pursuit of happiness, and are sustained only as long as they are fulfilling,' and which are 'based on voluntary commitment, mutual trust, equality, and reflexivity' (Valentine 2006: 366). The blogosphere is a network of such pure relationships and it extends the concept of intimacy beyond the domestic boundaries within which patriarchy attempts to confine mothers.

Maternal intimacies in momblogs: resistances, reassertions, affects

Why mothers need intimate connections

There are various psychological theories of intimacy which seek to explain why women are 'innately predisposed to intimate interaction': biological and evolutionary theories that locate the desire for intimacy in the maternal body, which is 'biologically prepared for childbearing and breastfeeding,' and the 'sex-role orientation' theory which states that women assume 'feminine roles concerning nurturance and primary care giving' and are hence 'primed for intimacy, whereas men are not' (Gaia 2002: 162). Even if we ignore the essentialising nature of these theories, we can still fruitfully use them to understand the popularity of momblogging and its appeal to mothers. Historical sources amply demonstrate how isolated and unprepared new mothers have always felt. In Rashsundari Devi's 1876 autobiography *Amaar Jibon*

(My Life), the earliest such writing by a woman in India, we read how alone and disconnected she felt as a new mother: 'I had not known before how great is the burden of pain for the mother who raises a child [. . .] Every human being should know of this but very few actually do' (quoted in Sarkar 2013: 191–192). New mothering, especially in urban, nuclear family locations, continues to be an isolating experience, and mothers feel the need for shared knowledge of mothering and companionship of mothers as keenly as Rashsundari Devi did so many years ago.

Blogger Lalitha Iyer of *Mommygolightly* writes that it was maternal loneliness that impelled her to blog, and that blogging has created a new network of intimacy that has sustained and supported her:

> I first started blogging about motherhood when I was lonely as a new mother [. . .] But I can say this with a lot of conviction that by putting myself and my child out there, we have only grown together. And in a good way. We have been recipients of a lot of kindness and love and affection, and that can't be a bad thing, can it? There are many occasions in parenting where you just don't know what to do; I often falter many times and hit a blank wall, and now I know I have this huge community of people to reach out to, some of who are not even parents. There is much wisdom in a collective consciousness.
>
> *(Iyer 2015b: Para 4–6)*

Blogging provides a new network of mothering intimacy that is often enabling and comforting. It is an effective way to connect with other mothers and functions both as support network and a parenting resource. Blogging also liberates mothers from both the isolation of mothering and the traditional subservient silences of motherhood. Blogger Preethi, founder of the group blog *Indian Mom Connect*, expresses this feeling of exhilaration, newly established companionship, and adventure:

> We are a new generation of mothers in India, of the information age. Of satellite TV and internet; Of smaller families and fewer children; Of mommy blogging and sharing stories. On the threshold of modernity and traditionalism. What is it like to parent at a time like this in India? Let's talk!
>
> *(Preethi 2011: Para 1)*

Blogger Roshni Chintalapati of *Indian American Mom* emphasises the diversity of maternal discourse, both mundane and serious, in the blogosphere and the emotional necessity of this 'me-time' when she writes about her experience in *Indiblogeshwari*, which is 'a group of women bloggers of Indian origin':

> So, what *do* we talk about, you ask? Practically everything under the sun from politics, to movies, to religion, to books, to beauty tips and beyond! There is always someone throwing in a unique perspective to a current event, or someone else sharing with us her grandmom's recipe for summer skincare!

> There is laughter, banter, dirty jokes, and virtual hugs. I especially love the personal stories from some of these strong women who have stood up for themselves and dared to walk out of abusive relationships, and who have single-handedly raised their children to mature, caring teens and adults.
>
> *(Chintalapati 2013a: Para 2)*

This is a discourse and a network that is chosen and shaped by mothers themselves, and is not determined by external agents. May Friedman identifies '[t]his capacity for a matricentric space' as 'a radical potential of the mamasphere' (Friedman 2013: 79). The question that now must be asked is, how far is the radical potential of the mamasphere realised by Indian mombloggers? Again, it needs to be stated that the matricentric space of Indian mombloggers is limited in terms of reach and impact, as it is predicated upon the 'social exclusion [of] non-blogging, non-wired and non-computer literate women' (Stadtman Tucker 2008: 207). Yet, within these limitations, mombloggers are articulating their resistances, both individually and collaboratively, to received motherhood norms and are discursively engaging with many of the uncomfortable, and therefore often marginalised, experiences of motherhood.

Practicing feminist mothering through blogging intimacies

At this juncture, I would like reference the concept of feminist mothering, as theorised by Andrea O'Reilly:

> A feminist practice/theory of mothering [. . .] functions as a counternarrative of motherhood: it seeks to interrupt the master narrative of motherhood to imagine and implement a view of mothering that is empowering to women. Feminist mothering is thus determined more by what it is not (i.e., patriarchal motherhood) rather than by what it is. Feminist mothering may refer to any practice of mothering that seeks to challenge and change various aspects of patriarchal motherhood that cause mothering to be limiting or oppressive to women.
>
> *(O'Reilly 2008: 4)*

According to this definition, feminist mothering is a sustained contestation of established patriarchal norms of motherhood, which also means that such mothering will focus upon issues that have been invisibilised from the normative discourse of motherhood. Along with offline practices, momblogs are rich sites where feminist mothering positions are articulated and debated.

Feminist mothering is by nature collaborative and it resists the isolating restrictions imposed upon mothers by patriarchal family structures and conventions through creation of networks of intimate and enabling friendships.

In a guest post (guest posting is a feature that is produced by the new mothering intimacies on the blogosphere) on *The Life and Times of an Indian Homemaker*,

Wordsetmefree differentiates between the family-dictated friendships that her mother formed and her own self-chosen networks of friends. For traditional women of her mother's generation, the support system was 'HER side of the family – her sister, her cousins, her aunts,' who provided a sense of belonging and empathy, but no inspiration or proactive support because 'relatives (in the Indian setting) cannot really be one's support system. They are subject to the same conditioning that the rest of us are. They have nothing new to offer' (Wordssetmefreee 2015: Para 5–7). In contrast, she finds that women of her generation actively seek and maintain female friendships beyond the family:

> I realised I needed friendship time without my husband and kids. I learnt to ask for it, advocate for it, and maintain it as an essential part of my life [. . .] And friendship with other women and having a good support system is the best defense against patriarchy. For feminism to thrive, friendships between women must thrive.
>
> *(Wordssetmefreee 2015: Para 23–25)*

The Life and Times of an Indian Homemaker, in a complete subversion of the associations of domesticity and docility implicit in 'homemaker,' is a mom-turned-activist blog that is a site for collaborative resistances to gender stereotypes and subjugations from an explicitly feminist location. One such discursively oriented strategy utilised by blogger Indian Home Maker is to publish emails sent to her by victims of institutional subjugation and encourage her readers to share their opinions and advice. She also opens up her blog to guestbloggers (as seen above) and deploys her authorial, curatorial, and editorial agency to create strategic and intimate networks of resistance by mothers and other women, paving way for possibilities of online intimate friendships that can translate into offline activism and empowerment. As Wordsetmefree states: 'This blog is a small example of the power of women supporting one another. *Imagine what is possible* with people we can meet and talk to and confide in and bond with in our daily lives' (Wordssetmefreee 2015: Para 24; emphasis mine). It is in this enabling of the mothers' imagination to visualise an alterity to regulatory, institutionalised motherhood that imbues the blogosphere with a radically feminist transformative potential.

Deconstructing the myth of good motherhood

Perhaps the most important contribution of mombloggers is to collaboratively resist the dominant and homogenising myth of good motherhood by reiterating the agency and autonomy of every individual mother and the plurality of mothering practices. Blogger Lalitha Iyer states that 'motherhood is the biggest dichotomy anyway. There are ways and ways of negotiating it and there is no right or wrong about any of them' (Iyer 2015a: Para 8). In a popular post that reviews the independent film 'The Bad Mother,' shared over 184 times, blogger Renu Jain Chandarana of the group blog *Masalamommas* explicitly shatters the myth of good motherhood by narrating her own experience of maternal frustration, exhaustion, ambivalence, and loss of independent selfhood:

> Motherhood can drive a woman mad. What other line of work could be so cruel to the mind, body and soul? Every mom has wracked her brain wondering, 'Am I doing enough?' Every mom has fallen into the comparison trap where she pits herself against the high-functioning, perfect-on-the-outside woman raising perfect kids. We all know this is not so, yet our minds take us there. We yearn for the days before kids [. . .] Those yesteryear days when life was easier, kinder, and we had more control.
>
> *(Chandarana 2015: Para 1)*

This is based on a deeply realised recognition of mothering as a complex, intricate experience that is both enabling and disabling. As blogger Lalitha Iyer of *Mommy Go-Lightly* writes, 'Yes, the moments of joy are pure and unparalleled. But so are the moments of frustration, despair and anxiety' (Iyer 2013: Para 12). The open and fearless sharing of such personal, intensely experienced maternal ambivalences through the intervention of digital media resonates with other mother-readers and creates new mothering intimacies where all the participants feel liberated from the compulsive bindings of motherhood constructs. This is evident in the readers' comments to such posts; the comments are almost all supportive and affirmative, and they are often confessional in nature, where the readers open up about their own lived experiences and ambivalences.

Discussing maternal guilt and the WOHM vs. SAHM divide

One area of maternal experience that feminist mothering explores in depth is that of maternal guilt, a guilt that is often experienced by working mothers who are conditioned to consider themselves as less than perfect because they are unable to live up to the norm of full-time, intensive motherhood. One of Roshni Chintalapati's most popular blog posts defends working-out-of-home mothers (or WOHMs) on the issue of maternal guilt, where she also resists the neo-liberal patriarchal binary that pits working mothers against stay-at-home mothers (or SAHMs) to the detriment of both: '*I did not write this post with the intention of debating the pros and cons of keeping your kids at home versus sending them to daycare. I merely wrote this to help some WOHMs who suffer the same feelings of inadequacy and guilt that I felt at the time mentioned*'(Chintalapati 2013b: Para 10).

Here, Chintalapati strategically uses the networks of intimacy on her blog to contest the false binary between working mothers and stay-at-home mothers and deliberately chooses to shift the focus to the shared feelings of inadequacy and guilt that both WOHMs and SAHMs suffer from, especially when they internalise the comparison with the media-circulated 'supermom' construct of maternal perfection. During the course of the rest of the blog-post, Chintalapati resolves the conundrum of maternal guilt by urging mothers to develop self-confidence in their choices; a self-confidence that is boosted by mutual support from both WOHMs and SAHMs who must refuse to accuse each other of inadequate mothering.

Reclaiming the maternal body

Another act of feminist mothering by mombloggers is to reclaim the rights to their own bodies. This is articulated in the numerous blog posts about breastfeeding decisions. Patriarchy-dictated generic expert advice prescribes exclusive breastfeeding as a mother's duty to the child, but, curiously, shames the public display of, or even open conversation about, such activity, resulting in further isolation of mothers. Breastfeeding is considered too intimate an act for public display or discussion. Mombloggers engage with this issue directly and publicly, reclaiming it as an act that has to be decided by the mother herself, and providing access to shared stories that can act as both practical resource and emotional support for other mothers having problems or doubts about breastfeeding.

A blogger who chooses to write under the pseudonym Mutteringsofmemyself at *Indian Moms Connect* rebelliously rejects any guilt that mothers unable to breastfeed are forced to feel, and extends her support to other mothers in similar situations: 'This is to all mothers with "soya" babies – It's fine if you want to breastfeed but can't! Do what's best for your kid and they turn out just as fine and love you just as much and bond just as well!' (Mutteringsofmemyself 2013: n.pag). A popular post that has been shared over 50 times by the readers, this is a direct debunking of the culturally prescribed motherhood intimacy that insists on breastfeeding being an integral but invisible part of maternal love, duty, and bonding. Blogger Rashmie Jaju, on the other hand, courageously posts photographs of herself breastfeeding her younger daughter, even as she gives a reasoned defence of her informed decision to breastfeed her daughter beyond 'the recommended norm' of six months (Jaju 2014: Para 1). By subverting the taboo on motherhood intimacy of breastfeeding in her public blogsite of new mothering intimacies, Jaju is able to reclaim control of her maternal body and reinscribe an intense and intimate mothering experience on her own terms.

Reassertions of motherhood stereotypes and silences

However, it is true that there are many taboos that continue to be left out of the Indian maternal blogging discourse. For instance, I could not find a single blogpost by any Indian momblogger that discussed queer mothering, although there are many such blogs in the United States, for example, that are specifically created for and by lesbian mothers. Also, while some Indian momblogs are discussing contentious topics like 'invisible divorce,' which is estrangement between parents although they continue to stay married as 'legal divorce is looked down upon,' the posts are written from the perspective of the impact on children, rather than the mother (MySahana 2014: Para 1). There are other matrifocal experiences like maternal rage or maternal desire that are largely neglected by Indian momblogs.

One reason for this reticence is located in the very structure of networked intimacy. When a blog is dependent on the network of its readers, when a blogger shares bonds of intimate friendship with her loyal readers, then the blogger will also have to conform to the predominant attitudes of the group. She can use persuasive methods to deconstruct stereotypes and follow her feminist mothering agenda, but outright radical debates that might offend her close circle of readers are mostly avoided. In a way, therefore, the network of intimacy that is created between blogger-readers can be restrictive as well as supportive. Reading through the momblogs by Indian mothers, we also often come across a number of posts that reassert the social construction of the good mother. Jessica Collett delineates some strategies adopted by mothers to reinforce their offline identity constructions of good motherhood: tactics of 'ingratiation' where mothers conform to the opinions of other mothers, use of 'self-enhancement to advertise her strengths and admirable qualities,' and managing their and 'their children's appearances' (Collett 2005: 330). Similar tactics are also deployed in the online contexts of the blogosphere.

The title of blogger Shilpa Jadhav's blog – *Being Mommee: Love It ... Like It ... Live It* – indicates her unresisting internalisation of the norms of good motherhood. In a blogpost titled 'My children means everything to me!!!,' she writes, 'I love being tired after running behind [my sons] Shourya and Naksh,' while displaying a picture of her sleeping sons, and also congratulates herself on 'doing it right' because she is tired (Jadhav 2013b: Para 1). Here she seemingly conforms to the stereotype of the self-sacrificing mother while trivialising the serious issue of maternal exhaustion that new mothers grapple with. Yet, although Jadhav chooses to represent herself as a traditional mother rather than a feminist one, her candid and intimate confessional posts also interrogate – perhaps unwittingly – the received ideal of motherhood she consciously chooses to project. In another post where she states that she loves 'this job, Job of Being Mom of Shourya and Naksh,' and that she was brought up by her parents to 'get married, have a kids, look after my home, my kids that's all,' she also voices her confusion about whether her prescribed role as 'just' a stay-at-home mother will fulfil her for 'the rest of [her] life': 'So many questions running in my mind and I am not able to find an answer' (Jadhav 2013a: Para 4). It is this subversive 'interrogation,' claims Friedman, and not her submissive identity, 'that is potentially empowering' (Friedman 2013: 54).

To take another instance of imbricated submission and subversion, let us consider the following statement by blogger Sangeetha Menon: 'For every woman, the greatest gift from Almighty is motherhood; to be the mother of a child' (S. Menon n.d: Para 5). In isolation, it appears to mimic the glorification of motherhood that is the staple of Indian patriarchy. Yet, in this same paragraph, Menon also states, 'Like all new moms I didn't know what or where to start from,' revealing the anxiety of mothering that is erased in traditional motherhood representations. In the next paragraph, Menon describes how this anxiety was the impetus to seek and create new intimacies with other mothers by becoming a 'professional parenting blogger':

> Being in a nuclear family away from home, I felt all alone. My life went upside down, changed completely both physically & psychologically. I realised all my

> thoughts & experiences should be penned down & need to be shared with each one of you. There started my blogging journey in the name of Bumps n Baby.
>
> *(S. Menon n.d.: Para 6)*

Thus, obedience and resistance to mainstream discourses of motherhood can, and does, coexist in the blogosphere, within a blog, and even within a single post. As May Friedman writes, 'The mamasphere can be viewed as a dynamic organism, bound by discourses of motherhood yet constantly emerging both to obey and resist these discourses in dialogue' (Friedman 2013: 81). The response of mothers to totalising motherhood discourses is to interrupt and fragment the overarching homogeneity of the discourse and to articulate nuanced and pluralised narratives of mothering intimacies that accommodate both docility and resistance.

Commodification of maternal intimacies

Another criticism that can be made is that the blogosphere, being a product and a part of neo-liberal, globalised market flows, is aimed not just at self-expression and creation of networks of belonging, but also at exploiting, commercialising, and commodifying these very networks for profit. Many of the Indian momblogs are monetised, many of them write sponsored posts, some, like *Indian Moms Connect*, provide online business opportunities for mompreneurs through their platforms like IMC Marketplace, and there are some like Sangeetha Menon, who position themselves as professional bloggers and mompreneurs. Constable suggests that 'internet technology,' assisted by the flows of globalisation, 'plays a central role in the commodification of intimacy': this also includes the use of new technology and e-commerce portals by migrant mothers to 'maintain a sense of intimacy with family members far away, as in the case of "long distance mothering"' (Constable 2009: 53). Other scholars dismantle the criticism against commercialised mom-blogs, arguing that such criticism extends the gendered assumption that mother-work should not have monetary value, and also pointing out the fallacy inherent in presuming that all commercialised intimacy is necessarily inauthentic and corrupt (Connors 2009: 95).

Sangeetha Menon of *Bumps n Baby* is a professional blogger, blogging for profit, selling mothering-related products via her blog, and posting sponsored reviews of mother/baby care products. Yet when she expresses that it was her desire to address 'common concerns' like 'feeding, food habits and weight loss post baby' in order to 'help' new mothers, she may also be deploying the networks of intimacy on her blog ('You appreciated all my posts and showered your love on me' – she also posts screenshots of comments by her readers who have been inspired by her) to attain an agential selfhood beyond stay-at-home motherhood (S. Menon 2014: Para 6). When *Indian Moms Connect* claims, at the launch of its IMC Marketplace platform, 'We hope to partner with you in your motherhood and life journey whether as a parenting platform or a place to start your business,' the profit-oriented venture may also be read as a transformative act that extends the emotional support provided by online intimacy to economic support structures that ameliorate the experience of mothering (Team IMC 2015: Para 5).

Is the concept of intimacy restricted only to those posts which reveal autobiographical details about the blogger? I will argue that this is not the case. There are many posts which are advisory in nature, where the blogger gives her opinions about various aspects of birthing and care work. These posts are similar to correspondence or online letters from the blogger to the reader. I would read them through the lens of Foucault's analysis of self-writing:

> To write is thus to 'show oneself,' to project oneself into view, to make one's own face appear in the other's presence. And by this it should be understood that the letter is both a gaze that one focuses on the addressee (through the missive he receives, he feels looked at) and a way of offering oneself to his gaze by what one tells him about oneself. In a sense, the letter sets up a face-to-face meeting.
>
> *(Foucault 1997: 216)*

On applying this Foucauldian analysis to the blogosphere, we can redefine all such advisory, and even commercialised, posts as a form of intimate exchange between the blogger and the reader. Sangeetha Menon's post discussed above is also epistolary in structure, addressed directly to her readers as 'you,' and she creates a personal bond between blogger and reader that seeks to redefine commercial transactions or generalised advice-giving as intimate interactions. As Constable states:

> Globalisation does not simply result in greater commodification of intimate sexual, marital, and reproductive relationships; it also offers opportunities for defining new sorts of relationships and for redefining spaces, meanings, and expressions of intimacy that can transform and transgress conventional gendered spaces and norms.
>
> *(Constable 2009: 58)*

Reading against the grain allows us to recast the debate on commodification and inauthenticity in a new format that regards networked intimacies as a tool for improving the agency and autonomy of mothers.

Affirming mother–daughter intimacies

How does the maternal support network on the internet impact the relationship between mother and daughter? Nancy Chodorow believes that it is the daughters' experiences of growing up under the nurturance of their mothers that makes them identify with, and later adopt, the 'maternal' role, extending and perpetuating the condition of maternity from the act of giving birth to the 'continuing responsibility of children' – which does not have to gender-specific (Chodorow 1999: 208). Yet,

Chodorow herself offers a possible way out of the oppressive cycle of gendered care that is perpetuated through mother-daughter intimacy. She comments: 'Mother-daughter relationships in which the mother is supported by a network of women kin and friends, and has meaningful work and self-esteem, produce daughters with capacities for nurturance and a strong sense of self' (Chodorow 1999: 213). By providing both meaningful work and female support in online spaces, blogs have the potential to radically transform mother-daughter intimacies from ambivalent and oppressive to empowering and affirmative.

Supported by intimate networks, blogging mothers can map a less pliant and more assertive future for their daughters. Blogger Preethi rejects 'Sita and Savitri and other self-sacrificing women' as role models and states, 'I want my daughter to be compassionate, kind and just [. . .] but I don't want her to be nice or try to please people for her happiness,' and she stresses the importance of taking care 'of our happiness first by doing what we like' (Preethi 2016: Para 2–5).

In another post, blogger Ramya Abhinand counters patriarchal son-preference by responding to the family priest's injunction to try for a son with a gentle but firm assertion: 'I am very happy with my two girls. Nothing more' (Abinand 2016: Para 3). Then, there are posts by Anjum Choudhry Nayyar of *Masalamommas* on 'helping daughters navigate body image' that gives tips to other mothers on how to 'start the dialogue with your daughter' and give her the 'tools to think critically' (Nayyar 2014: Para 4–9). By projecting an independent-thinking, self-respecting and self-determining maternal identity, some blogging mothers are refashioning mother-daughter intimacies in positive ways.

One important project of feminist mothering is to create motherlines between mothers and daughters. The motherline is a African-American mothering concept formulated by feminist psychologist Naomi Ruth Lowinsky which emphasises the connections built between daughters and their mothers, grandmothers and female ancestors through shared 'stories of life cycles that link generations of women' (Lowinsky 2009: 1). It is a feminist strategy that challenges the dominant narrative of ambivalent mother–daughter intimacies and chooses to replace it with more empowering intimacies. Lowinsky claims that motherlines provide women with 'carnal knowledge of her own body, its blood mysteries and their power' (Lowinsky 2009: 13). In the patriarchal construct of motherhood intimacy, all references to blood and bodily mysteries are sanitised through a culturally imposed silence on menstruation. Mombloggers have spoken out against such taboos. Blogger Mansi Zaveri of *Kids Stop Press* determines to openly share her menstrual knowledge with her daughter:

> While I have had to live with period related taboos as an Indian daughter, now as an Indian mom, I choose to make a change. I definitely don't want my daughter to suffer the same ordeal [. . .] I have decided to break the 'No touch period rule' for my daughter [. . .] I will make sure she knows about her monthly cycle.
>
> *(Zaveri 2016: Para 4)*

Momblogs, by acting as repositories where mothers can narrate, share, and archive their own maternal practices and experiences, act as a powerful resource for daughters to learn from and create their own motherlines. Daughters (and also, of course, sons) of mombloggers will 'see their mothers in communities' and will also 'see themselves as intimately connected to their parents in their own infancies and early childhoods' (Friedman 2013: 136). It is the intervention of the digital media, with its persistence, archival capacity, and rhizomatic multiplicity of points of entry and engagement, that will make this possible.

The effect and affect of momblogs

The multitudinous capacity of the blogosphere and the structural fluidity of blogs make any overarching categorisation – such as 'radical' or 'commercial' or 'normative' – slippery and incomplete. In a way, it is true that momblogs do not address the 'structural context of motherhood' or attempt to 'transform society' (Stadtman Tucker 2008: 208). Instead of a restructuring of the institution of motherhood, what we find are minor resistances from individual bloggers on specific issues at specific times. According to Foucault, it is the 'swarm of [such] points of resistance' that 'makes a revolution possible' (quoted in Friedman 2013: 53). That is in the realm of possibility. At present, however, instead of a unanimous contestation and radical redefinition of motherhood intimacies, what we find is a multivalent, nuanced, pluralised – and often contradictory – assemblage of responses to, and reconfigurations of, various categories of maternal intimacy – body, birthing, care work, family, community, and the maternal self. This very polyvocality of intimate maternal discourses, however, marks the blogosphere as a site which interrupts the hitherto unilaterally imposed norms of motherhood intimacy, and indicates how there is potential for change in engaging with maternal intimacies in contemporary Indian contexts.

Finally, looking beyond the theorising of maternity, intimacy, and the internet, I would like to end by discussing the pragmatic and affective benefits of maternal intimacy in the blogosphere. Psychologists have long considered 'emotional intimacy' as a 'critical need for healthy human development' (Gaia 2002: 151). How, then, has the intimate act of momblogging impacted the condition of mothers in contemporary India? It must be restated here that blogging is an activity restricted to privileged groups of mothers, and also that blogging itself is being both supplanted and supplemented by other forms of social networking. Social networking trends indicate that blogging is probably in a state of stagnation and gradual decline. Yet, within this limited ambit, I would like to link the blogosphere with the women's empowerment project of 'bodily integrity,' which not only reclaims the rights to the body but also creates 'spaces for women to enable them to experience a new sense of the self' (Mathur 2008: 63). The blogosphere can function as such a transformative and enabling space for maternal intimacies, leading to the improvement of the emotional well-being of mothers.

This view is echoed in the concept of 'inclusive intimacy' that Anne Cronin locates in the domestic friendships among mothers: an intimacy that is forged from shared experiences, emotions and challenges of mothering and a bonding which expands and shapes mothers' sense of self as profoundly relational and interconnected with others, lifting them out of the often-debilitating isolation of nuclear mothering (Cronin 2015). What Cronin investigates in the offline domain is also applicable in the online domain, especially since our offline and online selves have become so inextricably imbricated and co-dependent. Thus, the affective value of momblogs, as a therapeutic and supportive space where mothers come of their own choosing to share their stories and anxieties, and enhance their lived experience of mothering through self-created and self-determined bonds of mothering intimacy, is the very real, and tangible, gain for mothers.

To conclude on a particularly affective note, allow me to quote from Indian Home Maker's blog-post on her experience of maternal grief, as she tries to come to terms with the traumatic death of her teenage daughter:

> Connecting to others will help you heal. So thank you for your comments, posts, messages and emails. I have been reading them, and reading them out to my friends and family [. . .] I have found that words have immense power to provide comfort and strength. I am creating a special page to link all the posts remembering Tejaswee.
>
> *(Indian Home Maker 2010: n.pag)*

Maternal grief is an experience that has often been ceremonially ritualised, but its depths and intensities are often marginalised in genteel public discourse. Here Indian Home Maker breaks down barriers between public and private, between 'real' and 'virtual' and enmeshes these categories in a dense network of intimate support that helped her to heal. The value of momblogs from the blogger's perspective is located in this imbrication and supplementing of online and offline mothering intimacies and in the ability of blogs to document, archive and memorialise relationships and moments of intimacy for posterity. Reconfiguring the self, the family, the community through online intimacies is ultimately and deeply a project through which mothers attempt to understand and engage with mothering in affirmative and fulfilling ways.

References

Abinand, Ramya. 2016. 'I am Only Saying What is Written in the Scriptures' [Blog Entry], *Indian Moms Connect*. www.indianmomsconnect.com/2016/01/12/girl-child. Accessed 1 February 2016.

Barton, Bruce. 2009. 'Paradox as Process: Intermedial Anxiety and the Betrayals of Intimacy.' *Theatre Journal*, 61(4): 575–601.

Bhattacharji, Sukumari. 2010. 'Motherhood in Ancient India.' In Maithreyi Krishnaraj (ed.), *Motherhood in India: Glorification without Empowerment?*, pp. 44–72. New Delhi: Routledge.

Bose, Mandakranta. 2010. *Women in the Hindu Tradition: Rules, Roles and Exceptions*. London: Routledge.

Boyd, Carol J. 1989. 'Mothers and Daughter: A Discussion of Theory and Research.' *Journal of Marriage and Family*, 51(2): 291–301.

Carroli, Linda. 1997. 'Virtual Encounters: Community or Collaboration on the Internet?' *Leonardo*, 30(5): 359–363.

Chandarana, Renu Jain. 2015. 'What is "The Bad Mother"? A Film Review' [Blog Entry], *Masalamommas*. http://masalamommas.com/2015/11/03/what-is-the-bad-mother-a-film-review. Accessed 15 February 2016.

Chandler, Mielle. 2007. 'Emancipated Subjectivities and the Subjugation of Mothering Practices.' In Andrea O'Reilly (ed.), *Maternal Theory: Essential Readings*, pp. 529–541. Bradford: Demeter Press.

Chintalapati, Roshni. 2013a. 'The Quest to Take Back "me-time"!' [Blog Entry], *Indian American Mom*. www.indianamericanmom.com/2013/06/moms-and-me-time.html. Accessed 12 January 2016.

Chintalapati, Roshni. 2013b. 'WOHMs, Ditch the Mommy Guilt Already!' [Blog Entry], *Indian American Mom*. www.indianamericanmom.com/2013/06/moms-and-me-time.html. Accessed 12 January 2016.

Chodorow, Nancy J. 1999. *The Reproduction of Mothering: Psychoanalysis and the Sociology of Gender*. Berkeley, CA: University of California Press.

Collett, Jessica L. 2005. 'What Kind of Mother Am I? Impression Management and the Social Construction of Motherhood.' *Symbolic Interaction*, 28(3): 327–347.

Connors, Catherine. 2009. 'Meter Politikon: On the "Politics" of Mommyblogging.' In May Friedman and Shana L. Calixte (eds.), *Mothering and Blogging: The Radical Act of the Mommyblog*, pp. 91–111. Toronto: Demeter Press.

Constable, Nicole. 2009. 'The Commodification of Intimacy: Marriage, Sex, and Reproductive Labour.' *Annual Review of Anthropology*, 38: 49–64, doi: 10.1146/annurev.anthro.37.081407.085133. Accessed 22 February 2016.

Cronin, Anne M. 2015. '"Domestic friends": Women's Friendships, Motherhood and Inclusive Intimacy.' *The Sociological Review*, 63(3): 662–679, doi: 10.1111/1467–954X.12255. Accessed 12 January 2016.

Doniger, Wendy. 2011. *Hindus: An Alternative History*. New Delhi: Penguin.

Foucault, Michel. 1997. 'Self Writing.' In *Ethics: Subjectivity and Truth*, trans. Robert Hurley, pp. 207–222. New York: The New York Press.

Friedman, May. 2013. *Mommyblogs and the Changing Face of Motherhood*. Toronto: University of Toronto Press.

Gaia, Celeste, A. 2002. 'Understanding Emotional Intimacy: A Review of Conceptualisation, Assessment and the Role of Gender.' *International Social Science Review*, 77(3/4): 151–170.

Giddens, Antony. 1992. *The Transformation of Intimacy: Sexuality, Love and Eroticism in Modern Societies*. Cambridge: Polity Press.

Indian Home Maker. 2010. 'Thank You' [Blog Entry], *The Life and Times of an Indian Home Maker*. https://indianhomemaker.wordpress.com/ 2010/08/23/thank-you. Accessed 5 October 2014.

Iyer, Lalitha. 2013. 'Why have Children?' [Blog Entry], *Mommygolightly*. http://mommygolightly.com/2013/08/07/why-have-children-2. Accessed 12 January 2016.

Iyer, Lalitha. 2015a. 'Marissa Mayer's Maternity Leave Is Her Problem. Choosing Her as a Role Model Is Yours' [Blog Entry], *Mommygolightly*. http://mommygolightly.com/2015/09/09/marissa-mayers-maternity-leave-is-her-problem-choosing-her-as-a-role-model-is-yours. Accessed 12 January 2016.

Iyer, Lalitha. 2015b. 'Parenting Sharenting: Love, Hate and Social Media' [Blog Entry], *Mommygolightly*. http://mommygolightly.com/2015/07/27/parenting-sharenting-love-hate-and-social-media. Accessed 12 January 2016.

Jadhav, Shilpa. 2013a. 'Being Stay @ Home Mom. . . ' [Blog Entry], *Being Mommee: Love It . . . Like It . . . Live It*. beingmommee.blogspot.in/2013/08/being-stay-home-mom.html. Accessed 1 February 2016.

Jadhav, Shilpa. 2013b. 'My Children Means Everything to Me!!!' [Blog Entry], *Being Mommee: Love It . . . Like It . . . Live It*. beingmommee.blogspot.in/2013/10/my-children-means-everything-to-me.html. Accessed 1 February 2016.

Jaju, Rashmie. 2014. 'Why I Am Breastfeeding Exclusively (almost) My 8-Months Old' [Blog Entry], *Mommy Labs*. www.mommy-labs.com/creative-kids/nurture_culture/breastfeeding-exclusively-my-8-eight-month-old. Accessed 1 February 2016.

Johri, Rachana. 2013. 'From *Parayi* to *Apni*: Mothers' Love as Resistance.' In Jasjit K. Sangha and Tahira Gonsalves (eds.), *South Asian Mothering: Negotiating Culture, Family and Selfhood*, pp. 17–32. Bradford: Demeter Press.

Kakar, Sudhir. 1990. *Intimate Relations: Exploring Indian Sexuality*. New Delhi: Penguin.

Lowinsky, Naomi Ruth. 2009. *The Motherline: Every Woman's Journey to Find Her Female Roots*. Cheyenne: Fisher King Books.

Mathur, Kanchan. 2008. 'Body as Space, Body as Site: Bodily Integrity and Women's Empowerment in India.' *Economic and Political Weekly*, 43(17): 54–63.

Menon, Kalyani Devaki. 2012. *Everyday Nationalism: Women in the Hindu Right of India*. New Delhi: Social Science Press.

Menon, Sangeetha. n.d. 'About Me' [Blog Entry], *Bumps n Baby*, www.bumpsnbaby.com/about-me. Accessed 12 January 2016.

Menon, Sangeetha. 2014. 'Finally! I Quit My Hefty Paying Job to Be a Full Time Blogger' [Blog Entry], *Bumps n Baby*. www.bumpsnbaby.com/i-quit-my-job-full-time-blogger. Accessed 12 January 2016.

Miller, Daniel, Elisabetta Costa, Nell Haynes, Tom McDonald, Razvan Nicolescu, Jolynna Sinanan, Juliano Spyer, Shriram Venkatraman and Xinyuan Wang. 2016. *How the World Changed Social Media*. London: UCL Press.

Mutteringsofmemyself. 2013. 'Breastfeeding – Why It Was NOT an Option For Me!' [Blog Entry], *Indian Moms Connect*. www.indianmomsconnect.com/2013/07/06/ breastfeeding-why-it-was-not-an-option-for-me. Accessed 1 February 2016.

MySahana. 2014. 'The Invisible Divorce' [Blog Entry], *Masalamommas*. http://masala mommas.com/2014/06/25/invisible-divorce. Accessed 12 February 2016.

Nayyar, Anjum Choudhry. 2014. 'Helping Daughters Navigate Body Image' [Blog Entry], *Masalamommas*. http://masalamommas.com/2014/05/12/helping-daughters-navigate-body-image. Accessed 15 February 2016.

O'Reilly, Andrea (ed.). 2008. *Feminist Mothering*. Albany: State University of New York Press.

Preethi. 2011. 'Let's Talk Motherhood' [Blog Entry], *Indian Moms Connect*. www.indian momsconnect.com/2011/08/01/lets-talk. Accessed 3 March 2014.

Preethi. 2016. 'Why I Won't Raise My Daughter To Be Nice!' [Blog Entry], *Indian Moms Connect*. www.indianmomsconnect.com/2016/01/06/wont-raise-daughter-nice. Accessed 12 January 2016.

Raja, Ira and Kay Souter (eds.). 2010. *An Endless Winter's Night: An Anthology of Mother-Daughter Stories*. New Delhi: Women Unlimited.

Ramsukhdas, Swami. 2012. *How to Lead a Household Life*. Gorakhpur: Gita Press.

Rich, Adrienne. 1986. *Of Woman Born: Motherhood as Experience and Institution*. New York: W.W. Norton & Co.

Sarkar, Tanika. 2013. *Words to Win: The Making of Amar Jiban: A Modern Autobiography*. New Delhi: Zubaan.

Serfaty, Viviane. 2004. *The Mirror and the Veil: An Overview of American Online Diaries and Blogs*. Amsterdam: Rodopi Press.

Stadtman Tucker, Judith. 2008. 'Mothering in the Digital Age: Navigating the Personal and Political in the Virtual Sphere.' In Amber E. Kinser (ed.), *Mothering in the Third Wave*, pp. 199–212. Toronto: Demeter Press.

Team IMC. 2015. 'What's IMC Been Up To?' [Blog Entry], *Indian Moms Connect.* www.indianmomsconnect.com/2015/05/14/whats-imc-been-up-to. Accessed 18 August 2015.

Tharu, Susie and K. Lalitha (eds.). 1991. *Women Writing in India: Volume I (600 BC to the Early Twentieth Century).* New Delhi: Oxford University Press.

Valentine, Gill. 2006. 'Globalizing Intimacy: The Role of Information and Communication Technologies in Maintaining and Creating Relationships.' *Women's Studies Quarterly,* 34(1/2): 365–393.

'Writers and Contributors.' n.d. *Indian Moms Connect.* www.indianmomsconnect.com/contributors. Accessed 21 February 2016.

Wordssetmefreee. "Women and Friendship – Building a Support System" By Priya. April 15, 2015. https://indianhomemaker.wordpress.com/tag/friendship/ Accessed 15 February 2016.

Zaveri, Mansi. 2016. 'Is It Time for Indian Moms to Change Age Old Menstrual Rules with Their Daughters?' [Blog Entry], *Kids Stop Press.* www.kidsstoppress.com/2016/02/is-it-time-for-indian-moms-to-change-age-old-menstrual-rules-with-their-daughters. Accessed 15 February 2016.

15

ROUTING TECHNO INTIMACY, RISK, ANXIETY, AND THE AMBIENT POLITICAL

Geeta Patel

If you saunter along any *ilākā* in Delhi, from an upscale colony to a *bastī*, and stop people along your meanderings to ask them where they imagine their intimacies lie (*geherīdostī, khās rishtedārī, avaidya sambandh, khās sambandh*) and how they might be forged, one almost reflexive response describes relationships with and bonds between people as flesh, as blood, as bodies. Technology would appear nowhere in this portrayal, even as technologies are becoming more and more ubiquitous in South Asia. In fact, most common presumptions and conceptions of the place of technology are underscored by the routes through which technology stalls, disrupts, and intervenes in face-to-face encounters, even as technologies are touted as the ultimate enablers.[1] In the case of the central government in Delhi (a tweeting Prime Minister led Sarkar), technologies are envisaged as cleaner, clearer routes, veritable magical carpet rides that will obviate the need for people through people transactions and along the way clear away the underbrush of bureaucratic corruption which is said to divert/distract currency from its proper course and right destination; somehow mobile banking, paying by cards, an Aadhar number (a numerical avatar for a person) will manage what has stymied generations (and of course all these salvific technological modes) and the implicit critiques that underwrite their fantasies of success must be denuded of political economies – they are obedient, as can be expected, to that very peculiar and particular paradox in bureaucratic market politics (i.e. writing about the market sans political economies, so that bureaucracy makes way before some strange notion of market forces).

'Hey, why don't you marry your phone?,' an article by Sonal Kalra from the *Hindustan Times*, New Delhi, on February 7, 2016, includes two images: In one, two people are sitting on the bench, backs fused, but intent only on their phone screens. The second voices the plaint of every friend, lover, or acquaintance whose dinner, lunch, or coffee companion has sat hunched over their phones, oblivious (Kalra 2016). These and a third image, also from the *Hindustan Times*, from September 9,

2015, 'Give me a sec, I'm on phone: Don't snub your partner on dates,' sourced from the Press Trust of India, Washington, all hang on the same joke.[2] That the phone reroutes, detours, circumvents, bars, or jams the proper channels along which nose-to-nose yearning, seduction, fondness, sex, aversion, repugnance, and animosity must voyage and ultimately puts the kibosh on a relationship you might ardently crave or loathe (even if antipathy is sent via text, Twitter, and such). A term has even been coined for it: pphubbing (partner phone snubbing).[3]

All three images, with their deliberate allusions to a world outside South Asia peopled by more or less white, obviously heterosexual folk, evince feelings or their absence in the kash-ma-kash, the tug and pull between mesmerised absorption in a phone and the person glaring at the device wielding user.[4] In all three photographs, because we, as viewers have no clue about whom or what is on the phones, the phone transmutes into the object of desire which intrudes, perhaps inadvertently, in a possible relationship between two people. In each case the techno-lover is oblivious to their surroundings; it is as though their very absentmindedness, somatically charged into their device, gives them the fillip to forsake the human beside them, across from them, or even alongside them. In the first image the two characters who sit on a park bench, bodies curled in towards the phones in their hands, facing away from the other, their entire concentration on screens over which their fingers hover are lost to the putative joys of trees and leaves fading into the background. In the second two, the mise-en-scène is of a probable date between a young woman and man in a café or restaurant, the images graced with accoutrements that might signal this reading: coffee cups with logos or glasses of wine. In each of these two, the woman's attention is targeted at the man rapt in an encounter with or through a phone.

Do we love our anxiety?

Upper-middle-class Indians use phones incessantly: chatting and taping while at the movies; texting and photographing while eating out with friends; texting and social-media-ing in classrooms, where teachers sometimes ban electronic appendages in a vain attempt to stem or forestall the constant flickers of lost attention. For Indians who work at any middle-class occupation, or patch together a living with ad hoc jobs or labouring serially in households cleaning, cooking, managing, phones are their work line, tethering them to the daily schedules and occasional or constant vagaries of employment. But by picturing phones in stories that feature white people, or by reissuing stories that were composed for and from an elsewhere outside the subcontinent, something has been performed or perhaps prognosticated for news readers in India which does not necessarily issue from the present presences of phone use in India. These particular portrayals, precisely because they issue from Euro-America, become a promissory cautionary future, one which is likely to be inhabited by new entrants to the narrative ledger of feeling detours: along with the phone's pleasure or benefits comes ambivalence. One might imagine then, a refurbished catalogue, slowly and perhaps stodgily piling up with roundabouts – feelings that ought to be oriented in one direction sent off in another. The image narratives suggest a possible 'it might happen this way' from which we want to perhaps disengage, which we want to shove away. In other words, they show us technologies that are paradoxically keyed: into responses pulling in a way that one might not fancy or one might want to not crave. Can we conceive of them as diversionary intimacy prosthetics which could be tacked onto a list of impedimentary devices which are so much more familiar, such as family members whose interference and meddling in one's stabs at cosying up to lovers, friends, and marriage mates has a long, sometimes fraught, sometimes soppily congenial lineage (mothers-in-law are the most commonly recognisable, but so are mothers who attempt to ensure that their children are not geared towards the persons, things, or situations that might keep their young adult child in thrall).

Such devices become an anxiety generator, if one represents anxiety in the vein that the philosopher Soren Kierkegaard spoke of over and over again in his playful, heartrending text from the mid-nineteenth century, *Either/Or* (the Swedish term 'angst' is heavier, deeper, darker than the slightly diaphanous intent that many uses of the word anxiety might draw on, even though when one is gripped by it thoroughly one can feel as though one was blotted out or diminished and eroded). For Kierkegaard, anxiety is usually a route to something else, or elicited by something other than itself, or hovers between the tug and tussle of two things: sorrow, ebullience, completeness, loss, absence, and presence. Perhaps not quite as somatically volatile as the more capacious repertory culled from languages in South Asia. Just a smattering might include 'pareshānī' or 'vyākultā,' 'betāb,' 'becain,' 'bekal,' 'kshubdh,' 'vyāgratā,' 'beqarārī,' 'utsuktā,' 'cintā,' 'utkantth' and 'iztarābī' (zwaad): each expression is similarly coded but each also leans towards a subtly distinctive tangible graininess to register fear, terror and agitation, restiveness, or edginess. Grubby, grim, fractious, or thorny feelings have illustrious aesthetic lineages in South Asia and continue to be well fleshed out in contemporary song, poetry, prose, and dialogues from cinema, the plethora garnered from the poetics of love or war or life or in more recent lyric from politics. And many of the local words might satisfy Kierkegaard, whose stories parse anxiety, and they might also conform to Sigmund Freud's equally mobile deployment of the word (Kierkegaard 1920) as byways to something else. 'Pareshānī' or 'vyākultā' evoke the restlessness in which one is snagged, an inability to sit still; and behind or before them are so many other possible moods. A sequence of brief or quick or hurried moods (vyabhicāra) crescendoing (vibhāva begins and anubhāva ends the sequence) into an ampler one has a time honoured history in rasa theory. So how does the English word anxiety work its way into this lexicon? What of technologies such as statistics on health, wealth and death that are the harbingers of anxiety verging, in the work of the literary scholar Kathleen Woodward in her book *Statistical Panic*, on panic (Woodward 2009). Is anxiety symptomatic of the incursions of technology into everyday lives in South Asia? Does anxiety in the English also carry with it a smidgen of the furtive or delicious pleasure that knotty or barbed feelings from South Asian lyric might have and hold when doing their deals with passion? A sort of love of the symptom à la Slavoj Žižek?

Let's circle back to the newspaper articles with which we began. Each one of them tells a sorry tale of companionate love or companionate friendship. If one did not want the body across from us to laser focus on us as *their* person, would it even matter to us that they were distracted away from us by a competing object? Companionate friendship is tried and true in the annals of south Asian poetics: from *sakhīs* who may or may not want the same thing (or lover) we do, to the *rāzdān*, to the *yār*. Companionate love, especially on public display, brandished for all to see, has a much more foreshortened history. So then, does something weird or idiosyncratic or merely curious ensue when technology is the confidante, the buddy, the lover or when our lives and livelihoods are made over through technologies? Some of the dos and don'ts to which we are so addicted, that we seek so ardently might suggest that it does? Sonal Kalra, the writer of some of the pieces I have discussed, and doyen of the 'what you can and should not' genre for technologies now attached to us compulsively is very specific in her recommendations. Cautionary tales complement sales pitches for fetish objects which we want so avidly: the *Hindustan Times* runs articles on both. And a growing cluster of the ins and outs of investing, from insurance pedagogies from copious advice-givers such as money gurus and religious figures who tell you where to park your money while offering prayers of various sorts, to investment and pension specialists on call-in television, radio, and other news media, to the CEO whose pearls of wisdom grace the sidebars on finance pages of newspapers proffer profuse and prudent suggestions to their, shall I say it, anxious interlocutors. South Asians are fervent devotees of experts and advisors. But I am getting ahead of myself by bringing finance into this story. For the moment I want to stick to technologies housed as objects such as the phone or the computer and pick through various genres, if you will, of anxiety they might broker or trundle along with them.

One of sources of anxiety embedded in objects is whether or not they will stay alive (Freud 1920); whether they will break down (given that many people who buy phones purchase revamped ones), or run out of juice (given the ubiquitously erratic electricity). The shape anxiety takes here is as a niggle – not a necessarily or always consistent flow of worry but worries that hang over one's shoulders in stutters, which sporadically come and pass away. With the fuss and bother (even if it episodic) over an object's putative life span comes a sense that the entity is more than merely an item. Rather, it prolongs something, enables something, and makes something possible. In simpler language it is an extension of oneself – a prosthesis which recomposes one as a cyborg, as an amalgam of human and machine, not quite machine not quite human but both.[5]

Even if the machine is just something we deploys or turn to for keeping in touch with employers, losing that article means that an avenue of possibilities is blockaded or shut down. The machine is thus tied into wellness, a future that is larger than an close present, or an immediate present which continues to find fulfilment in a near future (my job is in 90 minutes) or a longer more lingering future (I clean this house every week at 10 in the morning), or I am trying to set something up which will give me a better life, pay for the week's food, help my family with our bills (deals need not be just for the middle or upper-middle-classes) – all of which make living possible either in an attenuated but necessary fashion or in a more capacious way.[6] I will return to these further along in this chapter.

But, for the moment, if we stick with physical machines as the most literal manifestations of technology, it is clear that machines ferry along all sorts of likelihoods: avenues for living that transform/transfigure some of our everyday habits, anoint us with abilities and knacks that make us feel grander than ourselves so that we appear to flourish, or we nudge open a smidgen of room in which to subsist or to manage a life adequately enough push us into slightly touched up stories that make up possible futures (Berlant 2007; Joseph 2014). But South Asians are acquainted with things falling apart, dwindling – these are much more familiar contours for life plots than fulsome ones. And they come along with anxiety, worry, and sometimes even blasé nonchalance: will something actually persist in working, what will I do if it doesn't, what strategies will I cobble together to help me? One can sense this sort of worry in fits and starts, or in apprehension and disquiet hunching in the recesses of one's mind relentlessly, dogging one's dreams.

So far, I have laid out two hues that anxiety might take. One is lodged in what the object can enable or disable, the other in keeping the object alive. In an era when people piece together a litany of jobs just to cope with everyday expenses, keeping abreast of tasks assumes an acute urgency, escorted by an interminable, almost itchy rankle. A phone can then mutate into a conduit that promises some respite from turmoil – anxiety, *pareshānī* about how one might eat, sleep, survive. All these can be downloaded onto the phone's capable avenues for communication, keeping in touch, tallying up work (and in the process losing it becomes more exigent). And so we beget the singular and unavoidable paradox hounding technologies housed in or amalgamated into brittle existences: that precisely because something has been handed the proficiency to forestall worry it becomes the thing that incites fretting.[7]

Anxiety is intriguing. It is clear from my remarks thus far, sifting through where and how it lives, that anxiety is not exactly a feeling. It may be reckoned as fleshy discomfort, as irritation, as a tangle, as a panicky edginess channelling to something or somewhere else. Anxiety is discombobulating; it can throw someone off kilter (Phillips 2010). And one can get stuck there, sucked into its vortex, unable to shed the dogged persistence of its inevitable arising even when that is fitful.[8] In the language of *rasa/dhvānī* theory the state of *vyabhicāra*, betweeness, might be said to be its most unfailing idiosyncrasy. It is as though one can never quite get away from it enough to land into delight or horror or lambent grief keyed as *anubhāva*, the enduring mode which crescendos into a finale as the more provisional feelings that lead to it or compose it fall or wear away. Under these circumstances, when one is anxious, moving it out, away from oneself, shedding it seems so very urgent. Downloading it or outsourcing it so one does not have to bear it anymore and it is assumed by someone or something else as their burden, or releasing it as catharsis becomes vital (even when the anxiety assuaging object onto which it has been downloaded spawns another line into disquiet).[9]

Technological others

Apocryphal moral fables of technological road blocks on the path to love (which also include ancillary side-stories of phone, net, computer addiction, as an early childhood infection or disease), are paradoxical. Even as they are cemented through assumptions and inferences about the truly appropriate orientations of desire towards mammals of various species (although one rarely encounters phone blocks to a happily domesticated caring for a dog), they inaugurate and institute techno intimacies in worlds overrun with technological apparatuses such as phones, computers, and such. But as they are doing this, particular genres of technology become the headliners for how technology is conceived – as prosthetic objects such as phones and computers that extend the reach of what it means to be human. Along the way, Marcel Mauss's early 1935 assay of technologies of the body (techniques of body as social, political, economic apparatuses and pedagogies with political economies underwriting them, that guide into commonplace, almost unheeded habits such as digging, walking, swimming, shitting, smiling), which Michel Foucault also picks up on in *Discipline and Punish*, seem to lose some of their purchase.[10] A point that many scholars have made about capitalism, might be of value here. It is as though one often falls prey to the objects one critiques; they become so much larger than life that they take over, or overtake analytical space.

In this essay I would like to reinvigorate the spirits of Maussian technologies and the ghosts labouring bodies from Foucault via Marx, disinter Althusser's ideological state apparatuses for a moment: by inviting finance into the ambit of the technological. This will enable me to think through how finance ferries along with it other byways to technological makeovers, such as those through risk, that underwrite personal, social, and political reconfigurations and rearrange or organise intimacies. Along the way this chapter will bare the configurations, such as anxiety, we fill in when we attend to, resort to, corral, or even absentmindedly implicate in the technological.

One contemporary instance becomes a sales pitch for the fiscal through the technological – a lure to bring people into banking in a country where banking is relatively scarce and the current central government under the prime minister Narendra Modi is also attempting to surveil monetary whereabouts by nudging all such transactions towards technology.[11]

BOB Mitra, is sold as your techno-animation friend who invites you like a huckster, to jig, jog, natter, and play with the Bank of Baroda in their ads, and tempt you to try your hand at techno-money (aka. hand them your hard-earned cash) with his help.[12]

Technological others: whither risk?

When I first stumbled into risk and began stalking it through its fiscal forms, that is, when risk appeared in the guise of the efflorescence, or perhaps even the vitalised ebullience of financial technologies over ten years ago – a cluster of seemingly disparate questions or events had pulled me in those directions.[13]

Pressured by international loan agencies that imagined that India might be faced with a deficit of trust, the economy had been 'opened' – to new investors in financial technologies such as insurance and loans who wanted to hawk them as promissory notes, life-lines to refurbished futures. The Swadeshi Jagran Manch (SJM) had been marshalling troops in and out of parliament to stop this inflow of the foreign via capital. In the general spirit of closing 'our' borders off to so-called alien influences, the right wing – the VHP, BJP, and Shiv Sena – had been on other rampages during this period. They levelled their ire against syncretic shrines, against the Pakistan cricket team playing in Mumbai, against portrayals of Saraswati by MF Hussain, against the film 'Fire.' The right wing combine shepherded into the fray arguments that had been pulled out of their pockets many times before and that are both brutally and banally familiar and underwritten by anxiety run rampant: about their hurt Hindu sentiments, Hindus violated and about Hinduism under siege, about the infections flowing in from the west. Their dictums were keyed through raging anxieties that capitalised on particular brands of Hinduism with nationalism held as a hostage (what it meant to be a citizen). The Naz Foundation was entering India and starting their work in India to address and offer health solutions to men likely to get HIV/AIDS. Lawrence Cohen and I ran one of the early workshops on MSM with them in the 1990s, under the auspices of Trikone, to 'train' them how to think about sexuality on the ground, so to speak.

At the time, I was teaching in and instituting local pedagogical initiatives through the University of Iowa, and the spate of suicides in that predominantly rural state, post the Reagan administration's so-called fiscal prudence drives, had led me to track farmer suicides in different countries, while grappling with what political-economic contingencies drove them there. These curiously unwieldy, contradictory flows (for want of a better term), events, mobilisations, matrices, I came to see as co-constitutive – in the ways that Theodore Adorno envisaged the empirical vibrant with, or Jacques Derrida imagined for *khôra*, the receptacle that is co-constitutive of the things it receives or accepts (picked up by Doreen Massey writing on space and place), or that Althusser animated through ideological apparatuses or that Michel Foucault brought into play with matrices composed of architecture, shape, and volume of rooms and furniture, their proper use, currents of traffic, textbooks, moral injunctions, playground proprieties, classroom pedagogies, parents, teachers, doctors, disease management, the ordering of a day with bells and flurries of transit in *History of Sexuality Volume One* when unfolding schooling (Derrida 1995; Massey 2005: 10; Foucault 1978).

Everything I have recounted which pertains to South Asia in the 1990s (along with the brief interposition on farming in the US), all speak to the ways in which neo-liberalism enters some arrangement of the everyday through what I left unspoken in that list.[14] They are constituted through risk or more explicitly they are shaped by risk. As risk becomes more habitual, it offers a conduit for anxiety, which is the modality that allows risk to insinuate itself – in the process anxiety as tangled into risk turns commonplace (Spivak 1985). As I will go on to show risk here is not quite the same as the inevitable things-falling-apart, not-exactly-working-as-expected to which South Asians are so accustomed. And I want to deploy risk itself as a technology in the more capacious sense. Risk taken in this emergent way that the technological can gesture towards furnishes us a vantage from which to grapple with what is happening in India right now; much of which is detoured through anxieties (qua anxiety).

How does curving towards risk as the vector through which one can transit into the vicious political exigencies that are besetting India at this moment equip us to attend to what we must notice? What do I understand risk to be? As a concept metaphor (Spivak) risk is enormously enticing at present, its little fingers reaching deep down into and grabbing hold of our intellectual and pedagogical projects. Its temptations invite certain categorical confusions or perhaps better, categorical conflations between two registers of risk.

Bear with me! One sort of risk, which has a long history, is the diffuse notion of danger/uncertainty that is specific and or inevitable, which daunts everyday life or work – such as death if one is not a divine presence or if one is engaged in a shipping venture the possibility of drowning or sinking as a clear-cut though amorphous danger. These are nucleus of older stories that accompany risk; some of them appear Lorraine Daston's writing on its history and here one might recall Gottfried Leibniz's earlier and Frank Knight's later invocations of judgement as the key to navigating one's way through the depredations that risk brings in its wake (Leibniz, Ariew, and Garber 1989; Daston 1995; Knight 1921). In other words, risk as an inchoate yet precise future that might or must fall upon us but we don't quite know when or where. Risk as *danger*, hazard, peril, or uncertainty, pervasive but perhaps not so easy to get a hold of, perhaps the always elusive future. Taken to South Asia, where scarcity is met every day with the intermittent peril of having things nose-dive, *pareshānī* or *vyākultā* are almost unremarkable somatic manifestations of consistently, dependably, regularly unreliable futures.

The other key in which risk appears that we often slide into the first is the *management* of danger or uncertainty – as the statistical collection of data, real or fantasised, on danger or on jeopardy that gives us some sense of, or purchase on the notion of a more likely future. In other words, uncertainty turned into data, so that its chanciness can be seemingly handled, supervised, and controlled. Here anxieties can be downloaded onto the numerical accretion of information to afford the illusion of managing them. Statistical likelihoods that then come to colour, orchestrate, or choreograph run-of-the-mill politics (in the guise of or the shape of friable, crumbly fiscal nationalism). Coping with a vague future by handing it over to number or nation: which morphs disaster away into something that feels as though it were merely and dangerously hazardous. *Vyākultā* or *pareshānī* turn less potent, and their grip on one's throat loosens slightly.[15] This form of risk is what I want to focus on in this essay – especially since it has become so paradoxically mundane for us all here and more and more so in all of South Asia, rather than just in India. It is here that we come to see the deep incorporation of, the flesh, skin and tendons, the incarnations of intimacy and the feelings that coalesce in them.

Let me explain what I mean. As financial technologies such as insurance, credit, and debt become more ordinary, the idea of managed risk is absorbed through them. Here lies the work of neo-liberalism – commonsensical neo-liberalism in which we are all complicit. Along with pensions, these fiscal technologies promise life futures, so I have clustered them, bundled them together into a composite I term 'life-finance.' 'Life-finance' keeps hope in place: Armān, wish, desire, hope, longing, eagerness, used as the sales pitch in a finance advertisement seems to suggest this. Do upper-middle-class white folk in Europe and the US have what Kierkegaard suggests – which is a kind of assumption of fullness, or repleteness?[16] Whereas in South Asia where everyone has to finesse their way through things not working quite the way one envisioned, this assumption is less likely to be commonplace. Banks, insurance companies and finance companies play on this in selling their wares. 'Life-finance' comes with the assurance that one won't have to hustle, fight, argue – one can buy into finance to make an easier, prettier life possible and in doing so be able to shelve (hand over to or off-load onto the financial company) the anxieties instigated by managing in this economy. They then annex our worries so that, though they might still lurk, they don't have quite the same muscle.[17] Can we call these economies 'make-over' ones, or 'anxiety-economies' or even 'anxiety-alleviation economies'?

Let's look first at insurance. Indians are being sold on purchasing protection against particular vulnerabilities or potential losses and are also being persuaded that buying into investment as life insurance provides cover (in the guise of a secure transaction (for which Indians, including OCIs get tax relief for the policies)). Other emblematic instances are the thriving ubiquity of credit/debt and private pensions. Both are either a genre of 'protective' finance, annuities/insurance instruments endorsed by the current government, with ample tax support from the 2016 budget, or a genre of future access to a better life. Both are being peddled as the tactics or vehicles through which risky lives become manageable or as inducements into dreaming oneself into the shinier economies of makeover consumption.[18] Credit and insurance, including that offered through development or rural banks or microcredit institutions or insurance providers can be turned over to protect your harvest or to buy seeds if you are a farmer imagining a more fulsome harvest while straining to make a new or less precarious future (your life at risk), or from government or private banks or insurance agencies to go on holiday or purchase a house, a car, a motor bike, fund an education or wedding if you are one of many middle-class consumers enticed into hope and promissory economies, that many recent authors term aspirational (Ramamurthy 2011). A recent advertisement by Hero (Honda) offers *umīd*, and many property ads open their salvos with *sapnā* – aspiration as both a hope and a dream. Fiscal technologies such as these effloresced under various Congress governments and continued unabated under NDA and BJP. Anxieties, worries about futures are downloaded onto fiscal technologies – and handled by corporations, banks, and the government in its various guises. They are outsourced. But at the same time what they sprout are the dreams and hopes of wellness – as promises.

Where exactly is risk in this? Insurance and loans risk pool, group and glue people together based on their 'risk profile' (as subjects at risk or subjects who generate risk) or collectivities coagulated through the risks that that they have in common and the anxieties that they share or that reside in that 'profile.' You profile yourself in political economies where profiling has become so regular that it escapes notice. Credit and investments are sold to variously pooled consumers as the ways through which they can alchemise themselves into less risky subjects whose worries taper or ebb, and can also restyle themselves into glossier versions. Capitalism cannibalises new terrains, and in consort with the policies and procedures of governance augments spaces where risk economies, which might well be named worry or anxiety economies, flourish. Ironically, wellness regimes offer some of these spaces.

Two species of fiscal entailments tug in different directions. We see ostensibly contradictory movements, yanking at each other but also composing each other. One is that of risk pooling – or risks and their attendant worries – based on loss, on vulnerability, on threats to life or livelihood. Pooling for things that will go amiss, in other words, losses to life and livelihoods that one or a community will endure (from STDs, to violence, to Hindutva – with its constant wail of Hinduism under siege). What is important to notice here is that the harms and bereavements have significance in express political economies, can be real as well as fantasised, their temporalities cusping past, present, and the future. And one might consider this as risk-loss pooling, coagulating constituencies through loss and the collective anxieties, 'pareshānī' or 'vyākultā,' which escort them.

The other is risk's smiling Janus face – alchemical wellness regimes. Mitigating risk through wellness routines, working remorselessly to produce better, salubrious, prettier, worthier lives that hold 'pareshānī' or 'vyākultā' at bay. Here we can clump and dump everyone from pedometer following people, to healthy food eaters to credit card consumers, to serial borrowers (whether they are Maharashtrian Dalit farmers striving to make their next harvest more fulsome, or upper-middle-class Delhi holiday goers hunting for the newest foreign location, or Vijay Mallya starting one company after another).

Both risk loss pooling and alchemical wellness regimes compel a peculiar self-generating commitment from subjects who live through them – a kind of neo Adam Smithian entrepreneurial subjectivity, floated on a sea of paper (or numerical) currency. And with them come family. Many of the ads that sold finance in the early twenty-first century banked on a corporation underwriting the nuclear family as a surrogate for the *māmā*, *kākā*, or *dādā* whom you might have once relied on for fiscal support and who were your resources in times of worry or difficulty – so they reinstituted, renewed the bankrolled family planning ad family (ham do hamāre do). Entrepreneurial alchemy at work. If I can make myself and my nuclear family over, finance the best self for a future, I myself (and they with me) will somehow be inured from danger and distress, perhaps even flout them, to become a happier, salubrious, livelier, richer, more outsource to them, count on their anxiety-alleviation measures, you could happily persevere as a nuclear family. Techno-intimacy ensues from risk loss pooling and wellness closeness. Along the way the lives of the parties to techno intimacies, corporations, banks and various configurations in which states appear, are ensured longevity. Consumers and citizens cache their hopes here. If their lives fail, or become risky, so do the projects of techno-intimacy ensured through them. And in so doing, corporations and states download their own friable futures onto consumers and citizens or citizen consumers.[19]

Citizen shapes

Continue to bear with me – I have thrown a bunch of provocations your way, and I would like to close with a few others that I hope will incite all of us to think together about the abbreviated scenarios with which I first started my forays into risk and what is happening today. What I would like to array before you is the question of citizenship, or more appropriately multiple sorts of citizenship that become actualised possibilities as risk infiltrates national, local, state, and community registers of belonging, so that risk becomes the technological byway through which intimacies in these venues are shaped.

These final thoughts build on many of the contemporary assays of neo-liberal citizenship.

Aihwa Ong's flexible citizenship and the organic body of Pheng Cheah's spectral nationality, Achille Mbembe's necropolitics and Jasbir Puar's maimed citizens belong here.[20] As do Lilly Irani's entrepreneurial citizens and Bill Maurer's nuanced mutation of the citizen from rights bearer, to share holder to risk sharer. Here we might also take account of feminist research done by Sri Lankan scholars such as Neloufer de Mel on the security state as the developmental state, and the emergence of the securitised citizen, subsisting on the state's promissory note to govern the constant disarrays of fiscal, social, political uncertainty promulgated by various factions in state bureaucracies.

My foray commences with the reformatting of the 1860's French constitution which absorbed the protections tendered through labour union based mutual funds. It traffics with various immigration acts including those in the US (the 1882 immigration acts such as the Chinese exclusion act) and tracks further back to Ernest Renan's early 1882 quest into lineaments of national feeling in the essay 'What is a nation?'[21] Turning to an idea of a daily plebiscite (nationalism as everyday habit), features held in common but also dropped from collective repositories (forgotten or forsaken) Renan dives directly into blood as the beating heart of national communities. But rather than what we might expect him to say – communities are composed of those who share blood – he suggests that it is bloodshed in common that makes nations, common losses that presses people into common projects.[22]

Taken into the contemporary key of risk and pooling we can rephrase Renan – and we can come to see the emergence of quotidian and exceptional forms of emergent fascisms through the invocation of blood. Risk pooling around common and in in many cases fantasised future/present/past losses – whether these are narrated as voluminous aggressions or petty grudges or chronic antipathies and slights – begins to orchestrate versions of belonging that are about bloodshed, not one's own blood but the blood of others. In the recent instance of a young 12-year-old boy hung by a go rakshak, one might see an allegorical metaphor in a sequence between protection and loss; *rakshanya* is, after all, the word in Sinhala for insurance. If one brought Slavoj Žižek into this conversation we might say that it is precisely what-will-never-happen brought into a fantasy that goads blood-letting. Here the illusion of harm that will never occur (loss to majoritarian communities who are in fact not losing anything) drives communities to virulently enforce forms of belonging, where belonging is squeezed out of the blood of those who are forcibly expurgated, excised, killed in a macabre ritual to ensure that a fantasy of possible who knows what. When a community orients their political through statistical possibilities sopped up into routine – they abide in the peculiar conundrum of feeling as though something were always likely to happen; a niggle swollen into a spate. This galvanises or triggers a politics of cathartic release for a sequence of worries that need never have been present; documenting supposedly realist events, as they often are, in fake form (Lebow 2006). Fantasies beget anxieties, which because they are based on realist fakes, cannot be easily downloaded or outsourced and so flood into blood-letting, supposedly cleansing through release. But because they are grounded in events which are fantasmatic, one release is never enough and must be lived over and over, in a horror show of compulsive replenishment. The constant possibility, the 'who knows when something will come or fail or disappear,' the we-are-always-worried futurity, which activates states of security, the alibis on which the security state and securitised states build their own futurities. Pre-emptive strikes are the interventions on citizens' behalf – statistical panic writ large – states prepone something they model as a future and intercede to suck anxiety out.

But are there countless and sundry loses that invite people to share the collective fantasy of loss in waiting, like someone standing along a wall anxiously awaiting their turn. More banally put, many other losses are displaced onto this form of loss. In other words, this genus of loss becomes the holding vehicle, the hamper basket, of other fields of loss. Risk then, reveals the voraciousness of capital, the mutability of capital, with ever newer featured losses and risky terrains, through which one can niggle, fret, and freak out, being pulled willy-nilly into its ambit. Is this then the ambient form of financialisation showing up in the get up of, and in fact as, the political?

Here lie the conditions for the eruption of fascism of the sort we saw in the examples from the 1990s with which I began and the genres of violence we have seen so recently. Loss based risk pooled politics ensue; and majoritarian constituencies who partake in these sorts of pooling envisage their wellness through the death of those who they fabricate as their others (the semi privatised form of the security state buoyed by, subsidised by nationalism).[23] But there is another sort of citizenship entrepreneurial alchemical citizenship, makeover citizens, who want from the state the pledge that they will get the conditions for making themselves over (a curious effect of privatisation of care and wellness that still emboldens state forms); make overs hold worry at bay. This finessed promise brought people to vote for the right wing, to lay their hopes in Modi – through it, development with little content but with the promise of becoming Gujarat, brought them to the BJP. It is for these projects and this register of citizenship that Modi produced prophylactic, panacea politics imagining that such politics would bind citizens to the BJP – from collective yoga, to turn in your gas connection, to tax relief for insurance/equity instruments, to smart cities, to a budget that asked farmers to buy yet more insurance coverage.

The two routes to risk-pooled, anxiety-fuelled techno-intimate citizenship – bloodshed and alchemical makeover – sometimes work in concert, sometimes in opposition.[24]Much has been forsaken along the way, justice, salvageable lives, sustainable futures. Can attending to the routes as well as what is dropped aside in the rush along them, help us craft responses to the many ways that which right-wing infiltrations are becoming more and more ordinary, lead us back along new paths to the hoary, crucial, insistent and pressing questions of justice: in the predicaments that have been raised by Burger women who lost their homes and families in Sri Lanka, incited by the hangings of children who were in the way, made so urgent by University of Hyderabad faculty, students and staff, and of course JNU.

Notes

1 'How Your Smartphone is Ruining Your Relationship.' http://time.com/4311202/smartphone-relationship-cell-phone/ Accessed 14 October 2017

2 'Give Me a Sec, I'm on Phone: Don't Snub your Partner on Dates.' www.hindustantimes.com/sex-and-relationships/give-me-a-sec-i-m-on-phone-don-t-snub-your-partner-on-dates/story-4PhY93ESx4SBba99MuTV3N.html Accessed 14 October 2017

3 'Science Says Your Cell Phone Use Could Be Hurting Your Relationship.' http://time.com/4057948/cell-phone-hurting-relationship/ Accessed 14 October 2017

4 'How Cellphone Use Can Disconnect Your Relationship.' www.psychologytoday.com/intl/blog/the-squeaky-wheel/201501/how-cellphone-use-can-disconnect-your-relationship.'Your Phone Habits May Be Damaging Your Relationship.' www.huffingtonpost.com/entry/cell-phone-hurts-relationships-phone-snub_us_560c0cdee4b0dd85030a1c4e. Pay attention to: 'How Your Cell Phone Hurts Your Relationships.' www.scientificamerican.com/article/how-your-cell-phone-hurts-your-relationships/.

'5 Ways Your Phone Will Get You Dumped.' www.menshealth.com/sex-women/how-cell-phones-hurt-relationships.

'Put Down That Phone! 'Technoference' May Be Hurting Your Relationship.' www.today.com/health/put-down-smartphone-technoference-can-hurt-your-relationship-1D80339938.

'Stop "Pphubbing": New Research Shows What Happens When You Focus More on Your Phone Than Your Lover.' www.essence.com/2015/10/05/stop-pphubbing-new-research-cell-phones-relationship.

'Your Smartphone May Be Powering Down Your Relationship.' www.cnn.com/2013/01/10/health/kerner-social-relationship/.

'How Smartphones Could Be Ruining Your Relationship.' http://liveboldandbloom.com/10/relationships/how-smartphones-could-be-ruining-your-relationship.

'Science Says Your Cell Phone Use Could Be Hurting Your Relationship.' http://time.com/4057948/cell-phone-hurting-relationship/ Accessed 15 October 2017.

5 Johanssen and Rambatan 2013. Donna Haraway, 'A Cyborg Manifesto.' In *Simians, Cyborgs and Women*. New York: Routledge, 1991. This essay began the discussion on cyborgs.

6 The most obvious tie into wellness is contained in small instruments such as pedometers and apps that read the body's movements and sleep, and make one feel that one holds the pulse of one's own wellness when one has them on.

7 Kierkegaard suggests that people who have everything understand the tenuous fantasy that everything is forever is always under possible erasure: here lies their angst. These routes of interrogation came out of conversations with Deborah Johnson and Anil Menon.

8 Anxiety has been medicalised: as a 'disorder' with a taxonomy of types and an entire arsenal of treatments for each sort.www.nimh.nih.gov/health/topics/anxiety-disorders/index.shtml dissects the disorder, which becomes a disorder when an anxious person is unable to live a life that is deemed conventional, filled with work and socialising.

9 I would like to fold my finessing of anxiety into Martin Heidegger's discussion on angst and care in Section VI of *Being and Time*. Albany: State University of New York Press, 1996. In some ways the registers of anxiety that are embedded in object (or tools or things in Heidegger's nomenclature) or in worrying about how one lives is closer to either fear (which is oriented toward external and internal things) or a sense of care taken in an ontic (rather than ontological) fashion. Care, as ontic, is a form of tranquilisation (see Walter Benjamin as well), means that one goes towards willing and wishing (perhaps what I call hope) as urge or predilection, rather than being ahead of oneself or already being in, and being together (180–183). This genre of (almost) care arouses 'a high degree of busyness in taking care of things' 'in such a way that there is an illusion of something happening.' (182). 'Being-in-the-world whose world is primarily projected as a wish-world has lost itself utterly in what is available, but in such a way that in the light of what is wished for, what is available (all the things at hand) is never enough. . . . Wishing . . . solely *hankers after* possibilities. This hankering after *closesoff* possibilities; what is "there" in such wishful hankering becomes the "real world." Ontologically, wishing presupposes care' (182). 'Predilection shows the character of being out for something. . . . The "toward" of predilection lets itself be attracted to what predilection hankers after. . . . the complete structure of care is modified. . . . It is "toward at any cost."' (182). Ontic care (worry, freneticness, constant searching after, yearning for) is what I am mainly alluding to in my descriptions, though being suspended in anxiety might come close to Heidegger's anxiety/angst, which is something other than ontic care. When a 'person,' as Dasein, unsticks themselves (or is precipitously unmoored) from the world lived in with other creatures, objects and tools in a perhaps hectic, perhaps harried or just oblivious fashion, and is thrown into cavernous aloneness as a result, that process gives them a breach through which they can flash on to another way of fathoming what the world they left behind is and might be. Anxiety arises as an unheimlich state; where unheimlich is uncanniness as a kind of un-homing (unheimlich is a concept that Freud also uses), as no longer being at home in this world because one has peeled oneself away from an unthinking absorption in its ordinariness. Angst, living in this bottomless solitude, is a profound, acute dread (khauf or bhay) that is redolent with possibilities because it offers a chance at release, a flight from everydayness so that one can return to everydayness, or what the flight is from, in a different key. Anxiety does not call for alleviation or downloading or outsourcing or catharsis for Heidegger. Rather, is it a state in which one must learn to reside to grasp what is so true about being alive – death.

10 *The essay by Marcel Mauss is called 'Techniques du corps.' The phrase can be translated as technae of the flesh, of body – and is also Mauss' title for the book in which it was published Les techniques du corps.* The essay was first published in Journal de Psychologie, XXXII: 3–4 (15 March–15 April 1936) after it had been given as a talk at the Société de Psychologie on 17 May 1934. Michel Foucault picks up on the technologies of the flesh in *Discipline and Punish* 2nd ed. Alan Sheridan (trans.) New York: Vintage Books, 1995, in which he, like Mauss, uses the figure of the soldier as one apocryphal instance of sculpting bodies through technologies/pedagogies See Althusser 1971.

11 The government is encouraging digital cash transfers and payments by offering financial compensation or support from them. One of many articles on the stories is ET Bureau, 'No Surcharge, Service Charge on Card Payments,' *Economic Times*, February26, 2016. http://economictimes.indiatimes.com/news/economy/policy/no-surcharge-service-charge-on-card-payments-cabinet/articleshow/51127090.cms

See also http://timesofindia.indiatimes.com/india/To-clamp-down-on-black-money-government-set-to-ban-cash-transactions-over-Rs-3-lakh/articleshow/53802260.cms http://timesofindia.indiatimes.com/business/india-business/Now-no-surcharge-on-card-digital-payments/articleshow/51128071.cms

12 www.bankofbaroda.com/newpage.asp Accessed 16 October 2017

13 Patel 2016. See Introduction, chapters 3 and 6. Some of the specificities that allude to are laid out here; and all three offer interrogations that parallel this essay.

14 I am using the rhetorical strategy that Anthony Giddens deploys to such good effect in his work – Giddens is the propagator of the notion of risk society. See also Patel, *Risky Bodies*, Chapter 6.

15 The implicit question here is: What are the anomalies when risk is sent off to, or absorbed into South Asia? One difference might be what I indicate – and which is organised through class. Do upper-middle-class white folk in Europe and the U.S. have what Kierkegaard suggests – which is a kind of assumption of fullness, or repleteness? Whereas in South Asia where everyone has to finesse their way through things not working quite the way one envisioned, this assumption is less likely to be commonplace. Banks, insurance companies and finance companies play on this in selling their wares. 'Life-finance' becomes a kind of promise that one won't have to hustle, fight, argue – one can buy into finance to make an easier, prettier life possible and in doing so be able to shelve (hand over to them) the anxieties instigated by managing in this economy.

16 For a stark contrast see the work of Joanne Barker, 'In Debt: The Dispossession of Manna-Hata.' Special issue of *Social Text* co-edited by Jodi A. Byrd, Alyosha Goldstein, and Jodi Kim (in review).

17 To use Lawrence Cohen felicitous term: Are we de-duplicating worries? Funnelling via technological repositories?

18 Here the word 'imagining' is key. Many articles and essays published in India on aspiration and aspirational futures rely on 'imagining' without ever quite speaking it. For one popular press article, see S. Mahindra Dev, 'An Aspirational New Generation and Future of India,' *Economic Times*, April 21, 2014. http://economictimes.indiatimes.com/opinion/et-commentary/an-aspirational-new-generation-and-future-of-india/articleshow/34020800.cms

19 This generates a very different notion of the public or the collective.

20 Pheng Cheah's organismic body ('polity as a political *body*') versus the mechanistic body ('mechanistic model' that underpinned Hobbes's Leviathan – the great artificial man of springs, strings, joints, and wheels ensouled by sovereignty') – allows for a different configuration of nationalism. His work emerges from Kant and German idealism which builds the metaphor (differentiating between sensible and phenomenal or moral). 'Metaphor of the organic body, but while this metaphor is essential to modern theories of freedom, it is also inherently unstable and prone to perform its own unravelling. The actualisation of freedom, conceived as the philosophical and political project of modernity, is, then, incapable of completion, and the nation, conceived as a body in which to incarnate the promise of freedom, remains necessarily spectral, neither simply living nor simply dead.' Pheng Cheah, *Spectral Nationality*. New York: Columbia University Press, 2003. Aihwa Ong, *Flexible Citizenship*. Durham: Duke University Press, 1999. Lilly Irani, 'Hackathons and the Making of Entrepreneurial Citizenship,' *Science, Technology and the Making of Human Values* 40(5) (September 2015): 799–824. Bill Maurer, 'Forget Locke: From Proprietor to Risk Bearer in the New Logics of Finance,' *Public Culture* 11(2) (1999): 365–385. Neloufer de Mel. For one example of the burgeoning literature on debt and citizenship see James Macdonald's useful though slanted opus *A Free Nation Deep in Debt: The Financial Roots of Democracy*. Princeton: Princeton University Press, 2006. Also Geeta Patel, 'Advertisements, Proprietary Heterosexuality, and Hundis: Postcolonial Finance, Nation-State Formations and the New Idealized Family,' *Rethinking Marxism* 24(4) (2002): 516–535. Achille Mbembe, 'Necropolitics,' *Public Culture* 15(1) (2003): 11–40. Jasbir Puar and Maya Mikdashi, 'Queer Theory and Permanent War,' *GLQ* 22(2) (2016): 215–222.

21 Ernest Renan, 'What is a Nation?' Lecture at Sorbonne, 11 March 1882 in Discours et Conferences, Paris, Caiman-Levy, 1887, pp. 277–310; also in Geoff Eley and Ronald

Grigor Suny, eds. *Becoming National: A Reader.* New York, Oxford: Oxford University Press, 1996, pp. 41–55.

22 Arjun Appadurai, *Fear of Small Numbers.* Durham: Duke University Press, 2006. I first presented this work at the University of Chicago and at Harvard University in the late 1990s; my conversations with Appadurai were not as significant as those with John Kelly on Renan and blood loss which sent me off to sift through the imbrication of loss and fiscal protection in order to generate something true about nationalism. The question of majoritarian claims to inadequate lives and their affective underpinnings and charge took a certain course under the Affect Group in the late 1990s.

23 When the electric charge of being subsidised by a welfare state is subdued or wanes, securitised development takes over. Complexes of securitisation sell shares in security, not merely as ambient but as the leverage on which legal authorisation for states to source cathartic murder is mandated.

24 Funnelling them through the stalemates that anxiety drags along in its wake. Outsourcing those stalemates to state actors and bureaucratic organs. Here I would like to mention the biological metaphorics from predatory, cellular, rhizome, and such which might be consorted with to good effect.

References

Althusser, Louis. 1971. 'Ideology and Ideological State Apparatuses.' In *Lenin and Philosophy.* 127–186, trans. Ben Brewster. London: New Left Books.

Appadurai, Arjun. 2006. *Fear of Small Numbers.* Durham: Duke University Press.

Berlant, Lauren. 2007. 'Slow Death: Sovereignty, Obesity, Lateral Agency.' *Critical Inquiry,* 33(4) (Summer): 754–780.

Cheah, Pheng. 2003. *Spectral Nationality.* New York: Columbia University Press.

Daston, Lorraine. 1995. *Classical Probability in the Enlightenment.* Princeton: Princeton University Press,

Derrida, Jacques. 1995. *On the Name,* ed. Thomas Dutoit. Stanford: Stanford University Press.

Eley, Geoff and Ronald Grigor Suny. (eds.). 1996. *Becoming National: A Reader.* New York, Oxford: Oxford University Press.

Foucault, Michel. 1978. *History of Sexuality Volume 1,* trans. Robert Hurley. New York: Pantheon Books.

Freud, Sigmund. 1920. *A General Introduction to Psychoanalysis,* trans. G. Stanley Hall. New York: Boni and Liveright.

Heidegger, Martin. 1996. *Being and Time.* Albany: State University of New York Press.

Irani, Lilly. 2015. "Hackathons and the Making of Entrepreneurial Citizenship." *Science, Technology and the Making of Human Values,*40(5) (September):799–824.

Johanssen, Jacob and Bonni Rambatan. (eds.). 2013. *Cyborg Subjects: Discourses on Digital Culture* (Shoestring Anthologies). CreateSpace Independent Publishing Platform, October.

Joseph, Miranda. 2014. *Debt to Society.* Minneapolis: University of Minnesota Press.

Kalra, Sonal. 2016. "Hey, Why Don't you Marry Your Phone?"*Hindustan Times,* New Delhi, 7 February 2016. www.hindustantimes.com/sex-and-relationships/hey-why-don-t-you-marry-your-phone/story-lVR9YP1gXoouv1llGw3OYM.html. Accessed 16 October 2017.

Kierkegaard, Soren. 1920. *Either/Or.* Sigmund Freud. *A General Introduction to Psychoanalysis,* trans. G. Stanley Hall. New York: Boni and Liveright.

Knight, Frank. 1921. *Risk, Uncertainty and Profit.* www.econlib.org/library/Knight/knRUP.html. Accessed 16 October 2017.

Lebow, Alisa. 2006. 'Faking What?' In Alexandra Juhasz and Jesse Lerner (eds.), *F is for Phony: Fake Documentary and Truth's Undoing,* 223–237. Minneapolis: University of Minnesota Press.

Leibniz, Gottfried, Roger Ariew and Daniel Garber. (eds.). 1989. *Philosophical Essays*. Indianapolis: Hackett.

Macdonald, James. 2006. *A Free Nation Deep in Debt: The Financial Roots of Democracy*. Princeton: Princeton University Press.

Massey, Doreen. 2005. *For Space*. London: Sage.

Maurer, Bill. 1999. 'Forget Locke: From Proprietor to Risk Bearer in the New Logics of Finance.' *Public Culture*, 11(2):365–385.

Mbembe, Achille. 2003. 'Necropolitics.' *Public Culture*, 15(1): 11–40.

Ong, Aihwa. 1999. *Flexible Citizenship*. Durham: Duke University Press.

Patel, Geeta. 2002. 'Advertisements, Proprietary Heterosexuality, and Hundis: Postcolonial Finance, Nation-State Formations and the New Idealized Family.' *Rethinking Marxism*, 24(4):516–535.

Patel, Geeta. 2016. *Risky Bodies & Techno-Intimacy*. New Delhi: Women Unlimited.

Phillips, Adam. 2010. *On Balance*. New York: Farrar, Strauss and Giroux.

Puar, Jasbir and Maya Mikdashi. 2016. 'Queer Theory and Permanent War.' *GLQ*, 22(2): 215–222.

Ramamurthy, Priti. 2011. 'Rearticulating Caste: The Global Cottonseed Commodity Chain and the Paradox of Smallholder Capitalism in South India.' *Environment and Planning A*, 43: 1035–1056.

Spivak, Gayatri. 1985. 'Scattered Speculations on the Question of Value.' *Diacritics*, 15(4) (Winter): 73–93.

Woodward, Kathleen. 2009. *Statistical Panic*. Durham: Duke University Press.

INDEX